phAc

W9-BHT-252

# Power of Attorney Handbook

## (+ CD-ROM)

*Sixth Edition*

Edward A. Haman

Attorney at Law

SPHINX® PUBLISHING
AN IMPRINT OF SOURCEBOOKS, INC.®
NAPERVILLE, ILLINOIS
www.SphinxLegal.com

2-09

Copyright © 1994, 1996, 1998, 2002, 2004, and 2006 by Edward Haman
Cover and internal design © 2006 by Sourcebooks, Inc.®

All rights reserved. No part of this book may be reproduced in any form or by any electronic or mechanical means including information storage and retrieval systems—except in the case of brief quotations embodied in critical articles or reviews—without permission in writing from its publisher, Sourcebooks, Inc. Purchasers of the book are granted license to use the forms contained herein for their own personal use. No claim of copyright is made to any government form reproduced herein. All brand names and product names used in this book are trademarks, registered trademarks, or trade names of their respective holders. Sourcebooks and the colophon are registered trademarks of Sourcebooks, Inc.

Sixth Edition: 2006

Published by: **Sphinx® Publishing, An Imprint of Sourcebooks, Inc.®**

<u>Naperville Office</u>
P.O. Box 4410
Naperville, Illinois 60567-4410
630-961-3900
Fax: 630-961-2168
www.sourcebooks.com
www.SphinxLegal.com

This publication is designed to provide accurate and authoritative information in regard to the subject matter covered. It is sold with the understanding that the publisher is not engaged in rendering legal, accounting, or other professional service. If legal advice or other expert assistance is required, the services of a competent professional person should be sought.

*From a Declaration of Principles Jointly Adopted by a Committee of the American Bar Association and a Committee of Publishers and Associations*

**This product is not a substitute for legal advice.**

*Disclaimer required by Texas statutes.*

**Library of Congress Cataloging-in-Publication Data**
Haman, Edward A.
  Power of attorney handbook + CD-ROM / by Edward A. Haman.-- 6th ed.
    p. cm.
  Includes index.
  ISBN-13: 978-1-57248-535-8 (pbk. : alk. paper)
  ISBN-10: 1-57248-535-3 (pbk. : alk. paper)
  1. Power of attorney--United States--Popular works. 2. Power of attorney--United States--Forms. I. Title.

KF1347.Z9H35 2006
346.7302'9--dc22
                                                                2006001898

Printed and bound in the United States of America.
SB — 10 9 8 7 6 5 4 3 2

346.73029 H171p 2006
Haman, Edward A.
Power of attorney handbook (
CD-ROM)

# Contents

How to Use the CD-ROM . . . . . . . . . . . . . . . . . . . . . . . v

Using Self-Help Law Books . . . . . . . . . . . . . . . . . . . . . vii

Introduction . . . . . . . . . . . . . . . . . . . . . . . . . . . . . . . . xi

**Chapter 1: Powers of Attorney, Generally** . . . . . . . . . . 1
Uses of Powers of Attorney
You as the Agent
Financial Powers of Attorney
Living Trusts
Health Care Powers of Attorney
Living Wills
The All-In-One Power of Attorney
Power of Attorney for Child Care
Choosing Your Agent

**Chapter 2: Power of Attorney Law** . . . . . . . . . . . . . . . 13
The Law in Your State
Legal Research

**Chapter 3: Financial Power of Attorney** . . . . . . . . . . **19**
   Your Agent
   Acceptance of Your Power of Attorney
   Limited Power of Attorney
   Real Estate
   Durable Financial Power of Attorney
   Affidavit of Attorney In Fact

**Chapter 4: Health Care Power of Attorney** . . . . . . . **33**
   Durable Power of Attorney for Health Care
   Your Health Care Agent
   Those Who can make Medical Treatment Decisions
   Living Wills
   Do Not Resuscitate Orders
   Anatomical Gifts

**Chapter 5: Other Power of Attorney Forms** . . . . . . . **47**
   Power of Attorney for Child Care
   Revoking a Power of Attorney

**Chapter 6: Lawyers** . . . . . . . . . . . . . . . . . . . . . . . . . . . . **51**
   Do You Want a Lawyer?
   Selecting a Lawyer
   Working with a Lawyer
   Firing Your Lawyer

**Glossary** . . . . . . . . . . . . . . . . . . . . . . . . . . . . . . . . . **59**

**Appendix A: State Laws** . . . . . . . . . . . . . . . . . . . . . **65**

**Appendix B: Blank Forms** . . . . . . . . . . . . . . . . . . . . **79**

**Index** . . . . . . . . . . . . . . . . . . . . . . . . . . . . . . . . . . . **347**

# How to Use
# the CD-ROM

Thank you for purchasing *Power of Attorney Handbook*. In this book, we have worked hard to compile exactly what you need to determine which powers of attorney you need, how to fill out the necessary forms, and how to file them. To make this material even more useful, we have included every document in the book on the CD-ROM that is attached to the inside back cover of the book.

You can use these forms just as you would the forms in the book. Print them out, fill them in, and use them however you need. You can also fill in the forms directly on your computer. Just identify the form you need, open it, click on the space where the information should go, and input your information. Customize each form for your particular needs. Use them over and over again.

The CD-ROM is compatible with both PC and Mac operating systems. (While it should work with either operating system, we cannot guarantee that it will work with your particular system and we cannot provide technical assistance.) To use the forms on your computer, you will need to use Microsoft Word or another word processing program that can read Word files. The CD-ROM does not contain any such program.

Insert the CD-ROM into your computer. Double-click on the icon representing the disc on your desktop or go through your hard drive to identify the drive that contains the disc and click on it.

Once opened, you will see the files contained on the CD-ROM listed as "Form #: [Form Title]." Open the file you need. You may print the form to fill it out manually at this point, or you can click on the appropriate line to fill it in using your computer. Once all your information is filled in, you can print your filled-in form.

•    •    •    •    •

Purchasers of this book are granted a license to use the forms contained in it for their own personal use. By purchasing this book, you have also purchased a limited license to use all forms on the accompanying CD-ROM. The license limits you to personal use only and all other copyright laws must be adhered to. No claim of copyright is made in any government form reproduced in the book or on the CD-ROM. You are free to modify the forms and tailor them to your specific situation.

The author and publisher have attempted to provide the most current and up-to-date information available. However, the courts, Congress, and your state's legislatures review, modify, and change laws on an ongoing basis, as well as create new laws from time to time. Due to the very nature of the information and the continual changes in our legal system, to be sure that you have the current and best information for your situation, you should consult a local attorney or research the current laws yourself.

This publication is designed to provide accurate and authoritative information in regard to the subject matter covered. It is sold with the understanding that the publisher is not engaged in rendering legal, accounting, or other professional service. If legal advice or other expert assistance is required, the services of a competent professional person should be sought.

> —*From a Declaration of Principles Jointly Adopted by a Committee of the American Bar Association and a Committee of Publishers and Associations*

This product is not a substitute for legal advice.

> —*Disclaimer required by Texas statutes*

# Using Self-Help Law Books

Before using a self-help law book, you should realize the advantages and disadvantages of doing your own legal work and understand the challenges and diligence that this requires.

**The Growing Trend**

Rest assured that you will not be the first or only person handling your own legal matter. For example, in some states, more than 75% of the people in divorces and other cases represent themselves. Because of the high cost of legal services, this is a major trend, and many courts are struggling to make it easier for people to represent themselves. However, some courts are not happy with people who do not use attorneys and refuse to help them in any way. For some, the attitude is, "Go to the law library and figure it out for yourself."

We write and publish self-help law books to give people an alternative to the often complicated and confusing legal books found in most law libraries. We have made the explanations of the law as simple and easy to understand as possible. Of course, unlike an attorney advising an individual client, we cannot cover every conceivable possibility.

**Cost/Value Analysis**

Whenever you shop for a product or service, you are faced with various levels of quality and price. In deciding what product or service to buy, you make a cost/value analysis on the basis of your willingness to pay and the quality you desire.

When buying a car, you decide whether you want transportation, comfort, status, or sex appeal. Accordingly, you decide among choices such as a Neon, a Lincoln, a Rolls Royce, or a Porsche. Before making a decision, you usually weigh the merits of each option against the cost.

When you get a headache, you can take a pain reliever (such as aspirin) or visit a medical specialist for a neurological examination. Given this choice, most people, of course, take a pain reliever, since it costs only pennies; whereas a medical examination costs hundreds of dollars and takes a lot of time. This is usually a logical choice because it is rare to need anything more than a pain reliever for a headache. But in some cases, a headache may indicate a brain tumor, and failing to see a specialist right away can result in complications. Should everyone with a headache go to a specialist? Of course not, but people treating their own illnesses must realize that they are betting on the basis of their cost/value analysis of the situation. They are taking the most logical option.

The same cost/value analysis must be made when deciding to do one's own legal work. Many legal situations are very straightforward, requiring a simple form and no complicated analysis. Anyone with a little intelligence and a book of instructions can handle the matter without outside help.

But there is always the chance that complications are involved that only an attorney would notice. To simplify the law into a book like this, several legal cases often must be condensed into a single sentence or paragraph. Otherwise, the book would be several hundred pages long and too complicated for most people. However, this simplification necessarily leaves out many details and nuances that would apply to special or unusual situations. Also, there are many ways to interpret most legal questions. Your case may come before a judge who disagrees with the analysis of our authors.

Therefore, in deciding to use a self-help law book and to do your own legal work, you must realize that you are making a cost/value analysis. You have decided that the money you will save in doing it yourself outweighs the chance that your case will not turn out to your satisfaction. Most people handling their own simple legal matters never have a problem, but occasionally people find that it ended up costing them more to have an attorney straighten out the situation than it would have if they had hired an attorney in the beginning. Keep this in mind while handling your case, and be sure to consult an attorney if you feel you might need further guidance.

**Local Rules**    The next thing to remember is that a book which covers the law for the entire nation, or even for an entire state, cannot possibly include every procedural difference of every jurisdiction. Whenever possible, we provide the exact form needed; however, in some areas, each county, or even each judge, may require unique forms and procedures. In our state books, our forms usually cover the majority of counties in the state or provide examples of the type of form that will be required. In our national books, our forms are sometimes even more general in nature but are designed to give a good idea of the type of form that will be needed in most locations. Nonetheless, keep in mind that your state, county, or judge may have a requirement, or use a form, that is not included in this book.

You should not necessarily expect to be able to get all of the information and resources you need solely from within the pages of this book. This book will serve as your guide, giving you specific information whenever possible and helping you to find out what else you will need to know. This is just like if you decided to build your own backyard deck. You might purchase a book on how to build decks. However, such a book would not include the building codes and permit requirements of every city, town, county, and township in the nation; nor would it include the lumber, nails, saws, hammers, and other materials and tools you would need to actually build the deck. You would use the book as your guide, and then do some work and research involving such matters as whether you need a permit of some kind, what type and grade of wood is available in your area, whether to use hand tools or power tools, and how to use those tools.

Before using the forms in a book like this, you should check with your court clerk to see if there are any local rules of which you should be aware or local forms you will need to use. Often, such forms will require the same information as the forms in the book but are merely laid out differently or use slightly different language. They will sometimes require additional information.

Besides being subject to local rules and practices, the law is subject to change at any time. The courts and the legislatures of all fifty states are constantly revising the laws. It is possible that while you are reading this book, some aspect of the law is being changed.

In most cases, the change will be of minimal significance. A form will be redesigned, additional information will be required, or a waiting period will be extended. As a result, you might need to revise a form, file an extra form, or wait out a longer time period. These types of changes will not usually affect the outcome of your case. On the other hand, sometimes a major part of the law is changed, the entire law in a particular area is rewritten, or a case that was the basis of a central legal point is overruled. In such instances, your entire ability to pursue your case may be impaired.

# Introduction

This book enables you to prepare your own power of attorney without hiring a lawyer. It explains the different types of powers of attorney, guides you in deciding which type you need, and shows you how to prepare it. Be sure to read the previous section on "Using Self-Help Law Books" for an overview of the purpose of this book.

The difficulty in covering any area of law on a national scale is that the law is different (and ever-changing) in each state. However, the general type of information found in most powers of attorney is very similar in each state. Appendix A of this book will give you some information about the specific laws of your state. Many states have officially approved forms, which are located in Appendix B, along with forms to use in states without officially approved forms.

The old saying that *knowledge is power* is especially true in the law. This book will give you a fair amount of that knowledge. However, if you become unsure at any time, Chapter 6 helps you understand how to select and work with a lawyer.

Read this entire book (including the listing for your state in Appendix A) before you prepare any papers. This will give you the information you need to decide what forms you need and how to fill them out. You may also want to visit your local law library to get more information. Chapter 2 provides information about doing your own legal research.

To complete the necessary forms, you will need to use the general instructions in the main part of this book, consult the listing for your state in Appendix A, and use the information from any additional reading and research you do. Chapter 1 is a general overview of powers of attorney, while Chapters 3 through 5 provide more specific information. Many of the official state forms also contain detailed instructions and valuable information.

# Powers of Attorney, Generally

A *power of attorney* is simply a paper giving another person (the *agent*) the legal authority to represent you and act on your behalf. This is necessary when some third person is asked to rely on that authority. In financial matters, this third party could be a bank; utility company; securities and investment broker; insurance company; mortgage lender; a company that provides materials or services to a business you own; or, numerous other individuals, business entities, or government agencies with whom you conduct personal or professional business. In the case of health care matters, this third party could be various types of health care providers, such as doctors, hospitals, physical therapists, dentists, and home health agencies.

Of course, a power of attorney is not necessary every time someone does something for you. For example, if you ask a friend to get a gallon of milk for you from the supermarket, your friend can do it without a power of attorney. He or she will be paying for it at the time of purchase, and the grocer has no concern about your arrangement.

It is an entirely different matter, however, if you ask your friend to go to your bank and borrow $5,000 in your name. The bank will want to be sure that you are legally obligated to repay the loan, and it will not just take your friend's word for it. The bank will want to protect itself, so it will require some kind of proof that you have authorized your friend to obligate you to repay the money. A power of attorney could provide the bank with the assurance it needs.

**NOTE:** *To understand a power of attorney, it is necessary to know a few terms. Most terms will be defined throughout this book and in the glossary.*

## USES OF POWERS OF ATTORNEY

In general, you need a power of attorney whenever you want someone else to act on your behalf in a matter of legal significance. The extent of the power you grant to another is up to you. You can limit what someone else can do for you and when someone else can act for you. Some of these limitations are discussed through this book, but a term you should be aware of now is *durable*. When you allow your agent to continue to act on your behalf after you become incapacitated, you have created a durable power of attorney. There are certain instances, discussed throughout the book, when a durable power of attorney is crucial.

**Finances**

You need a *financial power of attorney* any time you want someone else to conduct business for you. This may be necessary if you need to conduct business long-distance, or if you want your spouse or another family member to be able to conduct your business if you become physically or mentally unable to do so. Of course, some ability to act on your behalf can be created through joint bank accounts and brokerage accounts, but this will not work with all types of property. Furthermore, adding someone to your account can create other types of legal and tax problems that do not arise with a power of attorney.

---

**Example 1:**
Adding your spouse to the account may change presumptions about whether it is separate or joint property in the event of divorce.

**Example 2:**
Adding a child to your account might be considered a gift by the IRS, subjecting the transaction to the federal gift tax.

---

**Health Care**  You need a *health care power of attorney* if you want someone else to be able to make decisions about your health care in the event you are unable to make or communicate such decisions.

**Child Care**  If you are sending your child to live with someone else, either on a long-term basis or for a week or two, it may be a good idea to give that person the authority to make certain decisions regarding your child. This will typically include authority relating to whatever purpose you have in sending your child to live with the other person, as well as authority to make decisions in emergency situations.

**Avoiding Guardianship**  One important reason to have a power of attorney is to avoid having to go through a *guardianship proceeding* in the event you become incapacitated. A durable financial power of attorney and a health care power of attorney can allow someone you trust to take care of your affairs immediately in the event of your incapacitation. Without these documents, it will be necessary for someone to hire a lawyer (ultimately at your expense) and go through a court proceeding in order to be able to carry on your affairs by being named a guardian. The expenses of a guardianship reduce the assets available to be used on your behalf.

Being named a guardian places additional burdens upon that person. While an *agent* under a power of attorney does owe a duty to act in the *principal's* (your) best interest, the agent is relatively free to conduct business and account for his or her actions as he or she thinks appropriate. A guardian is under the continued observation of the court. The guardian must provide a specific type of accounting to the court on a periodic basis and may need to first get the judge's permission to do certain things.

One good reason to have a power of attorney is to avoid having to put your parents through the guardianship procedure. It can be a traumatic experience for elderly people to have a sheriff's deputy serve them with guardianship papers, appear in court and hear people talk about whether they are incompetent, and then have to see mental health professionals for a competency examination.

Many people with Alzheimer's disease simply and comfortably allow a spouse, child, or other family member to take over their affairs through a power of attorney. Putting such people through a guardianship procedure might not only be expensive and traumatic, but also might permanently damage the relationship with family members. There is also the very real possibility that the judge will decide a guardian is not necessary, even though it is clear to everyone who knows your parents that they are not able to manage without one. Now your relationship is seriously damaged and your parents are no better off than before.

## YOU AS THE AGENT

All of the uses mentioned for a power of attorney focus on you giving someone else authority to act for you. However, there is one common situation in which you need to suggest that someone give you (or some other responsible and trustworthy person) this authority.

**Aging Parents**   Many people today are facing the prospect of caring for their aging parents. Various ailments, such as a stroke, Alzheimer's disease, and Parkinson's disease, can render an elderly person unable to handle his or her financial affairs or make intelligent, informed decisions regarding medical care.

If your parents have not become aware of the possible need for a power of attorney, it may be necessary for you to take the initiative and suggest it. Too often, by the time it becomes obvious that a power of attorney is needed, the elderly person is no longer mentally competent to make one.

Whether your parents will be willing to execute a power of attorney at your suggestion will depend upon many things. These can include:

✪   your parents' attitude toward powers of attorney and giving up sole control;

✪ their attitude about life-prolonging procedures and someone making health care decisions for them;

✪ your relationship with your parents; and,

✪ whether they are willing to think about and discuss such issues.

It will be easiest if you have maintained a good and close relationship with your parents, and have earned their trust and confidence.

You may need to consider the possible reaction of your brothers or sisters. In some families, the siblings are close and on good terms, so these matters can be discussed and agreed upon. In other families, one sibling attempting to get the parents to sign powers of attorney can be viewed by the others as trying to get control of the money or deprive the others of their inheritance. In still other families, it is like pulling teeth to get any siblings to share in the responsibility of caring for elderly parents.

If you anticipate such family problems, you should still use a power of attorney. However, you may want to consider filing for guardianship in the long run. Even though there are many disadvantages to a guardianship proceeding, it would give you the added support of the court in the event a family member complains about the decisions you are making. See the section on pages 3–4 about guardianship for a discussion of some of the disadvantages.

**Questions to Ask Yourself**   You also need to be prepared for the burden of serving as an agent. You should ask yourself these questions before accepting this responsibility.

✪ Will you be reasonably comfortable making the types of decisions that may become necessary?

✪ Are you confident in your ability to manage your parents' financial affairs?

✪ Are you emotionally equipped to deal with making tough, possibly life-and-death, medical treatment decisions?

✪ Are you aware of your responsibilities as an agent?

(Be sure to read the section on "Choosing Your Agent" later in this chapter, the section on "Your Agent" in Chapter 3, and the section on "Your Health Care Agent" in Chapter 4.)

# FINANCIAL POWERS OF ATTORNEY

A *financial power of attorney* gives a person you designate the authority to act on your behalf in financial matters. This can be limited to one financial transaction or certain types of transactions, or it can include all types of transactions. You will need a financial power of attorney if you want someone to be able to act for you in some or all of your financial dealings. This is usually done when you have distant or numerous financial matters to attend to and cannot be there personally to transact all of the business. (Chapter 3 discusses the financial power of attorney in more detail.)

**Springing Power of Attorney**

Some states provide for a financial power of attorney that does not become effective until the principal becomes mentally or physically incapacitated. Such a document is called a *springing power of attorney* because it "springs" into effect upon the determination of one or more physicians that the principal has become incapacitated. This allows the principal to have a power of attorney in place for emergencies, without having to give the agent authority immediately.

(The listing for your state in Appendix A will indicate whether a springing power of attorney is permissible in your state.)

# LIVING TRUSTS

One alternative to a power of attorney you may want to consider is a *revocable living trust*. This is a good alternative, especially if your state does not provide for a springing power of attorney. Living trusts are beyond the scope of this book, but are mentioned here so that you are aware of this alternative. A living trust is a document in which you set up a separate legal entity, called a *trust*, and designate a *trustee* to manage the property. Ownership of your property is transferred to the trust. (For example, you would execute a deed to your real estate that transfers title from you to your trust.)

A *revocable* trust is one that you can cancel at any time in order to transfer the property back to your own name. An *irrevocable* trust is one in which you give up some control once you set it up. These distinctions are not important for purposes of the discussion here.

In a revocable living trust, you can designate yourself as the trustee and provide for a successor trustee to take over in the event you become incapacitated. This accomplishes the same thing as a springing power of attorney, in that you do not have to give someone else immediate authority to act on your behalf. Like a springing power of attorney, the other person can only act if you become incapacitated.

A living trust has other advantages, including avoiding probate upon death. On the other hand, a living trust is more complicated to set up than a power of attorney, it may require that a separate tax identification number be obtained and separate tax returns be filed, and it may not be subject to any deadline for creditors' claims. Also, in some states, it may result in the loss of classification as homestead property or the loss of a property tax homestead exemption.

## HEALTH CARE POWERS OF ATTORNEY

Documents expressing a person's desires regarding health care generally fall into two categories—health care powers of attorney and living wills. It is important to understand the difference between these two types of documents, as well as how they complement each other.

A *health care power of attorney* allows the agent to make decisions about the medical treatment for the principal. The agent may only act if the principal is unable to make such decisions for him- or herself. A health care power of attorney is most often used by a husband and wife or close family members, but it can also be used between good and trusted friends. Without a health care agent, doctors and hospitals may be reluctant to provide certain medical care if you are unable to give consent or help make decisions about various treatment options.

Many states have an official form in their laws. The forms are included in Appendix B. As mentioned in the following section, it is a good idea to have a living will *and* a health care power of attorney. (More about the health care powers of attorney and other health care matters is discussed in Chapter 4.)

## LIVING WILLS

A *living will* is a document in which a person states his or her desires regarding medical treatment in certain circumstances. You may see this called by other names, such as a *declaration regarding life-prolonging procedures*, an *advance directive*, or simply a *declaration*. Without a living will, doctors and hospitals may decide they are legally obligated to perform certain procedures that you may not desire, in the event you become seriously ill and are unable to communicate your desires.

The first living wills created simply provided a basic statement that the person did not want to be kept alive by machines or other artificial means if he or she had a terminal illness or injury. These documents did not include the appointment of any kind of agent. Since the person was expressing his or her wishes in writing, there was no need to appoint an agent to present the person's wishes.

As living wills developed, they came to include other serious situations, such as if the person is in a permanent coma. They also sometimes include the appointment of another person to assure that the living will is carried out. This person does not have the same powers as under a health care power of attorney, because his or her authority is limited to the types of medical conditions specified in the living will.

It is a good idea to have a living will *and* a health care power of attorney. If you only have a health care power of attorney and end up unable to communicate and express your wishes further, your agent will be relying on what you have said about what you want. If another family member disagrees with your agent's decision, your ultimate fate can end up in the hands of a judge. However, if you have expressed your wishes in a living will, your agent has written evidence to support his or her decision. (More about the living will, the health care power of attorney, and the withholding or withdrawal of life-prolonging procedures are discussed in Chapter 4.)

# THE ALL-IN-ONE POWER OF ATTORNEY

**NOTE:** *This section will only apply to you if you live in one of the following states: Connecticut, Indiana, Kentucky, Louisiana, Missouri, New Jersey, New Mexico, Ohio, Pennsylvania, South Dakota, Utah, Washington, or Wyoming. These states either have a statutory all-inclusive form (Connecticut, Indiana, and New Mexico) or do not have any statutory form for either a financial or health care power of attorney. If you live in any state not listed, you should use the specific statutory form(s) for your state. (See the table at the beginning of Appendix B for assistance in determining which form or forms to use.)*

If you intend to designate the same person as your agent for both financial and health care matters, you can do so in a single document. This works best if you are fairly certain that you will not want to change the agent, such as if you are naming your spouse or an adult child. The advantage is that this avoids any confusion that might occur in dealing with the preparation, signing, witnessing, notarizing, and storing of separate documents. However, there are two possible drawbacks to using a single document.

1.  If you later decide you want a different agent for financial or health care matters, trying to clearly indicate the change you want may get confusing, because you would be revoking only part of the original power of attorney. Some third parties might conclude that the entire document was revoked, and refuse to honor it. It may be necessary to revoke the entire original and create two new documents at that time.

2.  If your agent uses the power of attorney for one purpose, a third party who gets involved will know more than he or she needs to know.

---

**Example 1:**
If your agent uses the power of attorney to open a bank account for you, the bank officer will also be able to read

the part of the power of attorney regarding your medical care (which may have information revealing various medical conditions you have).

**Example 2:**
If you give your doctor a copy of the power of attorney so he or she knows who to contact in an emergency, your doctor will also be able to read the part relating to financial matters (which may contain information about your financial holdings that you would prefer to keep confidential).

---

If you live in Connecticut and decide that you want such an all-inclusive power of attorney, you can use form 23 in Appendix B. If you live in Indiana, use form 38. In New Mexico, use form 62. If you live in one of the other states listed at the beginning of this section and want an all-inclusive power of attorney, you can use form 1. Instructions for form 1 are provided in Chapter 3.

## POWER OF ATTORNEY FOR CHILD CARE

A *power of attorney for child care* allows someone to make decisions regarding the care of your minor child or children. You may want to have this type of power of attorney if your child will be spending prolonged periods of time living with a friend or relative, where you may not be able to be reached in an emergency. Doctors or hospitals may be reluctant to give medical treatment to a child without the consent of the parent. A power of attorney authorizing your friend or relative to consent to medical treatment for your child may resolve this problem. Also, if your child will be living with someone else, that person may need a power of attorney in order to enroll your child in school. You can use form 8 in Appendix B for this purpose.

## CHOOSING YOUR AGENT

As mentioned earlier, you need to be very careful when choosing an agent for your power of attorney. You need to select someone you can totally trust. Choosing the wrong agent for a financial power of attorney can bring you economic ruin. Naming the wrong agent in a health care power of attorney can cost you your life.

In a financial power of attorney, you need to name someone as your agent who will act in your best interest and who has the ability to handle finances.

### Example:

You may trust your husband not to take the money and run, but maybe he cannot balance a checkbook or always seems to make the wrong investment decisions.

In a health care power of attorney, you need to name someone as your agent who will act in your best interest, taking into account what you have expressed as your desires and not being controlled by what he or she wants.

### Example:

You may trust your wife not to have life support removed in order to collect your life insurance, but maybe she is so attached to you that she could not bring herself to order life support removed, even if she knows it is what you would want.

**Multiple Agents**

Instead of naming one agent, it is possible to name two or more agents. For example, if you have three children, you may not want two of them to feel left out if you name only one as your health care agent. You could name all three of them as agents. In such a case, you could provide in your power of attorney that decisions will be made by a majority vote. If you know that they all get along extremely well, you could provide that any one of them has the power to make decisions alone.

However, this may cause third parties to have doubts about the true authority of any agent seeking to act alone. In any type of decision-making arrangement, having multiple agents creates more potential for problems if disagreements arise between the agents. Such disagreements can lead to bad feelings among family members, and may even result in lawsuits as one agent sues another to try to stop him or her from implementing a decision. Such a lawsuit can result in financial loss to you or a delay in carrying out your wishes as to medical treatment. In most cases, the safest way is to stick with one agent.

**Separate Agents**

If you are creating a financial power of attorney and a health care power of attorney, there is no requirement that you name the same person as agent in both. Instead of having multiple agents acting on your behalf through one document, select the person best suited for the particular function you need.

---

### Example:

If you think that your wife, who is a nurse, would be the best one to make medical decisions for you, but your daughter the CPA would be better at handling your finances, you could designate your wife as your health care agent and name your daughter as your agent in your financial power of attorney.

---

**Successor Agents**

A *successor agent* is a backup agent—someone who will become your agent only if the first person you designate is unable or unwilling to act as your agent. The successor agent has no authority to act on your behalf unless the first agent is unable or unwilling. Having a successor agent does not pose the problems of multiple agents, but you should be just as confident in a successor agent as you are in the first agent you designate. If there are not two people in whom you have such confidence, you should stick with a single agent.

# Power of Attorney Law

## chapter 2

The basics of the law concerning powers of attorney are fairly simple. By signing a power of attorney, you are giving another person the authority to act on your behalf. Your power of attorney can give your agent broad powers or it can limit him or her to specific actions.

The law provides that other people may rely on your power of attorney in doing business with your agent. You will be bound by what your agent does through the power of attorney. This means that you must have a great deal of trust in the person you select as your agent.

The real reason for giving someone a power of attorney is to get some third party to believe that your agent really has authority to act on your behalf. Traditionally, and in many states even today, a third party can be left holding the bag if the agent does not really have authority. Therefore, many people and businesses are reluctant to honor a power of attorney. Some states have taken care of this problem by implementing the following three precautions:

1.  creating an official form in the state law;

2.  eliminating liability of a third party who relies on the power of attorney in the official form; and,

3. making it illegal for a third party to refuse to honor a power of attorney in the official form.

In other states, however, it may be difficult to get a bank, stock broker, or any others to do business based upon a power of attorney. (The law for specific types of powers of attorney is discussed in more detail in later chapters of this book.)

## THE LAW IN YOUR STATE

All states have some laws relating to powers of attorney. Some states provide detailed guidelines for creating a power of attorney, while others provide almost no guidelines. Some states have laws relating to financial powers of attorney, some have laws relating to health care powers of attorney, and some have laws relating to both types. To find out about the law for your state, refer to the listing for your state in Appendix A of this book.

Some states have laws making it illegal for a third party to refuse to honor a power of attorney. Other states do not specifically say this, but have other laws that refer to the recovery of attorney's fees, damages, and costs in lawsuits for an unreasonable refusal to honor a power of attorney. The general legal concepts relating to specific types of powers of attorney and living wills are discussed in more detail in later chapters.

Except for checking on any recent changes in your state's laws, you generally should not need to go beyond the information in this book. However, to help you check for any recent changes, or if you wish to study your state's laws on powers of attorney, the section in this chapter titled "Legal Research" gives you more information.

**Forms**  Many states have established approved forms for powers of attorney for financial matters, health care, or both. These documents are the states' official forms and should be used whenever possible to avoid potential problems of a third party questioning your power of attorney. These approved forms may be found in Appendix B. Other states have laws relating to powers of attorney, but do not provide an approved form. Appendix B also contains forms for use in states without an approved form. A chart is provided at the beginning of Appendix B to help you select the appropriate form for your state. More information about how to use Appendix A and the forms in Appendix B is found in later chapters and at the beginning of each appendix.

**Witnesses and Notaries**

The laws in the various states differ regarding matters such as how many witnesses are required, who may be a witness, and whether a particular type of power of attorney must be notarized. Generally, if your power of attorney may be used for purposes of buying or selling real estate, it should meet the witness and signature requirements for a deed. If your state has an approved form, you will be able to tell by looking at the form what is required in the way of witnesses and notarization.

If your state does not have an approved form, it is generally a good idea to sign your power of attorney before two witnesses and a notary public. A notary public can usually be found at your local bank. However, be sure to read the listing for your state in Appendix A to see if there are any specific requirements.

Carefully read the power of attorney form. It may provide information about who may serve as a witness. Generally, the person you name as your agent should *not* also be a witness.

Some states, particularly in relation to health care powers of attorney, have further limitations on who may or may not be a witness. More information about the qualifications of witnesses is discussed in later chapters.

# LEGAL RESEARCH

While every effort is made to ensure that the most recent information available is incorporated in this book, the law (including official forms) may change at any time. Therefore, it is advisable to check on the most current version of your state's laws before preparing and executing any forms. This can usually be done online or by visiting your local library.

If your public library does not have the most current version of your state's laws, you may need to visit a law library. Law libraries can usually be found at or near your local county courthouse, or at a law school. In most situations, you will not need to go beyond the information in this book. Ask the librarian to help you find what you need. The law librarian cannot give you legal advice, but can show you where to find your state's laws and other books on powers of attorney. Some typical sources are discussed in this section.

**Statutes or Code**

The main source of information is the set of books containing your state's laws. These are the *statutes*, or *code*, of your state (e.g., *Florida Statutes* or *Mississippi Code*). The title of the books may also include words such as *revised* or *annotated* (e.g., *Annotated California Code* or *Kentucky Revised Statutes*). The word *revised* means updated, and the word *annotated* means the book contains information that explains and interprets the laws. Titles may also include the publisher's name, such as *Purdon's Pennsylvania Consolidated Statutes Annotated*. The listing for your state in Appendix A gives the title of the set of laws for your state.

Each year, state legislatures meet and change the law. Therefore, it is important to be sure you have the most current version. The most common way to update laws is with a softcover *supplement*, found in the back of each volume. There will be a date on the cover to tell you when it was published, such as "2007 Cumulative Supplement." Laws are also updated with a supplemental volume (found at the end of the regular set of volumes) or a looseleaf binding (in which pages are removed and replaced).

Checking the most current law is probably all you will need to do. However, if you want to go further, the following sources may be helpful.

**Practice Manuals**

*Practice manuals* are books containing detailed information about various areas of the law. They usually include forms for all different situations, including powers of attorney.

**Digests**

A *digest* is a set of books that give summaries of appeals court cases. A digest for your state is best (e.g., *Florida Digest* or *California Digest*), as the national digest is difficult to use. Find information in the digest by looking in its index for the subject, such as "Power of

Attorney," "Principal and Agent," "Agency," "Health Care Power of Attorney," or "Life-prolonging procedures."

**Case Reporters**    *Case reporters* contain the full, written opinions of the appellate court cases. There will often be a set of case reporters specifically for your state (e.g., *Michigan Reports*). There are also *regional reporters* that include cases from a number of states in the same geographical area (e.g., *Southern Reporter* or *NorthWestern Reporter*).

Furthermore, many of the reporters are divided into two or more *series*. Rather than continue numbering volumes, at some point in time the publisher decided to label the volumes as the second series or third series, and started over with volume 1. For example, *NorthWestern Reporter, Second Series* (abbreviated *N.W.2d*).

**Legal Encyclopedia**    A *legal encyclopedia* is like a regular encyclopedia—you look up the subject you want (such as "power of attorney," "principal and agent," or "agency"), in alphabetical order. *American Jurisprudence* (abbreviated *Am. Jur.*) and *Corpus Juris Secundum* (*C.J.S.*) are the major sets. Some individual states have their own, such as *Florida Jurisprudence*. As with the reporters, you may find legal encyclopedias with a second series, such as *American Jurisprudence, Second Series* (abbreviated *Am. Jur. 2d*).

**Online Research**    The statutes of most states can be accessed online through **www.findlaw.com**. Make sure the "For Legal Professionals" tab is highlighted. Go to the box marked "Research the Law" and click on "Cases & Codes." Then, scroll down to the heading "U.S. State Laws," and click on the desired state, then click on the reference to that state's code or statutes. FindLaw will also give you links to state and federal court opinions, as well as numerous other legal resources.

# Financial Power of Attorney

## chapter 3

A *financial power of attorney* authorizes the agent to act on your behalf in financial matters. This may include such things as:

- ✪ buying and selling real estate or other property;

- ✪ entering into contracts;

- ✪ investing;

- ✪ engaging in banking transactions;

- ✪ operating a business; and,

- ✪ making decisions regarding lawsuits.

As discussed in Chapter 1, a financial power of attorney gives a person you designate the authority to act on your behalf in financial matters. This can be limited to one financial transaction or certain types of transactions, or it can include all types of transactions. You will need a financial power of attorney if you want someone to be able to act for you in some or all of your financial dealings. The power of attorney can be effective immediately or at some future date. This springing power of attorney allows you to have one in place in case of emergency.

Traditionally, a power of attorney was a long document that explained in detail all of the powers given to the agent. A **DURABLE FINANCIAL POWER OF ATTORNEY** is found in Appendix B. (see form 6, p.101.) The main drawback to such a power of attorney is the large number of pages. If you need to record the document, it can become costly, as you normally will pay a recording fee based on the number of pages. This can also be costly if you need to obtain certified copies of the recorded power of attorney. In most instances, you can get by with a more simplified form, such as the simplified version of the **DURABLE FINANCIAL POWER OF ATTORNEY**. (see form 7, p.106.)

To simplify things, some states have created shortened financial power of attorney forms. In these states, the state law spells out the details for each power. The powers are only generally referred to in the power of attorney document itself. Appendix B contains specific state forms for the following states: Alaska, Arkansas, California, Colorado, Connecticut, District of Columbia, Georgia, Illinois, Indiana, Minnesota, Montana, Nebraska, New Mexico, New York, North Carolina, Tennessee, Texas, and Wisconsin.

The law in Arizona requires a particular witness and notary provisions be included in a financial power of attorney, but does not provide an approved power of attorney form. Similarly, Maine requires that certain notices be included in a financial power of attorney, but does not provide a power of attorney form. These required provisions are included in Appendix B of this book. If you live in one of these states, you will use either form 6 or form 7. Be sure to attach your state's required provisions to it.

Instructions for these statutory forms are found in the forms themselves. If you do not live in one of these states, you will need to use one or more of the generic forms, such as form 6 or 7. Instructions for completing these forms can be found in the section of this chapter titled "Durable Financial Power of Attorney."

## YOUR AGENT

Your agent is not free to do anything he or she chooses. An agent's relationship to the principal is that of a *fiduciary*. This means the agent is in a position of trust and confidence. He or she has a duty to act in the best interest of the principal. Although an agent has this duty, you still need to be careful of your choice for an agent, including close family members. You should not execute a power of attorney unless you have complete faith in your agent.

You not only need to have faith that your agent has your best interests at heart, but also that he or she has the ability and knowledge to manage your financial affairs. The agent in a power of attorney has the ability to financially ruin the principal. It is true that you can sue your agent for misuse of the power of attorney, but once the funds or other assets are gone, a court judgment against the agent might not be worth the paper it is printed on.

## ACCEPTANCE OF YOUR POWER OF ATTORNEY

Encountering a third party who is reluctant to accept a power of attorney is more likely to occur with a financial power of attorney than with a health care power of attorney. As the principal, there are things you can do to ensure that your power of attorney will be accepted by certain third parties with whom you do regular business, such as banks, credit unions, or investment brokers. Take a copy of your power of attorney (either before or after you execute it) to the third parties and tell them you want to be sure there will be no problems having your agent act on your behalf. If they are aware of the power of attorney and have a copy on file, your agent should have no problems. You may also use the **AFFIDAVIT OF ATTORNEY IN FACT**, explained later in this chapter. (see form 11, p.111.)

## LIMITED POWER OF ATTORNEY

As discussed in Chapter 1, a power of attorney can be a very broad document, granting liberal power to your agent, or it can be a very limiting document, giving your agent the authority to do one specific thing. When you have a single transaction or other onetime deal to do, you should use a limited power of attorney that clearly identifies the specific transaction.

---

### Example:

You have agreed to sell your boat. The buyer will pick it up and pay you on Saturday, but you will be out of town. You could execute a power of attorney to give your friend the authority to sign a bill of sale or any title transfer documents, and to accept payment.

---

Form 10 in Appendix B may be used in such situations. Follow these steps to complete the **LIMITED POWER OF ATTORNEY**.

◈ In the first paragraph, type in your name and address on the first line and your agent's name and address on the second.

◈ In the blank space after the second paragraph, type in a description of what your agent is being authorized to do on your behalf. From the previous example, you might type in: "To do whatever is necessary to complete the sale to John Smith of my 2004 Tracker bass boat, Serial Number 1994837590, Registration Number FL 39920-C; including overseeing delivery of said boat, accepting payment, and executing any documents necessary to transfer title and ownership."

◈ Fill in the date and signature lines at the bottom.

> **NOTE:** *You may or may not need to attach a notary provision, depending upon what state you live in. Also, many states have their own forms for a power of attorney to transfer title to a motor vehicle or boat, so check with the state agency that handles such title or registration transfers before using the form in this book.*

## REAL ESTATE

A somewhat unique type of financial power of attorney concerns real estate. You may need such a power of attorney if you are purchasing or selling property in another state (or even in a distant area of your state) and you will not be there to sign the necessary papers.

You will need to comply with the requirements of the title insurance company or the lender. They will usually provide you with the form they require. For example, while there is no good reason why a general statement that grants your agent with the power "to purchase or sell any and all real estate as my agent sees fit" cannot be used, most lenders will require the power of attorney to specifically describe the particular piece of property being bought or sold.

**NOTE:** *Many of the power of attorney forms in various states include a general provision for real estate. However, this form may not be satisfactory to a lender. States that have such statutory forms usually provide in the law that the form is valid. Some states even make it illegal for the lender or title company to refuse to accept the approved form.*

*You could argue that the lender is violating the law if it does not accept the form, but it would probably not be worth your time to fight this out in court while your real estate deal waits. Also, these state forms do not limit the agent to a specific real estate transaction. These forms give the agent the power to conduct all real estate transactions, unless you add specific language placing restrictions on the agent.*

A power of attorney granting the power to buy or sell real estate will need to be executed in the same manner as required for a deed in the state where the property is located. This may require a certain number of witnesses, notarized signatures, and space requirements for recording information. Therefore, check with an attorney or real estate professional to determine what is required for your particular property.

The **POWER OF ATTORNEY FOR REAL ESTATE** is designed to appoint an agent for the purchase or sale of a single, specific piece of property. (see form 2, p.94.) You would use this form when you need to have someone represent you in connection with this transaction, but do not want to give your agent broad authority to conduct all of your business affairs or to engage in other real estate transactions.

Follow these directions to complete form 2.

◈ Type in your name and address on the first two lines in the first paragraph.

◈ Type in the name, address, and relationship to you, if any (such as wife, husband, or brother), of your agent on the third line.

◈ In the space following the first paragraph, type in the legal description of the property. The legal description should be the same as it will appear on the deed. If you do not have the legal description, type in as specific of a description as possible, which may simply be the street address. However, with a little effort, you should be able to obtain the legal description.

◈ If you wish to limit your agent's authority in any way, type in the limitations on the lines in paragraph 5.

◈ In paragraph 6, there is a line for you to fill in the date on which your agent's authority will end. If you do not wish to end this authority on any particular date, just cross out the words "or until _____, whichever occurs first."

◈ Sign before a notary on the line above the words "Signature of Principal." The notary will complete the rest of the form. Spaces are also provided for witnesses, which may be required in your state. Be sure to follow your state's requirements as to how a deed must be executed.

## DURABLE FINANCIAL POWER OF ATTORNEY

A *durable financial power of attorney* is the same as any other financial power of attorney, with one difference. A traditional (*nondurable*) power of attorney will end if you become incapacitated, whereas a durable power of attorney will continue to be effective. This can be important if you would want your agent, especially your spouse, to be able to conduct business for you if you become unable to do so yourself.

**Statutory Forms**   Several states have created an approved durable power of attorney form in their statutes. These statutory forms have some standard language and a list of the various types of powers you may give to your agent. If you live in one of the states with a statutory financial power of attorney form, use the specific form for your state found in Appendix B. These forms are fairly similar, and many contain detailed instructions, information, and disclosure statements.

Be sure to read each form carefully and be sure you understand all of the provisions and instructions. If your state does not have a statutory form, use form 6 in Appendix B. Form 6 is discussed in the next subsection of this chapter, titled "Generic Forms."

There are usually two types of statutory forms.

1. Forms on which you place a check mark or your initials on a line to indicate the powers you are giving to your agent.

2. Forms on which you place a check mark, your initials, or cross out a line to indicate the powers you are not giving your agent.

In the second type, you are automatically giving *all* possible powers to your agent, unless you indicate those you *do not* want him or her to have.

The following states have forms that give agents only the powers specifically designated in the power of attorney.

| | | |
|---|---|---|
| Arkansas | Minnesota | New Mexico |
| California | Montana | New York |
| Colorado | Nebraska | North Carolina |
| District of Columbia | | Wisconsin |

The form in Appendix B for Indiana is also this type of form, but it is not an official statutory form.

The following states have forms that give agents all powers, unless otherwise indicated: Alaska, Connecticut, Illinois, and Texas.

If you live in one of these states, use the form for your state in Appendix B (see the table at the beginning of the Appendix). If you do not live in one of these states, you can use form 6 or 7 in Appendix B.

The following provides some basic information to help you with the statutory forms for the states listed.

***Alaska (form 13).*** You need to cross out and initial any power you *do not* want to give your agent.

***Arizona (form 14).*** The witness and notary provisions that are required by Arizona law are included in Appendix B. There is not a statutory power of attorney form. Use form 6 or form 7, and attach form 14 as the last page.

***Arkansas (form 16).*** You need to initial only the powers you want to give your agent.

***California (form 18).*** You need to initial only the powers you want to give your agent.

***Colorado (form 20).*** You need to initial only the powers you want to give your agent. Form 21 is an affidavit for the agent to sign, swearing to the validity of the power of attorney. Blank copies of this affidavit should be made for the agent to use each time it is needed. This affidavit is signed at the time the agent seeks to use the power of attorney—not when the power of attorney is signed by the principal.

***Connecticut (form 23).*** You need to cross out and initial any power you *do not* want to give your agent. If you do not cross out and initial item "(L)," this will become a health care power of attorney (cross out all others to make this *only* for health care).

***District of Columbia (form 26).*** To grant fewer than all the powers, initial before every power granted. To grant all powers, initial item (N).

*Florida (form 28).* Florida does not have an official statutory form for a financial power of attorney. Therefore, you will need to use either form 6 or form 7. Form 28 is a form your physician can sign before a notary public to certify that you are medically unable to manage your finances, thereby allowing your agent to operate under a springing power of attorney.

*Georgia (form 31).* The directions on the form say: "To give the Agent the powers described in paragraphs 1 through 13, place your initials on the blank line at the end of each paragraph. If you DO NOT want to give a power to the agent, strike through the paragraph or line within the paragraph and place your initials beside the stricken paragraph or stricken line." Your initials go in different places depending upon whether you do or do not want to give a particular power to your agent.

If you are giving a power, you are instructed to place your initials "on the blank line at the end" of the paragraph. However, if you are not giving a power, you are instructed to place your initials "beside the stricken paragraph." You are also allowed to give a power, but cross out part of it.

A portion of the statutory form is shown below, designating paragraphs 5, 6, and 7. In paragraph 5, the power of "Stock and Bond Transactions" has been given, except that it has been modified to delete the authority to vote at meetings. The power has not been granted for paragraph 6. The full power has been given for paragraph 7.

---

 **5.    Stock and Bond Transactions:** To purchase, sell, exchange, surrender, assign, redeem, ~~vote at any meeting~~, or otherwise transfer any and all shares of stock, bonds, or other securities in any business, association, corporation, partnership, or other legal entity, whether private or public, now or hereafter belonging to me. _*JRS*_

 ~~**6.    Safe Deposits:** To have free access at any time or times to any safe deposit box or vault to which I might have access.~~
_____

**7.    Borrowing:** To borrow from time to time such sums of money as my Agent may deem proper and execute promissory notes, security deeds or agreements, financing statements, or other security instruments in such form as the lender may request and renew said notes and security instruments from time to time in whole or in part. _*JRS*_

On the last page of the Georgia form, there is a place for the agent to formally accept the appointment. This ACCEPTANCE OF APPOINT-MENT must be completed and signed by your agent before the power of attorney will be valid and effective.

*Illinois (form 36).* You need to cross out any power you *do not* want to give your agent.

*Indiana (form 38).* You need to initial only the powers you want to give your agent. By initialing item q, this becomes a health care power of attorney. There is not a statutory form, but form 38 meets the requirements of the Indiana statute.

*Maine (form 46).* Appendix B only includes the notices that are required by Maine law. There is not a statutory form. Use form 6 and attach it to form 46.

*Minnesota (form 50).* You need to place an "X" on the line in front of only the powers you want to give your agent.

*Montana (form 53).* You need to initial only the powers you want to give your agent. As this form is written, the power of attorney is effective immediately and is a durable power of attorney.

If you want to make it a springing power of attorney, on the lines under the heading "SPECIAL INSTRUCTIONS," type or print the following: "This power of attorney will only become effective if I become disabled, incapacitated, or incompetent."

If you do not want it to continue indefinitely, you will need to type or print an ending day on the "SPECIAL INSTRUCTIONS" lines, such as: "This power of attorney shall terminate at 11:59 p.m. on December 31, 2007."

If you do not want the power of attorney to be durable (i.e., to continue after you become disabled, incapacitated, or incompetent), you need to cross out that provision at the top of the second page of the form.

***Nebraska (form 56).*** You need to place an "X" in front of the powers you want to give your agent.

***New Hampshire (forms 59 and 60).*** The New Hampshire forms in Appendix B must be used along with either form 6 or form 7. Form 59 will be the first page of your power of attorney, and form 60 will be the last page.

***New Mexico (form 62).*** You need to initial only the powers you want to give your agent. You may give your agent all of the powers listed, including health care decision-making, by simply initialing item 17. This form also has an affidavit for the agent to sign, swearing to the validity of the power of attorney. Blank copies of this affidavit should be made for the agent to use each time it is needed. This affidavit is signed at the time the agent seeks to use the power of attorney—not when the power of attorney is signed by the principal. By initialing items 14 and 15, this becomes a health care power of attorney.

***New York (forms 64, 65, and 66).*** Instead of creating a single form with spaces to indicate when the power of attorney becomes effective and whether it is durable, New York has a separate form for each situation. On any of these forms you need to initial only the powers you want to give your agent. Form 67 is an affidavit for the agent to sign, swearing to the validity of the power of attorney. Blank copies of this affidavit should be made for the agent to use each time it is needed. This affidavit is signed at the time the agent seeks to use the power of attorney—not when the power of attorney is signed by the principal.

***North Carolina (form 69).*** You need to initial only the powers you want to give your agent.

***Oklahoma (form 73).*** The form included in Appendix B is just a signature page. Oklahoma does not have an official statutory form for a financial power of attorney, so you will need to attach form 73 to either form 6 or form 7.

***Pennsylvania (forms 76 and 77).*** The Pennsylvania forms in Appendix B must be used along with either form 6 or form 7. Form 76 will be the first page of your power of attorney, and form 77 will be the last page.

*Texas (form 85).* You need to cross out any power you *do not* want to give your agent.

*Wisconsin (form 95).* You need to initial only the powers you want to give your agent.

**Generic Forms**
Form 1 is for use in states that do not have a specific power of attorney form in their statutes for either financial or health care matters. Forms 6 and 7 are for use in those states that do not have a specific financial power of attorney form in their statutes. The following guidelines will help you decide which form or forms to use.

*Form 1.* (For general financial and health care matters.) Use this form if your state does not have a specific form in its statutes for a financial power of attorney or a health care power of attorney, and you want to give your agent broad powers to act in all types of financial matters and to act as your health care agent. If you decide to use form 1, be sure to read Chapter 4 for more information on the health care power of attorney.

*Form 6.* (For general financial matters.) Use this form if your state does not have a specific form in its statutes for a financial power of attorney and you want to give your agent broad powers to act in all types of financial matters, but do not want to include authority for health care decisions. This would be used either if you do not want to give anyone health care decision-making authority or if you wish to create a separate health care power of attorney document. Form 6 is basically the same as form 1, except the provisions for health care matters have been deleted.

*Form 7.* (Simplified form for general financial matters.) Use this form if your state does not have a specific form in its statutes for a financial power of attorney, you want to give your agent broad powers to act in all types of financial matters, and you wish to use a shorter, more simplified form than form 6.

*Instructions.* The following instructions will help you complete form 1, form 6, or form 7.

⬥  Type in your name on the first line in the first paragraph and your address on the second line.

⬥  Type in the name of your agent on the third line. You will also find spaces to designate successor agents, in the event your first choice is unable to act.

⬥  Check only one of the three boxes below the first paragraph, whichever reflects your wishes. If you want to give your agent authority immediately, check the first box (for a durable power of attorney). If you do not want your agent to have authority unless you become disabled or incapacitated, check the second box (for a springing power of attorney).

---

## – Warning –

Be sure to read the listing for your state in Appendix A. Under the heading "Financial," you will find a notation for many states that says either "Durable or springing" or "Durable." If it only says "Durable," a springing power of attorney is not specifically authorized in your state.

The law of the following states provides *only* for durable powers of attorney: Florida, Louisiana, Missouri, New Hampshire, Ohio, Oregon, Pennsylvania, and Virginia. If you live in one of these states, check the first or third box only. *Do not* check the second box.

The following states do not say one way or the other: Alabama, Arizona, Hawaii, Nevada, and Utah. If you live in one of these states and want to make a springing power of attorney, it would be a good idea to check the current status of the law (either by doing research on your own or by asking a lawyer if a springing power of attorney is permitted).

---

⬥  On the last page, type in the date in the last paragraph, beginning, "IN WITNESS WHEREOF."

➡ Type in the name and addresses of yourself and two witnesses, and your Social Security number, on the lines where indicated. If you intend to use this form to allow your agent to buy or sell real estate, remember to be sure it is executed in the manner required for a deed in the state where the property is located.

➡ You, your agent, and the witnesses sign before a notary, who will then complete the rest of the form.

## AFFIDAVIT OF ATTORNEY IN FACT

A third party that you are asking to honor a power of attorney may want some assurance that the power of attorney is currently valid. This may especially arise if the power of attorney was executed some time ago. Such assurance can often be provided by giving the third party an affidavit in which the agent states that the power of attorney is currently valid, that it has not been revoked by the principal or by operation of law, and that the principal is still alive. To do this, you can complete the **AFFIDAVIT OF ATTORNEY IN FACT**. (see form 11, p.111.) In some states, a third party has a legal right to ask for such an affidavit.

Follow these steps to complete form 11.

➡ After the lines "STATE OF" and "COUNTY OF," type in the state and county where the affidavit will be signed.

➡ Type in the agent's full name on the line in the first, unnumbered paragraph.

➡ In paragraph 1, type in the title of the power of attorney document on the first line (e.g., "Durable Power of Attorney," "Power of Attorney for Health Care"), the principal's name on the second line, and the date the power of attorney is being executed on the third line.

➡ Have the agent sign on the line marked "Affiant" in front of a notary public

➡ Have the notary complete the notary section at the bottom of the form.

# Health Care Power of Attorney

## chapter 4

This chapter discusses the following documents relating to health care issues:

- ✪ durable power of attorney for health care;

- ✪ living wills;

- ✪ do not resuscitate orders; and,

- ✪ anatomical gifts.

It also discusses what happens in the absence of any of these documents. This chapter is primarily concerned with the health care power of attorney, but you should also be aware of the other three issues that are discussed in the following pages.

# DURABLE POWER OF ATTORNEY FOR HEALTH CARE

A *durable power of attorney for health care* allows you to designate an agent to make all decisions about your health care if you are unable to make these decisions yourself. This applies to all health care decisions and for all types of medical conditions. It is much broader than a *living will*, which only expresses your desires if you become terminally ill or permanently unconscious and are unable to express your wishes regarding the use of life-prolonging procedures. (There are problems that may arise if you have a health care power of attorney, but do not also have a living will. These potential problems are explained in the section of this chapter on "Living Wills.")

The health care power of attorney is not limited to situations in which you are terminally ill, in a persistent vegetative state, or in some other condition narrowly defined in your state. It is not limited to life-prolonging procedures, either.

---

## Example:

Dave is in a automobile accident that leaves him in a coma. His physician expects him to eventually recover, so he is not in a terminal condition, end-stage condition, or persistent vegetative state. While Dave is in the coma, a question arises about whether he should have surgery. If he were not in a coma, Dave would be able to listen to the doctor's explanation of the relative risks and benefits of having the surgery or not having the surgery, and could make a decision. Since Dave is in a coma, he cannot make this decision.

Dave has a living will, but this does not come into play here because he is not in one of the three conditions provided for in a living will. As Dave does not have a health care power of attorney, his state's law allows his only son, Jim, to make the decision. Jim has an eighth grade education and is not someone Dave would trust to make important medical decisions. Dave would prefer to have his mother, who is a registered nurse, make such decisions, but under his state's law, a son outranks a parent. Dave should have made a health care power of attorney naming his mother as his agent.

---

Regarding the power of attorney for health care, the Terri Schiavo case from Florida has pointed out the importance of having this document. Because of the persistent intervention of the federal and state governments in this case, several additional significant terms have been added to the suggested health care power of attorney documents. It is also recommended that living will forms be used along with the health care power of attorney.

Due to the Schiavo case, a significant change is recommended regarding the manner in which you use these documents. Your health care agent should use only the health care power of attorney form initially. Your agent should show the health care power of attorney, but not your living will, to your health care providers. The living will should only be given to your health care agent, along with instructions that it is only to be used in the event someone raises a question as to your desires or intentions. In most cases, the health care power of attorney will be honored by health care providers, and your agent's instructions will be followed. The assumption here is that your agent is well aware of your beliefs and desires, and will act in your best interests. Only in the event of a challenge will it be necessary for your agent to produce the living will to reinforce his or her determination of what you would want.

Some may disagree with this advice. They would argue that the living will is the clearest expression of your wishes, and having your health care providers aware of this might prevent your health care agent from having a change of heart and going against what you would really want. This may be true. However, if you do not have full trust that the person you intend to name as your health care agent will follow your desires, perhaps you should select someone else.

Unless you live in a state that legally recognizes health care powers of attorney, you may have difficulty getting one accepted by doctors and hospitals. However, on the chance that one would be honored, it would still be better for you to have one. You can also ask your doctor or local hospital administrator whether they accept and honor health care powers of attorney.

**Statutory Forms**　The following states have created health care powers of attorney in their laws.

| | |
|---|---|
| Alabama | Nebraska |
| Arizona | Nevada |
| California | New Hampshire |
| Connecticut *(included in a general financial power of attorney)* | New Mexico *(both as part of the general financial power of attorney, and as a separate form)* |
| Delaware | |
| District of Columbia | New York |
| Florida | North Carolina |
| Georgia | North Dakota |
| Hawaii | Oklahoma |
| Idaho | Oregon |
| Illinois | Rhode Island |
| Indiana *(included in a general financial power of attorney)* | South Carolina |
| | Tennessee |
| Iowa | Texas |
| Kansas | Utah |
| Maine | Vermont |
| Maryland | Virginia |
| Minnesota | West Virginia |
| Mississippi | Wisconsin |

Forms specific for these states are found in Appendix B. There is also a form for Michigan in Appendix B, which was at one time an official form. The Michigan legislature chose to delete this from the Michigan Compiled Statutes, but it is still in compliance with Michigan law and is probably readily recognizable by health care providers in the state.

A few states have forms with titles that appear to be health care powers of attorney, but the content of these forms shows that they are really living wills that merely designate someone to communicate your living will desires to health care providers.

Health care authority is also provided as part of a general power of attorney form in Connecticut, Indiana, and New Mexico. You can use these forms for health care alone, either by only selecting the health care provision in the Indiana and New Mexico forms, or by deleting all other provisions in the Connecticut form.

If you live in one of the states listed previously as having a specific health care power of attorney form, locate the form for your state in Appendix B. All of the forms are fairly simple to complete. They all require you to fill in your name and identify your agent. Any other places to check or fill in information are very clear as to what is needed. Some forms include provisions for writing a living will, stating your desires regarding an autopsy and the donation of organs, and designating your primary physician. Some also contain detailed information about who may and may not serve as witnesses. In any case, be sure to carefully read your state's form, because many include detailed information and instructions to help you fill in the blanks. The following comments may help you with some specific forms.

***Connecticut (form 23).*** You do not need to do anything to give your agent authority to make health care decisions as stated in item (L). The Connecticut form gives the agent all powers listed, unless you delete them by drawing a line through the item and initialing the box opposite the item. Form 24 is a combination health care power of attorney and living will. It can be used if all you only want is to appoint an agent for health care decisions, or if you want to appoint one person as your agent for financial matters and a different person for health care decisions.

***Florida (form 29).*** In Florida, the agent is called the *surrogate*. The fourth paragraph is used to designate other people who will have a copy of your power of attorney for health care, so that other family members will be aware that someone has been given the power to make decisions for you. Form 30 is the official Florida statutory living will form, which should be used along with form 29.

***Georgia (form 32).*** Paragraph 6 allows you to suggest a person you want to be your guardian if a court is asked to appoint one for you. The last part of this form is to provide sample signatures of your agents. This is so the signatures may be compared to be sure the person claiming to be your agent is really your agent.

***Hawaii (forms 33 and 34).*** Form 33 is the official statutory form for a health care power of attorney. Form 34 is the official statutory form for a mental health care power of attorney, which deals with specific matters and treatments unique to mental health situations. You can use either, or both, of these forms.

*Illinois (form 37).* This form is designed to be a two-page, fill-in-the-blank form, with the statutes attached to it.

*Indiana (form 38).* Check item q. Also, read the paragraph regarding withholding health care and check the box if you agree with its provisions. The language of this paragraph must be in any health care power of attorney in Indiana if you want your agent to have the ability to refuse medical care on your behalf.

*New Mexico (forms 62 and 63).* Form 62 is an all-encompassing power of attorney. To give your agent authority to make health care decisions, initial the boxes opposite items 14 and 15. The last page is an affidavit for your agent to sign before a notary, to certify that he or she is not aware of anything that would make the power of attorney invalid. This affidavit should not be signed until it is needed in connection with a particular action your agent is taking on your behalf. Your agent may want to make several blank copies of the affidavit to be filled in and used at later dates. Form 63 is a specific power of attorney for health care that would be better to use if you only want to give your agent authority to make health care decisions.

*Ohio (form 72).* Form 72 provides notices required by law to be included in a health care power of attorney, although Ohio has not created an official health care power of attorney form. Therefore, you will need to attach form 3 to form 72. Be sure to read form 72, as it contains certain limits on the type of decisions your agent may make on your behalf.

*Oklahoma (form 74).* This form requires initials after each provision you select.

*Oregon (form 75).* Part E is a provision for your agent to sign accepting the appointment as your agent.

**Generic Forms**     If you do not live in a state with its own form, you may use the **DURABLE POWER OF ATTORNEY FOR HEALTH CARE**. (see form 3, p.95.) It is a health care power of attorney with living will provisions.

To complete the **DURABLE POWER OF ATTORNEY FOR HEALTH CARE** you need to do the following.

→ Type your name on the first line in the first paragraph, and your agent's name, address, and phone number on the second line of the paragraph.

→ If you wish to appoint an alternate agent in case your first choice is unable or unwilling to act, type in the alternate's name, address, and telephone number on the third line.

→ If you have any special instructions or limitations for your agent, type them in on the lines at the end of paragraph 3. You may want to read the powers of attorney for health care for the other states to get some ideas about what you may want to include here. If there are no instructions or limitations, type in the word "none."

→ In paragraph 4, select one of the three choices that expresses your desires. Check the box in front of your choice, and sign your name on the line after it.

> **NOTE:** *Choices 1 and 2 also have a box to check regarding the artificial delivery of food and water. This is a special issue, because food and water are not automatically included in most definitions of life-prolonging procedures. The withholding of food and water for a certain length of time can cause great pain and discomfort. You may want to discuss this matter with your doctor or another health care professional.*

→ In item 6, type in the name of your state on both lines.

→ Type in the date and sign your name on the signature line in front of two witnesses and a notary public.

→ Have two witnesses sign where indicated before the notary, and type in their names and addresses.

**The All-In-One Power of Attorney**

As discussed previously, it is possible to have one document serve as both a financial and health care power of attorney. If you wish to have such an all-inclusive power of attorney, see the section on "Durable Financial Power of Attorney" in Chapter 3. However, you will still need a living will, as explained later in this chapter. Also, if your state has a specific form in its statutes for a health care power of attorney, you should use your state's form. Check Appendix B to find out if there is a specific form for your state.

## YOUR HEALTH CARE AGENT

You should give careful thought to the choice of a health care agent. (Also referred to as surrogate in some health care power of attorney laws and forms.) After all, you may end up trusting this person with your life. Your agent should be someone you are close to and trust completely. An agent's responsibilities are often set forth in a state's laws. Generally, an agent may be expected to consult with health care providers and make informed decisions. Therefore, you should choose someone who is capable of understanding medical matters when explained by a doctor or other health care provider.

An agent is generally expected, or even required, to make decisions based upon what he or she believes you would decide under the circumstances. Therefore, you and your intended agent should discuss various possible injury and illness scenarios, and what type of treatment you would or would not want in certain circumstances. Some questions that should be asked and answered include the following.

- ✪ How do you feel about life-prolonging procedures?

- ✪ What types of medical procedures would you want or not want?

- ✪ Do you feel the same about these things in relation to being in a permanent coma as you do in relation to a terminal condition?

- ✪ If you were to be withdrawn from life-prolonging procedures, would you want that to include withholding water and feeding by artificial means?

These are just a few of the types of questions to be considered and discussed. You might also want to discuss your religious beliefs. All of this could help your agent make decisions for you. It might even help your agent defend his or her decision if challenged by another family member about what you would really want. Of course, one of the best ways to help your agent deal with certain conditions is to write down your wishes in a living will.

## THOSE WHO CAN MAKE MEDICAL TREATMENT DECISIONS

In some states, there is no law regarding who may make medical treatment decisions for another person. Other states have detailed laws on this subject. Of course, if you are mentally capable of understanding the options and expressing your wishes, then you always have the sole right to make the decision. However, if a patient is either mentally incapable of making the decision or is unable to communicate a decision, the following categories of people may be authorized to make decisions for the patient:

- ✪ an agent pursuant to a health care power of attorney;

- ✪ a court-appointed guardian who has been specifically authorized to make health care decisions;

- ✪ the patient's spouse;

- ✪ the patient's adult child, or a majority of his or her children;

- ✪ a parent of the patient;

- ✪ an adult brother or sister of the patient, or a majority of siblings;

- ✪ an adult relative of the patient; or,

- ✪ a close friend of the patient.

You may want to review this list and think about who might end up making life-or-death medical decisions for you. If this causes you some worry, a health care power of attorney—especially together with a living will—may alleviate your concern.

## LIVING WILLS

A *living will* is a legal document in which you express your wishes for the type of medical treatment you do or do not want in the event you suffer an illness or injury that leaves you in a particular type of medical condition. A living will typically only applies to what are considered *life-prolonging procedures* and only covers certain serious medical conditions that are defined by law.

Depending upon the state, laws generally provide for a living will to cover one or more of the following types of medical conditions:

- ✪ a *terminal condition*—typically defined as a condition caused by injury, disease, or illness from which there is no reasonable probability of recovery and that, without treatment, can be expected to cause death;

- ✪ a *persistent vegetative state*—typically defined as a permanent and irreversible condition of unconsciousness in which there is no voluntary action or cognitive behavior and an inability to communicate or interact purposefully with the environment; and,

- ✪ an *end-stage condition*—typically defined as a condition caused by injury, disease, or illness that has resulted in severe and permanent deterioration, indicated by incapacity and complete physical dependency, and for which, to a reasonable degree of medical certainty, treatment of the irreversible condition would be medically ineffective.

If at least one of the authorized conditions exists and you are either unable to make decisions or are unable to communicate your decisions, a living will expresses your decisions about whether you want to receive life-prolonging procedures. A typical definition of a life-prolonging procedure is:

*any medical procedure, treatment, or intervention, including artificially provided sustenance and hydration, that sustains, restores, or supplants a spontaneous vital function.*

The term does not include the administration of medication or performance of medical procedure, when such medication or procedure is deemed necessary to provide comfort care or to alleviate pain. To cover any other medical procedures, you would need a designation of health care agent.

Therefore, the following statements are true.

- As long as you are able to make and communicate decisions about your care, a living will has no effect.

- If at least one of the medical conditions described in your state's laws does not exist, a living will has no effect.

- If the medical procedure at issue is not a life-prolonging procedure, a living will has no effect.

If you have a health care power of attorney that authorizes your agent to make decisions about life-prolonging procedures, you may wonder why you need a living will. The answer is that a living will can help your agent make decisions based upon what you want. Your agent's duty is to make decisions based upon what he or she reasonably believes are your desires. Therefore, at some point, you need to tell your agent your desires in certain situations. This can be orally or in writing.

If there is no written direction, your agent will rely on conversations you had in which you expressed things such as what you would want if you were terminally ill or in a permanent vegetative state, as well as anything you may have said about your religious or philosophical beliefs. Through a living will, you can leave more concrete evidence of your wishes. The following case will show how this can be important.

### Example:

Jane and Bill are married. Jane has told Bill that if she were ever in a terminal condition or a permanent coma (i.e., permanent vegetative state), she would not want to be kept alive with any machines or feeding tubes. Jane is in an automobile accident that leaves her in what her doctors have deemed a permanent vegetative state.

After ten years of keeping her alive with a feeding tube, Bill finally decides that it is time to honor Jane's wishes and withdraw the feeding tube. Jane's parents, who cannot stand the thought of losing their daughter, and therefore refuse to accept that she is not going to recover, file a lawsuit to stop Bill from having the feeding tube removed. Jane's parents claim they have evidence that Jane never told Bill about her attitude toward the type of situation she is in.

It could take years for this case to wind its way through the various trial and appellate courts, while the feeding tube remains. If Jane had executed a living will, there would be little room to question her desires.

Some states' forms also allow you to designate a person to ensure that your wishes are carried out. However, unlike a health care power of attorney, a living will does not allow the person you designate to make health care decisions for you. It only allows that person to insist that your wishes expressed in the living will are followed. However, as discussed, a living will can be very helpful to support decisions made by your health care agent. Paragraph 4 in the **DURABLE POWER OF ATTORNEY FOR HEALTH CARE** is essentially a living will. (see form 3, p.95.)

## DO NOT RESUSCITATE ORDERS

A *do not resuscitate order* is a form that notifies medical care providers, such as hospital staff, nursing home or assisted living facility staff, and paramedics, that no resuscitation efforts are to be made in the event the patient's heart or breathing stops. You may also hear this referred to as a *no code order*, or abbreviated as *DNR*. Basically, do not resuscitate orders are used when the patient has a terminal condition and resuscitating the patient would do nothing more than briefly delay death and prolong discomfort.

A do not resuscitate order is typically signed by the patient's physician. In addition, depending upon the state, it may also be signed by:

- ✪   the patient;

- ✪   the patient's health care agent if the patient is incapacitated; or,

- ✪   the patient's court-appointed guardian who has the authority to make health care decisions.

This form is then posted in the patient's hospital or nursing home room, or somewhere in the patient's residence. Since this form will be provided by the physician, it is not included in the appendices.

---

## Example 1:

Bill is 95 years old, is mentally competent, and is suffering from severe congestive heart failure. He is only expected to live, at most, a few more months. Bill decides that if his heart stops, there is no point in the hospital staff resuscitating him, only for him to be in discomfort for a few more weeks and have to go through another heart attack. Bill and his doctor sign a do not resuscitate order.

## Example 2:

Margaret is 82 years old and has late-stage Alzheimer's Disease, leaving her bedridden with no quality of life. She has a health care power of attorney that appoints her daughter, Jean, as her surrogate. After consulting with Margaret's doctor, Jean decides that there would be no point in resuscitating Margaret so that she could continue in a vegetative state for a few more weeks or months. Jean and her mother's doctor sign a do not resuscitate order.

---

## ANATOMICAL GIFTS

An *anatomical gift* is when a patient, or other person with authority to make health care decisions, agrees to donate organs, other body parts, or the entire body upon death. In some states, such gifts are provided for on a person's driver's license. You may also have an opportunity to sign a document for an anatomical gift when being admitted to a hospital. Forms may also be available from various medical facilities, doctors, government agencies, organ banks, and so on.

# Other Power of Attorney Forms

## chapter 5

One of the best attributes of powers of attorney is their flexibility. In addition to allowing another to act on your behalf in matters related to your finances and health care, a power of attorney can be used to assist you in a child care situation. However, when giving another decision-making power regarding your child, you must be sure to monitor and limit that power.

This is also true for financial and health care powers of attorney. At times, it may be necessary to revoke the authority you bestow on another. This chapter discusses powers of attorney for child care and how to revoke a power of attorney once given.

## POWER OF ATTORNEY FOR CHILD CARE

A *power of attorney for child care* authorizes someone to make decisions regarding your child when you are not present to do so. This will usually be necessary if your child is going to live with a relative or friend, or will be on a prolonged visit to a relative or friend who lives far away from you.

People send their children to live with someone else for a variety or reasons, including:

○ making the child eligible for enrollment in a desired school;

○ ensuring adequate care for the child while the parent is working long hours or must be away for business;

○ maintaining adequate care for the child during the parent's serious illness;

○ sending a difficult child to someone better able to handle disciplinary problems;

○ keeping the child away from an abusive parent; or,

○ allowing the child a prolonged visit (such as summer vacation) with a friend or relative.

For whatever reason the child goes to live elsewhere, you will probably want that friend or relative to be able to enroll the child in school, sign permission slips for field trips, give consent to emergency or other medical care, and do whatever else is necessary for your child that would require parental consent. To accomplish this, a power of attorney may be needed. Such a form is provided in Appendix B of this book.

Follow these directions to complete a **LIMITED POWER OF ATTORNEY FOR CHILD CARE**. (see form 8, p.108.)

◈ Type in your name, your address, your child's name, and the name of the person you want as your agent on the lines in the first paragraph.

◈ Type in the date, time period, or other provision for when the power will end on the line in the last paragraph. If you want it to continue indefinitely, simply cross out the last line.

◈ Fill in the date where indicated, then sign on the signature line before a notary.

# REVOKING A POWER OF ATTORNEY

As mentioned earlier, your agent will have the authority to bind you by what he or she does on your behalf. To guard against your agent getting out of control, you must have the ability to end his or her right to represent you. There are specific ways to go about *revoking* a power of attorney.

Some powers of attorney provide that they end on a certain date. If such a provision is not part of your power of attorney, the agent's authority continues until you take some action to end it. Generally, you must sign another document revoking the power of attorney and give a copy of it to anyone who knows about, or has relied on, the power of attorney.

Anyone who is aware of the power of attorney and has conducted business with your agent may continue to assume your agent has authority until you notify them otherwise. Be sure to give them a copy of the revocation, preferably either by return-receipt mail, or by having them date and sign a copy so you have proof it was received.

Some of the power of attorney forms in Appendix B contain a provision for when the power of attorney terminates. These have optional provisions for termination. You will check the box for the provision you desire or write in a provision. The options are:

- ✪ termination upon written revocation by the principal;

- ✪ termination upon a particular date; or,

- ✪ termination upon a particular event.

Form 9 is a general **REVOCATION OF POWER OF ATTORNEY** form. (see form 9, p.109.) Be aware that this form has not been made a part of the law of any state.

Follow these steps to complete form 9.

- ◈ Type in your name and address on the first line in the main paragraph.

◈    Type in the title of the power of attorney you are revoking on the second line. This will be the title as it appears on the document, such as "Power of Attorney for Health Care," "Advance Health Care Directive," or "Statutory Power of Attorney."

◈    Type in the date of the power of attorney you are revoking on the third line.

◈    Type in the name of your agent on the fourth line.

◈    Type in the date on the line indicated and sign on the signature line (sign before a notary if the power of attorney you are revoking was also signed before a notary). Provisions are also included for two witnesses.

In addition to notifying your agent, you will need to notify certain people of your revocation. In the case of a financial power of attorney, you need to notify those people with whom your agent has conducted business on your behalf, as well as anyone else who is aware of the power of attorney. These people or businesses should be given a copy of the written revocation. In the case of a power of attorney for health care (or a living will), you need to notify your doctor, hospital, or other health care providers. Some state laws allow you to notify health care providers orally, although a written revocation is still the best way.

# Lawyers

## chapter 6

Whether or not you need an attorney depends upon many factors, such as how comfortable you feel handling the matter yourself and whether your situation is more complicated than usual. The purpose of a power of attorney is to allow someone you trust to act on your behalf when you are unable to do so. A power of attorney needs to accurately reflect your wishes and meet the legal requirements for it to be honored by others. The way most lawyers would approach this would be to consult your state laws, possibly consult a book such as this one, look at examples of other powers of attorney (that either they or other lawyers have prepared), and prepare a document to fit your situation. That is exactly what this book enables you to do for yourself.

However, there may be times when you should consult an attorney regarding your situation. The more complicated your financial affairs, or the more unique and specific your medical decisions are, having an attorney review your document could be helpful in making sure your wishes are what are described in your powers of attorney. This chapter helps you with using a lawyer in those situations requiring additional advice beyond this book.

# DO YOU WANT A LAWYER?

One of the first questions you will want to consider—and most likely the reason you are reading this book—is, *How much will an attorney cost?* Attorneys come in all ages, shapes, sizes, sexes, races, and ethnic groups—and price ranges. For a very rough estimate, you can expect an attorney to charge anywhere from $75 to $300 per hour. Some may prepare a power of attorney for a flat fee that may range anywhere from $50 to $500.

**Advantages to Hiring an Attorney**

There are several reasons using an attorney will be to your advantage. Some of those reasons would include the following.

✪ You can let your lawyer worry about all of the details. By having an attorney, you only need to become generally familiar with the contents of this book.

✪ Lawyers provide professional assistance with problems. It is an advantage to have an attorney in the event your situation is complicated or suddenly becomes complicated. It can also be comforting to have a lawyer to turn to for advice or to answer your questions.

**Advantages to Creating Your Own Power of Attorney**

There are, however, reasons why creating the power of attorney yourself will have distinct advantages. Some of those reasons include the following.

✪ You save the cost of a lawyer.

✪ You may get done faster. Two of the most frequent complaints about lawyers received by bar associations involve delay in completing the case and failure to return phone calls. Most lawyers have a heavy caseload that sometimes results in cases being neglected for various periods of time. If you are doing the work yourself, you can work at a faster pace.

✪ Selecting an attorney is not easy. As the next section shows, it is hard to know whether you are selecting an attorney you will be happy with.

**Middle Ground**    You may want to look for an attorney who is willing to accept an hourly fee to answer your questions and give you help as you need it. This way, you save some legal costs, but still get some professional assistance. Just be aware that lawyers tend to find fault with anything they did not personally prepare. For example, you can show a lawyer a document he or she prepared, and if the attorney does not remember preparing it, he or she will find things to change. A lawyer may tell you that you have done everything wrong and try to persuade you let him or her redo your power of attorney. Therefore, you may want to resort to seeing a lawyer only if you have encountered a problem with third parties.

## SELECTING A LAWYER

Selecting a lawyer is a two-step process. First, you need to decide which attorney to make an appointment with. Then, you need to decide if you want to hire that attorney.

**Finding Possible Lawyers**    There are many ways to find an attorney. Some of the ways may give you a little more confidence in your selection as you go to evaluate the lawyer, while others may provide a quick list to choose from with no other information. The following are some of the most common ways to find an attorney.

*Ask a friend.* A common—and frequently the best—way to find a lawyer is to ask someone you know to recommend one. This is especially helpful if the lawyer helped your friend create his or her power of attorney.

*Attorney referral service.* An attorney referral service is designed to match a client with an attorney handling cases in the area of law the client needs. The referral service, usually operated by a bar association, does not guarantee the quality of work, the level of experience, or the ability of the attorney. Finding a lawyer this way will at least connect you with one who is interested in power of attorney matters and probably has some experience in this area. You can find a referral service by looking in the Yellow Pages phone directory under "Attorney Referral Services" or "Attorneys."

***Yellow Pages.*** In addition to attorney referral services, you can look for lawyers in the Yellow Pages under the heading for "Attorneys." Many of the lawyers and law firms will place display ads here indicating their areas of practice and educational backgrounds. Look for ads for firms or lawyers that indicate they practice in areas such as living wills or powers of attorney.

***Ask another lawyer.*** If you have used the services of an attorney in the past for some other matter (for example, a real estate closing or traffic ticket), you may want to call and ask if he or she handles powers of attorney, or could refer you to an attorney whose ability in the area is respected.

**Evaluating a Lawyer**

After putting together a list of potential attorneys, you should select three to five lawyers worthy of further consideration. Your first step will be to call each attorney's office, explain that you are interested in having a power of attorney prepared, and ask the following questions.

- ✪ Does the attorney (or firm) handle powers of attorney?

- ✪ How much can you expect it to cost?

- ✪ How soon can you get an appointment?

If you like the answers you get, ask if you can speak to the attorney. Some offices will permit this, but others will require you to make an appointment. Make the appointment if that is what is required. Once you contact the attorney (either on the phone or at the appointment), ask the following questions.

- ✪ How long has the attorney been in practice?

- ✪ How long has the attorney been in practice in your state?

- ✪ What percentage of the attorney's cases involve powers of attorney? (Do not expect an exact answer, but you should get a rough estimate that is at least 20%.)

❂   How long will it take to have the powers of attorney prepared? (Do not expect an exact answer, but the attorney should be able to give you an average range and discuss things that may make a difference.)

❂   How much will it cost? (Do not expect an exact answer, but the attorney should be able to give you a range of costs and what could affect overall costs.)

If you get acceptable answers to these questions, it is time to ask yourself the following questions about the lawyer.

❂   Do you feel comfortable talking to the lawyer?

❂   Is the lawyer friendly toward you?

❂   Does the lawyer seem confident in him- or herself?

❂   Does the lawyer seem to be straightforward with you and able to explain things so you understand?

If you get satisfactory answers to all of these questions, you probably have a lawyer you will be able to work with. Most clients are happiest with an attorney they feel comfortable with.

## WORKING WITH A LAWYER

Once you hire your attorney, let your lawyer do his or her job. You will work best with your attorney if you listen to his or her instruction and keep an open, honest, and friendly attitude. You should also consider the following suggestions.

**Ask Questions**    If you want to know something, or if you do not understand something, ask your attorney. If you do not understand the answer, tell your attorney and ask that it be explained again. There are many points of law that even lawyers do not fully understand, so you should not be embarrassed to ask questions. Many people who say they had a bad experience with a lawyer either did not ask enough questions or had a lawyer who would not take the time to explain things to them. If your lawyer is not taking the time to explain what he or she is doing, it may be time to look for a new lawyer.

**Give Complete Information**

Anything you tell your attorney is confidential. An attorney can lose his or her license to practice if he or she reveals information without your permission, so do not hold back. Tell your lawyer everything, even if it does not seem important to you.

**Be Patient**

Be patient with the system (which is often slow), as well as with your attorney. Do not expect your lawyer to return your phone call within an hour. He or she may not be able to return it the same day, either. Most lawyers are very busy and overworked. It is rare that an attorney can maintain a full caseload and still make each client feel like the only client.

**Talk to the Secretary**

Your lawyer's secretary can be a valuable source of information. Be friendly and get to know him or her. Often, he or she will be able to answer your questions, and you will not get a bill for the time you talk to the secretary.

**Be on Time**

This applies to all appointments with your lawyer.

**Keep Your Attorney's Attention**

Many lawyers operate on the old principle of *the squeaking wheel gets the oil*. Work on a case tends to get put off until a deadline is near, an emergency develops, or the client calls. There is a reason for this. Many lawyers take more cases than can be effectively handled in order to increase their income. Your task is to become a squeaking wheel that does not squeak too much. Whenever you talk to your lawyer, ask the following questions.

- ✪ What is the next step?

- ✪ When do you expect it to be done?

- ✪ When should I talk to you next?

If you do not hear from the lawyer when you expect, call him or her the following day. Do not remind your lawyer that he or she did not call; just ask how things are going.

**Avoid Excess Fees**

Of course, you do not want to spend unnecessary money for an attorney. The following are a few things you can do to avoid excess legal fees.

- Do not make unnecessary phone calls to your lawyer.

- Give information to the secretary whenever possible.

- Direct your question to the secretary first. The secretary will refer it to the attorney if he or she cannot answer it.

- Plan your phone calls so you can get to the point and take less of your attorney's time.

- Do some of the legwork yourself, such as picking up and delivering papers yourself. Ask your attorney what you can do to assist him or her.

- Be prepared for appointments. Have all related papers with you and plan your visit to get to the point. Make an outline of what you want to discuss and what questions you want to ask.

**Pay Your Bill**

No client gets prompt attention like a client who pays his or her lawyer on time. You are entitled to an itemized bill, showing what the attorney did and how much time it took. Review your bill carefully. If your attorney asks for money in advance, you should be sure that you and the lawyer agree on what is to be done for this fee.

Many attorneys will have you sign an agreement that states how you will be charged, what is included in the hourly fee, and what is extra. Do not be surprised if your lawyer asks you to sign a fee agreement.

## FIRING YOUR LAWYER

If you find that you can no longer work with your lawyer or do not trust your lawyer, it is time to either continue alone or get a new attorney. You will need to send your lawyer a letter stating that you no longer desire his or her services, and that you are discharging him or her from your case.

Also state that you will be coming by his or her office the following day to pick up your file. The attorney does not have to give you his or her own notes, or other work in progress, but he or she must give you the essential contents of your file (such as copies of papers already filed or prepared and billed for, and any documents you provided). If the lawyer refuses to give you the file for any reason, contact your state's bar association about filing a complaint or grievance against the lawyer. Of course, you will need to settle any remaining fees charged.

# Glossary

This glossary provides general definitions. Any of these terms may be specifically defined by the laws of your state. If any term is specifically defined by the laws of your state, that definition will be used in interpreting any legal document you may use.

## A

**acknowledgment.** A statement, written or oral, made before a person authorized by law to administer oaths (such as a notary public).

**adult.** In most states, a person 18 years of age or older.

**advance directive.** (1) A general term used to describe any legally recognized written document or oral statement in which a person gives instructions concerning his or her health care. It includes a health care power of attorney, a living will, or an anatomical gift. (2) The title given to a health care power of attorney or living will in some states.

**affiant.** The legal term for the person who signs an affidavit.

**affidavit.** A person's written statement of facts, signed under oath before a person authorized to administer oaths (such as a notary public or court clerk).

**agent.** The person who is given authority by a power of attorney.

**anatomical gift.** The donation of an organ, other body part, or the entire body, upon death.

**attending physician.** The primary physician who has responsibility for the treatment and care of the patient.

**attorney-at-law.** A person who is licensed to practice law before state or federal courts. The term has no relationship to an attorney-in-fact.

**attorney-in-fact.** The person who is given authority by a power of attorney. This is another term for an *agent*. An attorney-in-fact does not have the power to represent anyone in court or to give legal advice.

# C

**chose in action.** A right to recover personal property, a debt, or damages by a lawsuit. A potential or pending lawsuit for the recovery of property or money.

**creditor.** A person or institution to whom money is owed.

# D

**debtor.** A person or institution who owes money.

**decedent.** A person who has died.

**do not resuscitate order.** A document signed by a patient's physician and by the patient, or someone having the proper legal authority to act on his or her behalf, that instructs medical personnel not to attempt resuscitation in the event the patient's heart or breathing ceases.

**donee.** One who is the recipient of a donation.

**donor.** One who makes a donation.

**durable power of attorney.** A power of attorney that continues after the principal becomes incapacitated.

# E

**end-stage condition.** A condition that is caused by injury, disease, or illness that has resulted in severe and permanent deterioration, indicated by incapacity and complete physical dependency. To a reasonable degree of medical certainty, treatment of the irreversible condition would be medically ineffective.

**execute.** To sign a legal document in the legally required manner (e.g., before witnesses or a notary public), thereby making it effective.

# F

**fiduciary.** A person having a duty, created by his or her own undertaking, to act primarily for the benefit of another.

**financial power of attorney.** A power of attorney giving the agent the power to act in financial matters, as opposed to health care matters.

# G

**general power of attorney.** A power of attorney that gives the agent very broad powers, generally to conduct all kinds of business on behalf of the principal.

**guardian of the person.** A person who is authorized by a court, pursuant to a guardianship proceeding, to make decisions regarding the care of another person.

**guardian of the property.** A person who is authorized by a court, pursuant to a guardianship proceeding, to handle the financial affairs of another person.

**guardianship.** (1) A legal proceeding to determine whether a person is legally incompetent and should have a guardian appointed to care for the person or the person's financial matters. (2) The legal relationship between a guardian and a ward.

# H

**health care advance directive.** The term used in some states for a health care power of attorney.

**health care power of attorney.** A special kind of power of attorney that gives the agent the authority to make decisions regarding the principal's medical care. The agent only has power in the event the principal is mentally unable to make intelligent decisions or is unable to communicate his or her decisions.

**homestead.** Real estate that is a person's primary place of residence. In some states, the homestead is given special treatment for property tax purposes, is exempt from the claims of creditors (other than a creditor holding a mortgage on the homestead property), and has various other privileges.

**hydration (artificial).** Providing a person with water through a feeding (gastrointestinal) or intravenous tube.

# I

**incapacitated or incapacity.** As used in this book, mentally unable to make intelligent, informed decisions, or mentally or physically unable to communicate.

**incompetent, incompetence, or incompetency.** A person is incompetent if he or she has been judicially determined to lack the capacity to manage at least some of his or her property, or to meet at least some of the essential health and safety requirements of taking care of one's self. This can be a little confusing, because some state laws use the word "incapacity." In this book, however, the word "incapacity" is used when there has not been a legal determination, and the word "incompetency" is used when there has been such a determination.

**institution.** Any type of business entity (e.g., corporation, partnership, limited liability company), organization, or other entity other than an individual person.

**instrument.** A legal term for a document.

**inter vivos trust.** *See living trust.*

**intestate.** When a person dies without leaving a will.

# J

**joint tenancy.** A way for two or more people to own property, so that when one owner dies, his or her interest in the property passes automatically to the remaining owner or owners.

# L

**lessee.** One who rents property from another.

**lessor.** One who rents property to another.

**life-prolonging procedure.** Any medical procedure, treatment, or intervention, including artificially provided sustenance and hydration, that sustains, restores, or supplants a spontaneous vital function. The term does not include the administration of medication or performance of medical procedure, when such medication or procedure is deemed necessary to provide comfort care or to alleviate pain.

**limited power of attorney.** A power of attorney that limits the agent's authority to certain specific areas or actions.

**living trust.** A legal relationship, established while the grantor is alive, in which one person (called the grantor) gives assets to another person or institution (called a trustee) to control for the benefit of the grantor or a third party (called the beneficiary). A living trust is set up while the grantor is alive, whereas a testamentary trust is set up after the grantor dies, as directed in the grantor's last will and testament.

**living will.** A document stating a person's desires regarding the use of life-prolonging procedures in the event he or she is in a certain medical condition—such as a terminal condition, an end-stage condition, or a permanent vegetative state—and is either unable to make his or her own decisions or is unable to communicate his or her wishes.

# N

**notary public.** A person who is legally authorized by the state to acknowledge signatures on legal documents.

**nutrition (artificial).** Providing a person with food through a feeding (gastrointestinal), or an intravenous, tube.

# P

**palliative care.** Medical care or treatment designed to alleviate pain or discomfort, rather than to cure or control the underlying illness or injury.

**pay-on-death account.** A financial account, such as a bank account or certificate of deposit, that is payable to a certain person upon the death of the account holder.

**persistent vegetative state.** A permanent and irreversible condition of unconsciousness in which there is the absence of voluntary action or cognitive behavior of any kind and an inability to communicate or interact purposefully with the environment.

**personal property.** All property other than land and things permanently attached to the land (such as buildings).

**proxy.** *See agent.*

**power of appointment.** A power, given by the owner of property to another person, to designate who will receive property or income from the property upon the death of the owner.

**power of attorney.** A document that gives one person (the agent) authority to act on behalf of another person (the principal).

**powers of attorney.** The plural form of power of attorney. Also, the various specific authorities granted to an agent in a power of attorney document.

**principal.** The person who executes a power of attorney, and thereby gives the agent the authority to act on his or her behalf.

# R

**recording.** The process of filing a deed, mortgage, or other legal document affecting title to land with the court clerk's office.

**revocation.** The recalling or cancellation of a previously granted power.

# S

**special power of attorney.** *See limited power of attorney.*

**springing power of attorney.** A power of attorney that does not become effective until a certain event occurs, such as the incapacity of the principal.

**surrogate.** Another term for the *agent*, used in some states.

# T

**tenancy by the entirety.** This is essentially the same as joint tenancy, but it can only occur between a husband and wife. Upon the death of one spouse, the property automatically passes to the surviving spouse. In states that do not have a tenancy by the entirety, spouses typically hold property as joint tenants with rights of survivorship.

**tenancy in common.** A way for two or more people to own property, whereby if one of the owners dies, his or her interest in the property passes to his or her heirs (not to the other co-owners).

**terminal condition.** A condition caused by injury, disease, or illness from which there is no reasonable probability of recovery, and which, without treatment, can be expected to cause death.

**third party.** As used in this book, a party who is neither a principal nor an agent under a power of attorney.

**title.** A document that proves ownership of property.

# W

**ward.** A person who has been declared incompetent and has a guardian appointed.

# State Laws

This appendix lists each state alphabetically and gives information about each state's laws concerning powers of attorney. You will find one or more of these three categories under each state as follows.

1.  *In General.* This contains any general power of attorney provisions that do not fall under one of the other categories.

2.  *Financial.* This references state laws concerning a financial power of attorney. Whether durable or springing powers of attorney are authorized by the state law is also indicated, along with the language suggested in the statute.

3.  *Health Care.* This references state laws concerning powers of attorney for health care, or living wills.

The first category will also give information about finding the state laws, including the full title of the set of law books with an example of how it is abbreviated.

**NOTE:** *The symbol "§" and the abbreviation "s." mean section, and "§§" means sections.*

# ALABAMA

*Financial:*   Michie's Alabama Code 1975, or Code of Alabama 1975; Title 26, Chapter 1, Section 26-1-2 (C.A. §26-1-2). Durable or springing: "This power of attorney shall not be affected by disability, incompetency, or incapacity of the principal" or "This power of attorney shall become effective upon the disability, incompetency, or incapacity of the principal." No statutory form. Can include a health care power of attorney if it meets the statutory requirements.

*Health Care:*   C.A. §22-8A-1. "Natural Death Act." Health care power of attorney is part of the Advance Directive for Health Care form found at C.A. §22-8A-4, which also includes living will provisions.

# ALASKA

*Financial:*   Alaska Statutes, Title 13, Section 13.26.332 (A.S. §13.26.332). Statutory form.

*Health Care:*   Health care is included in the statutory financial power of attorney form. Power of attorney for mental health treatment: A.S. §47.30.950; form at A.S. §47.30.970.

Living Will: A.S. §18.12.010, "Living Wills and Do Not Resuscitate Orders."

# ARIZONA

*Financial:*   Arizona Revised Statutes, Title 14, Section 14-5501 (A.R.S. §14-5501). Durable or springing: "This power of attorney is not affected by subsequent disability or incapacity of the principal or lapse of time," or "This power of attorney is effective on the disability or incapacity of the principal." No statutory form. To be valid, must: (1) clearly show intent to make a power of attorney and clearly designate an agent; (2) be dated and signed; (3) be notarized; and, (4) be witnessed by one person other than the agent, the agent's spouse, or the agent's children.

*Health Care:*   A.R.S. §36-3221; form at A.R.S. §36-3224. A separate mental health care power of attorney is provided for in A.R.S. §36-3281; form at A.R.S. §36-3286. Living will form found at A.R.S. §36-3262; and a "Prehospital Medical Care Directive" is found at A.R.S. §36-3251.

# ARKANSAS

*Financial:*   Arkansas Code of 1987 Annotated, Title 28, Chapter 68, Section 28-68-201 (A.C.A. §28-68-201). Form found at A.C.A. §28-68-401. Durable or springing: "This power of attorney shall not be affected by subsequent disability or incapacity of the principal," or "This power of attorney shall become effective upon the disability or incapacity of the principal," or similar language. Also see A.C.A. §28-68-301. Titled "Powers of Attorney for Small Property Interests." This is limited to (1) property with a gross value up to $20,000, not including homestead or capitalized value of any annual income, or (2) annual income up to $6,000.

*Health Care:*   Living Will: A.C.A. §20-17-201. Form found at A.C.A. §20-17-202.

# CALIFORNIA

*In General:*   *West's* Annotated California Probate Code, Section 4000 et seq. (A.C.P.C. §4000 et seq.)

*Financial:*   A.C.P.C. §4124. "Uniform Durable Power of Attorney Act." Durable or springing: "This power of attorney shall not be affected by subsequent incapacity of the principal," "This power of attorney shall become effective upon the incapacity of the principal," or similar language. Form may be found at A.C.P.C. §4401.

*Health Care:*   A.C.P.C. §4700, "Advance Health Care Directive Forms." Form may be found at A.C.P.C. §4701, which includes living will provisions.

## COLORADO

*Financial:*    *West's* Colorado Revised Statutes Annotated, Title 15, Section 15-1-1301 (C.R.S.A. §15-1-1301). "Uniform Statutory Form Power of Attorney Act." Form found at C.R.S.A. §15-1-1302. Durable: "This power of attorney will continue to be effective even though I become disabled, incapacitated, or incompetent" or similar language. "Uniform Durable Power of Attorney Act," C.R.S.A. §15-14-501, provides for durable or springing: "This power of attorney shall not be affected by disability of the principal," "This power of attorney shall become effective upon the disability of the principal," or similar language.

*Health Care:*    C.R.S.A. §15-14-506. Authorizes a "medical durable power of attorney," but no form is provided.

Living Will: C.R.S.A. §15-18-101. "Colorado Medical Treatment Decisions Act." Form may be found at C.R.S.A. §15-18-104.

The designation of a "proxy decision-maker" is authorized by C.R.S.A. §15-18.5-103. Organ donation provided for in C.R.S.A. §12-34-105.

## CONNECTICUT

*Financial:*    Connecticut General Statutes Annotated, Title 1, Section 1-42 (C.G.S.A. §1-42). "Connecticut Statutory Short Form Power of Attorney Act." Ignore "Chapter" numbers. Form found at C.G.S.A. §1-43. Durable power of attorney for bank accounts is found at C.G.S.A. §1-56b. Springing powers of attorney authorized by C.G.S.A. §1-56h. Affidavit for agent to certify that power of attorney is in full force and effect is found at C.G.S.A. §1-56i.

*Health Care:*    Health Care Power of Attorney may be found at C.G.S.A. §19a-575a.

Living Will: C.G.S.A. §19a-570, titled "Removal of Life Support Systems." Form may be found at C.G.S.A. §19a-575.

## DELAWARE

*In General:*    Delaware Code Annotated, Title 25, Section 171 (D.C.A. 25 §171). This applies to real estate.

*Financial:*    D.C.A. 12 §4901. Durable or springing: "This power of attorney shall not be affected by the subsequent disability or incapacity of the principal," "This power of attorney shall become effective upon the disability or incapacity of the principal," or similar language.

*Health Care:*    D.C.A. 16 §2501. Form found at D.C.A. 16 §2505. Requires two witnesses, who may not be related to the declarant, not be entitled to a share of the estate, not have any claims against the declarant, not have any financial responsibility for the declarant's medical care, and not be an employee of the hospital or other facility where the declarant is a patient. The witnesses must state in writing (this can be incorporated into the living will above their signature lines) that they "are not prohibited from being a witness under D.C.A. 16 §2503(b)."

## DISTRICT OF COLUMBIA

*Financial:*    District of Columbia Code, Title 21, Section 2081 (D.C.C. §21-2081). The spine of the book reads "D.C. Official Code." "Uniform Durable Power of Attorney Act." Durable or springing: "This power or attorney shall not be affected by subsequent disability or incapacity of the principal, or lapse of time," "This power of attorney shall become effective upon the disability or incapacity of the principal," or similar language. Also, D.C.C. §21-2102 provides for durable: "This power of attorney will continue to be effective if I become disabled, incapacitated, or incompetent." Form found at D.C.C. §21-2101.

*Health Care:*    D.C.C. §21-2201. "Health-Care Decisions." Form found at D.C.C. §21-2207.

# FLORIDA

*Financial:* Florida Statutes, Chapter 709, Section 709.08 (F.S. §709.08). Durable or springing. The language set forth in the statute initially appears to only provide for a durable power of attorney: "This durable power of attorney is not affected by subsequent incapacity of the principal except as provided in §709.08, Florida Statutes" or similar language. However, the statute also allows for a springing power of attorney, stating that: "if the durable power of attorney is conditioned upon the principal's lack of capacity to manage property as defined in s. 744.102(11)(a)," it is valid upon the delivery of certain affidavits from the agent and the principal's primary physician. Appropriate forms can be found in Appendix B. There is no statutory power of attorney form. It must be executed and witnessed in the same manner as documents for the transfer of real estate (i.e., signed before two witnesses and a notary). It can incorporate provisions for a health care surrogate. The statute provides for an award of attorney's fees to a party prevailing in a lawsuit to unreasonable refusal to honor a financial power of attorney.

*Health Care:* F.S. Chapter 765. Health Care Surrogate form found at F.S. §765.203.

Living Will: Form found at F.S. §765.303.

# GEORGIA

*Financial:* Official Code of Georgia Annotated, Title 10, Chapter 6, Section 10-6-1 (O.C.G.A. §10-6-1). This is titled "Agency," and deals with powers of attorney in general. Durable or springing options in official form. O.C.G.A. §10-6-6 authorizes springing power of attorney, and provides that principal can designate any person or persons to have the power to conclusively determine when the disability or other event has occurred that will make the document effective. Such persons must execute a declaration swearing that the event has occurred. Form may be found at O.C.G.A. §§10-6-141 and 10-6-142. (This is not the "Georgia Code," which is a separate and outdated set of books with a completely different numbering system.)

*Health Care:* O.C.G.A. §31-36-1. "Durable Power of Attorney for Health Care Act." Form found at O.C.G.A. §31-36-10. Includes living will provisions. Living will form found at O.C.G.A. §31-32-3.

# HAWAII

*In General:* Hawaii Revised Statutes, Section 501-174 (H.R.S. §501-174), and §502-84, concern requirements for filing a power of attorney for real estate with the land court and the bureau of conveyances. Ignore "Title" numbers.

*Financial:* H.R.S. §551D-1, "Uniform Durable Power of Attorney Act." Durable or springing: "This power of attorney shall not be affected by the disability of the principal" or "This power of attorney shall become effective upon the disability of the principal." No form.

*Health Care:* H.R.S. §327E-1, "Uniform Health-Care Decisions Act (Modified)." Form found at H.R.S. §327E-16. Includes living will provisions. Form for a mental health care power of attorney found at H.R.S. §327G-14.

# IDAHO

*Financial:* Idaho Code, Title 15, Chapter 5, Part 5, Section 15-5-501 (I.C. §15-5-501). "Uniform Durable Power of Attorney Act." Durable or springing: "This power or attorney shall not be affected by subsequent disability or incapacity of the principal," "This power of attorney shall become effective upon the disability or incapacity of the principal," or similar language.

*Health Care:*   Idaho Code, Title 39, Chapter 45, Section 39-4501 (I.C. §39-4501). "Medical Consent and Natural Death Act." Form found at I.C. §39-4510. Includes living will.

## ILLINOIS

*In General:*   *West's* Smith-Hurd Illinois Compiled Statutes Annotated, Chapter 755, Article 45, Section 1-1 (755 ILCS 45/1-1). "Illinois Power of Attorney Act." The financial and health care power of attorney provisions are subparts of this general law.

*Financial:*   755 ILCS 45/2-1, "Durable Power of Attorney Law;" and 755 ILCS 45/3-1, "Statutory Short Form Power of Attorney for Property Law." Statutory form is found at 755 ILCS 45/3-3, which includes durable or springing options.

*Health Care:*   755 ILCS 45/4-1, "Powers of Attorney for Health Care Law." Form is found at 755 ILCS 45/4-10. Form for living will found at 755 ILCS 35/3.

## INDIANA

*Financial:*   *West's* Annotated Indiana Code, Title 30, Article 5, Chapter 1, Section 30-5-1-1 (A.I.C. §30-5-1-1). Durable or springing authorized by A.I.C. §30-5-4-2, but no specific language in statute. Statute does not provide a form, but states that a form can be used that refers to the descriptive language in A.I.C. §§30-5-5-2 to 30-5-5-19 (these sections define each power that is generally referred to, and referenced, in the form). Statute provides that a power of attorney must be notarized.

*Health Care:*   A.I.C. §16-36-1-1. "Health Care Consent." Allows appointment of a "health care representative," but no form is provided. This can also be accomplished with the general power of attorney pursuant to A.I.C. §30-5-5-1, which includes a provision for health care powers.

Living Will: A.I.C. §16-36-4-1. Form for refusing life-prolonging procedures found at A.I.C. §16-36-4-10. Form for requesting life-prolonging procedures found at A.I.C. §16-36-4-11.

## IOWA

*Financial:*   Iowa Code Annotated, Section 633.705 (I.C.A. §633.705). "Powers of Attorney." Durable or springing: "This power of attorney shall not be affected by disability of the principal," "This power of attorney shall become effective upon the disability of the principal," or similar language.

*Health Care:*   I.C.A. §144B.1. Forms may be found at I.C.A. §144B.5 (Durable Power of Attorney for Health Care), and I.C.A. §144A.3 (Living Will).

## KANSAS

*In General:*   Kansas Statutes Annotated, Section 58-650 (K.S.A. §58-650). You may find these volumes as either "Vernon's Kansas Statutes Annotated," or "Kansas Statutes Annotated, Official." The supplement is a pocket part in Vernon's, and a separate softcover volume in the "Official." Both sets have very poor indexing systems.

*Financial:*   K.S.A. §58-650. "Kansas Power of Attorney Act." To be durable, it must be designated as a "durable power of attorney." Durable or springing: "This is a durable power of attorney and the authority of my attorney in fact shall not terminate if I become disabled or in the event of later uncertainty as to whether I am dead or alive" or "This is a durable power of attorney and the authority of my attorney in fact, when effective, shall not terminate or be void or voidable if I am or become disabled or in the event of later uncertainty as to whether I am dead or alive." Must be signed, dated, and notarized.

*Health Care:*    K.S.A. §58-625. "Durable Power of Attorney for Health Care Decisions." Form found at K.S.A. §58-632. Living will form found at K.S.A. §65-28,103.

## KENTUCKY

*Financial:*    Kentucky Revised Statutes, Chapter 386, Section 386.093 (K.R.S. §386.093). Durable or springing: "This power of attorney shall not be affected by subsequent disability or incapacity of the principal, or lapse of time," "This power of attorney shall become effective upon the disability of incapacity of the principal," or similar language. For recording a power of attorney for conveying real estate, see K.R.S. §382.370.

*Health Care:*    Living Will: K.R.S. §311.621, "Kentucky Living Will Directive Act." Form at K.R.S. §311.625.

## LOUISIANA

*In General:*    *West's* Louisiana Statutes Annotated. The set of Louisiana statutes is divided into topics, such as "Civil Code," "Revised Statutes," etc., so be sure you have the correct topic. For example, for the Civil Code, the book spines read "West's LSA Civil Code," and the front covers read "Louisiana Civil Code." In Louisiana, a power of attorney is also called a "mandate," "procuration," or "letter of attorney." The agent is also referred to as the "proxy" or "mandatary." L.S.A. Civil Code, Article 2989. No specific form is required, unless specified by a statute relating to a particular type of power of attorney. L.S.A. Civil Code, Art. 2993. Certain powers must be expressly given. L.S.A. Civil Code, Art. 2996 & 2997.

*Financial:*    A financial power of attorney is automatically durable, unless otherwise stated in the document. L.S.A. Civil Code, Art. 3026.

*Health Care:*    L.S.A. Revised Statutes §40:1299.53 provides that health care decisions can be made by "an agent acting pursuant to a valid mandate, specifically authorizing the agent to make health-care decisions." No statutory form.

Living Will: L.S.A. Revised Statutes §40:1299.58.1. "Natural Death Act." Form may be found at L.S.A. Rev. Stat. §40:1299.58.3; special form for military personnel stationed in the state may be found at L.S.A. Rev. Stat. §40:1299.61.

## MAINE

*Financial:*    Maine Revised Statutes Annotated, Title 18-A, Section 5-501 (18-A M.R.S.A. §5-501). Durable or springing: "This power of attorney is not affected by subsequent disability or incapacity of the principal or lapse of time" or "This power of attorney becomes effective upon the disability or incapacity of the principal." No statutory form. Notice requirements found at 18-A M.R.S.A. §5-508(c). Power of attorney must be notarized by either a notary public or an attorney.

*Health Care:*    18-A M.R.S.A. §5-801. "Uniform Health-Care Decisions Act." Form found at 18-A M.R.S.A. §5-804. Also provided for in 18-A M.R.S.A. §5-506, but no form in that statute.

## MARYLAND

*In General:*    Annotated Code of Maryland, Real Property, Section 4-107 (A.C.M., RP §4-107). Requires that a power of attorney for conveying real estate must be executed in the same manner as a deed, and must be recorded before or with the deed. These volumes are arranged by subject, so be sure you have the volume marked "Real Property" or whatever other volume is listed below.

*Financial:*    A.C.M., Estates & Trusts §13-601. Durable unless otherwise stated in the document. Be sure you have the volume marked "Estates and Trusts."

*Health Care:*  A.C.M., Health-General §5-601. Titled "Health Care Decision Act." Living Will and Power of Attorney form may be found at A.C.M., HG §5-603). Be sure you have the volume marked "Health-General."

## MASSACHUSETTS

*Financial:*  Annotated Laws of Massachusetts, Chapter 201B, Section 1 (A.L.M., C. 201B, §1). "Uniform "Durable Power of Attorney Act." Durable or springing: "This power of attorney shall not be affected by subsequent disability or incapacity of the principal," "This power of attorney shall become effective upon the disability or incapacity of the principal," or similar language.

*Health Care:*  A.L.M., C.201D. No form.

## MICHIGAN

*Financial:*  Michigan Compiled Laws Annotated, Section 700.5501 (M.C.L.A. §700.5501). Durable or springing: "This power of attorney is not affected by the principal's subsequent disability or incapacity, or by the lapse of time," "This power of attorney is effective upon the disability or incapacity of the principal," or similar language. The law specifically states that a general grant of power to buy or sell real estate is sufficient, and the legal property description is not required to be included in the power of attorney (M.C.L.A. §700.5502). Ignore the volume and chapter numbers, and look for section numbers. You may also see it referred to as a "letter of attorney."

*Health Care:*  M.C.L.A. §700.5506. Discusses "Designation of patient advocate," with some details as to what must be in the document; however, no form is provided in the statute. A witness may not be the patient's spouse, parent, child, grandchild, sibling, presumptive heir, known devisee at the time of the witnessing, physician, or patient advocate; nor an employee of a life or health insurance provider for the patient, of a health facility that is treating the patient, or of a home for the aged. The document must be made part of the patient's medical record with the patient's attending physician and, if applicable, with the facility where the patient is located.

## MINNESOTA

*Financial:*  Minnesota Statutes Annotated, Chapter 523, Section 523.07 (M.S.A. §523.07). Durable or springing: "This power of attorney shall not be affected by incapacity or incompetence of the principal" or "This power of attorney shall become effective upon the incapacity or disability of the principal." Form may be found at M.S.A. §523.23. Agent's affidavit may be found at M.S.A. §523.17.

*Health Care:*  M.S.A. §145C.01. "Durable Power of Attorney for Health Care." Form may be found at M.S.A. §145C.16.

Living Will: M.S.A. §145B.01. "Minnesota Living Will Act." Form found at M.S.A. §145B.04. Living will can be noted on driver's license. M.S.A. §171.07.

## MISSISSIPPI

*Financial:*  Mississippi Code 1972 Annotated, Title 87, Chapter 3, Section 87-3-9 (M.C. §87-3-9). Financial power of attorney: M.C. §§87-3-101 to 87-3-113. "Uniform Durable Power of Attorney Act." Durable or springing: "This power of attorney shall not be affected by subsequent disability or incapacity of the principal, or lapse of time," "This power of attorney shall become effective upon the disability or incapacity of the principal," or similar language.

*Health Care:*  M.C. §41-41-201. "Uniform Health Care Decisions Act." Form may be found at M.C. §41-41-209.

Living Will: M.C. §41-41-101, referred to as "Withdrawal of Life-Saving Mechanism." Form at M.C. §41-41-107. Revocation form at M.C. §41-41-109.

## MISSOURI

*Financial:*    *Vernon's* Annotated Missouri Statutes, Chapter 404, Section 404.700(A.M.S. §404.700). "Durable Power of Attorney Law of Missouri." Specifies which powers must be specifically stated at §404.710, but no form is provided. Durable power of attorney created by either titling the document "Durable Power of Attorney," or by including one of these provisions: "THIS IS A DURABLE POWER OF ATTORNEY AND THE AUTHORITY OF MY ATTORNEY IN FACT SHALL NOT TERMINATE IF I BECOME DISABLED OR INCAPACITATED, OR IN THE EVENT OF LATER UNCERTAINTY AS TO WHETHER I AM DEAD OR ALIVE" or "THIS IS A DURABLE POWER OF ATTORNEY AND THE AUTHORITY OF MY ATTORNEY IN FACT, WHEN EFFECTIVE, SHALL NOT TERMINATE OR BE VOID OR VOIDABLE IF I AM OR BECOME DISABLED OR INCAPACITATED OR IN THE EVENT OF LATER UNCERTAINTY AS TO WHETHER I AM DEAD OR ALIVE." A.M.S. §404.705. It must also be executed in the same manner as a deed.

*Health Care:*    A.M.S. §404.800. "Durable Power of Attorney for Health Care Act." No form provided.

Living Will: A.M.S. §459.010. Form found at A.M.S. §459.015.

## MONTANA

*Financial:*    Montana Code Annotated, Title 72, Chapter 31, Part 2, Section 72-31-201 (M.C.A. §72-31-201). Form found at M.C.A. §72-31-201. Durable: "This power of attorney will continue to be effective if I become disabled, incapacitated, or incompetent." M.C.A. §72-31-222.

*Health Care:*    No health care power of attorney form.

Living Will: M.C.A. §50-9-103. The Montana Attorney General maintains a health care declaration registry. (see M.C.A.§50-9-501.)

## NEBRASKA

*Financial:*    Revised Statutes of Nebraska, Chapter 49, Article 15 , Section 49-1501 (R.S.N. §49-1501). "Nebraska Short Form Act." Form found at R.S.N. §49-1522. Durable or springing: "This power of attorney shall not be affected by subsequent disability or incapacity of the principal," "This power of attorney shall become effective upon the disability or incapacity of the principal," or similar language. R.S.N. §30-2664.

*Health Care:*    R.S.N. §30-3401; form found at R.S.N. §30-3408.

## NEVADA

*Financial:*    Nevada Revised Statutes Annotated, Chapter 111, Section 111.460 (N.R.S.A. §111.460). Durable or springing: "This power of attorney is not affected by disability of the principal," "This power of attorney becomes effective upon the disability of the principal," or similar language. If used to convey real estate, must be executed and recorded in accordance with N.R.S.A. §111.450 (i.e., signed, acknowledged, notarized, and recorded).

*Health Care:*    N.R.S.A. §449.800. Form found at N.R.S.A. §449.830. Form for living will found at N.R.S.A. §449.610.

## NEW HAMPSHIRE

*Financial:*   New Hampshire Revised Statutes Annotated 1997, Chapter 506, Section 506:6 (N.H.R.S.A. §506:6). Ignore "title" numbers; look for "chapter" numbers. Durable only: "This power of attorney shall not be affected by the subsequent disability or incompetence of the principal." Statutes have suggested, but not required, disclosure statement. Statute also contains suggested form for acknowledgment by agent.

*Health Care:*   N.H.R.S.A. §137-J:1. Form found at N.H.R.S.A. §137-J:14 & 15.

Living Will: N.H.R.S.A. §137-H:1. Form found at N.H.R.S.A. §137-H:3.

## NEW JERSEY

*Financial:*   NJSA (for New Jersey Statutes Annotated), Title 46, Chapter 2B, Section 46:2B-8.1 (NJSA §46:2B-8.1). Durable or springing: "This power of attorney shall not be affected by disability or incapacity of the principal, or lapse of time," "This power of attorney shall become effective upon the disability or incapacity of the principal," or similar language. NJSA §46:2B-8.2.

*Health Care:*   NJSA §26:2H-53. "New Jersey Advance Directive for Health Care Act." No form. Requires two witnesses or notary. May supplement with video or audio recording. Woman may indicate desires for withholding or withdrawing life support in the event of pregnancy. NJSA §26:2H-56.

## NEW MEXICO

*Financial:*   New Mexico Statutes 1978 Annotated, Chapter 45, Section 45-5-501 (N.M.S.A. §45-5-501). Supplement is found at the end of each chapter. Durable or springing: "This power of attorney shall not be affected by subsequent incapacity of the principal, or lapse of time" or "This power of attorney shall become effective upon the incapacity of the principal." Form found at N.M.S.A. §45-5-602. The form includes provisions for end of life and health care decisions, but the separate "Optional Advance Health-Care Directive" is a more comprehensive form.

*Health Care:*   N.M.S.A. §24-7A-1. "Uniform Health-Care Decisions." Form found at N.M.S.A. §24-7A-4. Must be executed in the same manner as a will (with two witnesses and notarized).

## NEW YORK

*Financial:*   *McKinney's* Consolidated Laws of New York Annotated, General Obligation Law, Article 5, Title 15, Section 5-1501 (C.L.N.Y, Gen. Ob. §5-1501). This set of books is divided in subjects, so be sure you have the correct volume, such as "General Obligation Law" or "Public Health." Durable or springing: "This power of attorney shall not be affected by my subsequent disability or incompetence" or similar language (C.L.N.Y., Gen. Obl. §5-1505). Instead of one statutory form with options for various effective dates, New York has created separate forms for each type: Durable (C.L.N.Y., Gen. Ob. §5-1501, 1); Nondurable (§1501, 1-a); and Springing, called "effective at a future date," (§5-1506).

*Health Care:*   C.L.N.Y., Public Health, Article 29-C, §2980. "Health Care Agents and Proxies." Form found at §2981(d). Health care proxy may NOT be included in a general power of attorney. C.L.N.Y., Public Health §2981(e).

## NORTH CAROLINA

*Financial:*   General Statutes of North Carolina, Chapter 32A, Section 32A-1 (G.S.N.C. §32A-1). Durable or springing: "This power of attorney shall not be affected by my subsequent incapacity or mental incompetence," "This power of attorney shall become effective after I become incapacitated or incompetent," or similar language (G.S.N.C. §32A-8).

G.S.N.C. §32A-9(b) requires the power of attorney to be registered in the office of the register of deeds upon the principal becoming incapacitated or incompetent. G.S.N.C. §32A-11 also requires reporting to the court clerk with periodic accountings, unless this is waived in the power of attorney. Statutory form found at G.S.N.C. §32A-1.

*Health Care:*   G.S.N.C. §32A-15; form found at G.S.N.C. §32A-25. Provisions for "Health Care for Minor" found at G.S.N.C. §32A-34.

## NORTH DAKOTA

*Financial:*   North Dakota Century Code Annotated, Title 30.1, Chapter 30, Section 30.1-30-01 (N.D.C.C. §30.1-30-01). UDPAA. Durable or springing: "This power of attorney is not affected by subsequent disability or incapacity of the principal or by lapse of time" or "This power of attorney shall become effective upon the disability or incapacity of the principal."

*Health Care:*   N.D.C.C. §23-06.5-1. "Durable Power of Attorney for Health Care." Form found at N.D.C.C. §23-06.5-17.

## OHIO

*Financial:*   *Page's* Ohio Revised Code Annotated, Title 13, Chapter 1337, Section 1337.09 (O.R.S. §1337.09). Durable only: "This power of attorney shall not be affected by disability of the principal," "This power of attorney shall not be affected by disability of the principal or lapse of time," or similar language.

*Health Care:*   Discussed at O.R.S. §1337.11, including provisions requiring signature and date, two witnesses, and setting forth who can be an agent, but no form provided. Also see O.R.S. §2133.01. "Modified Uniform Rights of the Terminally Ill Act."

## OKLAHOMA

*Financial:*   Oklahoma Statutes Annotated, Title 58, Section 1071 (58 O.S.A. §1071). "Uniform Durable Power of Attorney Act." Durable or springing: "This power of attorney shall not be affected by subsequent disability or incapacity of the principal, or lapse of time," "This power of attorney shall become effective upon the disability or incapacity of the principal," or similar language. There is no statutory power of attorney form, but there is a form for signature, witnessing, and notarizing that will give the power of attorney the presumption of validity. See 58 O.S.A. §1072.2.

*Health Care:*   63 O.S.A. §3101. "Oklahoma Rights of the Terminally Ill or Persistently Unconscious Act." Mandatory form found at 63 O.S.A. §3101.4. Do not resuscitate consent form found at 63 O.S.A. §3131.5.

## OREGON

*Financial:*   Oregon Revised Statutes, Chapter 127, Section 127.005 (O.R.S. §127.005). A power of attorney is durable unless specifically limited.

*Health Care:*   Discussed at O.R.S. §1337.11, including requirements for signature and date, two witnesses, and setting forth who can be an agent. No form is provided, but §1337.17 sets forth a notice that must be included in all printed health care power of attorney forms offered to persons who do not consult an attorney. This notice must be attached as the first page of any health care power of attorney form you use. Also see O.R.S. §2133.01; "Modified Uniform Rights of the Terminally Ill Act."

## PENNSYLVANIA

*Financial:*   *Purdon's* Pennsylvania Consolidated Statutes Annotated, Title 20, Chapter 56, Section 20-5601 (20 Pa.C.S.A. §5601). A power of attorney is durable unless otherwise stated. 20 Pa.C.S.A. §5601.1. Statute provides forms for required Notice and Acceptance by agent.

*Health Care:*  No health care power of attorney provisions. Living Will: Pa.C.S.A. §20-5401. "Advance Directive for Health Care Act." Living will (called "Declaration") form found at Pa.C.S.A. §20-5404. This allows the appointment of a "surrogate," but only to make decisions if the principal is terminally ill or permanently unconscious; therefore, it is not a true power of attorney for health care.

## RHODE ISLAND

*Financial:*  General Laws of Rhode Island, Title 34, Chapter 34-22, Section 34-22-6.1 (G.L.R.I. §34-22-6.1). Durable or springing: "This power of attorney shall not be affected by the incompetency of the donor," "This power of attorney shall become effective upon the incompetency of the donor," or similar language.

*Health Care:*  G.L.R.I. §23-4.10-1, "Health Care Power of Attorney Act." G.L.R.I. §23-4.11-1, "Rights of the Terminally Ill Act." Form found at G.L.R.I. §23-4.10-2.

## SOUTH CAROLINA

*Financial:*  Code of Laws of South Carolina, Title 62, Chapter 5, Section 62-5-501 (C.L.S.C. §62-5-501). Durable or springing: "This power of attorney is not affected by physical disability or mental incompetence of the principal which renders the principal incapable of managing his own estate," "This power of attorney becomes effective upon the physical disability or mental incompetence of the principal," or similar language. According to C.L.S.C. §62-5-501(F)(1), a third party who is presented with a valid power of attorney, and has not received actual written notice of its revocation or termination, must not refuse to honor the power of attorney if it contains the following provision or a substantially similar provision: "No person who may act in reliance upon the representations of my attorney-in-fact for the scope of authority granted to the attorney-in-fact shall incur any liability as to me or to my estate as a result of permitting the attorney-in-fact to exercise this authority, nor is any such person who deals with my attorney-in-fact responsible to determine or ensure the proper application of funds or property."

*Health Care:*  C.L.S.C. §62-5-504. Form found at §62-5-504(D). Also see "Adult Health Care Consent Act," at C.L.S.C. §44-66-10 which discusses consent for medical treatment and states that this subject can be included in a durable power of attorney, but no form is provided.

Living Will: "Death With Dignity Act," C.L.S.C. §44-77-10. Form found at C.L.S.C. §44-77-50.

## SOUTH DAKOTA

*Financial:*  South Dakota Codified Laws, Title 59, Chapter 7, Section 59-7-2.1 (S.D.C.L. §59-7-2.1). Durable or springing: "This power of attorney shall not be affected by disability of the principal," "This power of attorney shall become effective upon the disability of the principal," or similar language.

*Health Care:*  Authorized by S.D.C.L. §§59-7-2.5 to 59-7-2.8, and 34-12C-3, but no forms are provided. Living will form found at S.D.C.L. §34-12D-3.

## TENNESSEE

*Financial:*  Tennessee Code Annotated, Title 34, Chapter 6, Section 34-6-101 (T.C.A. §34-6-101). "Uniform Durable Power of Attorney Act." Durable or springing: "This power of attorney shall not be affected by subsequent disability or incapacity of the principal," "This power of attorney shall become effective upon the disability or incapacity of the principal," or similar language. (T.C.A. §34-6-102.) No statutory form, but statute provides that a power of attorney may refer generally to the powers listed in the statute (T.C.A.

§34-6-109) without restating them. To completely understand what powers are included, and what limitations are placed on an agent, you should read the most current version of T.C.A. §§34-6-108 and 34-6-109.

*Health Care:* T.C.A. §34-6-203. "Durable Power of Attorney for Health Care." No statutory form. T.C.A. §34-6-205 has required warnings if power of attorney is not prepared by the principal.

Child Care: T.C.A. §34-6-301. "Durable Power of Attorney for Care of a Minor Child Act." Has limitations for when this can be used.

## TEXAS

*In General:* Some of the books containing Texas laws are titled Texas Civil Statutes, and others are titled Texas Codes Annotated.

*Financial:* *Vernon's* Texas Civil Statutes, Probate Code (Chapter XII), Section 481 (T.C.S., Probate Code §481). "Durable Power of Attorney Act." The T.C.S. is divided into subjects, so be sure you have the proper subject volume. Durable or springing: "This power of attorney is not affected by subsequent disability or incapacity of the principal" or "This power of attorney shall become effective on the disability or incapacity of the principal." T.C.S., Probate Code §482. Form found at T.C.S., Probate Code §490.

*Health Care:* Texas Codes Annotated, Health and Safety, Chapter 166, Section 166.151 (T.C.A., Health & Safety §166.151). "Medical Power of Attorney." Form and required notices may be found at T.C.A. §§166.163 & 166.164.

## UTAH

*Financial:* Pursuant to U.C.A. §75-5-503, a general power of attorney does not allow the agent to do any of the following, unless specifically stated in power of attorney: (1) create, modify, or revoke a revocable living trust created by the principal; (2) use the principal's property to fund a trust not created by the principal or by a person authorized to create a trust on behalf of the principal; (3) make or revoke a gift of the principal's property, in trust or otherwise; or, (4) designate or change the designation of beneficiaries to receive any property, benefit, or contract right on the principal's death.

*Health Care:* No provisions for a general power of attorney for health care. Living will form provided at U.C.A. §75-2-1104. Under U.C.A. §75-2-1106, you can execute a "Special Power of Attorney" that allows you to appoint someone to execute a living will for you if you are incapacitated.

## VERMONT

*In General:* Vermont Statutes Annotated, Title 27, (Chapter 5), Section 305 (27 V.S.A. §305). The chapter number is needed for online access, but is not included in the official statute designation. A power of attorney to convey real estate must be signed, have at least one witness, be acknowledged, and be recorded where a deed would be recorded.

*Financial:* Vermont Statutes Annotated, Title 14, (Chapter 123), Section 3501 (14 V.S.A. §3501). Durable or springing: Statute states that a power of attorney may become effective upon a future date or occurrence of a specific event, but only provides suggested language for durable: "This power of attorney shall not be affected by the subsequent disability or incapacity of the principal." 14 V.S.A. §3508.

*Health Care:* Vermont Statutes Annotated, Title 18, Section 5263. (18 V.S.A. §5263.) Titled "Durable Power of Attorney for Health Care." Form and required notices are found at 18 V.S.A.§§5276 and 5277.

Living Will: Covered at 18 V.S.A.§9700; referred to as a "terminal care document." Form found at 18 V.S.A. §9703.

## VIRGINIA

*Financial:*    Code of Virginia 1950, Title 11, Section 11-9.1 (C.V. §11-9.1). Durable or springing: Statute states that a power of attorney may become effective upon a future date or occurrence of a specific event (C.V. §11-9.4), but only provides suggested language for durable: "This power of attorney (or his authority) shall not terminate on disability of the principal."

*Health Care:*    C.V. §54.1-2981, form found at C.V. §54.1-2984.

## WASHINGTON

*Financial:*    *West's* Revised Code of Washington Annotated, Title 11, Chapter 94, Section 11.94.010 (R.C.W. §11.94.010). Found in chapter on "Power of Attorney." Durable or springing: "This power of attorney shall not be affected by disability of the principal," "This power of attorney shall become effective upon the disability of the principal," or similar language.

*Health Care:*    Health care power of attorney authorized by R.C.W. §11.94.010(3), but no form provided. Mental health power of attorney form found at R.C.W. §71.32.260.

Living Will: Covered at R.C.W. §70.122.010, "Natural Death Act."

## WEST VIRGINIA

*Financial:*    West Virginia Code, Chapter 39, Article 4, Section 39-4-1 (W.V.C. §39-4-1). Durable or springing: "This power of attorney shall not be affected by subsequent disability or incapacity of the principal" or "This power of attorney shall become effective upon the disability or incapacity of the principal."

*Health Care:*    W.V.C. §16-30-1. "West Virginia Health Care Decisions Act." Medical power of attorney and living will forms may be found at W.V.C. §16-30-4.

## WISCONSIN

*Financial:*    *West's* Wisconsin Statutes Annotated, Chapter 243, Section 243.01 (W.S.A. §243.01). Statutory form found at W.S.A. §243.10. Durable or springing: "This power of attorney shall not be affected by subsequent disability, incapacity or incompetency of the principal" or "This power of attorney shall become effective upon the subsequent disability, incapacity or incompetency of the principal."

*Health Care:*    W.S.A. §155.01, "Power of Attorney for Health Care." Form found at W.S.A. §155.30.

Living Will: Covered in W.S.A. §154.01.

## WYOMING

*In General:*    Wyoming Statutes Annotated, Title 34, Chapter 1, Section 34-1-103 (W.S.A. §34-1-103). Referred to as "letter of attorney." For powers of attorney in general see W.S.A. §§34-1-103 & 3-5-101. Husband and wife may give each other power of attorney, W.S.A. §34-1-129.

*Financial:*    W.S.A. §3-5-101. Durable or springing: "This power of attorney shall not become ineffective by my disability" or "This power of attorney shall become effective upon my disability."

*Health Care:*    W.S.A. §35-22-401. "Wyoming Health Care Decisions Act." Form found at W.S.A. §35-22-405. Authorization for psychiatric advance directives found at W.S.A. §35-22-301, but no form.

# Blank Forms

This appendix includes both statutory forms approved by various states and generic forms that may be used in states that do not have approved statutory forms.

It is suggested that you make photocopies of the forms in this Appendix and keep the originals blank to make additional copies in the event you make mistakes or need additional copies. You can also use the CD-ROM to fill in the forms or print blank copies as needed. (see "How to Use the CD-ROM" on page v.)

The table on page 81 will give you the number of the form or forms to use for your state (this is the form number—not the page number). Find your state, then read across to find which numbered form to use for the type of power of attorney you need. See *FIN.* for financial power of attorney, *H.C.* for health care power of attorney, and *COMB.* for the few states where you may want to use a combined financial and health care power of attorney. If there is no form number in the *COMB.* column, using a combined form is not recommended in your state.

For example, suppose you live in Illinois and want a health care power of attorney. Find Illinois on the table on the next page, then read across to the column titled *H.C.* This will tell you to use form 37. You would then locate form 37 in this appendix and fill it out.

A reference to "6 or 7" in the FIN. column means that you may either use the long form (form 6) or the short form (form 7) for financial power of attorney. Special notes on nine states are noted with symbols and are found immediately below the table. Remember, however, that the law and forms may change at any time.

The table of forms lists all of the forms in this appendix, including the form number, the name of the state to which it applies (if any), and the page number where the form may be found. You can also find the forms by referring to the form number in the upper, outside corner of each page. Just be sure you are using the correct form for your state. For example, the listing for form 13 is as follows.

**FORM 13: ALASKA: ALASKA GENERAL POWER OF ATTORNEY**
**(FINANCIAL)** . . . . . . . . . . . . . . . . . . . . . . . . . . . . . . . . . . . . . . . . **116**

This tells you that form 13 is for Alaska and is titled **ALASKA GENERAL POWER OF ATTORNEY**. As it may not be completely clear from the title what type of form this is, the notation **(FINANCIAL)** tells you it is a financial power of attorney form.

| STATE | FIN. | H.C. | COMB. |
|---|---|---|---|
| Alabama | 6 or 7 | 12 | |
| Alaska | 13 | 3 | |
| Arizona | * 6 or 7, & 14 | 15 | |
| Arkansas | 16 | 3 | |
| California | 18 | 19 | |
| Colorado | 20 | 3 or 22 | |
| Connecticut | 23 | 23 or 24 | 23 |
| Delaware | 6 or 7 | 25 | |
| District of Columbia | 26 | 27 | |
| Florida | 6 or 7 | 29 or 30 | |
| Georgia | 31 | 32 | |
| Hawaii | 6 or 7 | 33 or 34 | |
| Idaho | 6 or 7 | 35 | |
| Illinois | 36 | 37 | |
| Indiana | 38 | 38 | 38 |
| Iowa | 6 or 7 | 41 | |
| Kansas | 6 or 7 | 42 or 43 | |
| Kentucky | 6 or 7 | 3 or 44 | 1 |
| Louisiana | 6 or 7 | 3 or 45 | 1 |
| Maine | ^ 6 or 7, & 46 | 47 | |
| Maryland | 6 or 7 | 48 | |
| Massachusetts | 6 or 7 | 3 | |
| Michigan | 6 or 7 | 49 | |
| Minnesota | 50 | 51 | |
| Mississippi | 6 or 7 | 52 | |

| STATE | FIN. | H.C. | COMB. |
|---|---|---|---|
| Missouri | 6 or 7 | 3 | 1 |
| Montana | 53 | 54 or 55 | |
| Nebraska | 56 | 57 | |
| Nevada | 6 or 7 | 58 | |
| New Hampshire | # 6 or 7, & 59 & 60 | 61 | |
| New Jersey | 6 or 7 | 3 | 1 |
| New Mexico | 62 | 62 or 63 | 62 |
| New York | + 64, 65, or 66 | 68 | |
| North Carolina | 69 | 70 | |
| North Dakota | 6 or 7 | 71 | |
| Ohio | 6 or 7 | ✳ 3 & 72 | |
| Oklahoma | ❖ 6 or 7, & 73 | 74 | |
| Oregon | 6 or 7 | 75 | |
| Pennsylvania | ▲ 6 or 7, & 76 & 77 | 78 | |
| Rhode Island | 6 or 7 | 79 | |
| South Carolina | 6 or 7 | 80 | |
| South Dakota | 6 or 7 | 3 or 81 | 1 |
| Tennessee | 82 | 83 or 84 | |
| Texas | 85 | 86 or 87 | |
| Utah | 6 or 7 | ● 88 or 89 | |
| Vermont | 6 or 7 | 90 | |
| Virginia | 6 or 7 | 91 | |
| Washington | 6 or 7 | ■ 92 or 93 | |
| West Virginia | 6 or 7 | 94 | |
| Wisconsin | 95 | 96 | |
| Wyoming | 6 or 7 | 97 | |

* AZ: Take form 14 and staple it as the last page of either form 6 or form 7.

^ ME: Take form 46 and staple it as the first page of either form 6 or form 7.

# NH: Staple form 59 as the first page of either form 6 or form 7, and staple form 60 as the last page.

+ NY: Use form 64 if you want a durable power of attorney; form 66 if you want a nondurable power of attorney; and form 65 if you want a springing durable power of attorney.

✳ OH: Attach form 72 to form 3.

❖ OK: Staple form 73 to either form 6 or form 7.

▲ PA: Staple form 76 as the first page of either form 6 or form 7, and staple form 77 as the last page.

● UT: If all you wish to do is appoint an agent to execute a living will on your behalf, you can use form 89. If you want a more complete health care power of attorney, use form 88.

■ WA: If all you wish to do is create an advance directive for mental health matters, use form 92. If you want a more complete health care power of attorney, use form 93.

# TABLE OF FORMS

## *GENERAL USE FORMS*

FORM 1:   DURABLE POWER OF ATTORNEY
(FINANCIAL AND HEALTH CARE)............................87

FORM 2:   POWER OF ATTORNEY FOR REAL ESTATE ...................94

FORM 3:   DURABLE POWER OF ATTORNEY FOR HEALTH CARE ...........95

FORM 4:   LIVING WILL ...........................................97

FORM 5:   ADDENDUM TO LIVING WILL ..............................99

FORM 6:   DURABLE FINANCIAL POWER OF ATTORNEY.................101

FORM 7:   DURABLE FINANCIAL POWER OF ATTORNEY
(SIMPLIFIED FORM) ....................................106

FORM 8:   LIMITED POWER OF ATTORNEY FOR CHILD CARE ............108

FORM 9:   REVOCATION OF POWER OF ATTORNEY ....................109

FORM 10: LIMITED POWER OF ATTORNEY ...........................110

FORM 11: AFFIDAVIT OF ATTORNEY IN FACT........................111

## *INDIVIDUAL STATE FORMS*

FORM 12: ALABAMA: ADVANCE DIRECTIVE FOR HEALTH CARE ...........112

FORM 13: ALASKA: ALASKA GENERAL POWER OF ATTORNEY
(FINANCIAL)...........................................116

FORM 14: ARIZONA: WITNESS AND NOTARY PROVISIONS FOR
FINANCIAL POWER OF ATTORNEY .........................118

FORM 15: ARIZONA: HEALTH CARE POWER OF ATTORNEY...............119

FORM 16: ARKANSAS: STATUTORY POWER OF ATTORNEY
(FINANCIAL) ..........................................122

FORM 17: ARKANSAS: LIVING WILL ...............................124

FORM 18: CALIFORNIA: UNIFORM STATUTORY FORM
POWER OF ATTORNEY (FINANCIAL)........................125

FORM 19: CALIFORNIA: ADVANCE HEALTH CARE DIRECTIVE ...........128

FORM 20: COLORADO: COLORADO STATUTORY POWER OF ATTORNEY
FOR PROPERTY (FINANCIAL)..............................132

FORM 21: COLORADO: COLORADO AGENT'S AFFIDAVIT
REGARDING POWER OF ATTORNEY .........................135

FORM 22: COLORADO: COLORADO DECLARATION AS TO MEDICAL OR
SURGICAL TREATMENT ..................................136

FORM 23: CONNECTICUT: CONNECTICUT STATUTORY SHORT FORM
DURABLE POWER OF ATTORNEY
(FINANCIAL AND HEALTH CARE) .........................137

FORM 24: CONNECTICUT: HEALTH CARE INSTRUCTIONS................139

FORM 25: DELAWARE: ADVANCE HEALTH CARE DIRECTIVE . . . . . . . . . . . . . 141

FORM 26: DISTRICT OF COLUMBIA: STATUTORY POWER OF ATTORNEY
(FINANCIAL) . . . . . . . . . . . . . . . . . . . . . . . . . . . . . . . . 146

FORM 27: DISTRICT OF COLUMBIA: POWER OF ATTORNEY
FOR HEALTH CARE . . . . . . . . . . . . . . . . . . . . . . . . . . . . . 148

FORM 28: FLORIDA: AFFIDAVIT OF PHYSICIAN (FOR FINANCIAL) . . . . . . . . 150

FORM 29: FLORIDA: DESIGNATION OF HEALTH CARE SURROGATE . . . . . . . 151

FORM 30: FLORIDA: LIVING WILL . . . . . . . . . . . . . . . . . . . . . . . . . . . 152

FORM 31: GEORGIA: FINANCIAL POWER OF ATTORNEY . . . . . . . . . . . . . . . 153

FORM 32: GEORGIA: GEORGIA SHORT FORM DURABLE
POWER OF ATTORNEY FOR HEALTH CARE
(INCLUDES LIVING WILL) . . . . . . . . . . . . . . . . . . . . . . . . . 159

FORM 33: HAWAII: ADVANCE HEALTH CARE DIRECTIVE . . . . . . . . . . . . . . 162

FORM 34: HAWAII: ADVANCE MENTAL HEALTH CARE DIRECTIVE . . . . . . . . 166

FORM 35: IDAHO: LIVING WILL AND DURABLE POWER OF ATTORNEY
FOR HEALTH CARE . . . . . . . . . . . . . . . . . . . . . . . . . . . . . 171

FORM 36: ILLINOIS: ILLINOIS STATUTORY SHORT FORM
POWER OF ATTORNEY FOR PROPERTY . . . . . . . . . . . . . . . . . . 175

FORM 37: ILLINOIS: ILLINOIS STATUTORY SHORT FORM
POWER OF ATTORNEY FOR HEALTH CARE . . . . . . . . . . . . . . . . 181

FORM 38: INDIANA: POWER OF ATTORNEY
(FINANCIAL AND HEALTH CARE) . . . . . . . . . . . . . . . . . . . . . 186

FORM 39: INDIANA: LIVING WILL DECLARATION . . . . . . . . . . . . . . . . . . 188

FORM 40: INDIANA: LIFE PROLONGING PROCEDURES
DECLARATION . . . . . . . . . . . . . . . . . . . . . . . . . . . . . . . . 189

FORM 41: IOWA: DURABLE POWER OF ATTORNEY
FOR HEALTH CARE . . . . . . . . . . . . . . . . . . . . . . . . . . . . . 190

FORM 42: KANSAS: DURABLE POWER OF ATTORNEY FOR
HEALTH CARE DECISIONS . . . . . . . . . . . . . . . . . . . . . . . . . 191

FORM 43: KANSAS: DECLARATION (LIVING WILL) . . . . . . . . . . . . . . . . . . 193

FORM 44: KENTUCKY: LIVING WILL DIRECTIVE (LIVING WILL) . . . . . . . . . . 194

FORM 45: LOUISIANA: DECLARATION (LIVING WILL) . . . . . . . . . . . . . . . . 196

FORM 46: MAINE: DURABLE FINANCIAL POWER OF ATTORNEY
(NOTICES ONLY) . . . . . . . . . . . . . . . . . . . . . . . . . . . . . . . 197

FORM 47: MAINE: ADVANCE HEALTH-CARE DIRECTIVE . . . . . . . . . . . . . . 198

FORM 48: MARYLAND: HEALTH CARE DECISION MAKING FORMS . . . . . . . 202

FORM 49: MICHIGAN: DESIGNATION OF PATIENT ADVOCATE . . . . . . . . . . . 207

FORM 50: MINNESOTA: STATUTORY SHORT FORM POWER OF ATTORNEY
(FINANCIAL) . . . . . . . . . . . . . . . . . . . . . . . . . . . . . . . . . 209

FORM 51: MINNESOTA: HEALTH CARE DIRECTIVE . . . . . . . . . . . . . . . . . 212

FORM 52: MISSISSIPPI: ADVANCE HEALTH-CARE DIRECTIVE . . . . . . . . . . . 216

FORM 53: MONTANA: POWER OF ATTORNEY (FINANCIAL) . . . . . . . . . . . . . 222

FORM 54: MONTANA: DECLARATION (LIVING WILL WITH AGENT) . . . . . . . 225

FORM 55: MONTANA: DIRECTIVE TO PHYSICIANS
(LIVING WILL WITHOUT AGENT) . . . . . . . . . . . . . . . . . . . . . . . . 226

FORM 56: NEBRASKA: POWER OF ATTORNEY (FINANCIAL) . . . . . . . . . . . . . 227

FORM 57: NEBRASKA: POWER OF ATTORNEY FOR HEALTH CARE . . . . . . . . 228

FORM 58: NEVADA: DURABLE POWER OF ATTORNEY FOR
HEALTH CARE DECISIONS . . . . . . . . . . . . . . . . . . . . . . . . . . . 230

FORM 59: NEW HAMPSHIRE: NOTICE TO PRINCIPAL
(FINANCIAL) . . . . . . . . . . . . . . . . . . . . . . . . . . . . . . . . . . . . . . 234

FORM 60: NEW HAMPSHIRE: ACKNOWLEDGMENT OF AGENT
(FINANCIAL) . . . . . . . . . . . . . . . . . . . . . . . . . . . . . . . . . . . . . . 235

FORM 61: NEW HAMPSHIRE: DURABLE POWER OF ATTORNEY
FOR HEALTH CARE . . . . . . . . . . . . . . . . . . . . . . . . . . . . . . . . . 236

FORM 62: NEW MEXICO: STATUTORY POWER OF ATTORNEY
(FINANCIAL AND HEALTH CARE) . . . . . . . . . . . . . . . . . . . . . . 239

FORM 63: NEW MEXICO: OPTIONAL ADVANCE
HEALTH-CARE DIRECTIVE . . . . . . . . . . . . . . . . . . . . . . . . . . . 242

FORM 64: NEW YORK: DURABLE GENERAL POWER OF ATTORNEY
(FINANCIAL) . . . . . . . . . . . . . . . . . . . . . . . . . . . . . . . . . . . . . . 246

FORM 65: NEW YORK: DURABLE GENERAL POWER OF ATTORNEY
(FINANCIAL-SPRINGING) . . . . . . . . . . . . . . . . . . . . . . . . . . . 248

FORM 66: NEW YORK: NONDURABLE GENERAL POWER OF ATTORNEY
(FINANCIAL) . . . . . . . . . . . . . . . . . . . . . . . . . . . . . . . . . . . . . . 251

FORM 67: NEW YORK: AFFIDAVIT THAT POWER OF ATTORNEY
IS IN FULL FORCE . . . . . . . . . . . . . . . . . . . . . . . . . . . . . . . . . 253

FORM 68: NEW YORK: HEALTH CARE PROXY . . . . . . . . . . . . . . . . . . . . . . 254

FORM 69: NORTH CAROLINA: NORTH CAROLINA STATUTORY SHORT FORM
OF GENERAL POWER OF ATTORNEY (FINANCIAL) . . . . . . . . . . . . 255

FORM 70: NORTH CAROLINA: HEALTH CARE POWER OF ATTORNEY . . . . . . 257

FORM 71: NORTH DAKOTA: HEALTH CARE DIRECTIVE . . . . . . . . . . . . . . . . 262

FORM 72: OHIO: NOTICE FOR HEALTH CARE
POWER OF ATTORNEY . . . . . . . . . . . . . . . . . . . . . . . . . . . . . . 268

FORM 73: OKLAHOMA: SIGNATURE FORM FOR FINANCIAL
POWER OF ATTORNEY . . . . . . . . . . . . . . . . . . . . . . . . . . . . . . 272

FORM 74: OKLAHOMA: ADVANCE DIRECTIVE FOR HEALTH CARE . . . . . . . . 273

FORM 75: OREGON: ADVANCE DIRECTIVE (HEALTH CARE) . . . . . . . . . . . . 277

FORM 76: PENNSYLVANIA: NOTICE FOR FINANCIAL
POWER OF ATTORNEY . . . . . . . . . . . . . . . . . . . . . . . . . . . . . . 283

FORM 77: PENNSYLVANIA: ACKNOWLEDGMENT OF AGENT
(FINANCIAL) . . . . . . . . . . . . . . . . . . . . . . . . . . . . . . . . . . . . . .284

FORM 78: PENNSYLVANIA: DECLARATION (LIVING WILL) . . . . . . . . . . . . . . 285

FORM 79: RHODE ISLAND: STATUTORY FORM DURABLE
POWER OF ATTORNEY FOR HEALTH CARE. . . . . . . . . . . . . . . . . . 286

FORM 80: SOUTH CAROLINA: HEALTH CARE POWER OF ATTORNEY. . . . . . . 291

FORM 81: SOUTH DAKOTA: LIVING WILL DECLARATION . . . . . . . . . . . . . . . . 295

FORM 82: TENNESSEE: POWER OF ATTORNEY (FINANCIAL) . . . . . . . . . . . . . 297

FORM 83: TENNESSEE: DURABLE POWER OF ATTORNEY
FOR HEALTH CARE . . . . . . . . . . . . . . . . . . . . . . . . . . . . . . . . . . . . . 298

FORM 84: TENNESSEE: LIVING WILL. . . . . . . . . . . . . . . . . . . . . . . . . . . . . . . 300

FORM 85: TEXAS: STATUTORY DURABLE POWER OF ATTORNEY
(FINANCIAL). . . . . . . . . . . . . . . . . . . . . . . . . . . . . . . . . . . . . . . . . . 302

FORM 86: TEXAS: MEDICAL POWER OF ATTORNEY DESIGNATION
OF HEALTH CARE AGENT . . . . . . . . . . . . . . . . . . . . . . . . . . . . . . . 304

FORM 87: TEXAS: DIRECTIVE TO PHYSICIANS AND FAMILY
OR SURROGATES (LIVING WILL) . . . . . . . . . . . . . . . . . . . . . . . . . . 307

FORM 88: UTAH: SPECIAL POWER OF ATTORNEY (HEALTH CARE). . . . . . . . 314

FORM 89: UTAH: DIRECTIVE TO PHYSICIANS AND PROVIDERS OF
MEDICAL SERVICES (LIVING WILL) . . . . . . . . . . . . . . . . . . . . . . . . 315

FORM 90: VERMONT: DURABLE POWER OF ATTORNEY
FOR HEALTH CARE AND TERMINAL CARE DOCUMENT . . . . . . . . 316

FORM 91: VIRGINIA: ADVANCE MEDICAL DIRECTIVE. . . . . . . . . . . . . . . . . . 319

FORM 92: WASHINGTON: MENTAL HEALTH ADVANCE DIRECTIVE . . . . . . . 321

FORM 93: WASHINGTON: HEALTH CARE DIRECTIVE (LIVING WILL) . . . . . . . 331

FORM 94: WEST VIRGINIA: STATE OF WEST VIRGINIA
MEDICAL POWER OF ATTORNEY. . . . . . . . . . . . . . . . . . . . . . . . . . 332

FORM 95: WISCONSIN: WISCONSIN BASIC POWER OF ATTORNEY
FOR FINANCES AND PROPERTY . . . . . . . . . . . . . . . . . . . . . . . . . . 334

FORM 96: WISCONSIN: POWER OF ATTORNEY FOR HEALTH CARE. . . . . . . 338

FORM 97: WYOMING: ADVANCE HEALTH CARE DIRECTIVE . . . . . . . . . . . . . 342

# Durable Power of Attorney

I, _____(name), of_____
_____(address, including county and state)
hereby appoint _____(name), to serve as my agent ("Agent")
and to exercise the powers set forth below.  If said agent is unable or unwilling to act as my agent, then I
appoint the following as my successor agent(s) in the order named:
First Successor Agent: _____ (name);
Second Successor Agent: _____ (name).
This instrument shall be effective:

☐    Immediately upon the date of execution, and shall not be affected by my subsequent disability, incapacity or incompetence except as provided by statute.

☐    Upon my disability, incapacity or incompetence except as provided by statute.

☐    Immediately upon the date of execution, and shall terminate upon my disability, incapacity or incompetence.

I hereby revoke all powers of attorney, general or limited, previously granted by me, except for powers granted by me on forms provided by financial institutions granting the right to write checks on, deposit funds to and withdraw funds from accounts to which I am a signatory or granting access to a safe deposit, and except to any powers granted by me for health care decisions.

## ARTICLE I.

My Agent is authorized in my Agent's sole and absolute discretion at any time, with respect to any of my property, real (including homestead property or any other interest), personal, intangible and mixed, as follows:

(1)    To sell any property that I may own now or in the future, including but not limited to contingent and expectant interests, marital rights and any rights of survivorship incident to joint tenancy or tenancy by the entirety, upon such terms, conditions and security as my Agent shall deem appropriate and to grant options with respect to sales thereof; to make such disposition of the proceeds of such sales as my Agent shall deem appropriate;

(2)    To buy every kind of property, upon such terms and conditions as my Agent shall deem appropriate; to obtain options regarding such purchases; to arrange for appropriate disposition, use, safekeeping or insuring of any such property; to buy United States Government bonds redeemable at par in payment of the federal estate tax imposed at my death; to borrow money for the purposes described herein and to secure such borrowings in such manner as my Agent shall deem appropriate; to use any credit card held in my name to make such purchases and to sign such charge slips as may be necessary to use such credit cards; to repay from any funds belonging to me any money borrowed and to pay for any purchases made or cash advanced using credit cards issued to me;

(3)    To invest and reinvest all or any part of my property in any property or interests in property, wherever located, including without being limited to securities of all kinds, bonds, debentures, notes (secured or unsecured), stocks of corporations regardless of class, interests in limited partnerships, real estate or any interest in real estate whether or not productive at the time of investment, commodities contracts of all kinds, interests in trusts, investments trusts, whether of the open or closed fund types, and participation in common, collective or pooled trust funds or annuity contracts without being limited by any statute or rule of law concerning investments by fiduciaries; to sell (including short sales) and terminate any investments whether made by me or my Agent; to establish, utilize and terminate savings and money market accounts with financial institutions of all kinds; to establish, utilize and terminate accounts (including margin accounts) with securities brokers; to establish, utilize and terminate managing agency

accounts with corporate fiduciaries; to employ, compensate and terminate the services of financial and investment advisors and consultants;

(4)     With respect to real property (including but not limited to any real property I may hereafter acquire or receive and my personal residence) to lease, sublease, release; to eject, remove and relieve tenants or other persons from, and recover possession of by all lawful means; to accept real property as a gift or as security for a loan; to collect, sue for, receive and receipt for rents and profits and to conserve, invest or utilize any such rents, profits and receipts for the purposes described in this paragraph; to do any act of management and conservation, to pay, compromise, or to contest tax assessments and to apply for refunds in connections therewith; to employ laborers; to subdivide, develop, dedicate to public use without consideration, or dedicate easements over; to maintain, protect, repair, preserve, insure, build upon, demolish, alter or improve all or any part thereof; to obtain or vacate plats and adjust boundaries; to adjust differences in valuation on exchange or partition by giving or receiving consideration; to release or partially release real property from a lien; to sell and to buy real property; to mortgage or convey by deed of trust or otherwise encumber any real property now or hereafter owned by me, whether acquired by me or for me by my Agent;

(5)     With respect to personal property; to lease, sublease, and release; to recover possession of by all lawful means; to collect, sue for , receive and receipt for rents and profits therefrom; to maintain, protect, repair, preserve, insure, alter or improve all or any part thereof; to sell and to buy the same or other personal property; to mortgage, pledge or grant other security interests in any personal property or intangibles now or hereafter owned by me, whether acquired by me or for me by my Agent;

(6)     To exercise all rights with respect to corporate securities which I now own or may hereafter acquire, including the right to sell, grant security interests in, and to buy the same or different securities; to make such payments as my Agent deems necessary, appropriate, incidental or convenient to the owning and holding of such securities; to receive, retain, expend for my benefit, invest and reinvest or make such disposition of as my Agent shall deem appropriate all additional securities, cash or property (including the proceeds from the sales of my securities) to which I may be or become entitled by reason of my ownership of any securities; to vote at all meetings of security holders, regular or special; to lend money to any corporation in which I hold any shares and to guarantee or endorse loans made to such corporation by third parties;

(7)     To apply for, demand, arbitrate, settle, sue for, collect, receive, deposit, expend for my benefit, reinvest or make such other appropriate disposition of as my Agent deems appropriate, all cash, rights to the payment of cash, property (real, personal, intangible or mixed), debts, dues rights, accounts, legacies, bequests, devises, dividends, annuities, rights or benefits to which I am now or may in the future become entitled, regardless of the identity of the individual or public or private entity involved, including but not limited to benefits payable to or for my benefit by any governmental agency or body (such as Supplemental Social Security (SSI), Medicaid, Medicare, and Social Security Disability Insurance (SSDI), and for the purposes of receiving social security benefits, my Agent is hereby appointed my "Representative Payee"); to utilize all lawful means and methods to recover such assets or rights, qualify me for such benefits and claim such benefits on my behalf, and to compromise claims and grant discharges in regard to the matters described herein; to make such compromises, releases, settlements and discharges with respect thereto as my Agent shall deem appropriate;

(8)     To create and contribute to an employee benefit plan for my benefit; to select any payment option under any IRA or employee benefit plan in which I am a participant or to change options I have selected; to make voluntary contributions to such plans; to make "roll-overs" of plan benefits into other retirement plans; to apply for and receive payments and benefits; to waive rights given to non-employee spouses under state or federal law; to borrow money and purchase assets therefrom and sell assets thereto, if authorized by any such plans; to make and change beneficiary designations, including revocable or irrevocable designations; to consent or waive consent in connection with the designation of beneficiaries and the selection of joint and survivor annuities under any employee benefit plan;

(9)    To establish accounts of all kinds, including checking and savings, for me with financial institutions of any kind, including but not limited to banks and thrift institutions; to modify, terminate, make deposits to, write checks on,  make withdrawals from, or grant security interests in, all accounts in my name or with respect to which I am an authorized signatory, whether or not any such account was established by me or for me by my Agent; to negotiate, endorse or transfer any checks or other instruments with respect to any such accounts; to contract for any services rendered by any bank or financial institution;

(10)    To contract with any institution for the maintenance of a safe-deposit box in my name; to have access to all safe-deposit boxes in my name or with respect to which I am authorized signatory, whether or not the contract for such safe-deposit box was executed by me (either alone or jointly with others) or by my Agent in my name; to add to and remove from the contents of any such safe-deposit box and to terminate any contracts for such boxes;

(11)    To institute, supervise, prosecute, defend, intervene in, abandon, compromise, arbitrate, settle, dismiss, and appeal from any and all legal, equitable, judicial or administrative hearings, actions, suits, proceedings, attachments, arrests or distresses, involving me in any way, including but not limited to claims by or against me arising out of property damages or personal injuries suffered by or caused by me  or under such circumstances that the loss resulting therefrom will or may be imposed on me and otherwise engage in litigation involving me, my property or any interest of mine, including any property or interest of person for which or whom I have or may have any responsibility;

(12)    To borrow money from any lender for my account upon such terms and conditions as my Agent shall deem appropriate and to secure such borrowing by the granting of security interests in any property or interests in property which I may now or hereafter own; to borrow money upon any life insurance policies owned by me upon my life for any purpose and to grant a security interest in such policy to secure any such loans (including the assignment and delivery of any such policies as security); and no insurance company shall be under any obligation whatsoever to determine the need for such loan or the applications of the proceeds by my Agent;

(13)    To execute a revocable trust agreement with such trustee(s) as my Agent shall select which trust shall provide that all income and principal shall be paid to me, to some person for my benefit or applied for my benefit in such amounts as I or my Agent shall request or as the trustee(s) shall determine, and that on my death any remaining income and principal shall be paid to my personal representative, and that the trust may be revoked or amended by me or my Agent at any time, provided, however, that any amendment by my Agent must be such that by law or under the provisions of this instrument such amendment could have been included in the original trust agreement; to deliver and convey any or all of my assets to the trustee(s) thereof; to add any or all of my assets to such a trust already in existence at the time of the creation of this instrument or created by me or my Agent at any time thereafter; and my Agent may be sole trustee or one of several trustees; and to execute such instruments, documents and papers to effect the transfers described herein as may be necessary, appropriate, incidental or convenient; to make such transfers absolutely in fee simple or for my lifetime only with the remainder or reversion (of the property so transferred) remaining in me so that such property will be disposed of at my death by my will or by the intestacy laws of the state in which I shall die a resident;

(14)    To withdraw or receive the income or corpus of any trust over which I may have a right of receipt or withdrawal; to request and receive the income or corpus of any trust with respect to which the trustee thereof has the discretionary power to make distributions to or on my behalf, and to execute and deliver to such trustee a receipt and release or similar document for the income or corpus so received; to exercise (in whole or in part), release or let lapse any power of appointment held by me, whether general or special, or any power of amendment or revocation under any trust (including any trust with respect to which I may exercise any such power only with the consent of another person, even if my Agent is such other person), whether or not such power of appointment was created by me, subject however, to any restrictions upon such exercise imposed upon my Agent and set forth in other provisions of this instrument;

(15)    To purchase, maintain, surrender, collect, or cancel (a) life insurance or annuities of any kind on my life or the life of any one in whom I have an insurable interest; (b) liability insurance protecting me and my estate against third party claims; (c) hospital insurance, medical insurance, Medicare supplement insurance, custodial care insurance, and disability income insurance for me or any of my dependents; and (d) casualty insurance insuring assets of mine against loss or damage due to fire, theft, or other commonly ensured risk; to pay all insurance premiums, to select any options under such policies, to increase or decrease coverage under any such policy, to borrow against any such policy, to pursue all insurance claims on my behalf, to adjust insurance losses, and the foregoing powers shall apply to private and public plans, including but not limited to Medicare, Medicaid, SSI and Workers' Compensation;

(16)    To represent me in all tax matters; to prepare, sign, and file federal, state, or local income, gift and other tax returns of all kinds, including, where appropriate, joint returns, claims for refunds, requests for extensions of time to file returns or pay taxes, extensions and waivers of applicable periods of limitation, protests and petitions to administrative agencies or courts, including the tax court, regarding tax matters, and any and all other tax related documents, including but not limited to consents and agreements under Section 2032A of the Internal Revenue Code or any successor section thereto and consents to split gifts, closing agreements, and any power of attorney form required by the Internal Revenue Service or any state or local taxing authority; to pay taxes due, collect and make such disposition of refunds as my Agent shall deem appropriate, post bonds, receive confidential information and contest deficiencies determined by the Internal Revenue Service or any state or local taxing authority; to exercise any elections I may have under federal, state or local tax law; to allocate any generation-skipping tax exemption to which I am entitled, and generally to represent me or obtain professional representation for me in all tax matters and proceedings of all kinds and for all periods before all officers of the Internal Revenue Service or any state or local taxing authority and in all courts; to engage, compensate and discharge attorneys, accountants and other tax and financial advisors and consultants to represent or assist me in connection with all tax matters involving or in any way related to me or any property in which I have or may have an interest or responsibility.

## ARTICLE II.

My Agent is authorized in my Agent's sole and absolute discretion at any time to exercise the authority described below relating to matters involving the control and management of my person, and my health and medical care. In exercising the authority granted to my Agent herein, I first direct my Agent to try to discuss with me the specifics of any proposed decision regarding the control and management of my person or my health and medical care if I am able to communicate in any manner, however rudimentary. My Agent is further instructed that if I am unable to give an informed consent to medical treatment and my Agent cannot determine the treatment choice I would want made under the circumstances, my Agent shall give or withhold such consent for me based upon any treatment choices that I may previously have expressed on the subject while competent, whether under this instrument or otherwise. If my Agent cannot determine the treatment choice I would want made under the circumstances, then my Agent should make such choice for me based upon what my Agent believes to be in my best interests. Accordingly, my Agent is authorized as follows:

(1)    To request, receive and review any information, verbal or written, regarding my personal affairs or my physical or mental health, including medical and hospital records, and to execute any releases or other documents that may be required in order to obtain such information, and to disclose or deny such information to such persons, organizations, firms or corporations as my Agent shall deem appropriate;

(2)    To employ or discharge medical personal, including, but not limited to, physicians, psychiatrists, dentists, nurses, and therapists as my Agent shall deem necessary for my physical, mental, and emotional well-being, and to pay them (or cause them to be paid) reasonable compensation;

(3)    To give or withhold consent to any medical procedures, tests or treatments, including surgery; to arrange for my hospitalization, convalescent care, hospice or home care; to summon paramedics or other emergency medical personnel and seek emergency treatment for me, as my Agent shall deem appropriate; and under circumstances in which my Agent determines that certain medical procedures, tests or treatments are no longer of any benefit to me or where the benefits are outweighed by the burdens imposed, to revoke, withdraw, modify or change consent to such procedures, tests and treatments, as well as hospitalization, convalescent care, hospice or home care which I or my Agent have previously allowed or consented to or which may have been implied due to emergency conditions. My Agent's decisions should be guided by taking into account (a) the provisions of this instrument, (b) any reliable evidence of preferences that I may have expressed on the subject, whether before or after the execution of this document, (c) what my agent believes I would want done in the circumstances if I were able to express myself, and (d) any information given to my Agent by the physicians treating me as to my medical diagnosis and prognosis and the intrusiveness, pain, risks and side effects of the treatment;

(4)    To take whatever steps are necessary or advisable to enable me to remain in my personal residence as long as it is reasonable under the circumstances. I realize that my health may deteriorate so that it becomes necessary to have round-the-clock personal or nursing care, and I authorize my Agent to make all necessary arrangements, contractual or otherwise, for home health care, or care for me in any hospital, nursing home, assisted living facility, hospice, or similar establishment, and I direct my Agent to obtain such care (including any such equipment that might assist in my care) as is reasonable under the circumstances. Specifically, I want to remain in my personal residence as long as it is reasonable;

(5)    To exercise my right of privacy and my right to make decisions regarding my medical treatment; to consent to and arrange for the administration of pain-relieving drugs of any kind, or other surgical or medical procedures calculated to relieve pain, including unconventional pain-relief therapies which my Agent believes may be helpful to me; even though such actions may lead to permanent damage, addiction or even hasten the moment of (but not intentionally cause) my death;

(6)    To grant, in conjunction with any instructions given under this Article, releases to hospital staff, physicians, nurses and other medical and hospital administrative personnel who act in reliance on instructions given by my Agent or who render written opinions to my Agent in connection with any matter described in this Article from all liability for damages suffered or to be suffered by me; to sign documents titled or purporting to be a "Refusal to Permit Treatment" and "Leaving Hospital Against Medical Advice" as well as any necessary waivers of or releases from liability required by any hospital or physician to implement my wishes regarding medical treatment or nontreatment;

(7)    To assist and facilitate the carrying out of my wishes as set forth in any living will or life-prolonging procedures declaration I have executed; to request, require or consent to the writing of a "No-Code" or "Do Not Resuscitate" order by any attending physician.

(8)    I specifically DO NOT want the governor, state legislature, President of the United States, United States Congress, or any other individual, group, body, or agency of any local, state, or federal legislative or executive branch of government to be involved in any manner in the decision-making regarding my medical treatment, or the withholding or withdrawal of medical treatment. I specifically DO NOT want the following person(s) to be involved in any manner in the decision-making regarding my medical treatment, or the withholding or withdrawal of medical treatment: _____
_____.

## ARTICLE III.

(1)    In connection with the exercise of the powers herein described, my Agent is fully authorized and empowered to perform any acts and things and to execute and deliver any documents, instruments, and papers necessary, appropriate, incident or convenient to such exercise, including pursuing any legal or judicial remedies to which I would otherwise be entitled to pursue.

(2)      No person, organization, corporation or entity, who relies in good faith upon the authority of my Agent under this instrument, shall incur liability to me, my estate, my heirs or assigns, as a result of such reliance.

(3)      If any part of any provision of this instrument shall be invalid or unenforceable under applicable law, such part shall be ineffective to the extent of such invalidity only, without in any way affecting the remaining parts of such provision or the remaining provisions of this instrument.

(4)      In regard to medical decisions affecting me, I intend for this instrument to be honored in any jurisdiction where it may be presented and given the most liberal interpretation available for purposes of granting my Agent the fullest amount of discretion in making decisions on my behalf. Should any physician or health care institution fail to honor this instrument, then my Agent is authorized to terminate the services of such persons and institutions and to transfer my care to another physician or health care institution that will honor the instructions of my Agent.

(5)      If this instrument has been executed in multiple originals, each such counterpart original shall have equal force and effect. Any photocopy of this instrument shall have the same force and effect as an original.

(6)      This instrument and the actions taken by my Agent properly authorized hereunder shall be binding upon my heirs, successors, assigns, and personal representatives.

(7)      The powers granted to my Agent are nondelegable.

IN WITNESS WHEREOF, I have executed this Durable Power Of Attorney this_____ day of _____, _____.

Principal:

_____
Signature of Principal

Name:   _____
Address:  _____
_____
Soc. Sec. No.  _____

Witnesses:

_____
Signature of Witness
Name:   _____
Address: _____
          _____

_____
Signature of Witness
Name:   _____
Address: _____
          _____

STATE OF _____ )
COUNTY OF _____ )


On this_____ day of _____, _____ before
me, personally appeared _____, principal, and _____
and _____, witnesses, who are personally known to
me or who provided _____
_____ as identification, and signed the foregoing instrument in my presence.


_____
Notary Public

My Commission expires:


## ACKNOWLEDGMENT AND ACCEPTANCE BY AGENT

The undersigned accepts appointment as Agent and agrees to serve as Agent under this instrument.


_____
Signature of Agent
Name: _____
Address: _____
_____
Telephone: _____
Soc. Sec. No. _____

## Power of Attorney for Real Estate

I,_____ (name), of
_____ (address,
including county and state), do hereby appoint _____
_____ (name, address and
relationship if any), as my true and lawful attorney in fact, to bargain for, purchase, sell, convey, transfer, mortgage, maintain, or dispose of the real property described as follows:




    1.    Said attorney in fact shall have the full power and authority to do and perform all and every act that I may legally do, and every power necessary to carry out the purposes for which this power of attorney is granted.

    2.    Said attorney in fact shall have the full power and authority to negotiate and determine any and all terms, and to execute and sign any contracts, deeds, bills of sale, all necessary closing documents, mortgages, notes, leases, and any other necessary instruments in connection with the purchase, sale, management, or maintenance of said property on my behalf.

    3.    Said attorney in fact shall have the full power and authority to receive and accept any deed, bill of sale or other instrument of conveyance in connection with the purchase of said property, and to receive and accept any funds and proceeds from the sale of said property, on my behalf; and to approve and authorize the distribution of any such funds to third parties.

    4.    Said attorney in fact shall have the full power and authority to obtain, purchase, or contract for the purchase of any goods, services, or policies of insurance, which said attorney in fact may deem necessary or advisable, to repair, manage, maintain, preserve or protect said property owned by me.

    5.    I hereby revoke all previous powers of attorney relating to said property, and hereby ratify and confirm all actions of the attorney in fact appointed in this Power of Attorney.  This Power of Attorney is not to be construed as limiting or restricting the general powers granted herein, except:
_____.
_____

    6.    The powers and authority granted herein shall commence immediately, and shall continue until terminated in writing, or until _____,
whichever occurs first.

    DATED:_____


_____
Signature of Principal

Witness: _____          Witness: _____

Name: _____          Name: _____
Address: _____          Address: _____
_____          _____

    On this _____ day of _____, _____, personally appeared before me _____, to me personally known or who produced _____ as identification, who executed this Power of Attorney and acknowledged the same to be his/her free act and deed.


_____
Notary Public
My Commission Expires:

## Durable Power of Attorney for Health Care

1.        Appointment of Agent.  I, _____ , appoint
_____ , as my agent for health care decisions (called "Agent" in the rest of this document). If my Agent shall be unable or unwilling to make decisions pursuant to this Durable Power of Attorney for Health Care, I appoint as my alternate Agent _____ . I specifically DO NOT want the governor, state legislature, President of the United States, United States Congress, or any other individual, group, body, or agency of any local, state, or federal legislative or executive branch of government to be involved in any manner in the decision-making regarding my medical treatment, or the withholding or withdrawal of medical treatment. I specifically DO NOT want the following person(s) to be involved in any manner in the decision-making regarding my medical treatment, or the withholding or withdrawal of medical treatment: _____
_____.

2.        Effective Date and Durability.  My Agent may only act if I am unable to participate in making decisions regarding my medical treatment.   My attending physician and another physician or licensed psychologist shall determine, after examining me, when I am unable to participate in making my own medical decisions. This designation is suspended during any period when I regain the ability to participate in my own medical treatment decisions. I intend this document to be a Durable Power of Attorney for Health Care and it shall survive my disability or incapacity.

3.        Agent's Powers.  I grant my Agent full authority to make decisions for me.  In making such decisions, he or she should follow my expressed wishes, either written or oral, regarding my medical treatment. If my Agent cannot determine the choice I would want based on my written or oral statements, then he or she shall choose for me based on what he or she believes to be in my best interests. I direct that my Agent comply with the following instructions or limitations: _____
_____.

4.        Life-sustaining Treatment.  (CHOOSE ONLY ONE.)  I understand that I do not have to choose any of the instructions regarding life-sustaining treatment listed below. If I choose one, I will place a check mark by the choice and sign below my choice.  If I sign one of the choices listed below, I direct that reasonable measures be taken to keep me comfortable and to relieve pain.

[  ]    **CHOICE 1**: Life-sustaining treatment:  I grant discretion to my Agent.
        I do not want life-sustaining treatment (including artificial delivery of food and water except for artificial delivery of food and water) if any of the following medical conditions exist:
a.        I am in an irreversible coma or persistent vegetative state.
b.        I am terminally ill, and life-sustaining procedures would only serve to artificially delay my death.
c.        My medical condition is such that burdens of treatment outweigh the expected benefits.   In making this determination, I want my Patient Advocate to consider relief of my suffering, the expenses involved, and the quality of life, if prolonged.
        I expressly authorize my Agent to make decisions to withhold or withdraw treatment which would allow me to die, and I acknowledge such decisions could or would allow my death.

Signed: _____

OR

[  ]    **CHOICE 2:**  Life-sustaining treatment: withhold treatment only if I am in a coma or persistent vegetative state.
        I want life-sustaining treatment (____including artificial delivery of food and water ____except for artificial delivery of food and water) unless I am in a coma or persistent vegetative state that my physician reasonably believes to be irreversible.  Once my physician has reasonably concluded that I will remain unconscious for the rest of my life, I do not want life-sustaining treatment to be provided or continued.
        I expressly authorize my Agent to make decisions to withhold or withdraw treatment which would allow me to die, and I acknowledge such decisions could or would allow my death.

Signed: _____

OR

[  ]    **CHOICE 3:**  Directive for maximum treatment.
        I want my life to be prolonged to the greatest extent possible consistent with sound medical practice without regard to my condition, the chances I have for recovery, or the cost of the procedures, and I direct life-sustaining treatment to be provided in order to prolong my life.

Signed: _____

5.        Protection of third parties who rely on the instructions of my Agent.  No person or entity that relies in good faith on the instructions of my Agent pursuant to this document, without actual notice that this power has been revoked or amended, shall incur any liability to me or to my estate.  If I am unable to participate in making decisions for my care and there is no Agent to act for me, I request that the instructions I have given in this document be followed and be considered conclusive evidence of my wishes.

6.        Administrative provisions. I revoke any prior durable powers of attorney for health care that I may have executed to the extent that, and only to the extent that, they grant powers and authority within the scope of the powers granted to the Agent appointed in this document.

The document shall be governed by _____ law.  However, I intend for this durable power of attorney for health care to be honored in any jurisdiction where it is presented and for such jurisdiction to refer to _____ law to interpret and determine the validity and enforceability of this document.

Photocopies of this signed power of attorney shall be treated as original counterparts.

I am providing these instructions voluntarily and have not been required to give them to obtain treatment or to have care withheld or withdrawn.  I am at least eighteen years of age and of solid mind.


Dated: _____          _____
                                                                                         Signature


## WITNESS STATEMENT

I declare that the person who signed this Durable Power of Attorney for Health Care did so in my presence and appears to be of sound mind and under no duress, fraud or undue influence.  I am not the husband or wife, parent, child, grandchild, brother or sister of the person who signed this document.  Further, I am not his or her presumptive heir and , to the best of my knowledge, I am not a beneficiary to his or her will at the time of witnessing.  I am not the Agent, the physician or an employee of the life or health insurance provider for the person signing this document.  Nor am I an employee of the health care facility or home for the aged where the person signing this document resides or is being treated.


Dated: _____          _____
                                                                                         (signature)
                                                                                         Name: _____
                                                                                         Address: _____
                                                                                         _____


Dated: _____          _____
                                                                                         (signature)
                                                                                         Name: _____
                                                                                         Address: _____
                                                                                         _____


State of _____  )
County of _____  )

On this _____ day of _____, _____, before me personally appeared _____, principal, and _____ and _____, witnesses,  who  are  personally  known  to  me  or  who  produced  _____ _____ as identification, and signed the foregoing instrument in my presence.


_____
Notary Public
My Commission Expires:

# Living Will

I, _____, _____ (d/o/b) being of sound mind willfully and voluntarily make known my desires regarding my medical care and treatment under the circumstances as indicated below:

_____ 1.    If I should have an incurable or irreversible condition that will cause my death within a relatively short time, and if I am unable to make decisions regarding my medical treatment, I direct my attending physician to withhold or withdraw procedures that merely prolong the dying process and are not necessary to my comfort or to alleviate pain. This authorization includes, but is not limited to, the withholding or the withdrawal of the following types of medical treatment (subject to any special instructions in paragraph 5 below):

_____ a.    Artificial feeding and hydration.
_____ b.    Cardiopulmonary resuscitation (this includes, but is not limited to, the use of drugs, electric shock, and artificial breathing).
_____ c.    Kidney dialysis.
_____ d.    Surgery or other invasive procedures.
_____ e.    Drugs and antibiotics.
_____ f.    Transfusions of blood or blood products.
_____ g.    Other: _____
_____

_____ 2.    If I should be in an irreversible coma or persistent vegetative state that my attending physician reasonably believes to be irreversible or incurable, I direct my attending physician to withhold or withdraw medical procedures and treatment other than such medical procedures and treatment necessary to my comfort or to alleviate pain. This authorization includes, but is not limited to, the withholding or withdrawal of the following types of medical treatment (subject to any special instructions in paragraph 5 below):

_____ a.    Artificial feeding and hydration.
_____ b.    Cardiopulmonary resuscitation (this includes, but is not limited to, the use of drugs, electric shock, and artificial breathing).
_____ c.    Kidney dialysis.
_____ d.    Surgery or other invasive procedures.
_____ e.    Drugs and antibiotics.
_____ f.    Transfusions of blood or blood products.
_____ g.    Other: _____
_____

_____ 3.    If I have a medical condition where I am unable to communicate my desires as to treatment and my physician determines that the burdens of treatment outweigh the expected benefits, I direct my attending physician to withhold or withdraw medical procedures and treatment other than such medical procedures and treatment necessary to my comfort or to alleviate pain. This authorization includes, but is not limited to, the withholding or withdrawal of the following types of medical treatment (subject to any special instructions in paragraph 5 below):

_____ a. Artificial feeding and hydration.

_____ b. Cardiopulmonary resuscitation (this includes, but is not limited to, the use of drugs, electric shock, and artificial breathing).

_____ c. Kidney dialysis.

_____ d. Surgery or other invasive procedures.

_____ e. Drugs and antibiotics.

_____ f. Transfusions of blood or blood products.

_____ g. Other: _____

_____

_____ 4. I want my life prolonged to the greatest extent possible (subject to any special instructions in paragraph 5 below).

_____ 5. I specifically DO NOT want the governor, state legislature, President of the United States, United States Congress, or any other individual, group, body, or agency of any local, state, or federal legislative or executive branch of government to be involved in any manner in the decision-making regarding my medical treatment, or the withholding or withdrawal of medical treatment. I specifically DO NOT want the following person(s) to be involved in any manner in the decision-making regarding my medical treatment, or the withholding or withdrawal of medical treatment: _____.

_____ 6. Special instructions (if any) _____

_____

_____

_____

Signed this _____ day of _____, 200____.

_____

Signature

Address: _____

_____

The declarant is personally known to me and voluntarily signed this document in my presence.

Witness: _____     Witness: _____

Name: _____     Name: _____

Address: _____     Address: _____

_____     _____

State of _____ )

County of _____ )

On this _____ day of _____, 200____, before me, personally appeared _____, principal, and _____and _____, witnesses, who are personally known to me or who provided _____

_____

as identification, and signed the foregoing instrument in my presence.

_____

Notary Public

# Addendum to Living Will

I, _____, hereby execute this addendum to the _____ ("Living Will"), executed by me on _____, 200____. The sole purpose of this addendum is to more fully express my wishes regarding my medical treatment. If any or all of the terms of this addendum are determined to be invalid, my living will shall remain in effect. My desires regarding my medical care and treatment are as indicated below:

_____ 1.  If I should have an incurable or irreversible condition that will cause my death within a relatively short time without the administration of artificial life support procedures or treatment, and if I am unable to make decisions regarding my medical treatment, I direct my attending physician to withhold or withdraw procedures that merely prolong the dying process and are not necessary to my comfort or to alleviate pain. This authorization includes, but is not limited to, the withholding or withdrawal of the following types of medical treatment (subject to any special instructions in paragraph 5 below):

  _____ a.  Artificial feeding and hydration.
  _____ b.  Cardiopulmonary resuscitation (this includes, but is not limited to, the use of drugs, electric shock, and artificial breathing).
  _____ c.  Kidney dialysis.
  _____ d.  Surgery or other invasive procedures.
  _____ e.  Drugs and antibiotics.
  _____ f.  Transfusions of blood or blood products.
  _____ g.  Other: _____
              _____

_____ 2.  If I should be in an irreversible coma or persistent vegetative state that my physician reasonably believes to be irreversible or incurable, I direct my attending physician to withhold or withdraw medical procedures and treatment other than such medical procedures and treatment necessary to my comfort or to alleviate pain. This authorization includes, but is not limited to, the withholding or withdrawal of the following types of medical treatment (subject to any special instructions in paragraph 5 below):

  _____ a.  Artificial feeding and hydration.
  _____ b.  Cardiopulmonary resuscitation (this includes, but is not limited to, the use of drugs, electric shock, and artificial breathing).
  _____ c.  Kidney dialysis.
  _____ d.  Surgery or other invasive procedures.
  _____ e.  Drugs and antibiotics.
  _____ f.  Transfusions of blood or blood products.
  _____ g.  Other: _____
              _____

_____ 3.  If I should have a medical condition where I am unable to communicate my desires as to treatment and my physician determines that the burdens of treatment outweigh the expected benefits, I direct my attending physician to withhold or withdraw medical procedures and treatment other than such medical procedures and treatment necessary to my comfort or to alleviate pain This authorization includes, but is not limited to, the withholding or withdrawal of the following types of medical treatment (subject to any special instructions in paragraph 5 below):

  _____ a.  Artificial feeding and hydration.
  _____ b.  Cardiopulmonary resuscitation (this includes, but is not limited to, the use of drugs, electric shock, and artificial breathing).
  _____ c.  Kidney dialysis.

_____ d.     Surgery or other invasive procedures.
_____ e.     Drugs and antibiotics.
_____ f.     Transfusions of blood or blood products.
_____ g.     Other: _____
                                      _____

_____ 4.     I want my life prolonged to the greatest extent possible (subject to any special instructions in paragraph 5 below).

_____ 5.     I specifically DO NOT want the governor, state legislature, President of the United States, United States Congress, or any other individual, group, body, or agency of any local, state, or federal legislative or executive branch of government to be involved in any manner in the decision-making regarding my medical treatment, or the withholding or withdrawal of medical treatment. I specifically DO NOT want the following person(s) to be involved in any manner in the decision-making regarding my medical treatment, or the withholding or withdrawal of medical treatment: _____.

_____ 6.     Special instructions (if any) _____
           _____
           _____
           _____
           _____

Signed this _____ day of _____, 200____.

_____
Signature

Address: _____

_____

Each of the undersigned hereby witnesses the foregoing signature of the declarant, and attests that the declarant is personally known to me, that I believe the declarant to be of sound mind, and that the declarant voluntarily signed this document in my presence. I further attest that I am at least 18 years of age; that I am not related to the declarant by blood, marriage, or adoption; that I do not have a claim against any portion of the estate of the declarant; that I am not entitled to any portion of the declarant's estate by any will or codicil or by operation of law; that I am not the attending physician, nor an employee of the attending physician, of the declarant; that I am not employed by, an agent of, or a patient in, a health facility in which the declarant is a patient; that I am not directly responsible for the financial affairs or medical care of the declarant; that I did not sign this document on behalf of the declarant; and that I am not the declarant's health care representative or successor health care representative under a health care power of attorney.

Witness:_____    Witness:_____

Name:_____    Name:_____

Address:_____    Address:_____

# Durable Financial Power of Attorney

I, _____ (name), of _____

_____ (address, including county and state)

hereby appoint _____ (name), to serve as my agent ("Agent") and to exercise the powers set forth below.  If said agent is unable or unwilling to act as my agent, then I appoint the following as my successor agent(s) in the order named:

First Successor Agent: _____ (name);

Second Successor Agent: _____ (name).

This instrument shall be effective:

☐  Immediately upon the date of execution, and shall not be affected by my subsequent disability, incapacity or incompetence except as provided by statute.

☐  Upon my disability, incapacity or incompetence except as provided by statute.

☐  Immediately upon the date of execution, and shall terminate upon my disability, incapacity or incompetence.

I hereby revoke all powers of attorney, general or limited, previously granted by me, except for powers granted by me on forms provided by financial institutions granting the right to write checks on, deposit funds to and withdraw funds from accounts to which I am a signatory or granting access to a safe deposit, and except to any powers granted by me for health care decisions.

## ARTICLE I.

My Agent is authorized in my Agent's sole and absolute discretion at any time, with respect to any of my property, real (including homestead property or any other interest), personal, intangible and mixed, as follows:

(1)  To sell any property that I may own now or in the future, including but not limited to contingent and expectant interests, marital rights and any rights of survivorship incident to joint tenancy or tenancy by the entirety, upon such terms, conditions and security as my Agent shall deem appropriate and to grant options with respect to sales thereof; to make such disposition of the proceeds of such sales as my Agent shall deem appropriate;

(2)  To buy every kind of property, upon such terms and conditions as my Agent shall deem appropriate; to obtain options regarding such purchases; to arrange for appropriate disposition, use, safekeeping or insuring of any such property; to buy United States Government bonds redeemable at par in payment of the federal estate tax imposed at my death; to borrow money for the purposes described herein and to secure such borrowings in such manner as my Agent shall deem appropriate; to use any credit card held in my name to make such purchases and to sign such charge slips as may be necessary to use such credit cards; to repay from any funds belonging to me any money borrowed and to pay for any purchases made or cash advanced using credit cards issued to me;

(3)  To invest and reinvest all or any part of my property in any property or interests in property, wherever located, including without being limited to securities of all kinds, bonds, debentures, notes (secured or unsecured), stocks of corporations regardless of class, interests in limited partnerships, real estate or any interest in real estate whether or not productive at the time of investment, commodities contracts of all kinds, interests in trusts, investments trusts, whether of the open or closed fund types, and participation in common, collective or pooled trust funds or annuity contracts without being limited by any statute or rule of law concerning investments by fiduciaries; to sell (including short sales) and terminate any investments whether made by me or my Agent; to establish, utilize and terminate savings and money market accounts with financial institutions of all kinds; to establish, utilize and terminate accounts (including margin accounts) with securities brokers; to establish, utilize and terminate managing agency

accounts with corporate fiduciaries; to employ, compensate and terminate the services of financial and investment advisors and consultants;

(4)     With respect to real property (including but not limited to any real property I may hereafter acquire or receive and my personal residence) to lease, sublease, release; to eject, remove and relieve tenants or other persons from, and recover possession of by all lawful means; to accept real property as a gift or as security for a loan; to collect, sue for, receive and receipt for rents and profits and to conserve, invest or utilize any such rents, profits and receipts for the purposes described in this paragraph; to do any act of management and conservation, to pay, compromise, or to contest tax assessments and to apply for refunds in connections therewith; to employ laborers; to subdivide, develop, dedicate to public use without consideration, or dedicate easements over; to maintain, protect, repair, preserve, insure, build upon, demolish, alter or improve all or any part thereof; to obtain or vacate plats and adjust boundaries; to adjust differences in valuation on exchange or partition by giving or receiving consideration; to release or partially release real property from a lien; to sell and to buy real property; to mortgage or convey by deed of trust or otherwise encumber any real property now or hereafter owned by me, whether acquired by me or for me by my Agent;

(5)     With respect to personal property; to lease, sublease, and release; to recover possession of by all lawful means; to collect, sue for, receive and receipt for rents and profits therefrom; to maintain, protect, repair, preserve, insure, alter or improve all or any part thereof; to sell and to buy the same or other personal property; to mortgage, pledge or grant other security interests in any personal property or intangibles now or hereafter owned by me, whether acquired by me or for me by my Agent;

(6)     To exercise all rights with respect to corporate securities which I now own or may hereafter acquire, including the right to sell, grant security interests in, and to buy the same or different securities; to make such payments as my Agent deems necessary, appropriate, incidental or convenient to the owning and holding of such securities; to receive, retain, expend for my benefit, invest and reinvest or make such disposition of as my Agent shall deem appropriate all additional securities, cash or property (including the proceeds from the sales of my securities) to which I may be or become entitled by reason of my ownership of any securities; to vote at all meetings of security holders, regular or special; to lend money to any corporation in which I hold any shares and to guarantee or endorse loans made to such corporation by third parties;

(7)     To apply for, demand, arbitrate, settle, sue for, collect, receive, deposit, expend for my benefit, reinvest or make such other appropriate disposition of as my Agent deems appropriate, all cash, rights to the payment of cash, property (real, personal, intangible or mixed), debts, dues rights, accounts, legacies, bequests, devises, dividends, annuities, rights or benefits to which I am now or may in the future become entitled, regardless of the identity of the individual or public or private entity involved, including but not limited to benefits payable to or for my benefit by any governmental agency or body (such as Supplemental Social Security (SSI), Medicaid, Medicare, and Social Security Disability Insurance (SSDI), and for the purposes of receiving social security benefits, my Agent is hereby appointed my "Representative Payee"); to utilize all lawful means and methods to recover such assets or rights, qualify me for such benefits and claim such benefits on my behalf, and to compromise claims and grant discharges in regard to the matters described herein; to make such compromises, releases, settlements and discharges with respect thereto as my Agent shall deem appropriate;

(8)     To create and contribute to an employee benefit plan for my benefit; to select any payment option under any IRA or employee benefit plan in which I am a participant or to change options I have selected; to make voluntary contributions to such plans; to make "roll-overs" of plan benefits into other retirement plans; to apply for and receive payments and benefits; to waive rights given to non-employee spouses under state or federal law; to borrow money and purchase assets therefrom and sell assets thereto, if authorized by any such plans; to make and change beneficiary designations, including revocable or irrevocable designations; to consent or waive consent in connection with the designation of beneficiaries and the selection of joint and survivor annuities under any employee benefit plan;

(9)      To establish accounts of all kinds, including checking and savings, for me with financial institutions of any kind, including but not limited to banks and thrift institutions; to modify, terminate, make deposits to, write checks on,  make withdrawals from, or grant security interests in, all accounts in my name or with respect to which I am an authorized signatory, whether or not any such account was established by me or for me by my Agent; to negotiate, endorse or transfer any checks or other instruments with respect to any such accounts; to contract for any services rendered by any bank or financial institution;

(10)      To contract with any institution for the maintenance of a safe-deposit box in my name; to have access to all safe-deposit boxes in my name or with respect to which I am authorized signatory, whether or not the contract for such safe-deposit box was executed by me (either alone or jointly with others) or by my Agent in my name; to add to and remove from the contents of any such safe-deposit box and to terminate any contracts for such boxes;

(11)      To institute, supervise, prosecute, defend, intervene in, abandon, compromise, arbitrate, settle, dismiss, and appeal from any and all legal, equitable, judicial or administrative hearings, actions, suits, proceedings, attachments, arrests or distresses, involving me in any way, including but not limited to claims by or against me arising out of property damages or personal injuries suffered by or caused by me  or under such circumstances that the loss resulting therefrom will or may be imposed on me and otherwise engage in litigation involving me, my property or any interest of mine, including any property or interest of person for which or whom I have or may have any responsibility;

(12)      To borrow money from any lender for my account upon such terms and conditions as my Agent shall deem appropriate and to secure such borrowing by the granting of security interests in any property or interests in property which I may now or hereafter own; to borrow money upon any life insurance policies owned by me upon my life for any purpose and to grant a security interest in such policy to secure any such loans (including the assignment and delivery of any such policies as security); and no insurance company shall be under any obligation whatsoever to determine the need for such loan or the applications of the proceeds by my Agent;

(13)      To execute a revocable trust agreement with such trustee(s) as my Agent shall select which trust shall provide that all income and principal shall be paid to me, to some person for my benefit or applied for my benefit in such amounts as I or my Agent shall request or as the trustee(s) shall determine, and that on my death any remaining income and principal shall be paid to my personal representative, and that the trust may be revoked or amended by me or my Agent at any time, provided, however, that any amendment by my Agent must be such that by law or under the provisions of this instrument such amendment could have been included in the original trust agreement; to deliver and convey any or all of my assets to the trustee(s) thereof; to add any or all of my assets to such a trust already in existence at the time of the creation of this instrument or created by me or my Agent at any time thereafter; and my Agent may be sole trustee or one of several trustees; and to execute such instruments, documents and papers to effect the transfers described herein as may be necessary, appropriate, incidental or convenient; to make such transfers absolutely in fee simple or for my lifetime only with the remainder or reversion (of the property so transferred) remaining in me so that such property will be disposed of at my death by my will or by the intestacy laws of the state in which I shall die a resident;

(14)      To withdraw or receive the income or corpus of any trust over which I may have a right of receipt or withdrawal; to request and receive the income or corpus of any trust with respect to which the trustee thereof has the discretionary power to make distributions to or on my behalf, and to execute and deliver to such trustee a receipt and release or similar document for the income or corpus so received; to exercise (in whole or in part), release or let lapse any power of appointment held by me, whether general or special, or any power of amendment or revocation under any trust (including any trust with respect to which I may exercise any such power only with the consent of another person, even if my Agent is such other person), whether or not such power of appointment was created by me, subject however, to any restrictions upon such exercise imposed upon my Agent and set forth in other provisions of this instrument;

(15)     To purchase, maintain, surrender, collect, or cancel (a) life insurance or annuities of any kind on my life or the life of any one in whom I have an insurable interest; (b) liability insurance protecting me and my estate against third party claims; (c) hospital insurance, medical insurance, Medicare supplement insurance, custodial care insurance, and disability income insurance for me or any of my dependents; and (d) casualty insurance insuring assets of mine against loss or damage due to fire, theft, or other commonly ensured risk; to pay all insurance premiums, to select any options under such policies, to increase or decrease coverage under any such policy, to borrow against any such policy, to pursue all insurance claims on my behalf, to adjust insurance losses, and the foregoing powers shall apply to private and public plans, including but not limited to Medicare, Medicaid, SSI and Workers' Compensation;

(16)     To represent me in all tax matters; to prepare, sign, and file federal, state, or local income, gift and other tax returns of all kinds, including, where appropriate, joint returns, claims for refunds, requests for extensions of time to file returns or pay taxes, extensions and waivers of applicable periods of limitation, protests and petitions to administrative agencies or courts, including the tax court, regarding tax matters, and any and all other tax related documents, including but not limited to consents and agreements under Section 2032A of the Internal Revenue Code or any successor section thereto and consents to split gifts, closing agreements, and any power of attorney form required by the Internal Revenue Service or any state or local taxing authority; to pay taxes due, collect and make such disposition of refunds as my Agent shall deem appropriate, post bonds, receive confidential information and contest deficiencies determined by the Internal Revenue Service or any state or local taxing authority; to exercise any elections I may have under federal, state or local tax law; to allocate any generation-skipping tax exemption to which I am entitled, and generally to represent me or obtain professional representation for me in all tax matters and proceedings of all kinds and for all periods before all officers of the Internal Revenue Service or any state or local taxing authority and in all courts; to engage, compensate and discharge attorneys, accountants and other tax and financial advisors and consultants to represent or assist me in connection with all tax matters involving or in any way related to me or any property in which I have or may have an interest or responsibility.

## ARTICLE II.

(1)     In connection with the exercise of the powers herein described, my Agent is fully authorized and empowered to perform any acts and things and to execute and deliver any documents, instruments, and papers necessary, appropriate, incident or convenient to such exercise, including pursuing any legal or judicial remedies to which I would otherwise be entitled to pursue.

(2)     No person, organization, corporation or entity, who relies in good faith upon the authority of my Agent under this instrument, shall incur liability to me, my estate, my heirs or assigns, as a result of such reliance.

(3)     If any part of any provision of this instrument shall be invalid or unenforceable under applicable law, such part shall be ineffective to the extent of such invalidity only, without in any way affecting the remaining parts of such provision or the remaining provisions of this instrument.

(4)     In regard to medical decisions affecting me, I intend for this instrument to be honored in any jurisdiction where it may be presented and given the most liberal interpretation available for purposes of granting my Agent the fullest amount of discretion in making decisions on my behalf.  Should any physician or health care institution fail to honor this instrument, then my Agent is authorized to terminate the services of such persons and institutions and to transfer my care to another physician or health care institution that will honor the instructions of my Agent.

(5)     If this instrument has been executed in multiple originals, each such counterpart original shall have equal force and effect.  Any photocopy of this instrument shall have the same force and effect as an original.

(6) This instrument and the actions taken by my Agent properly authorized hereunder shall be binding upon my heirs, successors, assigns, and personal representatives.

(7) The powers granted to my Agent are nondelegable.

IN WITNESS WHEREOF, I have executed this Durable Power Of Attorney this _____ day of _____, _____.

Principal:

_____

Signature of Principal

Name: _____

Address: _____

_____

Soc. Sec. No. _____

Witnesses:

_____          _____

Signature of Witness                               Signature of Witness

Name: _____          Name: _____

Address: _____          Address: _____

_____                          _____

STATE OF _____ )

COUNTY OF _____ )

On this _____ day of _____, _____, before me, personally appeared _____, principal, and _____ and _____, witnesses, who are personally known to me or who provided _____ _____as identification, and signed the foregoing instrument in my presence.

_____

Notary Public

My Commission expires:

**ACKNOWLEDGMENT AND ACCEPTANCE BY AGENT**

The undersigned accepts appointment as Agent and agrees to serve as Agent under this instrument.

_____

Signature of Agent

Name: _____

Address: _____

_____

Telephone: _____

Soc. Sec. No. _____

## Durable Financial Power of Attorney

I, _____ (name), of _____
_____ (address, including county and
state), hereby appoint _____ (name) to serve as
my agent ("Agent") and to exercise the powers set forth below. If said Agent is unwilling or
unable to perform his or her duties, I hereby appoint _____
(name) as my successor agent, to exercise the powers set forth below. This power of attorney
shall be effective (check only one of the following):

__ Immediately upon the date of execution, and shall not be affected by subsequent disability,
incapacity, or incompetence, or lapse of time, except as provided by statute.

__ Upon my disability, incapacity, or incompetence, except as provided by statute.

__ Immediately upon the date of execution, and shall terminate upon my disability, incapacity,
or incompetence.

I hereby revoke all powers of attorney, general or limited, previously granted by me, except for
powers granted by me on forms provided by financial institutions granting the right to write
checks on, deposit funds to, and withdraw funds from accounts to which I am a signatory or
granting access to a safe deposit box.

My agent is authorized, in my agent's sole and absolute discretion at any time, with respect to
any of my property, real (including homestead property or any other interest), personal,
intangible, and mixed, as follows:

1.     To collect any money or property due me and endorse all checks or other instruments
payable to me; disclaim my interest in any real or personal property to which I am or become
entitled; and settle, pursue, or abandon any claim or property right I may now or later have.

2.     To pay any of my bills by signing checks to withdraw money from any checking account
and deposit and withdraw any other amounts held in my name in any bank or financial
institution, including individual retirement accounts (IRAs); establish, close, transfer, or in any
other way handle accounts of any type in financial institutions, including IRAs; and generally, in
my name, handle any property held by a financial institution, including property held by a bank
as trustee or a trust in which I have any interest and property stored in a safe-deposit box to
which I have access.

3.     To sell and transfer title to any real estate that I own or in which I have any interest;
purchase, hold, exchange, manage, and generally handle real estate; mortgage real estate;
and borrow money, whether or not in connection with any such mortgage.

4.     To sell, exchange, and transfer any personal property in which I have an interest,
including any motor vehicles, stocks, bonds, and other securities, whether or not in certificate
form; purchase, hold, operate, manage, and generally handle any personal property; and
exercise any right I may have in any insurance policy.

5.      To prepare and file any tax returns that I might be obligated to file, and represent me before any government or social service agency in connection with any tax I may owe or any rights or benefits to which I may be entitled, including, but not limited to, Social Security, Medicare, or Medicaid benefits.

6.      To establish, administer, amend, revoke (if applicable), and generally handle revocable or irrevocable trusts on my behalf; transfer all or part of my real or personal property to any trust; make gifts of real or personal property, outright or in trust; and make any decision regarding my property and the disposition of my property that I could make, even if the decision results in my being deprived of the beneficial ownership of that property.

7.      To do everything necessary to carry on my business affairs and provide for my health and welfare in the same way that I could if personally present.

I give my agent full power to do everything necessary to accomplish anything in the above list, and I confirm and ratify all that my agent lawfully does by virtue of this power. Any person or organization dealing with my agent may rely on this power and its presentation by my agent. No liability to me or my successors will result from this reliance if the person relying on this power has actual notice of its revocation or termination. The specification of particular powers is not intended to limit or restrict the general powers granted to my agent.

A photocopy of this power of attorney may be given to any person dealing with my agent and shall have the same effect as the original.

Dated: _____      _____

                                                                          Signature
                                                                          Social Security No.: _____

Witnesses:

_____      _____

Printed Name: _____      Printed Name: _____

STATE OF   _____  )
COUNTY OF  _____  )

On this _____ day of _____, 20___, personally appeared before me
_____, to me personally known or
who provided _____as identification, who executed this durable power of attorney and acknowledged the same to be his or her free act and deed.

_____
Notary Public
My commission expires:

# Limited Power of Attorney for Child Care

I/We, _____, presently residing at
_____, as the parent(s) of
_____, hereinafter referred to as my/our child(ren), hereby
delegate to _____, hereinafter referred to as my
agent, the authority to act in my place and stead with respect to each of the following powers:

1.    To enroll or withdraw my child from any school or similar institution;

2.    To consent to any necessary medical treatment, surgery, medication, therapy, hospitalization or other such care of or for my child;

3.    To employ, retain or discharge any person who may care for, counsel, treat or in any manner assist my child

4.    To exercise the same parental rights I may exercise with respect to the care, custody and control of my child, and the discretion to exercise the same rights in my agent's home or any other place selected by my agent in his or her discretion; and,

5.    To perform all other acts necessary, or incidental to the execution of the powers enumerated herein.

Any lawful act performed by my agent shall be binding upon myself, my heirs, beneficiaries, personal representatives and assigns. I reserve the right to amend or revoke this Limited Power of Attorney at any time hereafter; provided, however, any institution or other party dealing with my agent may rely upon this Limited Power of Attorney until receipt by it of a duly executed copy of my revocation thereof.

Any reproduced copy of this signed original shall be deemed to be an original counterpart of this Limited Power of Attorney. This Limited Power of Attorney shall not be affected by any legal incapacity during my lifetime, except as provided by statute.

This Limited Power of Attorney shall terminate upon a subsequent written revocation or on _____, whichever shall occur first.

Dated:_____          Dated: _____

_____                 _____
Signature                                        Signature

State of _____ )
County of _____ )

On this _____ day of _____, _____, before me, personally appeared
_____, principal(s), who is/are personally known to me
or who provided _____ as
identification, and signed the foregoing instrument in my presence.

_____
Notary Public
My Commission expires:

## Revocation of Power of Attorney

I, _____
_____ (name and address of principal), hereby revoke the
_____, which was executed by me on
_____, which appointed _____
(name of agent) as my agent.  Said agent no longer has authority to act on my behalf in any matter.  This revocation is effective immediately.

Date:_____

                                                    _____
                                                    Signature of Principal

Witnesses:

_____          _____
Signature of Witness                            Signature of Witness
Name:_____              Name:_____
Address:_____            Address:_____
_____          _____


State of _____ )
County of _____ )

    On this _____ day of _____, _____, before me,
personally appeared _____, who is
personally known to me or who provided _____
_____as identification, and signed the foregoing instrument in my presence.


                                                    _____
                                                    Notary Public

                                                    My Commission expires:

## Limited Power of Attorney

I, _____
_____ (your name and address), do hereby grant a limited and
specific power of attorney to _____
_____ (your agent's name and address), as
my attorney-in-fact (agent), giving said agent the full power and authority to undertake
and perform the following acts on my behalf to the same extent as if I had done so
personally:

The authority of my agent shall include such incidental acts as are reasonable
and necessary to carry out and perform the authorities and duties stated herein.

My agent agrees to accept this appointment subject to its terms, and agrees to
act in a fiduciary capacity consistent with my best interest, as my agent in his or her
discretion deems appropriate, and I hereby ratify all such acts of my agent.

This power of attorney may be revoked by me at any time, and will automatically
be revoked by my death; PROVIDED that any person relying on this power of attorney
before or after my death shall have full rights to accept the granted authority of my
agent until receipt of actual notice of revocation.

Signed this _____ day of _____, _____.


_____
Signature

## Affidavit of Attorney in Fact

STATE OF                   )

                                   )

COUNTY OF                )

Before me, the undersigned authority, personally appeared _____ ("Affiant"), who swore or affirmed that:

1. Affiant is the attorney in fact named in the _____ _____(title of document) executed by _____ ("Principal") on _____ (date).

2. This _____ (title of document) is currently exercisable by Affiant. The principal is domiciled in _____ (insert name of state, territory, or foreign country).

3. To the best of the Affiant's knowledge after diligent search and inquiry:

    a. The Principal is not deceased; and

    b. The Principal has not partially nor completely revoked or suspended the _____ _____ (title of document); and

    c. There has been no partial or complete termination by adjudication of incapacity or incompetence, by the occurrence of an event referenced in the _____ (title of document), nor any suspension by initiation of proceedings to determine incapacity or to appoint a guardian.

4. Affiant agrees not to exercise any powers granted by the _____ _____ (title of document) if Affiant attains knowledge that it has been partially or completely revoked, terminated, or suspended; or is no longer valid because of the death or adjudication of incapacity or incompetence of the Principal.


_____

(Affiant)


Sworn to (or affirmed) and subscribed before me this _____ day of _____, 20___, by _____ (name of person making statement).

# Advance Directive for Health Care
### (Living Will and Health Care Proxy)

This form may be used in the State of Alabama to make your wishes known about what medical treatment or other care you would or would not want if you become too sick to speak for yourself. You are not required to have an advance directive. If you do have an advance directive, be sure that your doctor, family, and friends know you have one and know where it is located.

### Section 1. Living Will.

I, _____, being of sound mind and at least 19 years old, would like to make the following wishes known. I direct that my family, my doctors and health care workers, and all others follow the directions I am writing down. I know that at any time I can change my mind about these directions by tearing up this form and writing a new one. I can also do away with these directions by tearing them up and by telling someone at least 19 years of age of my wishes and asking him or her to write them down.

I understand that these directions will only be used if I am not able to speak for myself.

IF I BECOME TERMINALLY ILL OR INJURED:

Terminally ill or injured is when my doctor and another doctor decide that I have a condition that cannot be cured and that I will likely die in the near future from this condition.

Life sustaining treatment—Life sustaining treatment includes drugs, machines, or medical procedures that would keep me alive but would not cure me. I know that even if I choose not to have life sustaining treatment, I will still get medicines and treatments that ease my pain and keep me comfortable.

Place your initials by either "yes" or "no":

I want to have life sustaining treatment if I am terminally ill or injured.
_____ Yes _____ No

Artificially provided food and hydration (Food and water through a tube or an IV)—I understand that if I am terminally ill or injured I may need to be given food and water through a tube or an IV to keep me alive if I can no longer chew or swallow on my own or with someone helping me.

Place your initials by either "yes" or "no":

I want to have food and water provided through a tube or an IV if I am terminally ill or injured.
_____ Yes _____ No

IF I BECOME PERMANENTLY UNCONSCIOUS:

Permanent unconsciousness is when my doctor and another doctor agree that within a reasonable degree of medical certainty I can no longer think, feel anything, knowingly move, or be aware of being alive. They believe this condition will last indefinitely without hope for improvement and have watched me long enough to make that decision. I understand that at least one of these doctors must be qualified to make such a diagnosis.

Life sustaining treatment—Life sustaining treatment includes drugs, machines, or other medical procedures that would keep me alive but would not cure me. I know that even if I choose not to have life sustaining treatment, I will still get medicines and treatments that ease my pain and keep me comfortable.

Place your initials by either "yes" or "no":

I want to have life-sustaining treatment if I am permanently unconscious.
\_\_\_\_ Yes \_\_\_\_No

Artificially provided food and hydration (Food and water through a tube or an IV)—I understand that if I become permanently unconscious, I may need to be given food and water through a tube or an IV to keep me alive if I can no longer chew or swallow on my own or with someone helping me.

Place your initials by either "yes" or "no":

I want to have food and water provided through a tube or an IV if I am permanently unconscious.
\_\_\_\_ Yes \_\_\_\_ No

OTHER DIRECTIONS:

Please list any other things you want done or not done.

In addition to the directions I have listed on this form, I also want the following:

_____
_____

If you do not have other directions, place your initials here: \_\_\_\_ No, I do not have any other directions.

## Section 2. If I need someone to speak for me.

This form can be used in the State of Alabama to name a person you would like to make medical or other decisions for you if you become too sick to speak for yourself. This person is called a health care proxy. You do not have to name a health care proxy. The directions in this form will be followed even if you do not name a health care proxy.

Place your initials by only one answer:

_____ I do not want to name a health care proxy. (If you check this answer, go to Section 3)

_____ I do want the person listed below to be my health care proxy. I have talked with this person about my wishes.

First choice for proxy: _____

Relationship to me: _____

Address: _____

City: _____ State: _____ Zip: _____

Day-time phone number: _____ Night-time phone number: _____

If this person is not able, not willing, or not available to be my health care proxy, this is my next choice:

Second choice for proxy: _____

Relationship to me: _____

Address: _____

City: _____ State: _____ Zip: _____

Day-time phone number: _____ Night-time phone number: _____

Instructions for Proxy

Place your initials by either "yes" or "no":

I want my health care proxy to make decisions about whether to give me food and water through a tube or an IV. _____ Yes _____ No

Place your initials by only one of the following:

_____ I want my health care proxy to follow only the directions as listed on this form.

_____ I want my health care proxy to follow my directions as listed on this form and to make any decisions about things I have not covered in the form.

_____ I want my health care proxy to make the final decision, even though it could mean doing something different from what I have listed on this form.

Section 3. The things listed on this form are what I want.

I understand the following:

If my doctor or hospital does not want to follow the directions I have listed, they must see that I get to a doctor or hospital who will follow my directions.

If I am pregnant, or if I become pregnant, the choices I have made on this form will not be followed until after the birth of the baby.

If the time comes for me to stop receiving life sustaining treatment or food and water through a tube or an IV, I direct that my doctor talk about the good and bad points of doing this, along with my wishes, with my health care proxy, if I have one, and with the following people:
_____

Section 4. My signature.

Your name: _____

The month, day, and year of your birth: _____

Your signature: _____

Date signed: _____

Section 5. Witnesses (need two witnesses to sign).

I am witnessing this form because I believe this person to be of sound mind. I did not sign the person's signature, and I am not the health care proxy. I am not related to the person by blood, adoption, or marriage and not entitled to any part of his or her estate. I am at least 19 years of age and am not directly responsible for paying for his or her medical care.

Name of first witness: _____

Signature: _____

Date: _____

Name of second witness: _____

Signature: _____

Date: _____

## Section 6. Signature of Proxy.

I, _____, am willing to serve as the health care proxy.

Signature: _____ Date: _____

Signature of Second Choice for Proxy:

I, _____, am willing to serve as the health care proxy if the first choice cannot serve.

Signature: _____ Date: _____

This advance directive for health care is made this _____ day of _____ (month, year). I, _____, being 19 years of age or older, of sound mind, hereby revoke any prior advance directive for health care, and in lieu thereof hereby willfully and voluntarily make known my desires by my instructions to others through my living will, or by my appointment of a health care proxy, or both, that my dying shall not be artificially prolonged under the circumstances set forth below, and do hereby declare:

# Alaska General Power of Attorney

THE POWERS GRANTED FROM THE PRINCIPAL TO THE AGENT OR AGENTS IN THE FOLLOWING DOCUMENT ARE VERY BROAD.  THEY MAY INCLUDE THE POWER TO DISPOSE, SELL, CONVEY, AND ENCUMBER YOUR REAL AND PERSONAL PROPERTY, AND THE POWER TO MAKE YOUR HEALTH CARE DECISIONS. ACCORDINGLY, THE FOLLOWING DOCUMENT SHOULD ONLY BE USED AFTER CAREFUL CONSIDERATION. IF YOU HAVE ANY QUESTIONS ABOUT THIS DOCUMENT, YOU SHOULD SEEK COMPETENT ADVICE.

YOU MAY REVOKE THIS POWER OF ATTORNEY AT ANY TIME.

Pursuant to AS 13.26.338–13.26.353, I, _____ (Name of principal), of _____ (Address of principal), do hereby appoint _____ _____ (Name and address of agent or agents), my attorney(s)-in-fact to act as I have checked below in my name, place, and stead in any way which I myself could do, if I were personally present, with respect to the following matters, as each of them is defined in AS 13.26.344, to the full extent that I am permitted by law to act through an agent:

THE AGENT OR AGENTS YOU HAVE APPOINTED WILL HAVE ALL THE POWERS LISTED BELOW UNLESS YOU DRAW A LINE THROUGH A CATEGORY AND INITIAL THE BOX OPPOSITE THAT CATEGORY.

(A)   real estate transactions............................................................( )
(B)   transactions involving tangible personal property, chattels, and goods.........( )
(C)   bonds, shares, and commodities transactions.......................................( )
(D)   banking transactions................................................................( )
(E)   business operating transactions.................................................( )
(F)   insurance transactions............................................................( )
(G)   estate transactions................................................................( )
(H)   gift transactions....................................................................( )
(I)   claims and litigation..............................................................( )
(J)   personal relationships and affairs................................................( )
(K)   benefits from government programs and military service............................( )
(L)   records, reports, and statements................................................( )
(M)   delegation.........................................................................( )
(N)   all other matters, including those specified as follows:                ( )

_____
_____
_____

IF YOU HAVE APPOINTED MORE THAN ONE AGENT, CHECK ONE OF THE FOLLOWING:
( )   Each agent may exercise the powers conferred separately, without the consent of any other agent.
( )   All agents shall exercise the powers conferred jointly, with the consent of all other agents.

TO INDICATE WHEN THIS DOCUMENT SHALL BECOME EFFECTIVE, CHECK ONE OF THE FOLLOWING:
( )   This document shall become effective upon the date of my signature.
( )   This document shall become effective upon the date of my disability and shall not otherwise be affected by my disability.

IF YOU HAVE INDICATED THAT THIS DOCUMENT SHALL BECOME EFFECTIVE ON THE DATE OF YOUR SIGNATURE, CHECK ONE OF THE FOLLOWING:
( )   This document shall not be affected by my subsequent disability.
( )   This document shall be revoked by my subsequent disability.

IF YOU HAVE INDICATED THAT THIS DOCUMENT SHALL BECOME EFFECTIVE UPON THE DATE OF YOUR SIGNATURE AND WANT TO LIMIT THE TERM OF THIS DOCUMENT, COMPLETE THE FOLLOWING:
This document shall only continue in effect for _____ (   ) years from the date of my signature.

YOU MAY DESIGNATE AN ALTERNATE ATTORNEY-IN-FACT. ANY ALTERNATE YOU DESIGNATE WILL BE ABLE TO EXERCISE THE SAME POWERS AS THE AGENT(S) YOU NAMED AT THE BEGINNING OF THIS DOCUMENT. IF YOU WISH TO DESIGNATE AN ALTERNATE OR ALTERNATES, COMPLETE THE FOLLOWING:
If the agent(s) named at the beginning of this document is unable or unwilling to serve or continue to serve, then I appoint the following agent to serve with the same powers:
First alternate or successor attorney-in-fact:_____
_____ (Name and address of alternate).

Second alternate or successor attorney-in-fact:_____
_____ (Name and address of alternate).

YOU MAY NOMINATE A GUARDIAN OR CONSERVATOR. IF YOU WISH TO NOMINATE A GUARDIAN OR CONSERVATOR, COMPLETE THE FOLLOWING:
In the event that a court decides that it is necessary to appoint a guardian or conservator for me, I hereby nominate _____
_____(name and address of person nominated) to be considered by the court for appointment to serve as my guardian or conservator, or in any similar representative capacity.

NOTICE OF REVOCATION OF THE POWERS GRANTED IN THIS DOCUMENT
You may revoke one or more of the powers granted in this document. Unless otherwise provided in this document, you may revoke a specific power granted in this power of attorney by completing a special power of attorney that includes the specific power in this document that you want to revoke. Unless otherwise provided in this document, you may revoke all the powers granted in this power of attorney by completing a subsequent power of attorney.

NOTICE TO THIRD PARTIES
A third party who relies on the reasonable representations of an attorney-in-fact as to a matter relating to a power granted by a properly executed statutory power of attorney does not incur any liability to the principal or to the principal's heirs, assigns, or estate as a result of permitting the attorney-in-fact to exercise the authority granted by the power of attorney. A third party who fails to honor a properly executed statutory form power of attorney may be liable to the principal, the attorney-in-fact, the principal's heirs, assigns, or estate for a civil penalty, plus damages, costs, and fees associated with the failure to comply with the statutory form power of attorney. If the power of attorney is one which becomes effective upon the disability of the principal, the disability of the principal is established by an affidavit, as required by law.

IN WITNESS WHEREOF, I have hereunto signed my name this ___day of____, _____.

_____
Signature of Principal
Acknowledged before me at _____ on _____.

_____
Signature of Officer or Notary

## Arizona Witness and Notary Provisions for Financial Power of Attorney

I, _____, the principal, sign my name to this power of attorney this _____ day of _____ and, being first duly sworn, do declare to the undersigned authority that I sign and execute this instrument as my power of attorney and that I sign it willingly, or willingly direct another to sign for me, that I execute it as my free and voluntary act for the purposes expressed in the power of attorney and that I am eighteen years of age or older, of sound mind and under no constraint or undue influence.

_____
Principal

I, _____, the witness, sign my name to the foregoing power of attorney being first duly sworn and do declare to the undersigned authority that the principal signs and executes this instrument as his/her power of attorney and that he/she signs it willingly, or willingly directs another to sign for him/her, and that I, in the presence and hearing of the principal, sign this power of attorney as witness to the principal's signing and that to the best of my knowledge the principal is eighteen years of age or older, of sound mind and under no constraint or undue influence.

_____
Witness

The State of _____
County of _____

Subscribed, sworn to and acknowledged before me by _____, the principal, and subscribed and sworn to before me by _____, witness, this _____ day of _____.

(seal)

(signed) _____

_____
(notary public)

**Health Care Power of Attorney**

### 1. **Health Care Power of Attorney**

I, _____, as principal, designate _____
_____ as my agent for all matters relating to my health care, including, without limitation, full power to give or refuse consent to all medical, surgical, hospital and related health care. This power of attorney is effective on my inability to make or communicate health care decisions. All of my agent's actions under this power during any period when I am unable to make or communicate health care decisions or when there is uncertainty whether I am dead or alive have the same effect on my heirs, devisees and personal representatives as if I were alive, competent and acting for myself.

If my agent is unwilling or unable to serve or continue to serve, I hereby appoint _____
_____ as my agent.

I have _____ I have not _____ completed and attached a living will for purposes of providing specific direction to my agent in situations that may occur during any period when I am unable to make or communicate health care decisions or after my death. My agent is directed to implement those choices I have initialed in the living will.

I have _____ I have not _____ completed a prehospital medical directive pursuant to § 36-3251, Arizona Revised Statutes.

This health care directive is made under § 36-3221, Arizona Revised Statutes, and continues in effect for all who may rely on it except those to whom I have given notice of its revocation.

### 2. **Autopsy (under Arizona law an autopsy may be required)**
If you wish to do so, reflect your desires below:
_____ 1. I do not consent to an autopsy.
_____ 2. I consent to an autopsy.
_____ 3. My agent may give consent to an autopsy.

### 3. **Organ Donation (Optional)**
(Under Arizona law, you may make a gift of all or part of your body to a bank or storage facility or a hospital, physician or medical or dental school for transplantation, therapy, medical or dental evaluation or research or for the advancement of medical or dental science. You may also authorize your agent to do so or a member of your family to make a gift unless you give them notice that you do not want a gift made. In the space below you may make a gift yourself or state that you do not want to make a gift. If you do not complete this section, your agent will have the authority to make a gift of a part of your body pursuant to law. Note: The donation elections you make in this health care power of attorney survive your death.)

If any of the statements below reflects your desire, initial on the line next to that statement. You do not have to initial any of the statements.

If you do not check any of the statements, your agent and your family will have the authority to make a gift of all or part of your body under Arizona law.

_____ I do not want to make an organ or tissue donation and do not want my
agent or family to do so.
_____ I have already signed a written agreement or donor card regarding organ and tissue
donation with the following individual or institution:_____
_____ Pursuant to Arizona law, I hereby give, effective on my death:
[  ] Any needed organ or parts.
[  ] The following part or organs listed:

_____
_____
_____

for (check one):
[  ] Any legally authorized purpose.
[  ] Transplant or therapeutic purposes only.

## 4. Physician Affidavit (Optional)

(Before initialing any choices above you may wish to ask questions of you physician regarding a particular treatment alternative. If you do speak with your physician it is a good idea to ask your physician to complete this affidavit and keep a copy for his file.)

I, Dr. _____ have reviewed this guidance document and have discussed with _____ any questions regarding the probable medical consequences of the treatment choices provided above. This discussion with the principal occurred on _____(date).
I have agreed to comply with the provisions of this directive.

_____
Signature of physician

## 5. Living Will (Optional)

(Some general statements concerning your health care options are outlined below. If you agree with one of the statements, you should initial that statement. **Read all of these statements carefully before you initial your selection**. You can also write your own statement concerning life-sustaining treatment and other matters relating to your health care. You may initial any combination of paragraphs 1, 2, 3 and 4, but if you initial paragraph 5 the others should not be initialed.)

_____ 1. If I have a terminal condition I **do not** want my life to be prolonged and I **do not** want life-sustaining treatment, beyond comfort care, that would serve **only** to artificially delay the moment of my death.

_____ 2. If I am in a terminal condition or an irreversible coma or a persistent vegetative state that my doctors reasonably feel to be irreversible or incurable, I **do** want the medical treatment necessary to provide care that would keep me comfortable, but I **do not** want the following:

   _____ (a) Cardiopulmonary resuscitation, for example, the use of drugs, electric shock and artificial breathing.

   _____ (b) Artificially administered food and fluids.

   _____ (c) To be taken to a hospital if at all avoidable.

_____ 3. Notwithstanding my other directions, if I am known to be pregnant, I do not want life-sustaining treatment withheld or withdrawn if it is possible that the embryo/fetus will develop to the point of live birth with the continued application of life-sustaining treatment.

_____ 4. Notwithstanding my other directions I **do** want the use of all medical care necessary to treat my condition until my doctors reasonably conclude that my condition is terminal or is irreversible and incurable or I am in a persistent vegetative state.

_____ 5. I **want** my life to be prolonged to the greatest extent possible.

**Other or additional statement of desires**

I have _____ I have not _____ attached additional special provisions or limitations to this document to be honored in the absence of my being able to give health care directions.

_____
Signature of Principal

Witness:_____

Address:_____

Witness:_____

Address:_____

_____

Date: _____

Time: _____

_____
Address of Agent

_____
Telephone of Agent

(Note: This document may be notarized instead of being witnessed.)

State of Arizona )
County of _____ )

     On this _____ day of _____, _____ before me, personally appeared _____ (name of principal), who is personally known to me or provided _____ as identification, and acknowledged that he or she executed it.

     [NOTARY SEAL]

_____
(signature of notary public)

## Statutory Power of Attorney

NOTICE: THE POWERS GRANTED BY THIS DOCUMENT ARE BROAD AND SWEEPING. THEY ARE EXPLAINED IN THE UNIFORM STATUTORY FORM POWER OF ATTORNEY ACT. IF YOU HAVE ANY QUESTIONS ABOUT THESE POWERS, OBTAIN COMPETENT LEGAL ADVICE. THIS DOCUMENT DOES NOT AUTHORIZE ANYONE TO MAKE MEDICAL AND OTHER HEALTH-CARE DECISIONS FOR YOU. YOU MAY REVOKE THIS POWER OF ATTORNEY IF YOU LATER WISH TO DO SO.

I _____ (insert your name and address) appoint _____ (insert the name and address of the person appointed) as my agent (attorney-in-fact) to act for me in any lawful way with respect to the following initialed subjects:

TO GRANT ALL OF THE FOLLOWING POWERS, INITIAL THE LINE IN FRONT OF (N) AND IGNORE THE LINES IN FRONT OF THE OTHER POWERS.

TO GRANT ONE OR MORE, BUT FEWER THAN ALL, OF THE FOLLOWING POWERS, INITIAL THE LINE IN FRONT OF EACH POWER YOU ARE GRANTING.

TO WITHHOLD A POWER, DO NOT INITIAL THE LINE IN FRONT OF IT. YOU MAY, BUT NEED NOT, CROSS OUT EACH POWER WITHHELD.
INITIAL

_____ (A)   Real property transactions.
_____ (B)   Tangible personal property transactions.
_____ (C)   Stock and bond transactions.
_____ (D)   Commodity and option transactions.
_____ (E)   Banking and other financial institution transactions.
_____ (F)   Business operating transactions.
_____ (G)   Insurance and annuity transactions.
_____ (H)   Estate, trust, and other beneficiary transactions.
_____ (I)   Claims and litigation.
_____ (J)   Personal and family maintenance.
_____ (K)   Benefits from social security, medicare, medicaid, or other governmental programs, or military service.
_____ (L)   Retirement plan transactions.
_____ (M)   Tax matters.
_____ (N)   ALL OF THE POWERS LISTED ABOVE. YOU NEED NOT INITIAL ANY OTHER LINES IF YOU INITIAL LINE (N).

SPECIAL INSTRUCTIONS: ON THE FOLLOWING LINES YOU MAY GIVE SPECIAL INSTRUCTIONS LIMITING OR EXTENDING THE POWERS GRANTED TO YOUR AGENT.

_____

UNLESS YOU DIRECT OTHERWISE ABOVE, THIS POWER OF ATTORNEY IS EFFECTIVE IMMEDIATELY AND WILL CONTINUE UNTIL IT IS REVOKED.

This power of attorney will continue to be effective even though I become disabled, incapacitated, or incompetent.

STRIKE THE PRECEDING SENTENCE IF YOU DO NOT WANT THIS POWER OF ATTORNEY TO CONTINUE IF YOU BECOME DISABLED, INCAPACITATED, OR INCOMPETENT.
I agree that any third party who receives a copy of this document may act under it. Revocation of the power of attorney is not effective as to a third party until the third party learns of the revocation. I agree to indemnify the third party for any claims that arise against the third party because of reliance on this power of attorney.

Signed this _____ day of _____, 20_____

_____
(Your Signature)

_____
(Your Social Security Number)

State of _____
(County) of _____

This document was acknowledged before me on _____
(Date) by _____ (Name of principal) _____

_____
(Signature of notarial officer)

(Seal, if any)

_____
(Title (and Rank))

[My commission expires: _____ ]

BY ACCEPTING OR ACTING UNDER THE APPOINTMENT, THE AGENT ASSUMES THE FIDUCIARY AND OTHER LEGAL RESPONSIBILITIES OF AN AGENT.

## Living Will
## (DECLARATION)

Initial and complete one or both of the following:

_____ If I should have an incurable or irreversible condition that will cause my death within a relatively short time, and I am no longer able to make decisions regarding my medical treatment, I direct my attending physician, pursuant to Arkansas Rights of the Terminally Ill or Permanently Unconscious Act, to [withhold or withdraw treatment that only prolongs the process of dying and is not necessary to my comfort or to alleviate pain] [follow the instructions of _____ whom I appoint as my health care proxy to decide whether life-sustaining treatment should be withheld or withdrawn].

_____ If I should become permanently unconscious I direct my attending physician, pursuant to Arkansas Rights of the Terminally Ill or Permanently Unconscious Act, to [withhold or withdraw treatment that only prolongs the process of dying and is not necessary to my comfort or to alleviate pain] [follow the instructions of _____ whom I appoint as my health care proxy to decide whether life-sustaining treatment should be withheld or withdrawn].

Initial and complete one of the following:

_____ It is my specific directive that nutrition may be withheld after consultation with my attending physician.
_____ It is my specific directive that nutrition may not be withheld.

Initial and complete one of the following:

_____ It is my specific directive that hydration may be withheld after consultation with my attending physician.
_____ It is my specific directive that hydration may not be withheld.

Signed this _____ day of _____, 200___.

Signature _____
Address _____
_____

The declarant voluntarily signed this writing in my presence.

Witness _____    Witness _____
Address _____    Address _____

# Uniform Statutory Form Power of Attorney

(California Probate Code Section 4401)

Notice to Person Executing Durable Power of Attorney

A durable power of attorney is an important legal document. By signing the durable power of attorney, you are authorizing another person to act for you, the principal. Before you sign this durable power of attorney, you should know these important facts:

Your agent (attorney-in-fact) has no duty to act unless you and your agent agree otherwise in writing. This document gives your agent the powers to manage, dispose of, sell, and convey your real and personal property, and to use your property as security if your agent borrows money on your behalf. This document does not give your agent the power to accept or receive any of your property, in trust or otherwise, as a gift, unless you specifically authorize the agent to accept or receive a gift.

Your agent will have the right to receive reasonable payment for services provided under this durable power of attorney unless you provide otherwise in this power of attorney.

The powers you give your agent will continue to exist for your entire lifetime, unless you state that the durable power of attorney will last for a shorter period of time or unless you otherwise terminate the durable power of attorney. The powers you give your agent in this durable power of attorney will continue to exist even if you can no longer make your own decisions respecting the management of your property.

You can amend or change this durable power of attorney only by executing a new durable power of attorney or by executing an amendment through the same formalities as an original. You have the right to revoke or terminate this durable power of attorney at any time, so long as you are competent.

This durable power of attorney must be dated and must be acknowledged before a notary public or signed by two witnesses. If it is signed by two witnesses, they must witness either (1) the signing of the power of attorney or (2) the principal's signing or acknowledgment of his or her signature. A durable power of attorney that may affect real property should be acknowledged before a notary public so that it may easily be recorded.

You should read this durable power of attorney carefully. When effective, this durable power of attorney will give your agent the right to deal with property that you now have or might acquire in the future. The durable power of attorney is important to you. If you do not understand the durable power of attorney, or any provision of it, then you should obtain the assistance of an attorney or other qualified person.

Notice to Person Accepting the Appointment as Attorney-in-Fact

By acting or agreeing to act as the agent (attorney-in-fact) under this power of attorney you assume the fiduciary and other legal responsibilities of an agent. These responsibilities include:

1. The legal duty to act solely in the interest of the principal and to avoid conflicts of interest.

2. The legal duty to keep the principal's property separate and distinct from any other property owned or controlled by you.

You may not transfer the principal's property to yourself without full and adequate consideration or accept a gift of the principal's property unless this power of attorney specifically authorizes you to transfer property to yourself or accept a gift of the principal's property. If you transfer the principal's property to yourself without specific authorization in the power of attorney, you may be prosecuted for fraud and/or embezzlement. If the principal is 65 years of age or older at the time that the property is transferred to you without authority, you may also be prosecuted for elder abuse under Penal Code Section 368. In addition to criminal prosecution, you may also be sued in civil court.

I have read the foregoing notice and I understand the legal and fiduciary duties that I assume by acting or agreeing to act as the agent (attorney-in-fact) under the terms of this power of attorney.

Date: _____

_____
(Signature of agent)

_____
(Print name of agent)

NOTICE: THE POWERS GRANTED BY THIS DOCUMENT ARE BROAD AND SWEEPING.  THEY ARE EXPLAINED IN THE UNIFORM STATUTORY FORM POWER OF ATTORNEY ACT (CALIFORNIA PROBATE CODE SECTIONS 4400–4465). IF YOU HAVE ANY QUESTIONS ABOUT THESE POWERS, OBTAIN COMPETENT LEGAL ADVICE. THIS DOCUMENT DOES NOT AUTHORIZE ANYONE TO MAKE MEDICAL AND OTHER HEALTHCARE DECISIONS FOR YOU.  YOU MAY REVOKE THIS POWER OF ATTORNEY IF YOU LATER WISH TO DO SO.

I, _____ (your name and address) appoint _____ _____ (name and address of the person appointed, or of each person appointed if you want to designate more than one) as my agent (attorney-in-fact) to act for me in any lawful way with respect to the following initialed subjects:

TO GRANT ALL OF THE FOLLOWING POWERS, INITIAL THE LINE IN FRONT OF (N) AND IGNORE THE LINES IN FRONT OF THE OTHER POWERS.

TO GRANT ONE OR MORE, BUT FEWER THAN ALL, OF THE FOLLOWING POWERS, INITIAL THE LINE IN FRONT OF EACH POWER YOU ARE GRANTING.

TO WITHHOLD A POWER, DO NOT INITIAL THE LINE IN FRONT OF IT. YOU MAY, BUT NEED NOT, CROSS OUT EACH POWER WITHHELD.

| | | |
|---|---|---|
| _____ | (A) | Real property transactions. |
| _____ | (B) | Tangible personal property transactions. |
| _____ | (C) | Stock and bond transactions. |
| _____ | (D) | Commodity and option transactions. |
| _____ | (E) | Banking and other financial institution transactions. |
| _____ | (F) | Business operating transactions. |
| _____ | (G) | Insurance and annuity transactions. |
| _____ | (H) | Estate, trust, and other beneficiary transactions. |
| _____ | (I) | Claims and litigation. |
| _____ | (J) | Personal and family maintenance. |
| _____ | (K) | Benefits from social security, medicare, medicaid, or other governmental programs, or civil or military service. |
| _____ | (L) | Retirement plan transactions. |
| _____ | (M) | Tax matters. |
| _____ | (N) | ALL OF THE POWERS LISTED ABOVE. |

YOU NEED NOT INITIAL ANY OTHER LINES IF YOU INITIAL LINE (N).

### SPECIAL INSTRUCTIONS:

ON THE FOLLOWING LINES YOU MAY GIVE SPECIAL INSTRUCTIONS LIMITING OR EXTENDING THE POWERS GRANTED TO YOUR AGENT.

_____
_____
_____
_____
_____

UNLESS YOU DIRECT OTHERWISE ABOVE, THIS POWER OF ATTORNEY IS EFFECTIVE IMMEDIATELY AND WILL CONTINUE UNTIL IT IS REVOKED.

This power of attorney will continue to be effective even though I become incapacitated.

STRIKE THE PRECEDING SENTENCE IF YOU DO NOT WANT THIS POWER OF ATTORNEY TO CONTINUE IF YOU BECOME INCAPACITATED.

## EXERCISE OF POWER OF ATTORNEY WHERE
## MORE THAN ONE AGENT DESIGNATED

If I have designated more than one agent, the agents are to act _____.
IF YOU APPOINTED MORE THAN ONE AGENT AND YOU WANT EACH AGENT TO BE ABLE TO ACT ALONE WITHOUT THE OTHER AGENT JOINING, WRITE THE WORD "SEPARATELY" IN THE BLANK SPACE ABOVE. IF YOU DO NOT INSERT ANY WORD IN THE BLANK SPACE, OR IF YOU INSERT THE WORD "JOINTLY," THEN ALL OF YOUR AGENTS MUST ACT OR SIGN TOGETHER.

I agree that any third party who receives a copy of this document may act under it. Revocation of the power of attorney is not effective as to a third party until the third party has actual knowledge of the revocation. I agree to indemnify the third party for any claims that arise against the third party because of reliance on this power of attorney.

Signed this _____ day of _____, _____.


_____
(your signature)


_____
(your Social Security number)


State of _____, County of _____,

BY ACCEPTING OR ACTING UNDER THE APPOINTMENT, THE AGENT ASSUMES THE FIDUCIARY AND OTHER LEGAL RESPONSIBILITIES OF AN AGENT.

## CERTIFICATE OF ACKNOWLEDGMENT OF NOTARY PUBLIC

State of California                         )
                                               )
County of _____    )

On this _____ day of _____, _____ before me, _____, (name of notary public) personally appeared _____, (name of principal) personally known to me (or proved to me on the basis of satisfactory evidence) to be the person whose name is subscribed to this instrument, and acknowledged that he/she executed it in his/her authorized capacity, and that by his/her signature on this instrument the person executed this instrument.

WITNESS my hand and official seal


_____
(signature of notary public)         (seal)

# Advance Health Care Directive
### (California Probate Code Section 4701)

### Explanation

You have the right to give instructions about your own health care. You also have the right to name someone else to make health care decisions for you. This form lets you do either or both of these things. It also lets you express your wishes regarding donation of organs and the designation of your primary physician. If you use this form, you may complete or modify all or any part of it. You are free to use a different form.

Part 1 of this form is a power of attorney for health care. Part 1 lets you name another individual as agent to make health care decisions for you if you become incapable of making your own decisions or if you want someone else to make those decisions for you now even though you are still capable. You may also name an alternate agent to act for you if your first choice is not willing, able, or reasonably available to make decisions for you. (Your agent may not be an operator or employee of a community care facility or a residential care facility where you are receiving care, or your supervising health care provider or employee of the health care institution where you are receiving care, unless your agent is related to you or is a coworker.)

Unless the form you sign limits the authority of your agent, your agent may make all health care decisions for you. This form has a place for you to limit the authority of your agent. You need not limit the authority of your agent if you wish to rely on your agent for all health care decisions that may have to be made. If you choose not to limit the authority of your agent, your agent will have the right to:

(a) Consent or refuse consent to any care, treatment, service, or procedure to maintain, diagnose, or otherwise affect a physical or mental condition.

(b) Select or discharge health care providers and institutions.

(c) Approve or disapprove diagnostic tests, surgical procedures, and programs of medication.

(d) Direct the provision, withholding, or withdrawal of artificial nutrition and hydration and all other forms of health care, including cardiopulmonary resuscitation.

(e) Make anatomical gifts, authorize an autopsy, and direct disposition of remains.

Part 2 of this form lets you give specific instructions about any aspect of your health care, whether or not you appoint an agent. Choices are provided for you to express your wishes regarding the provision, withholding, or withdrawal of treatment to keep you alive, as well as the provision of pain relief. Space is also provided for you to add to the choices you have made or for you to write out any additional wishes. If you are satisfied to allow your agent to determine what is best for you in making end-of-life decisions, you need not fill out Part 2 of this form.

Part 3 of this form lets you express an intention to donate your bodily organs and tissues following your death.

Part 4 of this form lets you designate a physician to have primary responsibility for your health care.

After completing this form, sign and date the form at the end. The form must be signed by two qualified witnesses or acknowledged before a notary public. Give a copy of the signed and completed form to your physician, to any other health care providers you may have, to any health care institution at which you are receiving care, and to any health care agents you have named. You should talk to the person you have named as agent to make sure that he or she understands your wishes and is willing to take the responsibility.

You have the right to revoke this advance health care directive or replace this form at any time.

* * * * * * * * * * * * * * * * *

### PART 1
### POWER OF ATTORNEY FOR HEALTH CARE

(1.1) DESIGNATION OF AGENT: I designate the following individual as my agent to make health care decisions for me:

_____
(name of individual you choose as agent)

_____
(address)                               (city)               (state)        (ZIP Code)

_____
(home phone)                                    (work phone)

OPTIONAL: If I revoke my agent's authority or if my agent is not willing, able, or reasonably available to make a health care decision for me, I designate as my first alternate agent:

_____

(name of individual you choose as first alternate agent)

_____

(address)                                    (city)           (state)        (ZIP Code)

_____

(home phone)                                 (work phone)

OPTIONAL: If I revoke the authority of my agent and first alternate agent or if neither is willing, able, or reasonably available to make a health care decision for me, I designate as my second alternate agent:

_____

(name of individual you choose as second alternate agent)

_____

(address)                                    (city)           (state)        (ZIP Code)

_____

(home phone)                                 (work phone)

(1.2) AGENT'S AUTHORITY: My agent is authorized to make all health care decisions for me, including decisions to provide, withhold, or withdraw artificial nutrition and hydration and all other forms of health care to keep me alive, except as I state here:

_____

_____

(Add additional sheets if needed.)

(1.3) WHEN AGENT'S AUTHORITY BECOMES EFFECTIVE: My agent's authority becomes effective when my primary physician determines that I am unable to make my own health care decisions unless I mark the following box.

If I mark this box (   ), my agent's authority to make health care decisions for me takes effect immediately.

(1.4) AGENT'S OBLIGATION: My agent shall make health care decisions for me in accordance with this power of attorney for health care, any instructions I give in Part 2 of this form, and my other wishes to the extent known to my agent. To the extent my wishes are unknown, my agent shall make health care decisions for me in accordance with what my agent determines to be in my best interest. In determining my best interest, my agent shall consider my personal values to the extent known to my agent.

(1.5) AGENT'S POSTDEATH AUTHORITY: My agent is authorized to make anatomical gifts, authorize an autopsy, and direct disposition of my remains, except as I state here or in Part 3 of this form:

_____

(Add additional sheets if needed.)

(1.6) NOMINATION OF CONSERVATOR: If a conservator of my person needs to be appointed for me by a court, I nominate the agent designated in this form. If that agent is not willing, able, or reasonably available to act as conservator, I nominate the alternate agents whom I have named, in the order designated.

## PART 2
## INSTRUCTIONS FOR HEALTH CARE

If you fill out this part of the form, you may strike any wording you do not want.

(2.1) END-OF-LIFE DECISIONS: I direct that my health care providers and others involved in my care provide, withhold, or withdraw treatment in accordance with the choice I have marked below:

☐  (a) Choice Not To Prolong Life. I do not want my life to be prolonged if (1) I have an incurable and irreversible condition that will result in my death within a relatively short time, (2) I become unconscious and, to a reasonable degree of medical certainty, I will not regain consciousness, or (3) the likely risks and burdens of treatment would outweigh the expected benefits, OR

☐  (b) Choice To Prolong Life. I want my life to be prolonged as long as possible within the limits of generally accepted health care standards.

(2.2) RELIEF FROM PAIN: Except as I state in the following space, I direct that treatment for alleviation of pain or discomfort be provided at all times, even if it hastens my death:

_____
_____
(Add additional sheets if needed.)

(2.3) OTHER WISHES: (If you do not agree with any of the optional choices above and wish to write your own, or if you wish to add to the instructions you have given above, you may do so here.) I direct that:

_____
_____
(Add additional sheets if needed.)

## PART 3
## DONATION OF ORGANS AT DEATH (OPTIONAL)

(3.1) Upon my death (mark applicable box):
☐ (a) I give any needed organs, tissues, or parts, OR
☐ (b) I give the following organs, tissues, or parts only.

_____
☐ (c) My gift is for the following purposes (strike any of the following you do not want):
    (1) Transplant
    (2) Therapy
    (3) Research
    (4) Education

## PART 4
## PRIMARY PHYSICIAN (OPTIONAL)

_____
(name of physician)

_____
(address)          (city)          (state)    (ZIP Code)

_____
(phone)

OPTIONAL: If the physician I have designated above is not willing, able, or reasonably available to act as my primary physician, I designate the following physician as my primary physician:

_____
(name of physician)

_____
(address)          (city)          (state)    (ZIP Code)

_____
(phone)

## PART 5

(5.1) EFFECT OF COPY: A copy of this form has the same effect as the original.

(5.2) SIGNATURE: Sign and date the form here:

_____    _____
(date)                          (sign your name)

_____    _____
(address)                     (print your name)

_____
(city)          (state)

(5.3) STATEMENT OF WITNESSES: I declare under penalty of perjury under the laws of California (1) that the individual who signed or acknowledged this advance health care directive is personally known to me, or that the individual's identity was proven to me by convincing evidence (2) that the individual signed or acknowledged this advance directive in my presence, (3) that the individual appears to be of sound mind and under no duress, fraud, or undue influence, (4) that I am not a person appointed as agent by this advance directive, and (5) that I am not the individual's health care provider, an employee of the individual's health care provider, the operator of a community care facility, an employee of an operator of a community care facility, the operator of a residential care facility for the elderly, nor an employee of an operator of a residential care facility for the elderly.

| | |
|---|---|
| First witness | Second witness |
| (print name) | (print name) |
| (address) | (address) |
| (city)            (state) | (city)            (state) |
| (signature of witness) | (signature of witness) |
| (date) | (date) |

(5.4) ADDITIONAL STATEMENT OF WITNESSES: At least one of the above witnesses must also sign the following declaration:

I further declare under penalty of perjury under the laws of California that I am not related to the individual executing this advance health care directive by blood, marriage, or adoption, and to the best of my knowledge, I am not entitled to any part of the individual's estate upon his or her death under a will now existing or by operation of law.

| | |
|---|---|
| (signature of witness) | (signature of witness) |

## PART 6
## SPECIAL WITNESS REQUIREMENT

(6.1) The following statement is required only if you are a patient in a skilled nursing facility--a health care facility that provides the following basic services: skilled nursing care and supportive care to patients whose primary need is for availability of skilled nursing care on an extended basis. The patient advocate or ombudsman must sign the following statement:

### STATEMENT OF PATIENT ADVOCATE OR OMBUDSMAN

I declare under penalty of perjury under the laws of California that I am a patient advocate or ombudsman as designated by the State Department of Aging and that I am serving as a witness as required by Section 4675 of the Probate Code.

| | |
|---|---|
| (date) | (sign your name) |
| (address) | (print your name) |
| (city)            (state) | |

# Colorado Statutory Power of Attorney for Property

NOTICE: UNLESS YOU LIMIT THE POWER IN THIS DOCUMENT, THIS DOCUMENT GIVES YOUR AGENT THE POWER TO ACT FOR YOU, WITHOUT YOUR CONSENT, IN ANY WAY THAT YOU COULD ACT FOR YOURSELF. THE POWERS GRANTED BY THIS DOCUMENT ARE BROAD AND SWEEPING. THEY ARE EXPLAINED IN THE "UNIFORM STATUTORY FORM POWER OF ATTORNEY ACT", PART 13 OF ARTICLE 1 OF TITLE 15, COLORADO REVISED STATUTES, AND PART 6 OF ARTICLE 14 OF TITLE 15, COLORADO REVISED STATUTES. IF YOU HAVE ANY QUESTIONS ABOUT THESE POWERS, OBTAIN COMPETENT LEGAL ADVICE. THIS DOCUMENT DOES NOT AUTHORIZE ANYONE TO MAKE MEDICAL AND OTHER HEALTH-CARE DECISIONS FOR YOU. YOU MAY REVOKE THIS POWER OF ATTORNEY IF YOU LATER WISH TO DO SO.

THE PURPOSE OF THIS POWER OF ATTORNEY IS TO GIVE THE PERSON YOU DESIGNATE (YOUR "AGENT") BROAD POWERS TO HANDLE YOUR PROPERTY AND AFFAIRS, WHICH MAY INCLUDE POWERS TO PLEDGE, SELL, OR OTHERWISE DISPOSE OF ANY REAL OR PERSONAL PROPERTY WITHOUT ADVANCE NOTICE TO YOU OR APPROVAL BY YOU. THIS FORM DOES NOT IMPOSE A DUTY ON YOUR AGENT TO EXERCISE GRANTED POWERS; BUT WHEN POWERS ARE EXERCISED, YOUR AGENT MUST USE DUE CARE TO ACT FOR YOUR BENEFIT AND IN ACCORDANCE WITH THE PROVISIONS OF THIS FORM AND MUST KEEP A RECORD OF RECEIPTS, DISBURSEMENTS, AND SIGNIFICANT ACTIONS TAKEN AS AGENT. YOU MAY NAME SUCCESSOR AGENTS UNDER THIS FORM BUT NOT CO-AGENTS. UNTIL YOU REVOKE THIS POWER OF ATTORNEY OR A COURT ACTING ON YOUR BEHALF TERMINATES IT, YOUR AGENT MAY EXERCISE THE POWERS GIVEN HERE THROUGHOUT YOUR LIFETIME, EVEN AFTER YOU MAY BECOME DISABLED, UNLESS YOU EXPRESSLY LIMIT THE DURATION OF THIS POWER IN THE MANNER PROVIDED BELOW.

YOU MAY HAVE OTHER RIGHTS OR POWERS UNDER COLORADO LAW NOT SPECIFIED IN THIS FORM.

I, _____, (insert your full name and address) appoint _____ _____ (insert the full name and address of the person appointed) as my agent (attorney-in-fact) to act for me in any lawful way with respect to the following initialed subjects:

TO GRANT ONE OR MORE OF THE FOLLOWING POWERS, INITIAL THE LINE IN FRONT OF EACH POWER YOU ARE GRANTING. TO WITHHOLD A POWER, DO <u>NOT</u> INITIAL THE LINE IN FRONT OF IT. YOU MAY, BUT NEED NOT, CROSS OUT EACH POWER WITHHELD.

| | | |
|---|---|---|
| _____ | (A) | Real estate transactions (when property recorded). |
| _____ | (B) | Tangible personal property transactions. |
| _____ | (C) | Stock and bond transactions. |
| _____ | (D) | Commodity and option transactions. |
| _____ | (E) | Banking and other financial institution transactions. |
| _____ | (F) | Business operating transactions. |
| _____ | (G) | Insurance and annuity transactions. |
| _____ | (H) | Estate, trust, and other beneficiary transactions. |
| _____ | (I) | Claims and litigation. |
| _____ | (J) | Personal and family maintenance. |
| _____ | (K) | Benefits from social security, medicare, medicaid, or other governmental programs or military service. |
| _____ | (L) | Retirement plan transactions. |
| _____ | (M) | Tax matters. |

UNLESS YOU DIRECT OTHERWISE ABOVE, THIS POWER OF ATTORNEY IS EFFECTIVE IMMEDIATELY AND WILL CONTINUE UNTIL IT IS REVOKED OR TERMINATED AS SPECIFIED BELOW. STRIKE THROUGH AND WRITE YOUR INITIALS TO THE LEFT OF THE FOLLOWING SENTENCE IF YOU DO <u>NOT</u> WANT THIS POWER OF ATTORNEY TO CONTINUE IF YOU BECOME DISABLED, INCAPACITATED, OR INCOMPETENT.

    1.    (    ) This power of attorney will continue to be effective even though I become disabled, incapacitated, or incompetent.

YOU MAY INCLUDE ADDITIONS TO AND LIMITATIONS ON THE AGENT'S POWERS IN THIS POWER OF ATTORNEY IF THEY ARE SPECIFICALLY DESCRIBED BELOW.

    2.    The powers granted above shall not include the following powers or shall be modified or limited in the following manner (here you may include any specific limitations you deem appropriate, such as a prohibition of or conditions on the sale of particular stock or real estate or special rules regarding borrowing by the agent):

_____

_____

_____

    3.    In addition to the powers granted above, I grant my agent the following powers (here you may add any other delegable powers, such as the power to make gifts, exercise powers of appointment, name or change beneficiaries or joint tenants, or revoke or amend any trust specifically referred to below):

_____

_____

_____

    4.    SPECIAL INSTRUCTIONS.  ON THE FOLLOWING LINES YOU MAY GIVE SPECIAL INSTRUCTIONS TO YOUR AGENT:

_____

_____

_____

YOUR AGENT WILL BE ENTITLED TO REIMBURSEMENT FOR ALL REASONABLE EXPENSES INCURRED IN ACTING UNDER THIS POWER OF ATTORNEY.  STRIKE THROUGH AND INITIAL THE NEXT SENTENCE IF YOU DO <u>NOT</u> WANT YOUR AGENT TO ALSO BE ENTITLED TO REASONABLE COMPENSATION FOR SERVICES AS AGENT.

    5.    (    ) My agent is entitled to reasonable compensation for services rendered as agent under this power of attorney.

THIS POWER OF ATTORNEY MAY BE AMENDED IN ANY MANNER OR REVOKED BY YOU AT ANY TIME.  ABSENT AMENDMENT OR REVOCATION, THE AUTHORITY GRANTED IN THIS POWER OF ATTORNEY IS EFFECTIVE WHEN THIS POWER OF ATTORNEY IS SIGNED AND CONTINUES IN EFFECT UNTIL YOUR DEATH, UNLESS YOU MAKE A LIMITATION ON DURATION BY COMPLETING THE FOLLOWING:

    6.    This power of attorney terminates on _____

_____ (Insert a future date or event, such as court determination of your disability, when you want this power to terminate prior to your death).

BY RETAINING THE FOLLOWING PARAGRAPH, YOU MAY, BUT ARE NOT REQUIRED TO, NAME YOUR AGENT AS GUARDIAN OF YOUR PERSON OR CONSERVATOR OF YOUR PROPERTY, OR BOTH, IF A COURT PROCEEDING IS BEGUN TO APPOINT A GUARDIAN OR CONSERVATOR, OR BOTH, FOR YOU. THE COURT WILL APPOINT YOUR AGENT AS GUARDIAN OR CONSERVATOR, OR BOTH, IF THE COURT FINDS THAT SUCH APPOINTMENT WILL SERVE YOUR BEST INTERESTS AND WELFARE. STRIKE THROUGH AND INITIAL PARAGRAPH 7 IF YOU DO <u>NOT</u> WANT YOUR AGENT TO ACT AS GUARDIAN OR CONSERVATOR, OR BOTH.

    7.    (    ) If a guardian of my person or a conservator for my property, or both, are to be appointed, I nominate the agent acting under this power of attorney as such guardian or conservator, or both, to serve without bond or security.

IF YOU WITH TO NAME SUCCESSOR AGENTS, INSERT THE NAME AND ADDRESS OF ANY SUCCESSOR AGENT IN THE FOLLOWING PARAGRAPH:

8.     If any agent named by me shall die, become incapacitated, resign, or refuse to accept the office of agent, I name the following each to act alone and successively, in the order named, as successor to such agent:

_____

_____

For purposes of this paragraph 8, a person is considered to be incapacitated if and while the person is a minor or a person adjudicated incapacitated or if the person is unable to give prompt and intelligent consideration to business matters, as certified by a licensed physician.

I agree that any third party who receives a copy of this document may act under it. Revocation of the power of attorney is not effective as to a third party until the third party learns of the revocation. I agree to indemnify the third party for any claims that arise against the third party because of reliance on this power of attorney.

Signed on _____, _____.

IF THERE IS ANYTHING ABOUT THIS FORM THAT YOU DO NOT UNDERSTAND, IT MAY BE IN YOUR BEST INTEREST TO CONSULT A COLORADO LAWYER RATHER THAN SIGN THIS FORM.

_____
(Your signature)

_____
(Your Social Security number)

YOU MAY, BUT ARE NOT REQUIRED TO, REQUEST YOUR AGENT AND SUCCESSOR AGENTS TO PROVIDE SPECIMEN SIGNATURES BELOW.  IF YOU INCLUDE SPECIMEN SIGNATURES IN THIS POWER OF ATTORNEY, YOU MUST COMPLETE THE CERTIFICATION OPPOSITE THE SIGNATURES OF THE AGENTS.

NOTICE TO AGENTS:  BY EXERCISING POWERS UNDER THIS DOCUMENT, THE AGENT ASSUMES THE FIDUCIARY AND OTHER LEGAL RESPONSIBILITIES OF AN AGENT UNDER COLORADO LAW.

Specimen signatures of agent                    I certify that the signatures of my agent
(and successors)                                         (and successors) are correct.

_____        _____
Agent                                                       Principal

_____        _____
Successor Agent                                         Principal

_____        _____
Successor Agent                                         Principal

STATE OF COLORADO                             )
                                                             ) ss.
COUNTY OF _____      )

This document was acknowledged before me on _____ (date) by _____
_____ (name of principal) (who certifies the correctness of the signature(s) of the agent(s).)  My commission expires: _____

_____
Notary public

# COLORADO AGENT'S AFFIDAVIT REGARDING POWER OF ATTORNEY

STATE OF COLORADO                          )
                                           ) ss.
County of _____           )


I, _____, whose address is _____ _____ of lawful age, pursuant to sections 15-1-1302, 15-14-501, and 15-14-502, Colorado Revised Statutes, state upon my oath that I am the attorney-in-fact and agent for_____ _____, principal, under the power of attorney dated _____, a copy of which is attached hereto and incorporated herein by this reference, that as of this date I have no actual knowledge of the [revocation or*] termination of the power of attorney by any act of the principal, or by the death, [disability, or incompetence*] of the principal, that my authority has not been terminated by a decree of dissolution of marriage or legal separation, and that to the best of my knowledge the power of attorney has not been so terminated and remains valid, in full force and effect.


Dated: _____          _____
                                        Attorney-in-Fact


The foregoing Affidavit was subscribed and sworn to before me on _____ _____, 20___, by _____, Agent. Witness my hand and official seal.


My Commission expires:_____


[SEAL]


Notary Public


*Strike "revocation or" and "disability or incompetence" if the power of attorney is durable and the principal is disabled or incompetent.

# COLORADO DECLARATION AS TO MEDICAL OR SURGICAL TREATMENT

I, _____, being of sound mind and at least eighteen years of age, direct that my life shall not be artificially prolonged under the circumstances set forth below and hereby declare that:

1.   If at any time my attending physician and one other qualified physician certify in writing that:

a.   I have an injury, disease, or illness which is not curable or reversible and which, in their judgment, is a terminal condition, and

b.   For a period of seven consecutive days or more, I have been unconscious, comatose, or otherwise incompetent so as to be unable to make or communicate responsible decisions concerning my person, then

I direct that, in accordance with Colorado law, life-sustaining procedures shall be withdrawn and withheld pursuant to the terms of this declaration, it being understood that life-sustaining procedures shall not include any medical procedure or intervention for nourishment considered necessary by the attending physician to provide comfort or alleviate pain. However, I may specifically direct, in accordance with Colorado law, that artificial nourishment be withdrawn or withheld pursuant to the terms of this declaration.

2.   In the event that the only procedure I am being provided is artificial nourishment, I direct that one of the following actions be taken:

_____ a.   Artificial nourishment shall not be continued when it is the only procedure being provided; or

_____ b.   Artificial nourishment shall be continued for _____ days when it is the only procedure being provided; or

_____ c.   Artificial nourishment shall be continued when it is the only procedure being provided.

3.   I execute this declaration, as my free and voluntary act, this _____ day of _____, 200___.

By _____
                        Declarant

The foregoing instrument was signed and declared by _____ to be his declaration, in the presence of us, who, in his presence, in the presence of each other, and at his request, have signed our names below as witnesses, and we declare that, at the time of the execution of this instrument, the declarant, according to our best knowledge and belief, was of sound mind and under no constraint or undue influence.

Dated at _____, Colorado, this _____ day of _____, 200___.

_____
Name and Address of Witness

_____
Name and Address of Witness

STATE OF COLORADO                          )
                                           ) ss.
COUNTY OF _____           )

SUBSCRIBED and sworn to before me by _____, the declarant, and _____ and _____, witnesses, as the voluntary act and deed of the declarant the _____ day of _____, 200____.

My commission expires:

_____
                        Notary Public

# Connecticut Statutory Short Form Durable Power of Attorney

**Notice: The powers granted by this document are broad and sweeping. They are defined in Connecticut Statutory Short Form Power of Attorney Act, section 1-42 to 1-56, inclusive, of the general statutes, which expressly permits the use of any other or different form of power of attorney desired by the parties concerned. The grantor of any power of attorney or the attorney-in-fact may make application to a court of probate for an accounting as provided in subsection (b) of section 45a-175.**

Know All Men by These Presents, which are intended to constitute a GENERAL POWER OF ATTORNEY pursuant to Connecticut Statutory Short Form Power of Attorney Act:

That I _____
_____(insert name and address of the principal)
do hereby appoint _____
_____
_____ (insert name and address of the agent, or each agents, if more than one is designated) my attorney(s)-in-fact TO ACT _____.

If more than one agent is designated and the principal wishes each agent alone to be able to exercise the power conferred, insert in the blank the word "severally". Failure to make any insertion or the insertion of the word "jointly" shall require the agents to act jointly.

First: In my name, place and stead in any way which I myself could do, if I were personally present, with respect to the following matters as each of them is defined in the Connecticut Statutory Short Form Power of Attorney Act to the extent that I am permitted by law to act through an agent:

(Strike out and initial in the opposite box any one or more of the subdivisions as to which the principal does NOT desire to give the agent authority. Such elimination of any one or more of subdivisions (A) to (L), inclusive, shall automatically constitute an elimination also of subdivision (M).)

To strike out any subdivision the principal must draw a line through the test of that subdivision AND write his initial in the box opposite.

| | | |
|---|---|---|
| (A) | real estate transactions;.................................................................... | (    ) |
| (B) | chattel and goods transactions;........................................................... | (    ) |
| (C) | bond, share and commodity transactions;............................................. | (    ) |
| (D) | banking transactions;........................................................................ | (    ) |
| (E) | business operating transactions;......................................................... | (    ) |
| (F) | insurance transactions;...................................................................... | (    ) |
| (G) | estate transactions;........................................................................... | (    ) |
| (H) | claims and litigation;.......................................................................... | (    ) |
| (I) | personal relationships and affairs;....................................................... | (    ) |
| (J) | benefits from military service;............................................................. | (    ) |
| (K) | records, reports and statements;......................................................... | (    ) |
| (L) | health care decisions;........................................................................ | (    ) |
| (M) | all other matters;.............................................................................. | (    ): |

_____
_____

(Special provisions and limitations may be included in the statutory short form power of attorney only if they conform to the requirements of the Connecticut Statutory Short Form Power of Attorney Act.)

Second: With full and unqualified authority to delegate any or all of the foregoing powers to any person or persons whom my attorney(s)-in-fact shall select;

Third: Hereby ratifying and confirming all that said attorney(s) or substitute(s) do or cause to be done.

IN WITNESS WHEREOF I have hereunto signed my name and affixed my seal this _____ day of _____, _____.

_____ (Signature of Principal) (Seal)

On the date written above, _____ declared to us that this instrument was [his/her] durable power of attorney, and requested us to act as witnesses to it. [He/She] signed it in our presence, all of us being present at the same time. We now sign this instrument as witnesses.

_____, Witness _____

_____, Witness _____

## ACKNOWLEDGMENT

State of _____

County of _____

The foregoing instrument was acknowledged before me this _____ by _____.

_____(Signature)

Title or Rank_____

Serial No. if any_____

**Health Care Instructions**

THESE ARE MY HEALTH CARE INSTRUCTIONS. MY APPOINTMENT OF A HEALTH CARE AGENT, MY APPOINTMENT OF AN ATTORNEY-IN-FACT FOR HEALTH CARE DECISIONS, THE DESIGNATION OF MY CONSERVATOR OF THE PERSON FOR MY FUTURE INCAPACITY AND MY DOCUMENT OF ANATOMICAL GIFT.

To any physician who is treating me: These are my health care instructions including those concerning the withholding or withdrawal of life support systems, together with the appointment of my health care agent and my attorney-in-fact for health care decisions, the designation of my conservator of the person for future incapacity and my document of anatomical gift. As my physician, you may rely on any decision made by my health care agent, attorney-in-fact for health care decisions or conservator of my person, if I am unable to make a decision for myself.

I, _____, the author of this document, request that, if my condition is deemed terminal or if I am determined to be permanently unconscious, I be allowed to die and not be kept alive through life support systems. By terminal condition, I mean that I have an incurable or irreversible medical condition which, without the administration of life support systems, will, in the opinion of my attending physician, result in death within a relatively short time. By permanently unconscious I mean that I am in a permanent coma or persistent vegetative state which is an irreversible condition in which I am at no time aware of myself or the environment and show no behavioral response to the environment. The life support systems which I do not want include, but are not limited to: Artificial respiration, cardiopulmonary resuscitation and artificial means of providing nutrition and hydration. I do want sufficient pain medication to maintain my physical comfort. I do not intend any direct taking of my life, but only that my dying not be unreasonably prolonged.

I appoint _____ to be my health care agent and my attorney-in-fact for health care decisions. If my attending physician determines that I am unable to understand and appreciate the nature and consequences of health care decisions and unable to reach and communicate an informed decision regarding treatment, my health care agent and attorney-in-fact for health care decisions is authorized to:

> (1) Convey to my physician my wishes concerning the withholding or removal of life support systems;

> (2) Take whatever actions are necessary to ensure that any wishes are given effect;

> (3) Consent, refuse or withdraw consent to any medical treatment as long as such action is consistent with my wishes concerning the withholding or removal of life support systems; and,

> (4) Consent to any medical treatment designed solely for the purpose of maintaining physical comfort.

If _____ is unwilling or unable to serve as my health care agent and my attorney-in-fact for health care decisions, I appoint _____ _____ to be my alternative health care agent and my attorney-in-fact for health care decisions. If a conservator of my person should need to be appointed, I designate _____ be appointed my conservator. If _____ is unwilling or unable to serve as my conservator, I designate _____. No bond shall be required of either of them in any jurisdiction.

I hereby make this anatomical gift, if medically acceptable, to take effect upon my death.

I give: (check one)

        ____ (1) any needed organs or parts

        ___(2)  only the following organs or parts _____ to
                 be donated for: (check one)
                 (1) ___ any of the purposes stated in subsection (a) of section 19a-279f of the
                     general statutes
                 (2) ___ these limited purposes _____.

These requests, appointments, and designations are made after careful reflection, while I am of sound mind. Any party receiving a duly executed copy or facsimile of this document may rely upon it unless such party has received actual notice of my revocation of it.

Date _____, 20___

                                     _____ L.S.

This document was signed in our presence by _____ the author of this document, who appeared to be eighteen years of age or older, of sound mind and able to understand the nature and consequences of health care decisions at the time this document was signed. The author appeared to be under no improper influence. We have subscribed this document in the author's presence and at the author's request and in the presence of each other.

_____        _____
(Witness)                                          (Witness)

_____        _____
(Number and Street)                             (Number and Street)

_____        _____
(City, State and Zip Code)                     (City, State and Zip Code)

STATE OF CONNECTICUT           )
                                   )ss.
COUNTY OF _____   )

We, the subscribing witnesses, being duly sworn, say that we witnessed the execution of these health care instructions, the appointments of a health care agent and an attorney-in-fact, the designation of a conservator for future incapacity and a document of anatomical gift by the author of this document; that the author subscribed, published and declared the same to be the author's instructions, appointments and designation in our presence; that we thereafter subscribed the document as witnesses in the author's presence, at the author's request, and in the presence of each other; that at the time of the execution of said document the author appeared to us to be eighteen years of age or older, of sound mind, able to understand the nature and consequences of said document, and under no improper influence, and we make this affidavit at the author's request this _____ day of _____, 20_____.

_____        _____
(Witness)                               (Witness)

Subscribed and sworn to before me this _____ day of _____, 20_____.

_____
Commissioner of the Superior Court

Notary Public

My commission expires: _____

## Advance Health-Care Directive

### EXPLANATION

You have the right to give instructions about your own health care. You also have the right to name someone else to make health-care decisions for you. This form lets you do either or both of these things. It also lets you express your wishes regarding anatomical gifts and the designation of your primary physician. If you use this form, you may complete or modify all or any part of it. You are free to use a different form.

Part 1 of this form is a power of attorney for health care. Part 1 lets you name another individual as agent to make health-care decisions for you if you become incapable of making your own decisions. You may also name an alternate agent to act for you if your first choice is not willing, able or reasonably available to make decisions for you. Unless related to you, an agent may not have a controlling interest in or be an operator or employee of a residential long-term health-care institution at which you are receiving care. If you do not have a qualifying condition (terminal illness/injury or permanent unconsciousness), your agent may make all health-care decisions for you except for decisions providing, withholding or withdrawing of a life sustaining procedure. Unless you limit the agent's authority, your agent will have the right to:

(a)        Consent or refuse consent to any care, treatment, service or procedure to maintain, diagnose or otherwise affect a physical or mental condition unless it's a life-sustaining procedure or otherwise required by law.

(b)        Select or discharge health-care providers and health-care institutions.

If you have a qualifying condition, your agent may make all health-care decisions for you, including, but not limited to:

(c)        The decisions listed in (a) and (b).

(d)        Consent or refuse consent to life sustaining procedures, such as, but not limited to, cardiopulmonary resuscitation and orders not to resuscitate.

(e)        Direct the providing, withholding or withdrawal of artificial nutrition and hydration and all other forms of health care.

Part 2 of this form lets you give specific instructions about any aspect of your health care. Choices are provided for you to express your wishes regarding the provision, withholding or withdrawal of treatment to keep you alive, including the provision of artificial nutrition and hydration as well as the provision of pain relief. Space is also provided for you to add to the choices you have made or for you to write out any additional instructions for other than end of life decisions.

Part 3 of this form lets you express an intention to donate your bodily organs and tissues following your death.

Part 4 of this form lets you designate a physician to have primary responsibility for your health care.

After completing this form, sign and date the form at the end. It is required that 2 other individuals sign as witnesses. Give a copy of the signed and completed form to your physician, to any other health-care providers you may have, to any health-care institution at which you are receiving care and to any health-care agents you have named. You should talk to the person you have named as agent to make sure that the person understands your wishes and is willing to take the responsibility.

You have the right to revoke this advance health-care directive or replace this form at any time.

* * * * * * * * * * * * * * * * * * * * *

### PART 1: POWER OF ATTORNEY FOR HEALTH CARE

(1)        DESIGNATION OF AGENT:  I designate the following individual as my agent to make health-care decisions for me:

_____
(name of individual you choose as agent)


_____
(address)                          (city)                          (state)                    (zip code)


_____
(home phone)                                          (work phone)

OPTIONAL: If I revoke my agent's authority or if my agent is not willing, able or reasonably available to make a health-care decision for me, I designate as my first alternate agent:

_____

(name of individual you choose as first alternate agent)

_____
(address)                (city)                (state)                (zip code)

_____
(home phone)                          (work phone)

OPTIONAL: If I revoke the authority of my agent and first alternate agent or if neither is willing, able or reasonably available to make a health-care decision for me, I designate as my second alternate agent:

_____

(name of individual you choose as second alternate agent)

_____
(address)                (city)                (state)                (zip code)

_____
(home phone)                          (work phone)

(2)     AGENT'S AUTHORITY: If I am not in a qualifying condition my agent is authorized to make all health-care decisions for me, except decisions about life-sustaining procedures and as I state here; and if I am in a qualifying condition, my agent is authorized to make all health-care decisions for me, except as I state here:

_____
_____
_____

(Add additional sheets if needed.)

(3)     WHEN AGENT'S AUTHORITY BECOMES EFFECTIVE: My agent's authority becomes effective when my primary physician determines I lack the capacity to make my own health-care decisions. As to decisions concerning the providing, withholding and withdrawal of life-sustaining procedures my agent's authority becomes effective when my primary physician determines I lack the capacity to make my own health-care decisions and my primary physician and another physician determine that I am in a terminal condition or permanently unconscious.

(4)     AGENT'S OBLIGATIONS: My agent shall make health-care decisions for me in accordance with this power of attorney for health care, any instructions I give in Part 2 of this form, and my other wishes to the extent known to my agent. To the extent my wishes are unknown, my agent shall make health-care decisions for me in accordance with what my agent determines to be in my best interest. In determining my best interest, my agent shall consider my personal values to the extent known to my agent.

(5)     NOMINATION OF GUARDIAN: If a guardian of my person needs to be appointed for me by a court, (please check one):

[   ]     I nominate the agent(s) whom I named in this form in the order designated to act as guardian.

[   ]     I nominate the following to be guardian in the order designated:

_____

[   ]     I do not nominate anyone to be guardian.

## PART 2: INSTRUCTIONS FOR HEALTH CARE

If you are satisfied to allow your agent to determine what is best for you in making end-of-life decisions, you need not fill out this part of the form. If you do fill out this part of the form, you may strike any wording you do not want.

(6)     END-OF-LIFE DECISIONS: If I am in a qualifying condition, I direct that my health-care providers and others involved in my care provide, withhold, or withdraw treatment in accordance with the choice I have marked below:

### Choice Not To Prolong Life

**I do not want my life to be prolonged if: (please check all that apply)**

_____(i)     I have a terminal condition (an incurable condition caused by injury, disease, or illness which, to a reasonable degree of medical certainty, makes death imminent and from which, despite the application of life-sustaining procedures, there can be no recovery) and regarding artificial nutrition and hydration, I make the following specific directions:

|  | I want used | I do not want used |
|---|---|---|
| Artificial nutrition through a conduit | _____ | _____ |
| Hydration through a conduit | _____ | _____ |

_____(ii)     I become permanently unconscious (a medical condition that has been diagnosed in accordance with currently accepted medical standards that has lasted at least 4 weeks and with reasonable medical certainty as total and irreversible loss of consciousness and capacity for interaction with the environment.  The term includes, without limitation, a persistent vegetative state or irreversible coma) and regarding artificial nutrition and hydration, I make the following specific directions:

|  | I want used | I do not want used |
|---|---|---|
| Artificial nutrition through a conduit | _____ | _____ |
| Hydration through a conduit | _____ | _____ |

### Choice To Prolong Life

_____     I want my life to be prolonged as long as possible within the limits of generally accepted health-care standards.

RELIEF FROM PAIN: Except as I state in the following space, I direct treatment for alleviation of pain or discomfort be provided at all times, even if it hastens my death: _____
_____
_____
_____

(7)     OTHER MEDICAL INSTRUCTIONS: (If you do not agree with any of the optional choices above and wish to write you own, or if you wish to add to the instructions you have given above, you may do so here.)  I direct that: _____
_____
_____

(Add additional sheets if necessary.)

### PART 3: ANATOMICAL GIFTS AT DEATH
#### (OPTIONAL)

(8)     I am mentally competent and 18 years or more of age.
     I hereby make this anatomical gift to take effect upon my death.  The marks in the appropriate squares and words filled into the blanks below indicate my desires.
     I give:  [   ] my body;  [   ] any needed organs or parts;
          [   ] the following organs or parts: _____
     To the following person or institutions:
          [   ] the physician in attendance at my death;
          [   ] the hospital in which I die;

[    ] the following named physician, hospital, storage bank or other medical institution:

_____

[    ] the following individual for treatment:

_____

for the following purposes:      [    ] any purpose authorized by law;
                  [    ] transplantation;      [    ] therapy;
                  [    ] research;           [    ] medical education.

### PART 4: PRIMARY PHYSICIAN
(OPTIONAL)

(9)      I designate the following physician as my primary physician:

_____

(name of physician)                        (phone)

_____

(address)         (city)         (state)         (zip code)

OPTIONAL: If the physician I have designated above is not willing, able or reasonably available to act as my primary physician, I designate the following physician as my primary physician:

_____

(name of physician)                        (phone)

_____

(address)         (city)         (state)         (zip code)

Primary Physician shall mean a physician designated by an individual or the individual's agent or guardian, to have primary responsibility for the individual's health care or, in the absence of a designation or if the designated physician is not reasonably available, a physician who undertakes the responsibility.

\* \* \* \* \* \* \* \* \* \* \* \* \* \* \* \* \* \* \* \*

(10)      EFFECT OF COPY: A copy of this form has the same effect as the original.

(11)      SIGNATURE: Sign and date the form here: I understand the purposes and effect of this document.

_____      _____

(date)                                   (sign your name)

_____      _____

(address)                               (print your name)

_____

(city)            (state)            (zip code)

(12) SIGNATURE OF WITNESSES:

Statement Of Witnesses

      SIGNED AND DECLARED by the above-named declarant as and for his/her written declaration under 16 Del.C. §§ 2502 and 2503, in our presence, who in his/her presence, at his/her request, and in the presence of each other, have hereunto subscribed our names as witnesses, and state:
      A.      That the Declarant is mentally competent.
      B.      That neither of them:

1. Is related to the declarant by blood, marriage or adoption;
2. Is entitled to any portion of the estate of the declarant under any will of the declarant or codicil thereto then existing nor, at the time of the executing of the advance health care directive, is so entitled by operation of law then existing;
3. Has, at the time of the execution of the advance health-care directive, a present or inchoate claim against any portion of the estate of the declarant;
4. Has a direct financial responsibility for the declarant's medical care;
5. Has a controlling interest in or is an operator or an employee of a residential long-term health-care institution in which the declarant is a resident; or
6. Is under eighteen years of age.

C. That if the declarant is a resident of a sanitarium, rest home, nursing home, boarding home or related institution, one of the witnesses, _____, is at the time of the execution of the advance health-care directive, a patient advocate or ombudsman designated by the Division of Services for Aging and Adults with Physical Disabilities or the Public Guardian.

First witness                                    Second witness


_____        _____
(print name)                                     (print name)


_____        _____
(address)                                        (address)


_____        _____
(city)                    (state)                (city)                    (state)


_____        _____
(signature of witness)                           (signature of witness)


_____        _____
(date)                                           (date)

I am not prohibited by §2503 of            I am not prohibited by §2503 of
Title 16 of the Delaware Code             Title 16 of the Delaware Code
from being a witness.                      from being a witness.

## STATUTORY POWER OF ATTORNEY

NOTICE: THE POWERS GRANTED BY THIS DOCUMENT ARE BROAD AND SWEEPING. THEY ARE EXPLAINED IN THE UNIFORM STATUTORY FORM POWER OF ATTORNEY ACT OF 1998. IF YOU HAVE ANY QUESTIONS ABOUT THESE POWERS, OBTAIN COMPETENT LEGAL ADVICE. THIS DOCUMENT DOES NOT AUTHORIZE ANYONE TO MAKE MEDICAL AND OTHER HEALTH-CARE DECISIONS FOR YOU. YOU MAY REVOKE THIS POWER OF ATTORNEY IF YOU LATER WISH TO DO SO.

I _____

_____ (insert your name and address) appoint

_____

_____ (insert the name and address of the person appointed) as my agent (attorney-in-fact) to act for me in any lawful way with respect to the following initialed subjects:

TO GRANT ALL OF THE FOLLOWING POWERS, INITIAL THE LINE IN FRONT OF (N) AND IGNORE THE LINES IN FRONT OF THE OTHER POWERS. TO GRANT ONE OR MORE, BUT FEWER THAN ALL, OF THE FOLLOWING POWERS, INITIAL THE LINE IN FRONT OF EACH POWER YOU ARE GRANTING. TO WITHHOLD A POWER, DO NOT INITIAL THE LINE IN FRONT OF IT. YOU MAY, BUT NEED NOT, CROSS OUT EACH POWER WITHHELD.

INITIAL

_____ (A)     Real property transactions, except transactions subject to D.C. Official Code §42-101.

_____ (B)     Tangible personal property transactions.

_____ (C)     Stock and bond transactions.

_____ (D)     Commodity and option transactions.

_____ (E)     Banking and other financial institution transactions.

_____ (F)     Business operating transactions.

_____ (G)     Insurance and annuity transactions.

_____ (H)     Estate, trust, and other beneficiary transactions.

_____ (I)     Claims and litigation.

_____ (J)     Personal and family maintenance.

_____ (K)     Benefits from social security, medicare, medicaid, or other governmental programs, or military service.

_____ (L)     Retirement plan transactions.

_____ (M)     Tax matters.

_____ (N)     ALL OF THE POWERS LISTED ABOVE.

YOU NEED NOT INITIAL ANY OTHER LINES IF YOU INITIAL LINE (N). If the line in front of line (N) is initialed, an initial on the line in front of any other power does not limit the powers granted by line (N).

SPECIAL INSTRUCTIONS: ON THE FOLLOWING LINES YOU MAY GIVE SPECIAL INSTRUCTIONS LIMITING OR EXTENDING THE POWERS GRANTED TO YOUR AGENT:

_____

_____

_____

UNLESS YOU DIRECT OTHERWISE ABOVE, THIS POWER OF ATTORNEY IS EFFECTIVE IMMEDIATELY AND WILL CONTINUE UNTIL IT IS REVOKED.

This power of attorney will continue to be effective even though I become disabled, incapacitated, or incompetent.

STRIKE THE PRECEDING SENTENCE IF YOU DO NOT WANT THIS POWER OF ATTORNEY TO CONTINUE IF YOU BECOME DISABLED, INCAPACITATED, OR INCOMPETENT.

I agree that any third party who receives a copy of this document may act under it. Revocation of the power of attorney is not effective as to a third party until the third party learns of the revocation. I agree to indemnify the third party for any claims that arise against the third party because of reliance on this power of attorney.

Signed this _____ day of _____, _____

_____
(Your Signature)

_____
(Your Social Security Number)

District of Columbia

This document was acknowledged before me on _____ (date) by _____ (name of principal).

_____
(Signature of notary public)

(Seal):
[My commission expires: _____]

BY ACCEPTING OR ACTING UNDER THE APPOINTMENT, THE AGENT ASSUMES THE FIDUCIARY AND OTHER LEGAL RESPONSIBILITIES OF AN AGENT.

**Power of Attorney For Health Care**

INFORMATION ABOUT THIS DOCUMENT

THIS IS AN IMPORTANT LEGAL DOCUMENT. BEFORE SIGNING THIS DOCUMENT, IT IS VITAL FOR YOU TO KNOW AND UNDERSTAND THESE FACTS:

THIS DOCUMENT GIVES THE PERSON YOU NAME AS YOUR ATTORNEY IN FACT THE POWER TO MAKE HEALTH-CARE DECISIONS FOR YOU IF YOU CANNOT MAKE THE DECISIONS FOR YOURSELF.

AFTER YOU HAVE SIGNED THIS DOCUMENT, YOU HAVE THE RIGHT TO MAKE HEALTH-CARE DECISIONS FOR YOURSELF IF YOU ARE MENTALLY COMPETENT TO DO SO. IN ADDITION, AFTER YOU HAVE SIGNED THIS DOCUMENT, NO TREATMENT MAY BE GIVEN TO YOU OR STOPPED OVER YOUR OBJECTION IF YOU ARE MENTALLY COMPETENT TO MAKE THAT DECISION.

YOU MAY STATE IN THIS DOCUMENT ANY TYPE OF TREATMENT THAT YOU DO NOT DESIRE AND ANY THAT YOU WANT TO MAKE SURE YOU RECEIVE.

YOU HAVE THE RIGHT TO TAKE AWAY THE AUTHORITY OF YOUR ATTORNEY IN FACT, UNLESS YOU HAVE BEEN ADJUDICATED INCOMPETENT, BY NOTIFYING YOUR ATTORNEY IN FACT OR HEALTH-CARE PROVIDER EITHER ORALLY OR IN WRITING. SHOULD YOU REVOKE THE AUTHORITY OF YOUR ATTORNEY IN FACT, IT IS ADVISABLE TO REVOKE IN WRITING AND TO PLACE COPIES OF THE REVOCATION WHEREVER THIS DOCUMENT IS LOCATED.

IF THERE IS ANYTHING IN THIS DOCUMENT THAT YOU DO NOT UNDERSTAND, YOU SHOULD ASK A SOCIAL WORKER, LAWYER, OR OTHER PERSON TO EXPLAIN IT TO YOU.

\* \* \* \* \*

YOU SHOULD KEEP A COPY OF THIS DOCUMENT AFTER YOU HAVE SIGNED IT. GIVE A COPY TO THE PERSON YOU NAME AS YOUR ATTORNEY IN FACT. IF YOU ARE IN A HEALTH-CARE FACILITY, A COPY OF THIS DOCUMENT SHOULD BE INCLUDED IN YOUR MEDICAL RECORD.

I, _____ , hereby appoint:

_____        _____
name                                    home address

_____        _____
home telephone number

_____
work telephone number

as my attorney in fact to make health-care decisions for me if I become unable to make my own health-care decisions. This gives my attorney in fact the power to grant, refuse, or withdraw consent on my behalf for any health-care service, treatment or procedure. My attorney in fact also has the authority to talk to health-care personnel, get information and sign forms necessary to carry out these decisions.

If the person named as my attorney in fact is not available or is unable to act as my attorney in fact, I appoint the following persons to serve in the order listed below:

1.  _____        _____
    name                                    home address

    _____        _____
    home telephone number

    _____
    work telephone number

2.  _____        _____
    name                                    home address

    _____        _____
    home telephone number

    _____
    work telephone number

With this document, I intend to create a power of attorney for health care, which shall take effect if I become incapable of making my own health-care decisions and shall continue during that incapacity.

My attorney in fact shall make health-care decisions as I direct below or as I make known to my attorney in fact in some other way.

(a) STATEMENT OF DIRECTIVES CONCERNING LIFE-PROLONGING CARE, TREATMENT, SERVICES, AND PROCEDURES:

_____
_____
_____

(b) SPECIAL PROVISIONS AND LIMITATIONS:

_____
_____
_____

BY MY SIGNATURE I INDICATE THAT I UNDERSTAND THE PURPOSE AND EFFECT OF THIS DOCUMENT.

I sign my name to this form on _____
                                                                (date)
at: _____
    (address)

_____
(Signature)

## WITNESSES

I declare that the person who signed or acknowledged this document is personally known to me, that the person signed or acknowledged this durable power of attorney for health care in my presence, and that the person appears to be of sound mind and under no duress, fraud, or undue influence. I am not the person appointed as the attorney in fact by this document, nor am I the health-care provider of the principal or an employee of the health-care provider of the principal.

First Witness

Signature: _____
Home Address: _____
Print Name: _____
Date: _____

Second Witness

Signature: _____
Home Address: _____
Print Name: _____
Date: _____

(AT LEAST 1 OF THE WITNESSES LISTED ABOVE SHALL ALSO SIGN THE FOLLOWING DECLARATION.)

I further declare that I am not related to the principal by blood, marriage or adoption, and, to the best of my knowledge, I am not entitled to any part of the estate of the principal under a currently existing will or by operation of law.

Signature: _____

Signature: _____

## Affidavit of Physician

STATE OF _____
COUNTY OF _____

Before me, the undersigned authority, personally appeared _____ _____ (name of physician), Affiant, who swore or affirmed that:

1. Affiant is a physician licensed to practice medicine in _____ _____ (name of state, territory, or foreign country).

2. Affiant is the primary physician who has responsibility for the treatment and care of _____ (principal's name).

3. To the best of Affiant's knowledge after reasonable inquiry, Affiant believes that the principal lacks the capacity to manage property, including taking those actions necessary to obtain, administer, and dispose of real and personal property, intangible property, business property, benefits, and income.

_____
(Affiant)

Sworn to (or affirmed) and subscribed before me this _____ day of _____, 20___, by _____ (name of person making statement).

_____
(Signature of Notary Public—State of Florida)

_____
(Print, Type, or Stamp Commissioned Name of Notary Public)

**Personally Known OR Produced Identification**

_____
(Type of Identification Produced)

**Designation of Health Care Surrogate**

Name: _____(Last)_____(First)_____(Middle Initial)

In the event that I have been determined to be incapacitated to provide informed consent for medical treatment and surgical and diagnostic procedures, I wish to designate as my surrogate for health care decisions:

Name: _____

Address: _____

Phone: _____         Zip Code: _____

If my surrogate is unwilling or unable to perform his or her duties, I wish to designate as my alternate surrogate:

Name: _____

Address: _____

Phone: _____         Zip Code: _____

I fully understand that this designation will permit my designee to make health care decisions, except for anatomical gifts, unless I have executed an anatomical gift declaration pursuant to law, and to provide, withhold, or withdraw consent on my behalf; to apply for public benefits to defray the cost of health care; and to authorize my admission to or transfer from a health care facility.

Additional instructions (optional): _____
_____
_____
_____

I further affirm that this designation is not being made as a condition of treatment or admission to a health care facility. I will notify and send a copy of this document to the following persons other than my surrogate, so they may know who my surrogate is.

Name: _____

Name: _____

Signed: _____

Date: _____

Witnesses:

1. _____

2. _____

## LIVING WILL

Declaration made this _____ day of _____, _____ (year) , I, _____, willfully and voluntarily make known my desire that my dying not be artificially prolonged under the circumstances set forth below, and I do hereby declare that, if at any time I am incapacitated and (please only initial one):

_____I have a terminal condition
**OR**
_____I have an end-stage condition
**OR**
_____I am in a persistent vegetative state

And if my attending or treating physician and another consulting physician have determined that there is no reasonable medical probability of my recovery from such condition, I direct that life-prolonging procedures be withheld or withdrawn when the application of such procedures would serve only to prolong artificially the process of dying, and that I be permitted to die naturally with only the administration of medication or the performance of any medical procedure deemed necessary to provide me with comfort care or to alleviate pain.

It is my intention that this declaration be honored by my family and physician as the final expression of my legal right to refuse medical or surgical treatment and to accept the consequences for such refusal.

In the event that I have been determined to be unable to provide express and informed consent regarding the withholding, withdrawal, or continuation of life-prolonging procedures, I wish to designate, as my surrogate to carry out the provisions of this declaration:

Name: _____

Address: _____

_____

_____

Zip Code: _____

Phone: _____

I understand the full import of this declaration, and I am emotionally and mentally competent to make this declaration.

Additional Instructions (optional):

Signed _____

| Witness 1 | Witness 2 |
|---|---|
| Address: _____ | Address: _____ |
| _____ | _____ |
| Phone: _____ | Phone: _____ |

# Financial Power of Attorney

## EXPLANATION FOR PRINCIPALS

WHAT IS A FINANCIAL POWER OF ATTORNEY? This document is called a "Financial Power of Attorney." It allows you to name one or more persons to help you handle your financial affairs. Depending on your individual circumstances, you can give this person or persons complete or limited power to act on your behalf. This document does not give someone the power to make medical decisions or personal decisions for you.

WHAT CAN MY AGENT DO? The "Agent" is the person you give power to handle your financial affairs. The "Principal" is you. Your decision to use this document is a very important one and you should think carefully about what financial decisions you want your Agent to make for you. With this document, you can give your Agent the right to make all financial decisions or only certain, limited decisions. For example, you can allow your Agent to handle all your financial affairs, including the power to sell, rent, or mortgage your home, pay your bills, cash or deposit checks, buy and sell your stock, investments, or personal items, or you can allow your Agent to handle only certain or specific financial affairs such as to pay your monthly bills.

DO I GIVE ALL MY POWERS AWAY? No. Even with this document, you can still handle your own financial affairs as long as you choose to or are able to. You need to talk to your Agent often about what you want and what he or she is doing for you using the document. If your Agent is not following your instructions or doing what you want, you may cancel or revoke the document and end your Agent's power to act for you.

HOW DO I REVOKE MY FINANCIAL POWER OF ATTORNEY? You may revoke your financial power of attorney by writing a signed and dated revocation of power of attorney and giving it to your Agent. You should also give it to anyone who has been relying upon the financial power of attorney and dealing with your Agent, such as your bank and investment institutions. Unless you notify all parties dealing with your Agent of your revocation, they may continue to deal with your Agent. You should contact a lawyer if your Agent continues to act after you have revoked the power of attorney.

WHEN DOES MY AGENT'S AUTHORITY END? As long as you are living, the financial power of attorney will remain in effect even if you become incapacitated or unable to communicate your wishes unless:
(1) A guardian is appointed for your property; or
(2) You include a date or specific occurrence when you want your document to be canceled.
However, upon your death or the death of your Agent or successor Agents, the document will be canceled and the Agent's power to act for you will end.
You can also include a date or a specific occurrence like your incapacity or illness as the time when you want your document to be canceled and your Agent's power to act for you to end.

WHEN DO THE POWERS TAKE EFFECT? Depending on your circumstances, you may wish to specify an occurrence or a future date for the document to become effective. Unless you do so, it becomes effective immediately.

MUST MY AGENT DO THOSE THINGS I AUTHORIZE? No. But if your Agent accepts this responsibility and agrees to act for you, he or she is required to sign and date the "Acceptance of Appointment" contained in the financial power of attorney form.

HOW DO I COMPLETE THIS DOCUMENT? Both the Principal and the Agent should read the full document carefully before initialing or signing. The Principal and the Agent should fully understand what powers are being granted to the Agent and what restrictions, if any, exist. Read each paragraph carefully. If you decide to give your Agent the power described in the paragraph, initial your name at the end of the paragraph. If you do not wish to give your Agent the power described in a paragraph, strike through and initial the paragraph or any line within a paragraph.

HOW DO I EXECUTE THE DOCUMENT? Two adult witnesses must watch you sign your name on the document. At least one witness cannot be the Principal's spouse or blood relative. After they witness you signing your name, the witnesses must sign their names. This document does not need to be notarized unless real property transactions such as leasing, selling, or mortgaging of property are authorized.

THIS DOCUMENT REFLECTS THE WISHES OF THE PRINCIPAL. Do not let anyone pressure you into making a financial power of attorney, naming an Agent, or granting a power unless it is your choice. If you do not understand any portion of this document, you should ask a lawyer to explain it to you.

County of _____

State of Georgia

I, _____, (hereinafter "Principal"), a resident of _____ County, Georgia, do hereby constitute and appoint _____ my true and lawful attorney-in-fact (hereinafter "Agent") for me and give such person the power(s) specified below to act in my name, place, and stead in any way which I, myself, could do if I were personally present with respect to the following matters:

(Directions: To give the Agent the powers described in paragraphs 1 through 13, place your initials on the blank line at the end of each paragraph. If you DO NOT want to give a power to the Agent, strike through the paragraph or a line within the paragraph and place your initials beside the stricken paragraph or stricken line. The powers described in any paragraph not initialed or which has been struck through will not be conveyed to the Agent. Both the Principal and the Agent must sign their full names at the end of the last paragraph.)

**1.	Bank and Credit Union Transactions:** To make, receive, sign, endorse, execute, acknowledge, deliver, and possess checks, drafts, bills of exchange, letters of credit, notes, stock certificates, withdrawal receipts and deposit instruments relating to accounts or deposits in, or certificates of deposit of banks, savings and loans, credit unions, or other institutions or associations. _____

**2.	Payment Transactions:** To pay all sums of money, at any time or times, that may hereafter be owing by me upon any account, bill of exchange, check, draft, purchase, contract, note, or trade acceptance made, executed, endorsed, accepted, and delivered by me or for me in my name, by my Agent. _____

**NOTE:** *If you initial paragraph 3 or paragraph 4, which follow, a notarized signature will be required on behalf of the principal.*

**3.	Real Property Transactions:** To lease, sell, mortgage, purchase, exchange, and acquire, and to agree, bargain, and contract for the lease, sale, purchase, exchange, and acquisition of, and to accept, take, receive, and possess any interest in real property whatsoever, on such terms and conditions, and under such covenants, as my Agent shall deem proper; and to maintain, repair, tear down, alter, rebuild, improve, manage, insure, move, rent, lease,, sell, convey, subject to liens, mortgages, and security deeds, and in any way or manner deal with all or any part of any interest in real property whatsoever, including specifically, but without limitation, real property lying and being situate in the State of Georgia, under such terms and conditions, and under such covenants, as my Agent shall deem proper and may for all deferred payments accept purchase money notes payable to me and secured by mortgages or deeds to secure debt, and may from time to time collect and cancel any of said notes, mortgages, security interests, or deeds to secure debt. _____

**4.** **Personal Property Transactions:** To lease, sell, mortgage, purchase, exchange, and acquire, and to agree, bargain, and contract for the lease, sale, purchase, exchange, and acquisition of, and to accept, take, receive, and possess any personal property whatsoever, tangible or intangible, or interest thereto, on such terms and conditions, and under such covenants, as my Agent shall deem proper; and to maintain, repair, improve, manage, insure, rent, lease, sell, convey, subject to liens or mortgages, or to take any other security interests in said property which are recognized under the Uniform Commercial Code as adopted at that time under the laws of Georgia or any applicable state, or otherwise hypothecate, and in any way or manner deal with all or any part of any real or personal property whatsoever, tangible or intangible, or any interest therein, that I own at the time of execution or may thereafter acquire, under such terms and conditions, and under such covenants, as my Agent shall deem proper. _____

**5.** **Stock and Bond Transactions:** To purchase, sell, exchange, surrender, assign, redeem, vote at any meeting, or otherwise transfer any and all shares of stock, bonds, or other securities in any business, association, corporation, partnership, or other legal entity, whether private or public, now or hereafter belonging to me. _____

**6.** **Safe Deposits:** To have free access at any time or times to any safe deposit box or vault to which I might have access. _____

**7.** **Borrowing:** To borrow from time to time such sums of money as my Agent may deem proper and execute promissory notes, security deeds or agreements, financing statements, or other security instruments in such form as the leader may request and renew said notes and security instruments from time to time in whole or in part. _____

**8.** **Business Operating Transactions:** To conduct, engage in, and otherwise transact the affairs of any and all lawful business ventures of whatever nature or kind that I may now or hereafter be involved in. _____

**9.** **Insurance Transactions:** To exercise or perform any act, power, duty, right, or obligation, in regard to any contract of life, accident, health, disability, liability, or other type of insurance or any combination of insurance; and to procure new or additional contracts of insurance to me to designate the beneficiary of same; provided, however, that my Agent cannot designate himself or herself as beneficiary of any such insurance contracts. _____

**10.** **Disputes and Proceedings:** To commence, prosecute, discontinue, or defend all actions or other legal proceedings touching my property, real or personal, or any part there or touching any matter in which I or my property, real or personal, may be in any way concerned. To defend, settle, adjust, make allowances, compound, submit to arbitration, and compromise all accounts, reckonings, claims, and demands whatsoever that now are, or hereafter shall be, pending between me and any person, firm, corporation, or other legal entity, in such manner and in all respects as my Agent shall deem proper. _____

**11.** **Hiring Representatives:** To hire accountants, attorneys at law, consultants, clerks, physicians, nurses, agents, servants, workmen, and others and to remove them, and to appoint others in their place, and to pay and allow the persons so employed such salaries, wages, or other remunerations, as my Agent shall deem proper. _____

**12.** **Tax, Social Security, and Unemployment**: To prepare, to make elections, to execute and to file all tax, social security, unemployment insurance, and informational returns required by the laws of the United States, or of any state or subdivision thereof, or of any foreign government; to prepare, to execute, and to file all other papers and instruments which the Agent shall think to be desirable or necessary for safeguarding of me against excess or illegal taxation or against penalties imposed for claimed violation of any law or other governmental regulation; and to pay, to compromise, or to contest or to apply for refunds in connection with any taxes or assessments for which I am or may be liable. _____

**13.   Broad Powers:** Without, in any way, limiting the foregoing, generally to do, execute, and perform any other act, deed, matter, or thing whatsoever, that should be done, executed, or performed, including but not limited to, powers conferred by Code Section 53-12-232 of the Official Code of Georgia Annotated, or that in the opinion of my Agent, should be done, executed, or performed, for my benefit or the benefit of my property, real or personal, and in my name of every nature and kind whatsoever, as fully and effectually as I could do if personally present.
_____

**14.   Effective Date:** This document will become effective upon the date of the Principal's signature unless the Principal indicates that it should become effective at a later date by completing the following, which is optional.

The powers conveyed in this document shall not become effective until the following time or upon the occurrence of the following event or contingency:

_____
_____

**NOTE:** *The Principal may choose to designate one or more persons to determine conclusively that the above-specified event or contingency has occurred. Such person or persons must make a written declaration under penalty of false swearing that such event or contingency has occurred in order to make this document effective. Completion of this provision is optional.*

The following person or persons are designated to determine conclusively that the above-specified event or contingency has occurred:

_____
_____

Signed: _____
                              Principal

_____
                              Agent

It is my desire and intention that this power of attorney shall not be affected by my subsequent disability, incapacity, or mental incompetence. However, I understand that it shall be revoked and the Agent's power canceled in the event a guardian is appointed for my property. As long as no such guardian is appointed, any and all acts done by the Agent pursuant to the powers conveyed herein during any period of my disability, incapacity, or mental incompetence shall have the same force and effect as if I were not disabled, incapacitated, or mentally incompetent.

I may, at any time, revoke this power of attorney, and it shall be canceled by my death. Otherwise, unless a guardian is appointed for my property, this power of attorney shall be deemed to be in full force and effect as to all persons, institutions, and organizations which shall act in reliance thereon prior to the receipt of written revocation thereof signed by me and prior to my death.

I do hereby ratify and confirm all acts whatsoever which my Agent shall do, or cause to be done, in or about the premises, by virtue of this power of attorney.

All parties dealing in good faith with my Agent may fully rely upon the power of and authority of my Agent to act for me on my behalf and in my name, and may accept and rely on agreements and other instruments entered into or executed by the agent pursuant to this power of attorney.

This instrument shall not be effective as a grant of powers to my Agent until my Agent has executed the Acceptance of Appointment appearing at the end of this instrument. This instrument shall remain effective until revocation by me or my death, whichever occurs first.

**Compensation of Agent.** (Directions: Initial the line following your choice.)

1. My Agent shall receive no compensation for services rendered. _____
2. My Agent shall receive reasonable compensation for services rendered. _____
3. My Agent shall receive $_____ for services rendered. _____

IN WITNESS WHEREOF, I have hereunto set my hand and seal on this _____ day of _____, _____.

_____
Principal

## WITNESSES

_____     _____

_____     _____
Signature and Address                   Signature and Address

**NOTE:** *A notarized signature is not required unless you have initialed paragraph 3 or 4 regarding property transactions.*

I, _____, a Notary Public, do hereby certify that _____ personally appeared before me this date and acknowledged the due execution of the foregoing Power of Attorney.

_____
Notary Public

State of Georgia

County of _____

## ACCEPTANCE OF APPOINTMENT

I, _____ (print name), have read the foregoing Power of Attorney and am the person identified therein as Agent for _____ _____ (name of grantor of power of attorney), the Principal named therein. I hereby acknowledge the following:

I owe a duty of loyalty and good faith to the Principal, and must use the powers granted to me only for the benefit of the Principal.

I must keep the Principal's funds and other assets separate and apart from my funds and other assets and titled in the name of the Principal. I must not transfer title to any of the Principal's funds or other assets into my name alone. My name must not be added to the title of any funds or other assets of the Principal, unless I am specifically designated as Agent for the Principal in the title.

I must protect and conserve, and exercise prudence and caution in my dealings with, the Principal's funds and other assets.

I must keep a full and accurate record of my acts, receipts, and disbursements on behalf of the Principal, and be ready to account to the Principal for such acts, receipts, and disbursements at all times. I must provide an annual accounting to the Principal of my acts, receipts, and disbursements, and must furnish an accounting of such acts, receipts, and disbursements to the personal representative of the Principal's estate within 90 days after the date of death of the Principal.

I have read the <u>Compensation of Agent</u> paragraph in the Power of Attorney and agree to abide by it.

I acknowledge my authority to act on behalf of the Principal ceases at the death of the Principal.

I hereby accept the foregoing appointment as Agent for the Principal with full knowledge of the responsibilities imposed on me, and I will faithfully carry out my duties to the best of my ability.


_____
(date)

              (Signature) _____

              (Address) _____


**NOTE:** *A notarized signature is not required unless the Principal initialed paragraph 3 or paragraph 4 regarding property transactions.*

I, _____, a Notary Public, do hereby certify that _____ personally appeared before me this date and acknowledged the due execution of the foregoing Acceptance of Appointment.


              _____
              Notary Public

## Georgia Statutory Short Form Durable Power of Attorney for Health Care

NOTICE: THE PURPOSE OF THIS POWER OF ATTORNEY IS TO GIVE THE PERSON YOU DESIGNATE (YOUR AGENT) BROAD POWERS TO MAKE HEALTH CARE DECISIONS FOR YOU, INCLUDING POWER TO REQUIRE, CONSENT TO, OR WITHDRAW ANY TYPE OF PERSONAL CARE OR MEDICAL TREATMENT FOR ANY PHYSICAL OR MENTAL CONDITION AND TO ADMIT YOU TO OR DISCHARGE YOU FROM ANY HOSPITAL, HOME, OR OTHER INSTITUTION; BUT NOT INCLUDING PSYCHOSURGERY, STERILIZATION, OR INVOLUNTARY HOSPITALIZATION OR TREATMENT COVERED BY TITLE 37 OF THE OFFICIAL CODE OF GEORGIA ANNOTATED. THIS FORM DOES NOT IMPOSE A DUTY ON YOUR AGENT TO EXERCISE GRANTED POWERS; BUT, WHEN A POWER IS EXERCISED, YOUR AGENT WILL HAVE TO USE DUE CARE TO ACT FOR YOUR BENEFIT AND IN ACCORDANCE WITH THIS FORM. A COURT CAN TAKE AWAY THE POWERS OF YOUR AGENT IF IT FINDS THE AGENT IS NOT ACTING PROPERLY. YOU MAY NAME CO-AGENTS AND SUCCESSOR AGENTS UNDER THIS FORM, BUT YOU MAY NOT NAME A HEALTH CARE PROVIDER WHO MAY BE DIRECTLY OR INDIRECTLY INVOLVED IN RENDERING HEALTH CARE TO YOU UNDER THIS POWER. UNLESS YOU EXPRESSLY LIMIT THE DURATION OF THIS POWER IN THE MANNER PROVIDED BELOW OR UNTIL YOU REVOKE THIS POWER OR A COURT ACTING ON YOUR BEHALF TERMINATES IT, YOUR AGENT MAY EXERCISE THE POWERS GIVEN IN THE POWER THROUGHOUT YOUR LIFETIME, EVEN AFTER YOU BECOME DISABLED, INCAPACITATED, OR INCOMPETENT. THE POWERS YOU GIVE YOUR AGENT, YOUR RIGHT TO REVOKE THOSE POWERS, AND THE PENALTIES FOR VIOLATING THE LAW ARE EXPLAINED MORE FULLY IN CODE SECTIONS 31-36-6, 31-36-9, AND 31-36-10 OF THE GEORGIA 'DURABLE POWER OF ATTORNEY FOR HEALTH CARE ACT' OF WHICH THIS FORM IS A PART (SEE THE BACK OF THIS FORM). THAT ACT EXPRESSLY PERMITS THE USE OF ANY DIFFERENT FORM OF POWER OF ATTORNEY YOU MAY DESIRE. IF THERE IS ANYTHING ABOUT THIS FORM THAT YOU DO NOT UNDERSTAND, YOU SHOULD ASK A LAWYER TO EXPLAIN IT TO YOU.

DURABLE POWER OF ATTORNEY made this _____ day of _____, _____.

1.     I, _____,
(insert name and address of principal)

hereby appoint _____
(insert name and address of agent)

as my attorney in fact (my agent) to act for me and in my name in any way I could act in person to make any and all decisions for me concerning my personal care, medical treatment, hospitalization, and health care and to require, withhold, or withdraw any type of medical treatment or procedure, even though my death may ensue. My agent shall have the same access to my medical records that I have, including the right to disclose the contents to others. My agent shall also have full power to make a disposition of any part or all of my body for medical purposes, authorize an autopsy of my body, and direct the disposition of my remains.

THE ABOVE GRANT OF POWER IS INTENDED TO BE AS BROAD AS POSSIBLE SO THAT YOUR AGENT WILL HAVE AUTHORITY TO MAKE ANY DECISION YOU COULD MAKE TO OBTAIN OR TERMINATE ANY TYPE OF HEALTH CARE, INCLUDING WITHDRAWAL OF NOURISHMENT AND FLUIDS AND OTHER LIFE-SUSTAINING OR DEATH-DELAYING MEASURES, IF YOUR AGENT BELIEVES SUCH ACTION WOULD BE CONSISTENT WITH YOUR INTENT AND DESIRES. IF YOU WISH TO LIMIT THE SCOPE OF YOUR AGENT'S POWERS OR PRESCRIBE SPECIAL RULES TO LIMIT THE POWER TO MAKE AN ANATOMICAL GIFT, AUTHORIZE AUTOPSY, OR DISPOSE OF REMAINS, YOU MAY DO SO IN THE FOLLOWING PARAGRAPHS.

2.     The powers granted above shall not include the following powers or shall be subject to the following rules or limitations (here you may include any specific limitations you

deem appropriate, such as your own definition of when life-sustaining or death-delaying measures should be withheld; a direction to continue nourishment and fluids or other life-sustaining or death-delaying treatment in all events; or instructions to refuse any specific types of treatment that are inconsistent with your religious beliefs or unacceptable to you for any other reason, such as blood transfusion, electroconvulsive therapy, or amputation):

_____

_____

THE SUBJECT OF LIFE-SUSTAINING OR DEATH-DELAYING TREATMENT IS OF PARTICULAR IMPORTANCE. FOR YOUR CONVENIENCE IN DEALING WITH THAT SUBJECT, SOME GENERAL STATEMENTS CONCERNING THE WITHHOLDING OR REMOVAL OF LIFE-SUSTAINING OR DEATH-DELAYING TREATMENT ARE SET FORTH BELOW. IF YOU AGREE WITH ONE OF THESE STATEMENTS, YOU MAY INITIAL THAT STATEMENT, BUT DO NOT INITIAL MORE THAN ONE:

I do not want my life to be prolonged nor do I want life-sustaining or death-delaying treatment to be provided or continued if my agent believes the burdens of the treatment outweigh the expected benefits. I want my agent to consider the relief of suffering, the expense involved, and the quality as well as the possible extension of my life in making decisions concerning life-sustaining or death-delaying treatment.

Initialed_____

I want my life to be prolonged and I want life-sustaining or death-delaying treatment to be provided or continued unless I am in a coma, including a persistent vegetative state, which my attending physician believes to be irreversible, in accordance with reasonable medical standards at the time of reference. If and when I have suffered such an irreversible coma, I want life-sustaining or death-delaying treatment to be withheld or discontinued.

Initialed_____

I want my life to be prolonged to the greatest extent possible without regard to my condition, the chances I have for recovery, or the cost of the procedures.

Initialed_____

THIS POWER OF ATTORNEY MAY BE AMENDED OR REVOKED BY YOU AT ANY TIME AND IN ANY MANNER WHILE YOU ARE ABLE TO DO SO. IN THE ABSENCE OF AN AMENDMENT OR REVOCATION, THE AUTHORITY GRANTED IN THIS POWER OF ATTORNEY WILL BECOME EFFECTIVE AT THE TIME THIS POWER IS SIGNED AND WILL CONTINUE UNTIL YOUR DEATH AND WILL CONTINUE BEYOND YOUR DEATH IF ANATOMICAL GIFT, AUTOPSY, OR DISPOSITION OF REMAINS IS AUTHORIZED, UNLESS A LIMITATION ON THE BEGINNING DATE OR DURATION IS MADE BY INITIALING AND COMPLETING EITHER OR BOTH OF THE FOLLOWING:

3. ( ) This power of attorney shall become effective on_____ _____(insert a future date or event during your lifetime, such as court determination of your disability, incapacity, or incompetency, when you want this power to first take effect).

4. ( ) This power of attorney shall terminate on_____ _____(insert a future date or event, such as court determination of your disability, incapacity, or incompetency, when you want this power to terminate prior to your death).

IF YOU WISH TO NAME SUCCESSOR AGENTS, INSERT THE NAMES AND ADDRESSES OF SUCH SUCCESSORS IN THE FOLLOWING PARAGRAPH:

5. If any agent named by me shall die, become legally disabled, incapacitated, or incompetent, or resign, refuse to act, or be unavailable, I name the following (each to act successively in the order named) as successors to such agent:

_____

_____

IF YOU WISH TO NAME A GUARDIAN OF YOUR PERSON IN THE EVENT A COURT DECIDES THAT ONE SHOULD BE APPOINTED, YOU MAY, BUT ARE NOT REQUIRED TO, DO SO BY INSERTING THE NAME OF SUCH GUARDIAN IN THE FOLLOWING PARAGRAPH. THE COURT WILL APPOINT THE PERSON NOMINATED BY YOU IF THE COURT FINDS THAT SUCH APPOINTMENT WILL SERVE YOUR BEST INTERESTS AND WELFARE. YOU MAY , BUT ARE NOT REQUIRED TO, NOMINATE AS YOUR GUARDIAN THE SAME PERSON NAMED IN THIS FORM AS YOUR AGENT.

     6.     If a guardian of my person is to be appointed, I nominate the following to serve as such guardian:

_____
          (insert name and address of nominated guardian of the person)

     7.     I am fully informed as to all the contents of this form and understand the full import of this grant of powers to my agent.

     Signed_____(Principal)

The principal has had an opportunity to read the above form and has signed the above form in our presence. We, the undersigned, each being over 18 years of age, witness the principal's signature at the request and in the presence of the principal, and in the presence of each other, on the day and year above set out.

Witnesses:                               Addresses:

_____     _____

_____     _____

Additional witness required when health care agency is signed in a hospital or skilled nursing facility.

I hereby witness this health care agency and attest that I believe the principal to be of sound mind and to have made this health care agency willingly and voluntarily.

Witness:_____   Address:_____
           Attending Physician

YOU MAY, BUT ARE NOT REQUIRED TO, REQUEST YOUR AGENT AND SUCCESSOR AGENTS TO PROVIDE SPECIMEN SIGNATURES BELOW. IF YOU INCLUDE SPECIMEN SIGNATURES IN THIS POWER OF ATTORNEY, YOU MUST COMPLETE THE CERTIFICATION OPPOSITE THE SIGNATURES OF THE AGENTS.

Specimen signatures of agent         I certify that the signature of my agent and
and successor(s)                   successor(s) is correct.

_____     _____
(Agent)                             (Principal)

_____     _____
(Successor agent)               (Principal)

_____     _____
(Successor agent)                (Principal)

# Advance Health-Care Directive

### Explanation

You have the right to give instructions about your own health care. You also have the right to name someone else to make health-care decisions for you. This form lets you do either or both of these things. It also lets you express your wishes regarding the designation of your health-care provider. If you use this form, you may complete or modify all or any part of it. You are free to use a different form.

Part 1 of this form is a power of attorney for health care. Part 1 lets you name another individual as agent to make health-care decisions for you if you become incapable of making your own decisions or if you want someone else to make those decisions for you now even though you are still capable. You may name an alternate agent to act for you if your first choice is not willing, able, or reasonably available to make decisions for you. Unless related to you, your agent may not be an owner, operator, or employee of a health-care institution where you are receiving care.

Unless the form you sign limits the authority of your agent, your agent may make all health-care decisions for you. This form has a place for you to limit the authority of your agent. You need not limit the authority of your agent if you wish to rely on your agent for all health-care decisions that may have to be made. If you choose not to limit the authority of your agent, your agent will have the right to:

(1) Consent or refuse consent to any care, treatment, service, or procedure to maintain, diagnose, or otherwise affect a physical or mental condition;

(2) Select or discharge health-care providers and institutions;

(3) Approve or disapprove diagnostic tests, surgical procedures, programs of medication, and orders not to resuscitate; and

(4) Direct the provision, withholding, or withdrawal of artificial nutrition and hydration and all other forms of health care.

Part 2 of this form lets you give specific instructions about any aspect of your health care. Choices are provided for you to express your wishes regarding the provision, withholding, or withdrawal of treatment to keep you alive, including the provision of artificial nutrition and hydration, as well as the provision of pain relief medication. Space is provided for you to add to the choices you have made or for you to write out any additional wishes.

Part 4 of this form lets you designate a physician to have primary responsibility for your health care. After completing this form, sign and date the form at the end and have the form witnessed by one of the two alternative methods listed below. Give a copy of the signed and completed form to your physician, to any other health-care providers you may have, to any health-care institution at which you are receiving care, and to any health-care agents you have named. You should talk to the person you have named as agent to make sure that he or she understands your wishes and is willing to take the responsibility. You have the right to revoke this advance health-care directive or replace this form at any time.

## PART 1
## DURABLE POWER OF ATTORNEY FOR HEALTH-CARE DECISIONS

(1) DESIGNATION OF AGENT: I designate the following individual as my agent to make health-care decisions for me:

_____

(name of individual you choose as agent)

_____

(address)                         (city)                    (state)              (zip code)

_____

(home phone)                                    (work phone)

OPTIONAL: If I revoke my agent's authority or if my agent is not willing, able, or reasonably available to make a health-care decision for me, I designate as my first alternate agent:

_____
(name of individual you choose as first alternate agent)

_____
(address)                    (city)                    (state)              (zip code)

_____
(home phone)                              (work phone)

OPTIONAL: If I revoke the authority of my agent and first alternate agent or if neither is willing, able, or reasonably available to make a health-care decision for me, I designate as my second alternate agent:

_____
(name of individual you choose as second alternate agent)

_____
(address)                    (city)                    (state)              (zip code)

_____
(home phone)                              (work phone)

(2) AGENT'S AUTHORITY: My agent is authorized to make all health-care decisions for me, including decisions to provide, withhold, or withdraw artificial nutrition and hydration, and all other forms of health care to keep me alive, except as I state here:

_____
_____
(Add additional sheets if needed.)

(3) WHEN AGENT'S AUTHORITY BECOMES EFFECTIVE: My agent's authority becomes effective when my primary physician determines that I am unable to make my own health-care decisions unless I mark the following box. If I mark this box [ ], my agent's authority to make health-care decisions for me takes effect immediately.

(4) AGENT'S OBLIGATION: My agent shall make health-care decisions for me in accordance with this power of attorney for health care, any instructions I give in Part 2 of this form, and my other wishes to the extent known to my agent. To the extent my wishes are unknown, my agent shall make health-care decisions for me in accordance with what my agent determines to be in my best interest. In determining my best interest, my agent shall consider my personal values to the extent known to my agent.

(5) NOMINATION OF GUARDIAN: If a guardian needs to be appointed for me by a court, I nominate the agent designated in this form. If that agent is not willing, able, or reasonably available to act as guardian, I nominate the alternate agents whom I have named, in the order designated.

# PART 2
# INSTRUCTIONS FOR HEALTH CARE

If you are satisfied to allow your agent to determine what is best for you in making end-of-life decisions, you need not fill out this part of the form. If you do fill out this part of the form, you may strike any wording you do not want.

(6) END-OF-LIFE DECISIONS: I direct that my health-care providers and others involved in my care provide, withhold, or withdraw treatment in accordance with the choice I have marked below: (Check only one box.)

[ ] (a) Choice Not To Prolong Life

I do not want my life to be prolonged if (i) I have an incurable and irreversible condition that will result in my death within a relatively short time, (ii) I become unconscious and, to a reasonable degree of medical certainty, I will not regain consciousness, or (iii) the likely risks and burdens of treatment would outweigh the expected benefits, OR

[ ] (b) Choice To Prolong Life

I want my life to be prolonged as long as possible within the limits of generally accepted health-care standards.

(7) ARTIFICIAL NUTRITION AND HYDRATION: Artificial nutrition and hydration must be provided, withheld or withdrawn in accordance with the choice I have made in paragraph (6) unless I mark the following box. If I mark this box [ ], artificial nutrition and hydration must be provided regardless of my condition and regardless of the choice I have made in paragraph (6).

(8) RELIEF FROM PAIN: If I mark this box [ ], I direct that treatment to alleviate pain or discomfort should be provided to me even if it hastens my death.

(9) OTHER WISHES: (If you do not agree with any of the optional choices above and wish to write your own, or if you wish to add to the instructions you have given above, you may do so here.) I direct that:

_____

_____

(Add additional sheets if needed.)

# PART 3
## DONATION OF ORGANS AT DEATH (OPTIONAL)

(10) Upon my death: (mark applicable box)
[ ] (a) I give any needed organs, tissues, or parts, OR
[ ] (b) I give the following organs, tissues, or parts only
[ ] (c) My gift is for the following purposes (strike any of the following you do not want)
     (i) Transplant
     (ii) Therapy
     (iii) Research
     (iv) Education

# PART 4
## PRIMARY PHYSICIAN (OPTIONAL)

(11) I designate the following physician as my primary physician:

_____
(name of physician)

_____
(address)                          (city)                          (state)                          (zip code)

_____
(phone)

OPTIONAL: If the physician I have designated above is not willing, able, or reasonably available to act as my primary physician, I designate the following physician as my primary physician:

_____
(name of physician)

_____
(address)                          (city)                          (state)                          (zip code)

_____
(phone)

(12) EFFECT OF COPY: A copy of this form has the same effect as the original.

(13) SIGNATURES: Sign and date the form here:

_____
(date)                                              (sign your name)

_____
(address)                                              (print your name)

_____
(city)                                              (state)

(14) WITNESSES: This power of attorney will not be valid for making health-care decisions unless it is either (a) signed by two qualified adult witnesses who are personally known to you and who are present when you sign or acknowledge your signature; or (b) acknowledged before a notary public in the State.

# ALTERNATIVE NO. 1

## Witness

I declare under penalty of false swearing pursuant to section 710-1062, Hawaii Revised Statutes, that the principal is personally known to me, that the principal signed or acknowledged this power of attorney in my presence, that the principal appears to be of sound mind and under no duress, fraud, or undue influence, that I am not the person appointed as agent by this document, and that I am not a health-care provider, nor an employee of a health-care provider or facility. I am not related to the principal by blood, marriage, or adoption, and to the best of my knowledge, I am not entitled to any part of the estate of the principal upon the death of the principal under a will now existing or by operation of law.

_____     _____
(date)                                       (signature of witness)

_____     _____
(address)                                    (printed name of witness)

_____     _____
(city)                                       (state)

## Witness

I declare under penalty of false swearing pursuant to section 710-1062, Hawaii Revised Statutes, that the principal is personally known to me, that the principal signed or acknowledged this power of attorney in my presence, that the principal appears to be of sound mind and under no duress, fraud, or undue influence, that I am not the person appointed as agent by this document, and that I am not a health-care provider, nor an employee of a health-care provider or facility.

_____     _____
(date)                                       (signature of witness)

_____     _____
(address)                                    (printed name of witness)

_____     _____
(city)                                       (state)

# ALTERNATIVE NO. 2

State of Hawaii
County of _____

On this _____ day of _____, in the year _____, before me,
_____ (insert name of notary public) appeared _____, personally
known to me (or proved to me on the basis of satisfactory evidence) to be the person whose name is subscribed
to this instrument, and acknowledged that he or she executed it.


Notary Seal


_____
(Signature of Notary Public)

# ADVANCE MENTAL HEALTH CARE DIRECTIVE

### Explanation

You have the right to give instructions about your own mental health care. You also have the right to name someone else to make mental health treatment decisions for you. This form lets you do either or both of these things. It also lets you express your wishes regarding the designation of your health care providers. If you use this form, you may complete or modify all or any part of it. You are free to use a different form.

Part 1 of this form is a list of options you may designate as part of your mental health care and treatment. For ease of designating specific instructions, mark those options in Part 1.

Part 2 of this form is a power of attorney for mental health care. This lets you name another individual as your agent to make mental health treatment decisions for you, if you become incapable of making your own decisions, or if you want someone else to make those decisions for you now, even though you are still capable of making your own decisions. You may name alternate agents to act for you if your first choice is not willing, able, or reasonably available to make decisions for you. Unless related to you, your agent may not be an owner, operator, or employee of a health care institution where you are receiving care.

You may allow your agent to make all mental health treatment decisions for you. However, if you wish to limit the authority of your agent, you may specify those limitations on the form. If you do not limit the authority of your agent, your agent will have the right to:

(1) Consent or refuse consent to any care, treatment, service, or procedure to maintain, diagnose, or otherwise affect a mental condition;

(2) Select or discharge health care providers and institutions;

(3) Approve or disapprove diagnostic tests, surgical procedures, and programs of medication; and

(4) Approve or disapprove of electroconvulsive treatment.

Part 3 of this form lets you give specific instructions about any aspect of your mental health care and treatment. Choices are provided for you to express your wishes regarding the provision, withholding, or withdrawal of medication and treatment. Space is provided for you to add to the choices you have made or for you to write out any additional wishes.

Part 4 of this form must be completed in order to activate the advance mental health care directive. After completing this form, sign and date the form at the end and have the form witnessed by one or both of the two methods listed below. Give a copy of the signed and completed form to your physician, to any other health care providers you may have, to any health care institution at which you are receiving care, and to any mental health care agents you have named. You should talk to the persons you have named as agents to make sure that they understand your wishes and are willing to take the responsibility.
You have the right to revoke this advance mental health care directive or replace this form at any time, unless otherwise specified in writing in the advance mental health care directive.

If you are in imminent danger of causing bodily harm to yourself or others, or have been involuntarily committed to a health care institution for mental health treatment, the advance mental health care directive will not apply.

# PART 1
## CHECKLIST OF MENTAL HEALTH CARE OPTIONS

**NOTE TO PROVIDER:** *The following is a checklist of selections I have made regarding my mental health care and treatment. I include this statement to express my strong desire for you to acknowledge and abide by my rights, under state and federal laws, to influence decisions about the care I will receive.*

(Declarant: Put a check mark in the left-hand column for each section you have completed.)

___ Designation of my mental health care agent(s).
___ Authority granted to my agent(s).
___ My preference for a court appointed guardian.
___ My preference of treating facility and alternatives to hospitalization.
___ My preferences about the physicians or other mental health care providers who will treat me if I am hospitalized.
___ My preferences regarding medications.
___ My preferences regarding electroconvulsive therapy (ECT or shock treatment).
___ My preferences regarding emergency interventions (seclusion, restraint, medications).
___ Consent for experimental drugs or treatments.
___ Who should be notified immediately of my admission to a facility.
___ Who should be prohibited from visiting me.
___ My preferences for care and temporary custody of my children or pets.
___ Other instructions about mental health care and treatment.

# PART 2
## DURABLE POWER OF ATTORNEY FOR
## MENTAL HEALTH TREATMENT DECISIONS

(1) DESIGNATION OF AGENT: I designate the following individual as my agent to make mental health care decisions for me:

_____
(name of individual you choose as agent)

_____
(address)                    (city)              (state)         (zip code)

_____
(home phone)                          (work phone)

OPTIONAL: If I revoke my agent's authority or if my agent is not willing, able, or reasonably available to make a mental health care decision for me, I designate as my first alternate agent:

_____
(name of individual you choose as first alternate agent)

_____
(address)                    (city)              (state)         (zip code)

_____
(home phone)                          (work phone)

OPTIONAL: If I revoke the authority of my agent and first alternate agent or if neither is willing, able, or reasonably available to make a mental health care decision for me, I designate as my second alternate agent:

_____
(name of individual you choose as second alternate agent)

_____
(address)                    (city)              (state)          (zip code)

_____
(home phone)                        (work phone)

(2) AGENT'S AUTHORITY: My agent is authorized to make all mental health care treatment decisions for me, including decisions to provide, withhold, or withdraw medication and treatment, and all other forms of mental health care, except as I state here: _____
_____
_____
_____
(Add additional sheets if needed.)

(3) WHEN AGENT'S AUTHORITY BECOMES EFFECTIVE: My agent's authority becomes effective when my supervising health care provider who is a physician and one other physician or licensed psychologist determine that I am unable to make my own mental health care decisions.

(4) AGENT'S OBLIGATION: My agent shall make mental health care decisions for me in accordance with this power of attorney for mental health care, any instructions I give in Part 2 of this form, and my other wishes to the extent known to my agent. To the extent my wishes are unknown, my agent shall make mental health care decisions for me in accordance with what my agent determines to be in my best interest. In determining my best interest, my agent shall consider my personal values to the extent known to my agent.

(5) NOMINATION OF GUARDIAN: If a guardian of the person needs to be appointed for me by a court, I nominate the agent designated in this form. If that agent is not willing, able, or reasonably available to act as guardian, I nominate the alternate agents whom I have named, in the order designated.

# PART 3
# INSTRUCTIONS FOR MENTAL HEALTH CARE AND TREATMENT

If you are satisfied to allow your agent to determine what is best for you, you need not fill out this part of the form. If you do fill out this part of the form, you may strike any wording you do not want.

(6) My preference of treating facility and alternatives to hospitalization:
_____

(7) My preferences about the physicians or other mental health care providers who will treat me if I am hospitalized:
_____
_____

(8) My preferences regarding medications:
_____

(9) My preferences regarding electroconvulsive therapy (ECT or shock treatment):
_____
_____

(10) My preferences regarding emergency interventions (seclusion, restraint, medications):

_____
_____
_____

(11) Consent for experimental drugs or treatments:

_____

(12) Who should be notified immediately of my admission to a facility:

_____

(13) Who should be prohibited from visiting me:

_____

(14) My preferences for care and temporary custody of my children or pets:

_____
_____

(15) My preferences about revocation of my advance mental health care directive during a period of incapacity:

_____
_____

(16) OTHER WISHES: (If you do not agree with any of the optional choices above and wish to write your own, or if you wish to add to the instructions you have given above, you may do so here.) I direct that:

_____
_____

(Add additional sheets if needed.)

## PART 4
## WITNESSES AND SIGNATURES

(17) EFFECT OF COPY: A copy of this form has the same effect as the original.

(18) SIGNATURES: Sign and date the form here:

_____          _____
(date)                                    (sign your name)


_____          _____
(address)                                 (print your name)


_____
(city)                    (state)


(19) WITNESSES: This power of attorney will not be valid for making mental health care decisions unless it is either: (a) signed by two qualified adult witnesses who are personally known to you and who are present when you sign or acknowledge your signature; or (b) acknowledged before a notary public in the State.

# AFFIRMATION OF WITNESSES

## Witness 1

I declare under penalty of false swearing pursuant to section 710-1062, Hawaii Revised Statutes, that the principal is personally known to me, that the principal signed or acknowledged this power of attorney in my presence, that the principal appears to be of sound mind and under no duress, fraud, or undue influence, that I am not the person appointed as agent by this document, and that I am not a health care provider, nor an employee of a health care provider or facility. I am not related to the principal by blood, marriage, or adoption, and to the best of my knowledge, I am not entitled to any part of the estate of the principal upon the death of the principal under a will now existing or by operation of law.

_____
(date)

_____
(address)

_____
(city)                    (state)

_____
(sign your name)

_____
(print your name)

## Witness 2

I declare under penalty of false swearing pursuant to section 710-1062, Hawaii Revised Statutes, that the principal is personally known to me, that the principal signed or acknowledged this power of attorney in my presence, that the principal appears to be of sound mind and under no duress, fraud, or undue influence, that I am not the person appointed as agent by this document, and that I am not a health care provider, nor an employee of a health care provider or facility. I am not related to the principal by blood, marriage, or adoption, and to the best of my knowledge, I am not entitled to any part of the estate of the principal upon the death of the principal under a will now existing or by operation of law.

_____
(date)

_____
(address)

_____
(city)                    (state)

_____
(sign your name)

_____
(print your name)

## DECLARATION OF NOTARY

State of Hawaii
County of _____

On this _____ day of _____, in the year _____, before me, _____ (insert name of notary public) appeared _____, personally known to me (or proved to me on the basis of satisfactory evidence) to be the person whose name is subscribed to this instrument, and acknowledged that he or she executed it.


(Seal)


_____
(Signature of Notary Public)

# LIVING WILL AND DURABLE POWER OF ATTORNEY FOR HEALTH CARE

Date of Directive: _____

Name of person executing Directive: _____

Address of person executing Directive: _____

## A LIVING WILL
A Directive to Withhold or to Provide Treatment

1. Being of sound mind, I willfully and voluntarily make known my desire that my life shall not be prolonged artificially under the circumstances set forth below. This Directive shall only be effective if I am unable to communicate my instructions and:

a. I have an incurable injury, disease, illness or condition and two (2) medical doctors who have examined me have certified:

    1. That such injury, disease, illness or condition is terminal; and
    2. That the application of artificial life-sustaining procedures would serve only to prolong artificially my life; and
    3. That my death is imminent, whether or not artificial life-sustaining procedures are utilized; or

b. I have been diagnosed as being in a persistent vegetative state.

In such event, I direct that the following marked expression of my intent be followed, and that I receive any medical treatment or care that may be required to keep me free of pain or distress.

Check one box and initial the line after such box:

☐ I direct that all medical treatment, care and procedures necessary to restore my health, sustain my life, and to abolish or alleviate pain or distress be provided to me. Nutrition and hydration, whether artificial or nonartificial, shall not be withheld or withdrawn from me if I would likely die primarily from malnutrition or dehydration rather than from my injury, disease, illness or condition.

## OR

☐ I direct that all medical treatment, care and procedures, including artificial life-sustaining procedures, be withheld or withdrawn, except that nutrition and hydration, whether artificial or nonartificial shall not be withheld or withdrawn from me if, as a result, I would likely die primarily from malnutrition or dehydration rather than from my injury, disease, illness or condition, as follows: (If none of the following boxes are checked and initialed, then both nutrition and hydration, of any nature, whether artificial or nonartificial, shall be administered.)

Check one box and initial the line after such box.

☐ Only hydration, of any nature, whether artificial or nonartificial, shall be administered;

☐ Only nutrition, of any nature, whether artificial or nonartificial, shall be administered;

☐ Both nutrition and hydration, of any nature, whether artificial or nonartificial shall be administered.

## OR

_____ I direct that all medical treatment, care and procedures be withheld or withdrawn, including withdrawal of the administration of artificial nutrition and hydration.

2.  This Directive shall be the final expression of my legal right to refuse or accept medical and surgical treatment, and I accept the consequences of such refusal or acceptance.

3.  If I have been diagnosed as pregnant, this Directive shall have no force during the course of my pregnancy.

4.  I understand the full importance of this Directive and am mentally competent to make this Directive. No participant in the making of this Directive or in its being carried into effect shall be held responsible in any way for complying with my directions.

## A DURABLE POWER OF ATTORNEY FOR HEALTH CARE

1.  DESIGNATION OF HEALTH CARE AGENT. None of the following may be designated as your agent: (1) your treating health care provider; (2) a nonrelative employee of your treating health care provider; (3) an operator of a community care facility; or (4) a nonrelative employee of an operator of a community care facility. If the agent or an alternate agent designated in this Directive is my spouse, and our marriage is thereafter dissolved, such designation shall be thereupon revoked.

I do hereby designate and appoint the following individual as my attorney in fact (agent) to make health care decisions for me as authorized in this Directive. (Insert name, address and telephone number of one individual only as your agent to make health care decisions for you.)

Name of Health Care Agent: _____
Address of Health Care Agent: _____
Telephone Number of Health Care Agent: _____

For the purposes of this Directive, "health care decision" means consent, refusal of consent, or withdrawal of consent to any care, treatment, service or procedure to maintain, diagnose or treat an individual's physical condition.

2.  CREATION OF DURABLE POWER OF ATTORNEY FOR HEALTH CARE. By this portion of this Directive, I create a durable power of attorney for health care. This power of attorney shall not be affected by my subsequent incapacity. This power shall be effective only when I am unable to communicate rationally.

3.  GENERAL STATEMENT OF AUTHORITY GRANTED. Subject to any limitations in this Directive, including as set forth in paragraph 2 immediately above, I hereby grant to my agent full power and authority to make health care decisions for me to the same extent that I could make such decisions for myself if I had the capacity to do so. In exercising this authority, my agent shall make health care decisions that are consistent with my desires as stated in this Directive or otherwise made known to my agent including, but not limited to, my desires concerning obtaining or refusing or withdrawing life-prolonging care, treatment, services and procedures, including such desires set forth in a living will or similar document executed by me, if any. (If you want to limit the authority of your agent to make health care decisions for you, you can state the limitations in paragraph 4 ("Statement of Desires, Special Provisions, and Limitations") below. (You can indicate your desires by including a statement of your desires in the same paragraph.)

4.  STATEMENT OF DESIRES, SPECIAL PROVISIONS, AND LIMITATIONS. (Your agent must make health care decisions that are consistent with your known desires. You can, but are not required to, state your desires in the space provided below. You should consider whether you want to include a statement of your desires concerning life-prolonging care, treatment, services and procedures. You can also include a statement of your desires concerning other matters

relating to your health care, including a list of one or more persons whom you designate to be able to receive medical information about you and/or to be allowed to visit you in a medical institution. You can also make your desires known to your agent by discussing your desires with your agent or by some other means. If there are any types of treatment that you do not want to be used, you should state them in the space below. If you want to limit in any other way the authority given your agent by this Directive, you should state the limits in the space below. If you do not state any limits, your agent will have broad powers to make health care decisions for you, except to the extent that there are limits provided by law.) In exercising the authority under this durable power of attorney for health care, my agent shall act consistently with my desires as stated below and is subject to the special provisions and limitations stated in a living will or similar document executed by me, if any. Additional statement of desires, special provisions, and limitations:

_____

_____

(You may attach additional pages or documents if you need more space to complete your statement.)

5. INSPECTION AND DISCLOSURE OF INFORMATION RELATING TO MY PHYSICAL OR MENTAL HEALTH.

A. General Grant of Power and Authority. Subject to any limitations in this Directive, my agent has the power and authority to do all of the following: (1) Request, review and receive any information, verbal or written, regarding my physical or mental health including, but not limited to, medical and hospital records; (2) Execute on my behalf any releases or other documents that may be required in order to obtain this information; (3) Consent to the disclosure of this information; and (4) Consent to the donation of any of my organs for medical purposes. (If you want to limit the authority of your agent to receive and disclose information relating to your health, you must state the limitations in paragraph 4 ("Statement of Desires, Special Provisions, and Limitations") above.)

B. HIPAA Release Authority. My agent shall be treated as I would be with respect to my rights regarding the use and disclosure of my individually identifiable health information or other medical records. This release authority applies to any information governed by the Health Insurance Portability and Accountability Act of 1996 (HIPAA), 42 U.S.C. 1320d and 45 CFR 160 through 164. I authorize any physician, health care professional, dentist, health plan, hospital, clinic, laboratory, pharmacy, or other covered health care provider, any insurance company, and the Medical Information Bureau, Inc. or other health care clearinghouse that has provided treatment or services to me, or that has paid for or is seeking payment from me for such services, to give, disclose and release to my agent, without restriction, all of my individually identifiable health information and medical records regarding any past, present or future medical or mental health condition, including all information relating to the diagnosis of HIV/AIDS, sexually transmitted diseases, mental illness, and drug or alcohol abuse. The authority given my agent shall supersede any other agreement that I may have made with my health care providers to restrict access to or disclosure of my individually identifiable health information. The authority given my agent has no expiration date and shall expire only in the event that I revoke the authority in writing and deliver it to my health care provider.

6. SIGNING DOCUMENTS, WAIVERS AND RELEASES. Where necessary to implement the health care decisions that my agent is authorized by this Directive to make, my agent has the power and authority to execute on my behalf all of the following: (a) Documents titled, or purporting to be, a "Refusal to Permit Treatment" and/or a "Leaving Hospital Against Medical Advice"; and (b) Any necessary waiver or release from liability required by a hospital or physician.

7. DESIGNATION OF ALTERNATE AGENTS. (You are not required to designate any alternate agents but you may do so. Any alternate agent you designate will be able to make the same health care decisions as the agent you designated in paragraph 1 above, in the event that agent

is unable or ineligible to act as your agent. If an alternate agent you designate is your spouse, he or she becomes ineligible to act as your agent if your marriage is thereafter dissolved.) If the person designated as my agent in paragraph 1 is not available or becomes ineligible to act as my agent to make a health care decision for me or loses the mental capacity to make health care decisions for me, or if I revoke that person's appointment or authority to act as my agent to make health care decisions for me, then I designate and appoint the following persons to serve as my agent to make health care decisions for me as authorized in this Directive, such persons to serve in the order listed below:

A.  First Alternate Agent:
Name _____
Address _____
Telephone Number _____

B.  Second Alternate Agent:
Name _____
Address _____
Telephone Number _____

C.  Third Alternate Agent:
Name _____
Address _____
Telephone Number _____

8.  PRIOR DESIGNATIONS REVOKED. I revoke any prior durable power of attorney for health care. DATE AND SIGNATURE OF PRINCIPAL. (You must date and sign this Living Will and Durable Power of Attorney for Health Care.)

I sign my name to this Statutory Form Living Will and Durable Power of Attorney for Health Care on the date set forth at the beginning of this Form at _____ (City, State).

_____
Signature

# Illinois Statutory Short Form Power of Attorney for Property

(NOTICE: THE PURPOSE OF THIS POWER OF ATTORNEY IS TO GIVE THE PERSON YOU DESIGNATE (YOUR "AGENT") BROAD POWERS TO HANDLE YOUR PROPERTY, WHICH MAY INCLUDE POWERS TO PLEDGE, SELL OR OTHERWISE DISPOSE OF ANY REAL OR PERSONAL PROPERTY WITHOUT ADVANCE NOTICE TO YOU OR APPROVAL BY YOU. THIS FORM DOES NOT IMPOSE A DUTY ON YOUR AGENT TO EXERCISE GRANTED POWERS; BUT WHEN POWERS ARE EXERCISED, YOUR AGENT WILL HAVE TO USE DUE CARE TO ACT FOR YOUR BENEFIT AND IN ACCORDANCE WITH THIS FORM AND KEEP A RECORD OF RECEIPTS, DISBURSEMENTS AND SIGNIFICANT ACTION TAKEN AS AGENT. A COURT CAN TAKE AWAY THE POWERS OF YOUR AGENT IF IT FINDS THE AGENT IS NOT ACTING PROPERLY. YOU MAY NAME SUCCESSOR AGENTS UNDER THIS FORM BUT NOT CO-AGENTS. UNLESS YOU EXPRESSLY LIMIT THE DURATION OF THIS POWER IN THE MANNER PROVIDED BELOW, UNTIL YOU REVOKE THIS POWER OR A COURT ACTING ON YOUR BEHALF TERMINATES IT, YOUR AGENT MAY EXERCISE THE POWERS GIVEN HERE THROUGHOUT YOUR LIFETIME, EVEN AFTER YOU BECOME DISABLED. THE POWERS YOU GIVE YOUR AGENT ARE EXPLAINED MORE FULLY IN SECTION 3-4 OF THE ILLINOIS "STATUTORY SHORT FORM POWER OF ATTORNEY FOR PROPERTY LAW" OF WHICH THIS FORM IS A PART (SEE ATTACHED). THAT LAW EXPRESSLY PERMITS THE USE OF ANY DIFFERENT FORM OF POWER OF ATTORNEY YOU MAY DESIRE. IF THERE IS ANYTHING ABOUT THIS FORM THAT YOU DO NOT UNDERSTAND, YOU SHOULD ASK A LAWYER TO EXPLAIN IT TO YOU.)

POWER OF ATTORNEY made this _____ day of _____.

(month)          (year)

1.  I, _____

_____(insert name and address of principal),

hereby appoint _____

_____(insert name and address of agent)

as my attorney-in-fact (my "agent") to act for me and in my name (in any way I could act in person) with respect to the following powers, as defined in Section 3-4 of the "Statutory Short Form Power of Attorney for Property Law" (including all amendments), but subject to any limitation on or additions to the specified powers inserted in paragraph 2 or 3 below:

(YOU MUST STRIKE OUT ANY ONE OR MORE OF THE FOLLOWING CATEGORIES OF POWERS YOU DO NOT WANT YOUR AGENT TO HAVE. FAILURE TO STRIKE THE TITLE OF ANY CATEGORY WILL CAUSE THE POWERS DESCRIBED IN THAT CATEGORY TO BE GRANTED TO THE AGENT. TO STRIKE OUT A CATEGORY YOU MUST DRAW A LINE THROUGH THE TITLE OF THAT CATEGORY.)

|     |     |
| --- | --- |
| (a) | Real estate transactions. |
| (b) | Financial institution transactions. |
| (c) | Stock and bond transactions. |
| (d) | Tangible personal property transactions. |
| (e) | Safe deposit box transactions. |
| (f) | Insurance and annuity transactions. |
| (g) | Retirement plan transactions. |
| (h) | Social Security, employment and military service benefits. |
| (i) | Tax matters. |
| (j) | Claims and litigation. |
| (k) | Commodity and option transactions. |
| (l) | Business operations. |
| (m) | Borrowing transactions. |
| (n) | Estate transactions. |
| (o) | All other property powers and transactions. |

(LIMITATIONS ON AND ADDITIONS TO THE AGENT'S POWERS MAY BE INCLUDED IN THIS POWER OF ATTORNEY IF THEY ARE SPECIFICALLY DESCRIBED BELOW.)

2.      The powers granted above shall not include the following powers or shall be modified or limited in the following particulars (here you may include any specific limitations you deem appropriate, such as a prohibition or conditions on the sale of a particular stock or real estate or special rules on borrowing by the agent):

_____
_____
_____

3.      In addition to the powers granted above, I grant my agent the following powers (here you may add any other delegable powers including, without limitation, the power to make gifts, exercise powers of appointment, name or change beneficiaries or joint tenants or revoke or amend any trust specifically referred to below):

_____
_____
_____

(YOUR AGENT WILL HAVE AUTHORITY TO EMPLOY OTHER PERSONS AS NECESSARY TO ENABLE THE AGENT TO PROPERLY EXERCISE THE POWERS GRANTED IN THIS FORM, BUT YOUR AGENT WILL HAVE TO MAKE ALL DISCRETIONARY DECISIONS.  IF YOU WANT TO GIVE YOUR AGENT THE RIGHT TO DELEGATE DISCRETIONARY DECISION-MAKING POWERS TO OTHERS, YOU SHOULD KEEP THE NEXT SENTENCE, OTHERWISE IT SHOULD BE STRUCK OUT.)

4.      My agent shall have the right by written instrument to delegate any or all of the foregoing powers involving discretionary decision-making to any person or persons whom my agent may select, but such delegation may be amended or revoked by an agent (including any successor) named by me who is acting under this power of attorney at the time of reference.

(YOUR AGENT WILL BE ENTITLED TO REIMBURSEMENT FOR ALL REASONABLE EXPENSES INCURRED IN ACTING UNDER THIS POWER OF ATTORNEY.  STRIKE OUT THE NEXT SENTENCE IF YOU DO NOT WANT YOUR AGENT TO ALSO BE ENTITLED TO REASONABLE COMPENSATION FOR SERVICES AS AGENT.)

5.      My agent shall be entitled to reasonable compensation for services rendered as agent under this power of attorney.

(THIS POWER OF ATTORNEY MAY BE AMENDED OR REVOKED BY YOU AT ANY TIME AND IN ANY MANNER.  ABSENT AMENDMENT OR REVOCATION, THE AUTHORITY GRANTED IN THIS POWER OF ATTORNEY WILL BECOME EFFECTIVE AT THE TIME THIS POWER IS SIGNED AND WILL CONTINUE UNTIL YOUR DEATH UNLESS A LIMITATION ON THE BEGINNING DATE OR DURATION IS MADE BY INITIALING AND COMPLETING EITHER (OR BOTH) OF THE FOLLOWING:)

6. (          ) This power of attorney shall become effective on _____
_____ (insert a future date or event during your lifetime, such as court determination of your disability, when you want this power to first take effect)

7. (          ) This power of attorney shall terminate_____
_____ (insert a future date or event, such as court determination of your disability, when you want this power to terminate prior to your death)

(IF YOU WISH TO NAME SUCCESSOR AGENTS, INSERT THE NAME(S) AND ADDRESS(ES) OF SUCH SUCCESSOR(S) IN THE FOLLOWING PARAGRAPH.)

8.      If any agent named by me shall die, become incompetent, resign or refuse to accept the office of agent, I name the following (each to act alone and successively, in the order named) as successor(s) to such agent:

_____

_____

For purposes of this paragraph 8, a person shall be considered to be incompetent if and while the person is a minor or an adjudicated incompetent or disabled person or the person is unable to give prompt and intelligent consideration to business matters, as certified by a licensed physician.

(IF YOU WISH TO NAME YOUR AGENT AS GUARDIAN OF YOUR ESTATE, IN THE EVENT A COURT DECIDES THAT ONE SHOULD BE APPOINTED, YOU MAY, BUT ARE NOT REQUIRED TO, DO SO BY RETAINING THE FOLLOWING PARAGRAPH. THE COURT WILL APPOINT YOUR AGENT IF THE COURT FINDS THAT SUCH APPOINTMENT WILL SERVE YOUR BEST INTERESTS AND WELFARE. STRIKE OUT PARAGRAPH 9 IF YOU DO NOT WANT YOUR AGENT TO ACT AS GUARDIAN.)

9.      If a guardian of my estate (my property) is to be appointed, I nominate the agent acting under this power of attorney as such guardian, to serve without bond or security.

10.     I am fully informed as to all the contents of this form and understand the full import of this grant of powers to my agent.

Signed _____

(principal)

(YOU MAY, BUT ARE NOT REQUIRED TO, REQUEST YOUR AGENT AND SUCCESSOR AGENTS TO PROVIDE SPECIMEN SIGNATURES BELOW. IF YOU INCLUDE SPECIMEN SIGNATURES IN THIS POWER OF ATTORNEY, YOU MUST COMPLETE THE CERTIFICATION OPPOSITE THE SIGNATURES OF THE AGENTS.)

Specimen signatures of agent              I certify that the signatures of my
(and successors)                          agent (and successors) are correct.

_____     _____

(agent)                                     (principal)

_____     _____

(successor agent)                         (principal)

_____     _____

(successor agent)                         (principal)

(THIS POWER OF ATTORNEY WILL NOT BE EFFECTIVE UNLESS IT IS NOTARIZED, USING THE FORM BELOW.)

State of _____          )
                                               ) SS.
County of _____           )

      The undersigned, a notary public in and for the above county and state, certifies that _____, known to me to be the same person whose name is subscribed as principal to the foregoing power of attorney, appeared before me in person and acknowledged signing and delivering the instrument as the free and voluntary act of the principal, for the uses and purposes therein set forth (and certified to the correctness of the signature(s) of the agent(s)).

Dated: _____ (SEAL)

                                  _____

                                  Notary Public
                                  My commission expires_____

THE NAME AND ADDRESS OF THE PERSON PREPARING THIS FORM SHOULD BE INSERTED IF THE AGENT WILL HAVE POWER TO CONVEY ANY INTEREST IN REAL ESTATE.

      This document was prepared by: _____

_____

### Illinois Statutory Short Form Power of Attorney for Property Law

§3-4.  Explanation of powers granted in the statutory short form power of attorney for property. This Section defines each category of powers listed in the statutory short form power of attorney for property and the effect of granting powers to an agent.  When the title of any of the following categories is retained (not struck out) in a statutory property power form, the effect will be to grant the agent all of the principal's rights, powers and discretions with respect to the types of property and transactions covered by the retained category, subject to any limitations on the granted powers that appear on the face of the form.  The agent will have authority to exercise each granted power for and in the name of the principal with respect to all of the principal's interests in every type of property or transaction covered by the granted power at the time of exercise, whether the principal's interests are direct or indirect, whole or fractional, legal, equitable or contractual, as a joint tenant or tenant in common or held in any other form; but the agent will not have power under any of the statutory categories (a) through (o) to make gifts of the principal's property, to exercise powers to appoint to others or to change any beneficiary whom the principal has designated to take the principal's interests at death under any will, trust, joint tenancy, beneficiary form or contractual arrangement.  The agent will be under no duty to exercise granted powers or to assume control of or responsibility for the principal's property or affairs; but when granted powers are exercised, the agent will be required to use due care to act for the benefit of the principal in accordance with the terms of the statutory property power and will be liable for negligent exercise.  The agent may act in person or through others reasonably employed by the agent for that purpose and will have authority to sign and deliver all instruments, negotiate and enter into all agreements and do all other acts reasonably necessary to implement the exercise of the powers granted to the agent.

(a)  Real estate transactions.  The agent is authorized to:  buy, sell, exchange, rent and lease real estate (which term includes, without limitation, real estate subject to a land trust and all beneficial interests in and powers of direction under any land trust); collect all rent, sale proceeds and earnings from real estate; convey, assign and accept title to real estate; grant easements, create conditions and release rights of homestead with respect to real estate; create land trusts and exercise all powers under land trusts; hold, possess, maintain, repair, improve, subdivide, manage, operate and insure real estate; pay, contest, protest and compromise real estate taxes and assessments; and, in general, exercise all powers with respect to real estate which the principal could if present and under no disability.

(b)  Financial institution transactions.  The agent is authorized to:  open, close, continue and control all accounts and deposits in any type of financial institution (which term includes, without limitation, banks, trust companies, savings and building and loan associations, credit unions and brokerage firms); deposit in and withdraw from and write checks on any financial institution account or deposit; and, in general, exercise all powers with respect to financial institution transactions which the principal could if present and under no disability.

(c)  Stock and bond transactions.  The agent is authorized to:  buy and sell all types of securities (which term includes, without limitation, stocks, bonds, mutual funds and all other types of investment securities and financial instruments); collect, hold and safe keep all dividends, interest, earnings, proceeds of sale, distributions, shares, certificates and other evidence of ownership paid or distributed with respect to securities; exercise all voting rights with respect to securities in person or by proxy, enter into voting trusts and consent to limitations on the right to vote; and, in general, exercise all powers with respect to securities which the principal could if present and under no disability.

(d)  Tangible personal property transactions.  The agent is authorized to: buy and sell, lease, exchange, collect, possess and take title to all tangible personal property; move, store, ship, restore, maintain, repair, improve, manage, preserve, insure and safe keep tangible personal property; and, in general, exercise all powers with respect to tangible personal property which the principal could if present and under no disability.

(e)  Safe deposit box transactions.  The agent is authorized to: open, continue and have access to all safe deposit boxes; sign, renew, release or terminate any safe deposit contract; drill or surrender any safe deposit box; and, in general, exercise all powers with respect to safe deposit matters which the principal could if present and under no disability.

(f)  Insurance and annuity transactions.  The agent is authorized to:  procure, acquire, continue, renew, terminate or otherwise deal with any type of insurance or annuity contract (which terms include, without limitation, life, accident, health, disability, automobile casualty, property or liability insurance); pay premiums or assessments on or surrender and collect all distributions, proceeds or benefits payable under any insurance or annuity contract; and, in general, exercise all powers with respect to insurance and annuity contracts which the principal could if present and under no disability.

(g)  Retirement plan transactions.  The agent is authorized to:  contribute to, withdraw from and deposit funds in any type of retirement plan (which term includes, without limitation, any tax qualified or unqualified pension, profit sharing, stock bonus, employee savings and other retirement plan, individual retirement account, deferred compensation plan and any other type of employee benefit plan); select and change payment options for the principal under any retirement plan; make rollover contributions from any retirement plan to other retirement plans or individual retirement accounts; exercise all investment powers available under any type of self-directed retirement plan; and, in general, exercise all powers with respect to retirement plans and retirement plan account balances which the principal could if present and under no disability.

(h)  Social Security, unemployment and military service benefits.  The agent is authorized to: prepare, sign and file any claim or application for Social Security, unemployment or military service benefits; sue for, settle or abandon any claims to any benefit or assistance under any federal, state, local or foreign statute or regulation; control, deposit to any account, collect, receipt for, and take title to and hold all benefits under any Social Security, unemployment, military service or other state, federal, local or foreign statute or regulation; and, in general, exercise all powers with respect to Social Security, unemployment, military service and government benefits which the principal could if present and under no disability.

(i) Tax matters. The agent is authorized to: sign, verify and file all the principal's federal, state and local income, gift, estate, property and other tax returns, including joint returns and declarations of estimated tax; pay all taxes; claim, sue for and receive all tax refunds; examine and copy all the principal's tax returns and records; represent the principal before any federal, state or local revenue agency or taxing body and sign and deliver all tax powers of attorney on behalf of the principal as required to settle, pay and determine all tax liabilities; and, in general, exercise all powers with respect to tax matters which the principal could if present and under no disability.

(j) Claims and litigation. The agent is authorized to: institute, prosecute, defend, abandon, compromise, arbitrate, settle and dispose of any claim in favor of or against the principal or any property interests of the principal; collect and receipt for any claim or settlement proceeds and waive or release all rights of the principal; employ attorneys and others and enter into contingency agreements and other contracts as necessary in connections with litigation; and, in general, exercise all powers with respect to claims and litigation which the principal could if present and under no disability.

(k) Commodity and option transactions. The agent is authorized to: buy, sell, exchange, assign, convey, settle and exercise commodities futures contracts and call and put options on stocks and stock indices traded on a regulated options exchange and collect and receipt for all proceeds of any such transactions; establish or continue option accounts for the principal with any securities or futures broker; and, in general, exercise all powers with respect to commodities and options which the principal could if present and under no disability.

(l) Business operations. The agent is authorized to: organize or continue any business (which term includes, without limitation, any farming, manufacturing, service, mining, retailing or other type of business operation) in any form, whether as a proprietorship, joint venture, partnership, corporation, trust or other legal entity; operate, buy, sell, expand, contract, terminate or liquidate any business; direct, control, supervise, manage or participate in the operation of any business and engage, compensate and discharge business managers, employees, agents, attorneys, accountants and consultants; and, in general, exercise all powers with respect to business interests and operations which the principal could if present and under no disability.

(m) Borrowing transactions. The agent is authorized to: borrow money; mortgage or pledge any real estate or tangible or intangible personal property as security for such purposes; sign, renew, extend, pay and satisfy any notes or other forms of obligation; and, in general, exercise all powers with respect to secured and unsecured borrowing which the principal could if present and under no disability.

(n) Estate transactions. The agent is authorized to: accept, receipt for, exercise, release, reject, renounce, assign, disclaim, demand, sue for, claim and recover any legacy, bequest, devise, gift or other property interest or payment due or payable to or for the principal; assert any interest in and exercise any power over any trust, estate or property subject to fiduciary control; establish a revocable trust solely for the benefit of the principal that terminates at the death of the principal and is then distributed to the legal representative of the estate of the principal; and, in general, exercise all powers with respect to estates and trusts which the principal could if present and under no disability; provided, however, that the agent may not make or change a will and may not revoke or amend a trust revocable or amendable by the principal or require the trustee of any trust for the benefit of the principal to pay income or principal to the agent unless specific authority to that end is given, and specific reference to the trust is made, in the statutory property power form.

# Illinois Statutory Short Form Power of Attorney for Health Care

(NOTICE: THE PURPOSE OF THIS POWER OF ATTORNEY IS TO GIVE THE PERSON YOU DESIGNATE (YOUR "AGENT") BROAD POWERS TO MAKE HEALTH CARE DECISIONS FOR YOU, INCLUDING POWER TO REQUIRE, CONSENT TO OR WITHDRAW ANY TYPE OF PERSONAL CARE OR MEDICAL TREATMENT FOR ANY PHYSICAL OR MENTAL CONDITION AND TO ADMIT YOU TO OR DISCHARGE YOU FROM ANY HOSPITAL, HOME OR OTHER INSTITUTION. THIS FORM DOES NOT IMPOSE A DUTY ON YOUR AGENT TO EXERCISE GRANTED POWERS; BUT WHEN POWERS ARE EXERCISED, YOUR AGENT WILL HAVE TO USE DUE CARE TO ACT FOR YOUR BENEFIT AND IN ACCORDANCE WITH THIS FORM AND KEEP A RECORD OF RECEIPTS, DISBURSEMENTS AND SIGNIFICANT ACTIONS TAKEN AS AGENT. A COURT CAN TAKE AWAY THE POWERS OF YOUR AGENT IF IT FINDS THE AGENT IS NOT ACTING PROPERLY. YOU MAY NAME SUCCESSOR AGENTS UNDER THIS FORM BUT NOT CO-AGENTS, AND NO HEALTH CARE PROVIDER MAY BE NAMED. UNLESS YOU EXPRESSLY LIMIT THE DURATION OF THIS POWER IN THE MANNER PROVIDED BELOW, UNTIL YOU REVOKE THIS POWER OR A COURT ACTING ON YOUR BEHALF TERMINATES IT, YOUR AGENT MAY EXERCISE THE POWERS GIVEN HERE THROUGHOUT YOUR LIFETIME, EVEN AFTER YOU BECOME DISABLED. THE POWERS YOU GIVE YOUR AGENT, YOUR RIGHT TO REVOKE THOSE POWERS AND THE PENALTIES FOR VIOLATING THE LAW ARE EXPLAINED MORE FULLY IN SECTIONS 4-5, 4-6, 4-9 AND 4-10(b) OF THE ILLINOIS "POWERS OF ATTORNEY FOR HEALTH CARE LAW" OF WHICH THIS FORM IS A PART (SEE ATTACHED). THAT LAW EXPRESSLY PERMITS THE USE OF ANY DIFFERENT FORM OF POWER OF ATTORNEY YOU MAY DESIRE. IF THERE IS ANYTHING ABOUT THIS FORM THAT YOU DO NOT UNDERSTAND, YOU SHOULD ASK A LAWYER TO EXPLAIN IT TO YOU.)

POWER OF ATTORNEY made this _____ day of _____
                                                                                      (month)                    (year)

1.    I, _____

_____

_____,
                                 (insert name and address of principal)

hereby appoint:

_____

_____
                                 (insert name and address of agent)

as my attorney-in-fact (my "agent") to act for me and in my name (in any way I could act in person) to make any and all decisions for me concerning my personal care, medical treatment, hospitalization and health care and to require, withhold or withdraw any type of medical treatment or procedure, even though my death may ensue. My agent shall have the same access to my medical records that I have, including the right to disclose the contents to others. My agent shall also have full power to make a disposition of any part or all of my body for medical purposes, authorize an autopsy and direct the disposition of my remains.

(THE ABOVE GRANT OF POWER IS INTENDED TO BE AS BROAD AS POSSIBLE SO THAT YOUR AGENT WILL HAVE AUTHORITY TO MAKE ANY DECISION YOU COULD MAKE TO OBTAIN OR TERMINATE ANY TYPE OF HEALTH CARE, INCLUDING WITHDRAWAL OF FOOD AND WATER AND OTHER LIFE-SUSTAINING MEASURES, IF YOUR AGENT BELIEVES SUCH ACTION WOULD BE CONSISTENT WITH YOUR INTENT AND DESIRES. IF YOU WISH TO LIMIT THE SCOPE OF YOUR AGENT'S POWERS OR PRESCRIBE SPECIAL RULES OR LIMIT THE POWER TO MAKE AN ANATOMICAL GIFT, AUTHORIZE AUTOPSY OR DISPOSE OF REMAINS, YOU MAY DO SO IN THE FOLLOWING PARAGRAPHS.)

2.     The powers granted above shall not include the following powers or shall be subject to the following rules or limitations (here you may include any specific limitations you deem appropriate, such as: your own definition of when life-sustaining measures should be withheld; a direction to continue food and fluids or life-sustaining treatment in all events; or instructions to refuse any specific types of treatment that are inconsistent with your religious beliefs or unacceptable to you for any other reason, such as blood transfusion, electro-convulsive therapy, amputation, psychosurgery, voluntary admission to a mental institution, etc.):

_____

_____

(THE SUBJECT OF LIFE-SUSTAINING TREATMENT IS OF PARTICULAR IMPORTANCE. FOR YOUR CONVENIENCE IN DEALING WITH THAT SUBJECT, SOME GENERAL STATEMENTS CONCERNING THE WITHHOLDING OR REMOVAL OF LIFE-SUSTAINING TREATMENT ARE SET FORTH BELOW. IF YOU AGREE WITH ONE OF THESE STATEMENTS, YOU MAY INITIAL THAT STATEMENT; BUT DO NOT INITIAL MORE THAN ONE:)

I do not want my life to be prolonged nor do I want life-sustaining treatment to be provided or continued if my agent believes the burdens of the treatment outweigh the expected benefits. I want my agent to consider the relief of suffering, the expense involved and the quality as well as the possible extension of my life in making decisions concerning life sustaining treatment.

Initialed _____

I want my life to be prolonged and I want life-sustaining treatment to be provided or continued unless I am in a coma which my attending physician believes to be irreversible, in accordance with reasonable medical standards at the time of reference. If and when I have suffered irreversible coma, I want life-sustaining treatment to be withheld or discontinued.

Initialed _____

I want my life to be prolonged to the greatest extent possible without regard to my condition, the chances I have for recovery or the cost of the procedures.

Initialed _____

(THIS POWER OF ATTORNEY MAY BE AMENDED OR REVOKED BY YOU IN THE MANNER PROVIDED IN SECTION 4-6 OF THE ILLINOIS "POWERS OF ATTORNEY FOR HEALTH CARE LAW" (SEE THE END OF THIS FORM). ABSENT AMENDMENT OR REVOCATION, THE AUTHORITY GRANTED IN THIS POWER OF ATTORNEY WILL BECOME EFFECTIVE AT THE TIME THIS POWER IS SIGNED AND WILL CONTINUE UNTIL YOUR DEATH, AND BEYOND IF ANATOMICAL GIFT, AUTOPSY OR DISPOSITION OF REMAINS IS AUTHORIZED, UNLESS A LIMITATION ON THE BEGINNING DATE OR DURATION IS MADE BY INITIALING AND COMPLETING EITHER OR BOTH OF THE FOLLOWING:)

3. (         ) This power of attorney shall become effective on _____
_____ (insert a future date or event during your lifetime, such as court determination of your disability, when you want this power to first take effect)

4. (         ) This power of attorney shall terminate on _____
_____ (insert a future date or event, such as court determination of your disability, when you want this power to terminate prior to your death)

(IF YOU WISH TO NAME SUCCESSOR AGENTS, INSERT THE NAMES AND ADDRESSES OF SUCH SUCCESSORS IN THE FOLLOWING PARAGRAPH.)

5.      If any agent named by me shall die, become incompetent, resign, refuse to accept the office of agent or be unavailable, I name the following (each to act alone and successively, in the order named) as successors to such agent:_____

_____

For purposes of this paragraph 5, a person shall be considered to be incompetent if and while the person is a minor or an adjudicated incompetent or disabled person or the person is unable to give prompt and intelligent consideration to health care matters, as certified by a licensed physician.

(IF YOU WISH TO NAME YOUR AGENT AS GUARDIAN OF YOUR PERSON, IN THE EVENT A COURT DECIDES THAT ONE SHOULD BE APPOINTED, YOU MAY, BUT ARE NOT REQUIRED TO, DO SO BY RETAINING THE FOLLOWING PARAGRAPH. THE COURT WILL APPOINT YOUR AGENT IF THE COURT FINDS THAT SUCH APPOINTMENT WILL SERVE YOUR BEST INTERESTS AND WELFARE. STRIKE OUT PARAGRAPH 6 IF YOU DO NOT WANT YOUR AGENT TO ACT AS GUARDIAN.)

6.      If a guardian of my person is to be appointed, I nominate the agent acting under this power of attorney as such guardian, to serve without bond or security. (insert name and address of nominated guardian of the person)

7.      I am fully informed as to all the contents of this form and understand the full import of this grant of powers to my agent.


Signed _____
                        (principal)

The principal has had an opportunity to read the above form and has signed the form or acknowledged his or her signature or mark on the form in my presence.

_____          Residing at_____
              (witness)                  _____

(YOU MAY, BUT ARE NOT REQUIRED TO, REQUEST YOUR AGENT AND SUCCESSOR AGENTS TO PROVIDE SPECIMEN SIGNATURES BELOW. IF YOU INCLUDE SPECIMEN SIGNATURES IN THIS POWER OF ATTORNEY YOU MUST COMPLETE THE CERTIFICATION OPPOSITE THE SIGNATURES OF THE AGENTS.)

Specimen signatures of agent                I certify that the signatures of my agent (and
(and successors)                            successors) are correct.


_____          _____
              (agent)                                  (principal)


_____          _____
         (successor agent)                             (principal)


_____          _____
         (successor agent)                             (principal)

# Illinois Statutory Short Form Power of Attorney for Health Care Law

§ 4-5.    Limitations on health care agencies. Neither the attending physician nor any other health care provider may act as agent under a health care agency; however, a person who is not administering health care to the patient may act as health care agent for the patient even though the person is a physician or otherwise licensed, certified, authorized, or permitted by law to administer health care in the ordinary course of business or the practice of a profession.

§4-6. Revocation and amendment of health care agencies.
    (a)    Every health care agency may be revoked by the principal at any time, without regard to the principal's mental or physical condition, by any of the following methods:
    1.    By being obliterated, burnt, torn or otherwise destroyed or defaced in a manner indicating intention to revoke;
    2.    By a written revocation of the agency signed and dated by the principal or person acting at the direction of the principal; or
    3.    By an oral or any other expression of the intent to revoke th agency in the presence of a witness 18 years of age or older who signs and dates a writing confirming that such expression of intent was made.
    (b)    Every health care agency may be amended at any time by a written amendment signed and dated by the principal or person acting at the direction of the principal.
    (c)    Any person, other than the agent, to whom a revocation or amendment is communicated or delivered shall make all reasonable efforts to inform the agent of that fact as promptly as possible.

§4-9.    Penalties. All persons shall be subject to the following sanctions in relation to health care agencies, in addition to all other sanctions applicable under any other law or rule of professional conduct:
    (a)    Any person shall be civilly liable who, without the principal's consent, wilfully conceals, cancels or alters a health care agency or any amendment of revocation of the agency or who falsifies or forges a health care agency, amendment or revocation.
    (b)    A person who falsifies or forges a health care agency or wilfully conceals or withholds personal knowledge of an amendment or revocation of a health care agency with the intent to cause a withholding or withdrawal of life-sustaining or death-delaying procedures contrary to the intent of the principal and thereby, because of such act, directly causes life-sustaining or death-delaying procedures to be withheld or withdrawn and death to the patient to be hastened shall be subject to prosecution for involuntary manslaughter.
    (c)    Any person who requires or prevents execution of a health care agency as a condition of insuring or providing any type of health care services to the patient shall be civilly liable and guilty of a Class A misdemeanor.

§ 4-10(b).    The statutory short form power of attorney for health care (the "statutory health care power") authorizes the agent to make any and all health care decisions on behalf of the principal which the principal could make if present and under no disability, subject to any limitations on the granted powers that appear on the face of the form, to be exercised in such manner as the agent deems consistent with the intent and desires of the principal. The agent will be under no duty to exercise granted powers or to assume control of or responsibility for the principal's health care; but when granted powers are exercised, the agent will be required to use due care to act for the benefit of the principal in accordance with the terms of the statutory health care power and will be liable for negligent exercise. The agent may act in person or through others reasonably employed by the agent for that purpose but may not delegate authority to make health care decisions. The agent may sign and deliver all instruments, negotiate and enter into all agreements and do all other acts reasonably necessary to implement the exercise of the powers granted to the agent. Without limiting the generality of the foregoing, the statutory health care power shall include the following powers, subject to any limitations appearing on the face of the form:

(1)      The agent is authorized to give consent to and authorize or refuse, or to withhold or withdraw consent to, any and all types of medical care, treatment or procedures relating to the physical or mental health of the principal, including any medication program, surgical procedures, life-sustaining treatment or provision of food and fluids for the principal.

(2)      The agent is authorized to admit the principal to or discharge the principal from any and all types of hospitals, institutions, homes, residential or nursing facilities, treatment centers and other health care institutions providing personal care or treatment for any type of physical or mental condition. The agent shall have the same right to visit the principal in the hospital or other institution as is granted to a spouse or adult child of the principal, any rule of the institution to the contrary notwithstanding.

(3)      The agent is authorized to contract for any and all types of health care services and facilities in the name of and on behalf of the principal and to bind the principal to pay for all such services and facilities, and to have an exercise those powers over the principal's property as are authorized under the statutory property power, to the extent the agent deems necessary to pay health care costs; and the agent shall not be personally liable for any services or care contracted for on behalf of the principal.

(4)      At the principal's expense and subject to reasonable rules of the health care provider to prevent disruption of the principal's health care, the agent shall have the same right th principal has to examine and copy and consent to disclosure of all the principal's medical records that the agent deems relevant to the exercise of the agent's powers, whether the records relate to mental health or any other medical condition and whether they are in the possession of or maintained by any physician, psychiatrist, psychologist, therapist, hospital, nursing home or other health care provider.

(5)      The agent is authorized: to direct that an autopsy be made pursuant to Section 2 of "An Act in relation to autopsy of dead bodies," approved August 13, 1965, including all amendments; to make a disposition of any part or all of the principal's body pursuant to the Uniform Anatomical Gift Act, as now or hereafter amended; and to direct the disposition of the principal's remains.

# Power of Attorney

I, _____
_____(insert your name and address),
appoint _____
_____ (insert the name and address
of the person appointed) as my agent (attorney-in-fact) to act for me in any lawful way with
respect to the following initialed subjects, as each subject is defined and described in the
Annotated Indiana Code, which is incorporated by reference herein:

TO GRANT ONE OR MORE OF THE FOLLOWING POWERS, INITIAL THE LINE IN
FRONT OF EACH POWER YOU ARE GRANTING.  TO WITHHOLD A POWER, DO NOT
INITIAL THE LINE IN FRONT OF IT. YOU MAY, BUT NEED NOT, CROSS OUT EACH POWER
WITHHELD. THE ANNOTATED INDIANA CODE SECTIONS NOTED ARE INCORPORATED BY
REFERENCE.

INITIALS

| | | |
|---|---|---|
| _____ | a. | ALL POWERS (b THROUGH r) LISTED BELOW. |
| _____ | b | Real property transactions.  (Ann. Ind. Code § 30-5-5-2) |
| _____ | c. | Tangible personal property transactions.  (Ann. Ind. Code § 30-5-5-3) |
| _____ | d. | Bond, share and commodity transactions.  (Ann. Ind. Code § 30-5-5-4) |
| _____ | e. | Retirement plans.  (Ann. Ind. Code § 30-5-5-4.5) |
| _____ | f. | Banking transactions.  (Ann. Ind. Code § 30-5-5-5) |
| _____ | g. | Business operating transactions.  (Ann. Ind. Code § 30-5-5-6) |
| _____ | h. | Insurance transactions.  (Ann. Ind. Code § 30-5-5-7) |
| _____ | i. | Beneficiary transactions.  (Ann. Ind. Code § 30-5-5-8) |
| _____ | j. | Gift transactions.  (Ann. Ind. Code § 30-5-5-9) |
| _____ | k. | Fiduciary transactions.  (Ann. Ind. Code § 30-5-5-10) |
| _____ | l. | Claims and litigation.  (Ann. Ind. Code § 30-5-5-11) |
| _____ | m. | Family maintenance.  (Ann. Ind. Code § 30-5-5-12) |
| _____ | n. | Benefits from military service.  (Ann. Ind. Code § 30-5-5-13) |
| _____ | o. | Records, reports, and statements.  (Ann. Ind. Code § 30-5-5-14) |
| _____ | p. | Estate transactions.  (Ann. Ind. Code § 30-5-5-15) |
| _____ | q. | Health care powers.  (Ann. Ind. Code §30-5-5-16) |
| _____ | r. | Delegation of authority. (Ann. Ind. Code §30-5-5-18) |
| _____ | s. | General authority as to all other matters. (Ann. Ind. Code §30-5-5-19) |

If you checked "Health care powers," and wish your agent to be able to withdraw or
withhold health care  as described below, check the following box:

☐        I authorize my health care representative to make decisions in my best interest
concerning withdrawal or withholding of health care (pursuant to Ann. Ind. Code §§30-5-5-17, 16-
36-1, and 16-36-4).  If at any time based on my previously expressed preferences and the
diagnosis and prognosis my health care representative is satisfied that certain health care is not
or would not be beneficial or that such health care is or would be excessively burdensome, then
my health care representative may express my will that such health care be withheld or
withdrawn and may consent on my behalf that any or all health care be discontinued or not
instituted, even if death may result.

My health care representative must try to discuss this decision with me.  However, if I am
unable to communicate, my health care representative may make such a decision for me, after
consultation with my physician or physicians and other relevant health care givers.  To the extent
appropriate, my health care representative may also discuss this decision with my family and
others to the extent they are available.

CHECK ONE OF THE FOLLOWING BOXES:

☐      This power of attorney shall terminate upon my disability, incapacity or incompetence.

☐      This power of attorney is effective immediately, and shall not be affected by my disability, incapacity or incompetence.

☐      This power of attorney will become effective upon my disability, incapacity or incompetence.

Signed this _____ day of _____, _____.

_____      _____
(Your signature)                          (Your Social Security number)

State of _____
(County) of _____

On this _____ day of _____, _____, before me, personally appeared _____ (name of principal), who is personally known to me or provided _____ as identification, and acknowledged that he or she executed it.

_____
Notary Public

## LIVING WILL DECLARATION

Declaration made this _____ day of _____ (month, year). I, _____, being at least eighteen (18) years of age and of sound mind, willfully, and voluntarily make known my desires that my dying shall not be artificially prolonged under the circumstances set forth below, and I declare:

If at any time my attending physician certifies in writing that: (1) I have an incurable injury, disease, or illness; (2) my death will occur within a short time; and (3) the use of life prolonging procedures would serve only to artificially prolong the dying process, I direct that such procedures be withheld or withdrawn, and that I be permitted to die naturally with only the performance or provision of any medical procedure or medication necessary to provide me with comfort care or to alleviate pain, and, if I have so indicated below, the provision of artificially supplied nutrition and hydration. (Indicate your choice by initialing or making your mark before signing this declaration):

_____ I wish to receive artificially supplied nutrition and hydration, even if the effort to sustain life is futile or excessively burdensome to me.

_____ I do not wish to receive artificially supplied nutrition and hydration, if the effort to sustain life is futile or excessively burdensome to me.

_____ I intentionally make no decision concerning artificially supplied nutrition and hydration, leaving the decision to my health care representative appointed under IC 16-36-1-7 or my attorney in fact with health care powers under IC 30-5-5.

In the absence of my ability to give directions regarding the use of life prolonging procedures, it is my intention that this declaration be honored by my family and physician as the final expression of my legal right to refuse medical or surgical treatment and accept the consequences of the refusal.

I understand the full import of this declaration.

Signed _____

_____
City, County, and State of Residence

The declarant has been personally known to me, and I believe (him/her) to be of sound mind. I did not sign the declarant's signature above for or at the direction of the declarant. I am not a parent, spouse, or child of the declarant. I am not entitled to any part of the declarant's estate or directly financially responsible for the declarant's medical care. I am competent and at least eighteen (18) years of age.

Witness _____    Date _____

Witness _____    Date _____

# LIFE PROLONGING PROCEDURES DECLARATION

Declaration made this _____ day of _____ (month, year). I, _____, being at least eighteen (18) years of age and of sound mind, willfully and voluntarily make known my desire that if at any time I have an incurable injury, disease, or illness determined to be a terminal condition I request the use of life prolonging procedures that would extend my life. This includes appropriate nutrition and hydration, the administration of medication, and the performance of all other medical procedures necessary to extend my life, to provide comfort care, or to alleviate pain.

In the absence of my ability to give directions regarding the use of life prolonging procedures, it is my intention that this declaration be honored by my family and physician as the final expression of my legal right to request medical or surgical treatment and accept the consequences of the request.

I understand the full import of this declaration.

Signed _____

_____
City, County, and State of Residence

The declarant has been personally known to me, and I believe (him/her) to be of sound mind. I am competent and at least eighteen (18) years of age.

Witness_____ Date_____

Witness_____ Date_____

## Durable Power of Attorney for Health Care

I hereby designate _____ as my attorney in fact (my agent) and give to my agent the power to make health care decisions for me. This power exists only when I am unable, in the judgment of my attending physician, to make those health care decisions. The attorney in fact must act consistently with my desires as stated in this document or otherwise made known.

Except as otherwise specified in this document, this document gives my agent the power, where otherwise consistent with the law to this state, to consent to my physician not giving health care or stopping health care which is necessary to keep me alive.

This document gives my agent power to make health care decisions on my behalf, including to consent, to refuse to consent, or to withdraw consent to the provision of any care, treatment, service, or procedure to maintain, diagnose, or treat a physical or mental condition. This power is subject to any statement of my desires and any limitations included in this document.

My agent has the right to examine my medical records and to consent to disclosure of such records.

The powers granted by this document are subject to the following instructions and limitations (if none, type in "none"): _____
_____
_____

In the event my designated agent is unable or unwilling to serve, I designate the following alternative attorneys in fact (agents), to serve in the order stated below:

First Alternative Agent: _____

Second Alternative Agent: _____

Signature: _____

# Durable Power of Attorney for Health Care Decisions

I, _____ , designate and appoint:

Name _____

Address: _____
_____

Telephone Number: _____

to be my agent for health care decisions and pursuant to the language stated below, on my behalf to:

    (1)    consent, refuse consent, or withdraw consent to any care, treatment, service or procedure to maintain, diagnose or treat a physical or mental condition, and to make decisions about organ donation, autopsy and disposition of the body;

    (2)    make all necessary arrangements at any hospital, psychiatric hospital or psychiatric treatment facility, hospice, nursing home or similar institution; to employ or discharge health care personnel to include physicians, psychiatrists, psychologists, dentists, nurses, therapists or any other person who is licensed, certified or otherwise authorized or permitted by the laws of this state to administer health care as the agent shall deem necessary for my physical, mental; and emotional well being; and

    (3)    request, receive and review any information, verbal or written, regarding my personal affairs or physical or mental health including medical and hospital records and to execute any releases of other documents that may be required in order to obtain such information.

In exercising the grant of authority set forth above my agent for health care decisions shall:

_____

_____

*(Here may be inserted any special instructions or statement of the principal's desires to be followed by the agent in exercising the authority granted).*

## Limitations of Authority

    (1)    The powers of the agent herein shall be limited to the extent set out in writing in this durable power of attorney for health care decisions, and shall not include the power to revoke or invalidate any previously existing declaration made in accordance with the natural death act.

    (2)    The agent shall be prohibited from authorizing consent for the following items:

_____

_____

    (3)    This durable power of attorney for health care decisions shall be subject to the additional following limitations:

_____

_____

## Effective Time

This power of attorney for health care decisions shall become effective (check one):

    ☐    immediately and shall not be affected by my subsequent disability or incapacity.

    ☐    upon the occurrence of my disability or incapacity.

## Revocation

Any durable power of attorney for health care decisions I have previously made is hereby revoked.

This durable power of attorney for health care decisions shall be revoked (check one):

☐     by an instrument in writing executed, witnessed or acknowledged in the same manner as required herein.

☐     _____

           (set out another manner of revocation, if desired.)

## Execution

Executed this _____, at _____, Kansas.

_____
Principal

     This document must be: (1) Witnessed by two individuals of lawful age who are not the agent, not related to the principal by blood, marriage or adoption, not entitled to any portion of the principal's estate and not financially responsible for principal's health care; OR (2) acknowledged by a notary public.

_____      _____
Witness                        Witness

_____      _____
Address                       Address

(OR)

STATE OF _____ )

                                SS.

COUNTY OF _____ )

This instrument was acknowledged before me on _____, by _____.

_____
Signature of notary public

(Seal, if any)           My appointment expires: _____

# DECLARATION

Declaration made this _____ day of _____ (month, year). I, _____, being of sound mind, willfully and voluntarily make known my desire that my dying shall not be artificially prolonged under the circumstances set forth below, do hereby declare:

If at any time I should have an incurable injury, disease, or illness certified to be a terminal condition by two physicians who have personally examined me, one of whom shall be my attending physician, and the physicians have determined that my death will occur whether or not life-sustaining procedures are utilized and where the application of life-sustaining procedures would serve only to artificially prolong the dying process, I direct that such procedures be withheld or withdrawn, and that I be permitted to die naturally with only the administration of medication or the performance of any medical procedure deemed necessary to provide me with comfort care.

In the absence of my ability to give directions regarding the use of such life-sustaining procedures, it is my intention that this declaration shall be honored by my family and physician(s) as the final expression of my legal right to refuse medical or surgical treatment and accept the consequences from such refusal.

I understand the full import of this declaration and I am emotionally and mentally competent to make this declaration.

Signed _____

City, County and State of Residence _____

The declarant has been personally known to me and I believe the declarant to be of sound mind. I did not sign the declarant's signature above for or at the direction of the declarant. I am not related to the declarant by blood or marriage, entitled to any portion of the estate of the declarant according to the laws of intestate succession or under any will of declarant or codicil thereto, or directly financially responsible for declarant's medical care.

Witness _____

Witness _____

(OR)

STATE OF _____ )

_____ss.

COUNTY OF _____ )

This instrument was acknowledged before me on _____ (date) by _____ (name of person)

_____
(Signature of notary public)

(Seal, if any)

My appointment expires: _____

# Living Will Directive

My wishes regarding life-prolonging treatment and artificially provided nutrition and hydration to be provided to me if I no longer have decisional capacity, have a terminal condition, or become permanently unconscious have been indicated by checking and initialing the appropriate lines below. By checking and initialing the appropriate lines, I specifically:

_____ Designate _____ as my health care surrogate(s) to make health care decisions for me in accordance with this directive when I no longer have decisional capacity. If _____ refuses or is not able to act for me, I designate _____ as my health care surrogate(s).

Any prior designation is revoked.

If I do not designate a surrogate, the following are my directions to my attending physician. If I have designated a surrogate, my surrogate shall comply with my wishes as indicated below:

_____ Direct that treatment be withheld or withdrawn, and that I be permitted to die naturally with only the administration of medication or the performance of any medical treatment deemed necessary to alleviate pain.

_____ DO NOT authorize that life-prolonging treatment be withheld or withdrawn.

_____ Authorize the withholding or withdrawal of artificially provided food, water, or other artificially provided nourishment or fluids.

_____ DO NOT authorize the withholding or withdrawal of artificially provided food, water, or other artificially provided nourishment or fluids.

_____ Authorize my surrogate, designated above, to withhold or withdraw artificially provided nourishment or fluids, or other treatment if the surrogate determines that withholding or withdrawing is in my best interest; but I do not mandate that withholding or withdrawing.

_____ Authorize the giving of all or any part of my body upon death for any purpose specified in KRS 311.185.

_____ DO NOT authorize the giving of all or any part of my body upon death.

In the absence of my ability to give direction regarding the use of life-prolonging treatment and artificially provided nutrition and hydration, it is my intention that this directive shall be honored by my attending physician, my family, and any surrogate designated pursuant to this directive as the final expression of my legal right to refuse medical or surgical treatment and I accept the consequences of the refusal.

If I have been diagnosed as pregnant and that diagnosis is known to my attending physician, this directive shall have no force or effect during the course of my pregnancy.

I understand the full import of this directive and I am emotionally and mentally competent to make this directive.

Signed this _____ day of _____, 200_____.

_____
Signature

_____

Address

In our joint presence, the grantor, who is of sound mind and eighteen (18) years of age, or older, voluntarily dated and signed this writing or directed it to be dated and signed for the grantor.

_____     _____

Signature of witness                Signature of witness

_____     _____

Address                             Address

OR

STATE OF KENTUCKY                    )

_____ COUNTY )

Before me, the undersigned authority, came the grantor who is of sound mind and eighteen (18) years of age, or older, and acknowledged that he voluntarily dated and signed this writing or directed it to be signed and dated as above.

Done this _____ day of _____, 200_____.

_____

Signature of Notary Public or other officer

Date commission expires: _____

Execution of this document restricts withholding and withdrawing of some medical procedures. Consult Kentucky Revised Statutes or your attorney.

# DECLARATION

Declaration made this _____ day of _____, _____ (month, year).

I, _____, being of sound mind, willfully and voluntarily make known my desire that my dying shall not be artificially prolonged under the circumstances set forth below and do hereby declare:

If at any time I should have an incurable injury, disease or illness, or be in a continual profound comatose state with no reasonable chance of recovery, certified to be a terminal and irreversible condition by two physicians who have personally examined me, one of whom shall be my attending physician, and the physicians have determined that my death will occur whether or not life-sustaining procedures are utilized and where the application of life-sustaining procedure would serve only to prolong artificially the dying process, I direct (initial one only):

___That all life-sustaining procedures, including nutrition and hydration, be withheld or withdrawn so that food and water will not be administered invasively.

___That life-sustaining procedures, except nutrition and hydration, be withheld or withdrawn so that food and water can be administered invasively.

I further direct that I be permitted to die naturally with only the administration of medication or the performance of any medical procedure deemed necessary to provide me with comfort care.

In the absence of my ability to give directions regarding the use of such life-sustaining procedures, it is my intention that this declaration shall be honored by my family and physician(s) as the final expression of my legal right to refuse medical or surgical treatment and accept the consequences from such refusal.

I understand the full import of this declaration and I am emotionally and mentally competent to make this declaration.

Signed _____

City, Parish, and State of Residence _____

The declarant has been personally known to me and I believe him or her to be of sound mind.

Witness _____

Witness _____

## Durable Financial Power of Attorney

Notice to the Principal: As the "Principal," you are using this Durable Power of Attorney to grant power to another person (called the "Agent" or "Attorney-in-fact") to make decisions about your money, property or both and to use your money, property or both on your behalf. If this written Durable Power of Attorney does not limit the powers that you give your Agent, your Agent will have broad and sweeping powers to sell or otherwise dispose of your property and spend your money without advance notice to you or approval by you. Under this document, your Agent will continue to have these powers after you become incapacitated, and you may also choose to authorize your Agent to use these powers before you become incapacitated. The powers that you give your Agent are explained more fully in the Maine Revised Statutes, Title 18-A, sections 5-501 to 5-508 and in Maine case law. You have the right to revoke or take back this Durable Power of Attorney at any time as long as you are of sound mind. If there is anything about this Durable Power of Attorney that you do not understand, you should ask a lawyer to explain it to you.

Notice to the Agent: As the "Agent" or "Attorney-in-fact," you are given power under this Durable Power of Attorney to make decisions about the money, property or both belonging to the Principal and to spend the Principal's money, property or both on that person's behalf in accordance with the terms of this Durable Power of Attorney. This Durable Power of Attorney is valid only if the Principal is of sound mind when the Principal signs it. As the Agent, you are under a duty (called a "fiduciary duty") to observe the standards observed by a prudent person dealing with the property of another. The duty is explained more fully in the Maine Revised Statutes, Title 18-A, sections 5-501 to 5-508 and 7-302 and in Maine case law. As the Agent, you are not entitled to use the money or property for your own benefit or to make gifts to yourself or others unless the Durable Power of Attorney specifically gives you the authority to do so. As the Agent, your authority under this Durable Power of Attorney will end when the Principal dies and you will not have the authority to administer the estate unless you are authorized to do so in accordance with the Maine Probate Code. If you violate your fiduciary duty under this Durable Power of Attorney, you may be liable for damages and may be subject to criminal prosecution. If there is anything about this Durable Power of Attorney or your duties under it that you do not understand, you should ask a lawyer to explain it to you.

This language does not confer powers not otherwise contained in the durable financial power of attorney.

# Advance Health-Care Directive

## Explanation

You have the right to give instructions about your own health care. You also have the right to name someone else to make health-care decisions for you. This form lets you do either or both of these things. It also lets you express your wishes regarding donation of organs and the designation of your primary physician. If you use this form, you may complete or modify all or any part of it. You are free to use a different form.

Part 1 of this form is a power of attorney for health care. Part 1 lets you name another individual as agent to make health-care decisions for you if you become incapable of making your own decisions or if you want someone else to make those decisions for you now even though you are still capable. You may also name an alternate agent to act for you if your first choice is not willing, able or reasonably available to make decisions for you. Unless related to you, your agent may not be an owner, operator or employee of a residential long-term health-care institution at which you are receiving care.

Unless the form you sign limits the authority of your agent, your agent may make all health-care decisions for you. This form has a place for you to limit the authority of your agent. You need not limit the authority of your agent if you wish to rely on your agent for all health-care decisions that may have to be made. If you choose not to limit the authority of your agent, your agent will have the right to:

    (a)     Consent or refuse consent to any care, treatment, service or procedure to maintain, diagnose or otherwise affect a physical or mental condition;

    (b)     Select or discharge health-care providers and institutions;

    (c)     Approve or disapprove diagnostic tests, surgical procedures, programs of medication and orders not to resuscitate; and

    (d)     Direct the provision, withholding or withdrawal of artificial nutrition and hydration and all other forms of health care, including life-sustaining treatment.

Part 2 of this form lets you give specific instructions about any aspect of your health care. Choices are provided for you to express your wishes regarding the provision, withholding or withdrawal of treatment to keep you alive, including the provision of artificial nutrition and hydration, as well as the provision of pain relief. Space is also provided for you to add to the choices you have made or for you to write out any additional wishes.

Part 3 of this form lets you express an intention to donate your bodily organs and tissues following your death.

Part 4 of this form lets you designate a physician to have primary responsibility for your health care.

After completing this form, sign and date the form at the end. You must have 2 other individuals sign as witnesses. Give a copy of the signed and completed form to your physician, to any other health-care providers you may have, to any health-care institution at which you are receiving care and to any health-care agents you have named. You should talk to the person you have named as agent to make sure that he or she understands your wishes and is willing to take the responsibility.

You have the right to revoke this advance health-care directive or replace this form at any time.

\*    \*    \*    \*    \*    \*    \*    \*    \*    \*    \*    \*    \*    \*    \*    \*    \*    \*    \*

# PART 1.  POWER OF ATTORNEY FOR HEALTH CARE

(1)      DESIGNATION OF AGENT:  I designate the following individual as my agent to make health-care decisions for me:

_____
(name of individual you choose as agent)


_____
(address)                    (city)                    (state)          (zip code)


_____
(home phone)                                (work phone)

OPTIONAL:   If I revoke my agent's authority or if my agent is not willing, able or reasonably available to make a health-care decision for me, I designate as my first alternate agent:

_____
(name of individual you choose as first alternate agent)


_____
(address)                    (city)                    (state)          (zip code)


_____
(home phone)                                (work phone)

OPTIONAL:  If I revoke the authority of my agent and first alternate agent or if neither is willing, able or reasonably available to make a health-care decision for me, I designate as my second alternate agent:



_____
(name of individual you choose as second alternate agent)


_____
(address)                    (city)                    (state)          (zip code)


_____
(home phone)                                (work phone)

(2)      AGENT'S AUTHORITY:   My agent is authorized to make all health-care decisions for me, including decisions to provide, withhold or withdraw artificial nutrition and hydration and all other forms of health care to keep me alive, except as I state here:
_____
_____
_____
(Add additional sheets if needed)

(3)      WHEN AGENT'S AUTHORITY BECOMES EFFECTIVE:  My agent's authority becomes effective when my primary physician determines that I am unable to make my own health-care decisions unless I mark the following box.  If I mark this box [      ], my agent's authority to make health-care decisions for me takes effect immediately.

(4)      AGENT'S OBLIGATION:  My agent shall make health-care decisions for me in accordance with this power of attorney for health care, any instructions I give in Part 2 of this form and my other wishes to the extent known to my agent.  To the extent my wishes are unknown, my

agent shall make health-care decisions for me in accordance with what my agent determines to be in my best interest. In determining my best interest, my agent shall consider my personal values to the extent known to my agent.

(5)     NOMINATION OF GUARDIAN:   If a guardian of my person needs to be appointed for me by a court, I nominate the agent designated in this form.  If that agent is not willing, able or reasonably available to act as guardian, I nominate the alternate agents whom I have named, in the order designated.

## PART 2.  INSTRUCTIONS FOR HEALTH CARE

If you are satisfied to allow your agent to determine what is best for you in making end-of-life decisions, you need not fill out this part of the form.  If you do fill out this part of the form, you may strike any wording you do not want.

(6)     END-OF-LIFE DECISIONS:  I direct that my health-care providers and others involved in my care provide, withhold or withdraw treatment in accordance with the choice I have marked below:

[ ]     (a)     Choice Not To Prolong Life:  I do not want my life to be prolonged if (i) I have an incurable and irreversible condition that will result in my death within a relatively short time, (ii) I become unconscious and, to a reasonable degree of medical certainty, I will not regain consciousness, or (iii) the likely risks and burdens of treatment would outweigh the expected benefits, OR

[ ]     (b)     Choice To Prolong Life:  I want my life to be prolonged as long as possible within the limits of generally accepted health-care standards.

(7)     ARTIFICIAL NUTRITION AND HYDRATION:  Artificial nutrition and hydration must be provided, withheld or withdrawn in accordance with the choice I have made in paragraph (6) unless I mark the following box.  If I mark this box [ ], artificial nutrition and hydration must be provided regardless of my condition and regardless of the choice I have made in paragraph (6).

(8)     RELIEF FROM PAIN:  Except as I state in the following space, I direct that treatment for alleviation of pain or discomfort be provided at all times, even if it hastens my death:

_____

_____

(9)     OTHER WISHES:  (If you do not agree with any of the optional choices above and wish to write your own, or if you wish to add to the instructions you have given above, you may do so here.)  I direct that:

_____

_____

(Add additional sheets if needed)

## PART 3.  DONATION OF ORGANS AT DEATH (OPTIONAL)

(10)    Upon my death (mark applicable box)

[ ]     (a)     I give needed organs, tissues or parts OR

[ ]     (b)     I give the following organs, tissues or parts only

_____

[ ]     (c)     My gift is for the following purposes (strike any of the following you do not want)

(i)     Transplant         (iii)    Research

(ii)    Therapy            (iv)    Education

## PART 4.  PRIMARY PHYSICIAN (OPTIONAL)

(11)     I designate the following physician as my primary physician:

_____
(name of physician)                                            (phone)

_____
(address)                    (city)                    (state)        (zip code)

OPTIONAL:  If the physician I have designated above is not willing, able or reasonably available to act as my primary physician, I designate the following physician as my primary physician:

_____
(name of physician)                                            (phone)

_____
(address)                    (city)                    (state)        (zip code)

\*   \*   \*   \*   \*   \*   \*   \*   \*   \*   \*   \*   \*   \*   \*   \*   \*

(12)     EFFECT OF COPY:  A copy of this form has the same effect as the original.

(13)     SIGNATURES:  Sign and date the form here:

_____        _____
(date)                                              (sign your name)

_____        _____
(address)                                          (print your name)

_____
(city)                    (state)

SIGNATURES OF WITNESSES:

First witness                                      Second witness

_____        _____
(print name)                                        (print name)

_____        _____
(address)                                            (address)

_____        _____
(city)                    (state)                    (city)                    (state)

_____        _____
(signature of witness)                        (signature of witness)

_____        _____
(date)                                              (date)

# Health Care Decision Making Forms

The following forms allow you to make some decisions about future health care issues. Form I, called a "Living Will," allows you to make decisions about life-sustaining procedures if, in the future, your death from a terminal condition is imminent despite the application of life-sustaining procedures or you are in a persistent vegetative state. Form II, called an "Advance Directive," allows you to select a health care agent, give health care instructions, or both. If you use the advance directive, you can make decisions about life-sustaining procedures in the event of terminal condition, persistent vegetative state, or end-stage condition. You can also use the advance directive to make any other health care decisions.

These forms are intended to be guides. You can use one form or both, and you may complete all or only part of the forms that you use. Different forms may also be used.

Please note: If you decide to select a health care agent that person may not be a witness to your advance directive. Also, at least one of your witnesses may not be a person who may financially benefit by reason of your death.

## Form I
## Living Will
## (Optional Form)

If I am not able to make an informed decision regarding my health care, I direct my health care providers to follow my instructions as set forth below. (Initial those statements you wish to be included in the document and cross through those statements which do not apply.)

a.　If my death from a terminal condition is imminent and even if life-sustaining procedures are used there is no reasonable expectation of my recovery—

_____ I direct that my life not be extended by life-sustaining procedures, including the administration of nutrition and hydration artificially.

_____ I direct that my life not be extended by life-sustaining procedures, except that, if I am unable to take food by mouth, I wish to receive nutrition and hydration artificially.

_____ I direct that, even in a terminal condition, I be given all available medical treatment in accordance with accepted health care standards.

b.　If I am in a persistent vegetative state, that is if I am not conscious and am not aware of my environment nor able to interact with others, and there is no reasonable expectation of my recovery within a medically appropriate period—

_____ I direct that my life not be extended by life-sustaining procedures, including the administration of nutrition and hydration artificially.

_____ I direct that my life not be extended by life-sustaining procedures, except that, if I am unable to take food by mouth, I wish to receive nutrition and hydration artificially.

_____ I direct that I be given all available medical treatment in accordance with accepted health care standards.

c.　If I am pregnant my agent shall follow these specific instructions: _____

_____

_____

_____

d.　Upon my death, I wish to donate:

_____ Any needed organs, tissues, or eyes.

_____ Only the following organs, tissues, or eyes: _____

I authorize the use of my organs, tissues, or eyes:
\_\_\_\_ For transplantation
\_\_\_\_ For therapy
\_\_\_\_ For research
\_\_\_\_ For medical education
\_\_\_\_ For any purpose authorized by law.

I understand that before any vital organ, tissue, or eye may be removed for transplantation, I must be pronounced dead. After death, I direct that all support measures be continued to maintain the viability for transplantation of my organs, tissues, and eyes until organ, tissue, and eye recovery has been completed.

I understand that my estate will not be charged for any costs associated with my decision to donate my organs, tissues, or eyes or the actual disposition of my organs, tissues, or eyes.

By signing below, I indicate that I am emotionally and mentally competent to make this living will and that I understand its purpose and effect.

_____    _____
(Date)    (Signature of Declarant)

The declarant signed or acknowledged signing this living will in my presence and based upon my personal observation the declarant appears to be a competent individual.

_____    _____
(Witness)    (Witness)

(Signature of Two Witnesses)

## Form II
## Advance Directive

### Part A
### Appointment of Health Care Agent
### (Optional Form)

(Cross through if you do not want to appoint a health care agent to make health care decisions for you.  If you do want to appoint an agent, cross through any items in the form that you do not want to apply.)

(1)    I, _____, residing at _____ _____, appoint the following individual as my agent to make health care decisions for me_____ _____
(Full Name, Address, and Telephone Number)

Optional:  If this agent is unavailable or is unable or unwilling to act as my agent, then I appoint the following person to act in this capacity _____
_____
(Full Name, Address, and Telephone Number)

(2)    In accordance with the Health Insurance Portability and Accountability Act, a health care agent is a personal representative and is entitled to request and receive protected health information.

(3)     My agent has full power and authority to make health care decisions for me, including the power to:

      a.     In accordance with the Health Insurance Portability and Accountability Act and as mypersonal representative, request, receive, and review any information, oral or written, regarding my physical or mental health, including, but not limited to, medical and hospital records, and other protected health information, and consent to disclosure of this information;

      b.     Employ and discharge my health care providers;

      c.     Authorize my admission to or discharge from (including transfer to another facility) any hospital, hospice, nursing home, adult home, or other medical care facility; and

      d.     Consent to the provision, withholding, or withdrawal of health care, including, in appropriate circumstances, life-sustaining procedures.

(4)     The authority of my agent is subject to the following provisions and limitations:-_____

_____

_____

_____

(5)     My agent's authority becomes operative (initial the option that applies):

_____ When my attending physician and a second physician determine that I am incapable of making an informed decision regarding my health care, provided however, when this document is signed, each individual identified in paragraph (1) is, in accordance with the Health Insurance Portability and Accountability Act, my personal representative for all purposes related to any assessment of my capacity to make an informed decision regarding my health care; or

_____ When this document is signed.

(6)     My agent is to make health care decisions for me based on the health care instructions I give in this document and on my wishes as otherwise known to my agent. If my wishes are unknown or unclear, my agent is to make health care decisions for me in accordance with my best interest, to be determined by my agent after considering the benefits, burdens, and risks that might result from a given treatment or course of treatment, or from the withholding or withdrawal of a treatment or course of treatment.

(7)     My agent shall not be liable for the costs of care based solely on this authorization.

      By signing below, I indicate that I am emotionally and mentally competent to make this appointment of a health care agent and that I understand its purpose and effect.

_____      _____
         (Date)                           (Signature of Declarant)

      The declarant signed or acknowledged signing this appointment of a health care agent in my presence and based upon my personal observation appears to be a competent individual.

_____      _____
       (Witness)                            (Witness)

(Signature of Two Witnesses)

# Part B
## Advance Medical Directive
## Health Care Instructions
## (Optional Form)

(Cross through if you do not want to complete this portion of the form. If you do want to complete this portion of the form, initial those statements you want to be included in the document and cross through those statements that do not apply.)

If I am incapable of making an informed decision regarding my health care, I direct my health care providers to follow my instructions as set forth below.
(Initial all those that apply.)

(1)     If my death from a terminal condition is imminent and even if life-sustaining procedures are used there is no reasonable expectation of my recovery—
_____ I direct that my life not be extended by life-sustaining procedures, including the administration of nutrition and hydration artificially.
_____ I direct that my life not be extended by life-sustaining procedures, except that, if I am unable to take food by mouth, I wish to receive nutrition and hydration artificially.

(2)     If I am in a persistent vegetative state, that is, if I am not conscious and am not aware of my environment or able to interact with others, and there is no reasonable expectation of my recovery —
_____ I direct that my life not be extended by life-sustaining procedures, including the administration of nutrition and hydration artificially.
_____ I direct that my life not be extended by life-sustaining procedures, except that, if I am unable to take food by mouth, I wish to receive nutrition and hydration artificially.

(3)     If I have an end-stage condition, that is a condition caused by injury, disease, or illness, as a result of which I have suffered severe and permanent deterioration indicated by incompetency and complete physical dependency and for which, to a reasonable degree of medical certainty, treatment of the irreversible condition would be medically ineffective—
_____ I direct that my life not be extended by life-sustaining procedures, including the administration of nutrition and hydration artificially.
_____ I direct that my life not be extended by life-sustaining procedures, except that, if I am unable to take food by mouth, I wish to receive nutrition and hydration artificially.

(4)     I direct that no matter what my condition, medication not be given to me to relieve pain and suffering, if it would shorten my remaining life.

(5)     I direct that no matter what my condition, I be given all available medical treatment in accordance with accepted health care standards.

(6)     If I am pregnant, my decision concerning life-sustaining procedures shall be modified as follows: _____
_____

(7)     Upon my death, I wish to donate:
\_\_\_\_ Any needed organs, tissues, or eyes.
\_\_\_\_ Only the following organs, tissues, or eyes: _____

I authorize the use of my organs, tissues, or eyes:
_____ For transplantation
_____ For therapy
_____ For research
_____ For medical education
_____ For any purpose authorized by law.

      I understand that before any vital organ, tissue, or eye may be removed for transplantation, I must be pronounced dead. After death, I direct that all support measures be continued to maintain the viability for transplantation of my organs, tissues, and eyes until organ, tissue, and eye recovery has been completed.

      I understand that my estate will not be charged for any costs associated with my decision to donate my organs, tissues, or eyes or the actual disposition of my organs, tissues, or eyes.

(8)     I direct (in the following space, indicate any other instructions regarding receipt or nonreceipt of any health care) _____

_____

_____

      By signing below, I indicate that I am emotionally and mentally competent to make this advance directive and that I understand the purpose and effect of this document.

_____      _____
(Date)              (Signature of Declarant)

      The declarant signed or acknowledged signing the foregoing advance directive in my presence and based upon personal observation appears to be a competent individual.

_____      _____
(Witness)             (Witness)

(Signature of Two Witnesses)

## Designation of Patient Advocate and Living Will

I, _____, appoint _____,
whose address is _____,
and whose telephone number is _____, as my patient advocate
pursuant to M.C.L.A., Section 700.5506, et seq. If said patient advocate is unable or unwilling to act,
then I appoint _____, whose address is _____
_____ and whose telephone number is _____, as
my successor patient advocate. I authorize my patient advocate to make medical or mental health
treatment decisions for me when I am unable to participate in medical or mental health decisions,
including decisions to withhold or withdraw medical treatment, even if such withholding or withdrawal
could or would allow me to die. I understand the consequences of appointing a patient advocate.

I direct that my patient advocate comply with the following instructions or limitations:

_____
_____
_____

I also direct that my patient advocate have the authority to make decisions regarding the
enforcement of my intentions regarding life-prolonging procedures as stated below:

I, _____, being of sound mind, willfully and voluntarily
make known my desire that my dying shall not be artificially prolonged under the circumstances set
forth below:

If I should have an incurable or irreversible condition that will cause my death within a
relatively short time, and if I am unable to make decisions regarding my medical treatment, I direct my
attending physician to withhold or withdraw procedures that merely prolong the dying process and are
not necessary to my comfort, or to alleviate pain.

This authorization [check only one box]  ☐ includes     ☐ does not include
the withholding or withdrawal of artificial feeding and hydration.

With respect to mental health treatment decision, I [check only one box] ☐ do  ☐ do not waive
my right to revoke this designation of patient advocate

Anatomical Gifts: In the event of my death, my patient advocate shall have the authority to
make an anatomical gift. Upon my death, I wish to donate:
_____ Any needed organs, tissues, or eyes.
_____ Only the following organs, tissues, or eyes: _____

I authorize the use of my organs, tissues, or eyes:
_____ For transplantation
_____ For therapy
_____ For research
_____ For medical education
_____ For any purpose authorized by law.

I understand that before any vital organ, tissue, or eye may be removed for transplantation, I
must be pronounced dead. After death, I direct that all support measures be continued to maintain the
viability for transplantation of my organs, tissues, and eyes until organ, tissue, and eye recovery has
been completed. I understand that my estate will not be charged for any costs associated with my
decision to donate my organs, tissues, or eyes or the actual disposition of my organs, tissues, or eyes.

The authority conferred by this document is exercisable only when I am unable to participate
in medical or mental health treatment decisions and, in the case of the authority to make an anatomical
gift the authority remains exercisable after my death.

Signed this _____ day of _____, 20___.

_____
Signature
Address: _____
_____

The declarant is personally known to me, voluntarily signed this document in my presence, and appeared to be of sound mind and under no duress, fraud, or undue influence.

Witness: _____       Witness: _____

Name: _____       Name: _____

Address: _____       Address: _____

### Acceptance of Patient Advocate

I, _____, hereby accept the designation of Patient Advocate for _____and understand that:

    1.    This designation is not effective unless the patient is unable to participate in decisions regarding the patient's medical or mental health, as applicable. If this patient advocate designation includes the authority to make an anatomical gift as described in section 5506, the authority remains exercisable after the patient's death.

    2.    A patient advocate shall not exercise powers concerning the patient's care, custody, and medical or mental health treatment that the patient, if the patient were able to participate in the decision, could not have exercised on his or her own behalf.

    3.    This patient advocate designation cannot be used to make a medical treatment decision to withhold or withdraw treatment from a patient who is pregnant that would result in the pregnant patient's death.

    4.    A patient advocate may make a decision to withhold or withdraw treatment that would allow a patient to die only if the patient has expressed in a clear and convincing manner that the patient advocate is authorized to make such a decision, and that the patient acknowledges that such a decision could or would allow the patient's death.

    5.    A patient advocate shall not receive compensation for the performance of his or her authority, rights, and responsibilities, but a patient advocate may be reimbursed for actual and necessary expenses incurred in the performance of his or her authority, rights, and responsibilities.

    6.    A patient advocate shall act in accordance with the standards of care applicable to fiduciaries when acting for the patient and shall act consistent with the patient's best interests. The known desires of the patient expressed or evidenced while the patient is able to participate in medical or mental health treatment decisions are presumed to be in the patient's best interests.

    7.    A patient may revoke his or her designation at any time and in any manner sufficient to communicate an intent to revoke.

    8.    A patient may waive his or her right to revoke the patient advocate designation as to the power to make mental health treatment decisions, and if such a waiver is make, his or her ability to revoke as to certain treatment will be delayed for 30 days after the patient communicates his or her intent to revoke.

    9.    A patient advocate may revoke his or her acceptance to the designation at any time and in any manner sufficient to communicate an intent to revoke.

    10.    A patient admitted to a health facility or agency has the rights enumerated in section 20201 of the public health code, 1978 PA 368, MCL 333.20201.

Date: _____       _____
                                                       (Signature)

## STATUTORY SHORT FORM POWER OF ATTORNEY
## MINNESOTA STATUTES, SECTION 523.23

**IMPORTANT NOTICE: The powers granted by this document are broad and sweeping. They are defined in Minnesota Statutes, section 523.24. If you have any questions about these powers, obtain competent advice. This power of attorney may be revoked by you if you wish to do so. This power of attorney is automatically terminated if it is to your spouse and proceedings are commenced for dissolution, legal separation, or annulment of your marriage. This power of attorney authorizes, but does not require, the attorney-in-fact to act for you.**

PRINCIPAL (Name and Address of Person Granting the Power)

_____

ATTORNEY(S)-IN-FACT
(Name and Address)

SUCCESSOR ATTORNEY(S)-IN-FACT
(Optional) To act if any named attorney-in-fact dies, resigns, or is otherwise unable to serve.
(Name and Address)

First Successor _____

_____     _____
_____
_____     Second Successor _____
_____
_____     _____
_____

NOTICE:  If more than one attorney-in-fact is designated, make a check or "x" on the line in front of one of the following statements:

_____     Each attorney-in-fact may independently exercise the powers granted.

EXPIRATION DATE (Optional)
_____, _____
Use Specific Month  Day  Year Only

_____     All attorneys-in-fact must jointly exercise the powers granted.

I, (the above-named Principal) hereby appoint the above named Attorney(s)-in-Fact to act as my attorney(s)-in-fact:

FIRST: To act for me in any way that I could act with respect to the following matters, as each of them is defined in Minnesota Statutes, section 523.24:

(To grant to the attorney-in-fact any of the following powers, make a check or "x" on the line in front of each power being granted. You may, but need not, cross out each power not granted. Failure to make a check or "x" on the line in front of the power will have the effect of deleting the power unless the line in front of the power of (N) is checked or x-ed.)

Check or "x"

_____ (A)     real property transactions;
         I choose to limit this power to real property in _____ County, Minnesota,
described as follows: (Use legal description.  Do not use street address.)
         (If more space is needed, continue on the back or on an attachment.)
_____ (B)     tangible personal property transactions;
_____ (C)     bond, share, and commodity transactions;
_____ (D)     banking transactions;
_____ (E)     business operating transactions;
_____ (F)     insurance transactions;
_____ (G)     beneficiary transactions;
_____ (H)     gift transactions;
_____ (I)     fiduciary transactions;
_____ (J)     claims and litigation;
_____ (K)     family maintenance;
_____ (L)     benefits from military service;
_____ (M)     records, reports, and statements;
_____ (N)     all of the powers listed in (A) through (M) above and all other matters.

SECOND: (You must indicate below whether or not this power of attorney will be
         effective if you become incapacitated or incompetent. Make a check or "x" on
         the line in front of the statement that expresses your intent.)

_____ This power of attorney shall continue to be effective if I become incapacitated or
incompetent.

_____ This power of attorney shall not be effective if I become incapacitated or
incompetent.

THIRD: (You must indicate below whether or not this power of attorney authorizes the
         attorney-in-fact to transfer your property to the attorney-in-fact. Make a check or
         "x" on the line in front of the statement that expresses your intent.)

_____ This power of attorney authorizes the attorney-in-fact to transfer my property to
the attorney-in-fact.

_____ This power of attorney does not authorize the attorney-in-fact to transfer my
property to the attorney-in-fact.

FOURTH: (You may indicate below whether the attorney-in-fact is required to make an
         accounting. Make a check or "x" on the line in front of the statement that
         expresses your intent.)

_____ My attorney-in-fact need not render an accounting unless I request it or the
accounting is otherwise required by Minnesota Statutes, section 523.21.
_____ My attorney-in-fact must render _____
                                         (Monthly, Quarterly, Annual)
accountings to me or _____
                              (Name and Address)
during my lifetime, and a final accounting to the personal representative of my estate, if
any is a Appointed, after my death.

In Witness Whereof I have hereunto signed my name this _____ day of _____, 20____.

_____
(Signature of Principal)

(Acknowledgment of Principal)

STATE OF MINNESOTA    )
                                         )ss.
COUNTY OF                  )

The foregoing instrument was acknowledged before me this _____ day of _____, _____, by _____
　　　　　　　(Insert Name of Principal)

_____
(Signature of Notary Public or other Official)

This instrument was drafted by:

Specimen Signature of Attorney(s)-in-Fact
(Notarization not required)

_____          _____

_____          _____

_____          _____

# Health Care Directive

I, _____, understand this document allows me to do ONE OR BOTH of the following:

PART I: Name another person (called the health care agent) to make health care decisions for me if I am unable to decide or speak for myself.  My health care agent must make health care decisions for me based on the instructions I provide in this document (Part II), if any, the wishes I have made known to him or her, or must act in my best interest if I have not made my health care wishes known.

AND/OR

PART II: Give health care instructions to guide others making health care decisions for me.  If I have named a health care agent, these instructions are to be used by the agent. These instructions may also be used by my health care providers, others assisting with my health care and my family, in the event I cannot make decisions for myself.

## PART I:  APPOINTMENT OF HEALTH CARE AGENT

THIS IS WHO I WANT TO MAKE HEALTH CARE DECISIONS FOR ME IF I AM UNABLE TO DECIDE OR SPEAK FOR MYSELF

(I know I can change my agent or alternate agent at any time and I know I do not have to appoint an agent or an alternate agent)

NOTE: If you appoint an agent, you should discuss this health care directive with your agent and give your agent a copy. If you do not wish to appoint an agent, you may leave Part I blank and go to Part II.

When I am unable to decide or speak for myself, I trust and appoint _____
_____ to make health care decisions for me. This person is called my health care agent.

Relationship of my health care agent to me: _____

Telephone number of my health care agent: _____

Address of my health care agent: _____

(OPTIONAL) APPOINTMENT OF ALTERNATE HEALTH CARE AGENT:  If my health care agent is not reasonably available, I trust and appoint _____ to be my health care agent instead.

Relationship of my alternate health care agent to me: _____

Telephone number of my alternate health care agent: _____

Address of my alternate health care agent: _____

THIS IS WHAT I WANT MY HEALTH CARE AGENT TO BE ABLE TO DO IF I AM UNABLE TO DECIDE OR SPEAK FOR MYSELF (I know I can change these choices)

My health care agent is automatically given the powers listed below in (A) through (D).  My health care agent must follow my health care instructions in this document or any other instructions I have given to my agent. If I have not given health care instructions, then my agent must act in my best interest.

Whenever I am unable to decide or speak for myself, my health care agent has the power to:

(A) Make any health care decision for me. This includes the power to give, refuse, or withdraw consent to any care, treatment, service, or procedures. This includes deciding whether to stop or not start health care that is keeping me or might keep me alive, and deciding about intrusive mental health treatment.

(B) Choose my health care providers.

(C) Choose where I live and receive care and support when those choices relate to my health care needs.

(D) Review my medical records and have the same rights that I would have to give my medical records to other people.

If I DO NOT want my health care agent to have a power listed above in (A) through (D) OR if I want to LIMIT any power in (A) through (D), I MUST say that here:

_____

_____

My health care agent is NOT automatically given the powers listed below in (1) and (2). If I WANT my agent to have any of the powers in (1) and (2), I must INITIAL the line in front of the power; then my agent WILL HAVE that power.

_____ (1) To decide whether to donate any parts of my body, including organs, tissues, and eyes, when I die.

_____ (2) To decide what will happen with my body when I die (burial, cremation).

If I want to say anything more about my health care agent's powers or limits on the powers, I can say it here:

_____

_____

## PART II: HEALTH CARE INSTRUCTIONS

NOTE: Complete this Part II if you wish to give health care instructions. If you appointed an agent in Part I, completing this Part II is optional but would be very helpful to your agent. However, if you chose not to appoint an agent in Part I, you MUST complete some or all of this Part II if you wish to make a valid health care directive. These are instructions for my health care when I am unable to decide or speak for myself. These instructions must be followed (so long as they address my needs).

THESE ARE MY BELIEFS AND VALUES ABOUT MY HEALTH CARE (I know I can change these choices or leave any of them blank)

I want you to know these things about me to help you make decisions about my health care:

My goals for my health care: _____

_____

My fears about my health care: _____

_____

My spiritual or religious beliefs and traditions: _____

_____

My beliefs about when life would be no longer worth living: _____

_____

My thoughts about how my medical condition might affect my family: _____

_____

THIS IS WHAT I WANT AND DO NOT WANT FOR MY HEALTH CARE (I know I can change these choices or leave any of them blank)

Many medical treatments may be used to try to improve my medical condition or to prolong my life. Examples include artificial breathing by a machine connected to a tube in the lungs, artificial feeding or fluids through tubes, attempts to start a stopped heart, surgeries, dialysis, antibiotics, and blood transfusions. Most medical treatments can be tried for a while and then stopped if they do not help.

I have these views about my health care in these situations: (Note: You can discuss general feelings, specific treatments, or leave any of them blank)

If I had a reasonable chance of recovery, and were temporarily unable to decide or speak for myself, I would want: _____

_____

If I were dying and unable to decide or speak for myself, I would want: _____

_____

If I were permanently unconscious and unable to decide or speak for myself, I would want: _____

_____

If I were completely dependent on others for my care and unable to decide or speak for myself, I would want:

_____

In all circumstances, my doctors will try to keep me comfortable and reduce my pain.  This is how I feel about pain relief if it would affect my alertness or if it could shorten my life: _____

_____

There are other things that I want or do not want for my health care, if possible:

Who I would like to be my doctor: _____

_____

Where I would like to live to receive health care: _____

_____

Where I would like to die and other wishes I have about dying: _____

_____

My wishes about donating parts of my body when I die: _____

_____

My wishes about what happens to my body when I die (cremation, burial): _____

_____

Any other things: _____

_____

## PART III:  MAKING THE DOCUMENT LEGAL

This document must be signed by me.  It also must either be verified by a notary public (Option 1) OR witnessed by two witnesses (Option 2). It must be dated when it is verified or witnessed.

I am thinking clearly, I agree with everything that is written in this document, and I have made this document willingly.

_____
My Signature

Date signed: _____

Date of birth: _____

Address: _____

If I cannot sign my name, I can ask someone to sign this document for me.

_____
Signature of the person who I asked to sign this document for me.

_____
Printed name of the person who I asked to sign this document for me.

## Option 1: Notary Public

In my presence on _____ (date), _____ (name) acknowledged his/her signature on this document or acknowledged that he/she authorized the person signing this document to sign on his/her behalf. I am not named as a health care agent or alternate health care agent in this document.

_____
(Signature of Notary)

(Notary Stamp)

## Option 2: Two Witnesses

Two witnesses must sign.  Only one of the two witnesses can be a health care provider or an employee of a health care provider giving direct care to me on the day I sign this document.

Witness One:

(i) In my presence on _____ [date], _____ [name] acknowledged his/her signature on this document or acknowledged that he/she authorized the person signing this document to sign on his/her behalf.
(ii) I am at least 18 years of age.
(iii) I am not named as a health care agent or an alternate health care agent in this document.
(iv) If I am a health care provider or an employee of a health care provider giving direct care to the person listed above in (A), I must initial this box: [      ]
I certify that the information in (i) through (iv) is true and correct.

_____
(Signature of Witness One)

Address: _____

Witness Two:

(i) In my presence on _____ [date], _____ [name] acknowledged his/her signature on this document or acknowledged that he/she authorized the person signing this document to sign on his/her behalf.
(ii) I am at least 18 years of age.
(iii) I am not named as a health care agent or an alternate health care agent in this document.
(iv) If I am a health care provider or an employee of a health care provider giving direct care to the person listed above in (A), I must initial this box: [      ]
I certify that the information in (i) through (iv) is true and correct.

_____
(Signature of Witness Two)

Address: _____

REMINDER: Keep this document with your personal papers in a safe place (not in a safe deposit box). Give signed copies to your doctors, family, close friends, health care agent, and alternate health care agent. Make sure your doctor is willing to follow your wishes. This document should be part of your medical record at your physician's office and at the hospital, home care agency, hospice, or nursing facility where you receive your care.

## ADVANCE HEALTH CARE DIRECTIVE

### Explanation

You have the right to give instructions about your own health care. You also have the right to name someone else to make health care decisions for you. This form lets you do either or both of these things. It also lets you express your wishes regarding the designation of your primary physician. If you use this form, you may complete or modify all or any part of it. You are free to use a different form.

Part 1 of this form is a power of attorney for health care. Part 1 lets you name another individual as agent to make health care decisions for you if you become incapable of making your own decisions or if you want someone else to make those decisions for you now even though you are still capable. You may name an alternate agent to act for you if your first choice is not willing, able or reasonably available to make decisions for you. Unless related to you, your agent may not be an owner, operator, or employee of a residential long-term health care institution at which you are receiving care.

Unless the form you sign limits the authority of your agent, your agent may make all health care decisions for you. This form has a place for you to limit the authority of your agent. You need not limit the authority of your agent if you wish to rely on your agent for all health care decisions that may have to be made. If you choose not to limit the authority of your agent, your agent will have the right to:

(a) Consent or refuse consent to any care, treatment, service, or procedure to maintain, diagnose, or otherwise affect a physical or mental condition;

(b) Select or discharge health care providers and institutions;

(c) Approve or disapprove diagnostic tests, surgical procedures, programs of medication, and orders not to resuscitate; and

(d) Direct the provision, withholding, or withdrawal of artificial nutrition and hydration and all other forms of health care.

Part 2 of this form lets you give specific instructions about any aspect of your health care. Choices are provided for you to express your wishes regarding the provision, withholding, or withdrawal of treatment to keep you alive, including the provision of artificial nutrition and hydration, as well as the provision of pain relief. Space is provided for you to add to the choices you have made or for you to write out any additional wishes.

Part 3 of this form lets you designate a physician to have primary responsibility for your health care.

Part 4 of this form lets you authorize the donation of your organs at your death, and declares that this decision will supersede any decision by a member of your family.

After completing this form, sign and date the form at the end and have the form witnessed by one of the two alternative methods listed below. Give a copy of the signed and completed form to your physician, to any other health care providers you may have, to any health care institution at which you are receiving care, and to any health care agents you have named. You should talk to the person you have named as agent to make sure that he or she understands your wishes and is willing to take the responsibility.

You have the right to revoke this advance health care directive or replace this form at any time.

# PART 1
# POWER OF ATTORNEY FOR HEALTH CARE

(1) DESIGNATION OF AGENT: I designate the following individual as my agent to make health care decisions for me:

_____
(name of individual you choose as agent)

_____
(address)            (city)         (state)     (zip code)

_____
(home phone)            (work phone)

OPTIONAL: If I revoke my agent's authority or if my agent is not willing, able, or reasonably available to make a health care decision for me, I designate as my first alternate agent:

_____
(name of individual you choose as first alternate agent)

_____
(address)             (city)         (state)     (zip code)

_____
(home phone)            (work phone)

OPTIONAL: If I revoke the authority of my agent and first alternate agent or if neither is willing, able, or reasonably available to make a health care decision for me, I designate as my second alternate agent:

_____
(name of individual you choose as second alternate agent)

_____
(address)             (city)         (state)     (zip code)

_____
(home phone)            (work phone)

(2) AGENT'S AUTHORITY: My agent is authorized to make all health care decisions for me, including decisions to provide, withhold, or withdraw artificial nutrition and hydration, and all other forms of health care to keep me alive, except as I state here:

_____

_____

_____
(Add additional sheets if needed.)

(3) WHEN AGENT'S AUTHORITY BECOMES EFFECTIVE: My agent's authority becomes effective when my primary physician determines that I am unable to make my own health care decisions unless I mark the following box. If I mark this box [ ], my agent's authority to make health care decisions for me takes effect immediately.

(4) AGENT'S OBLIGATION: My agent shall make health care decisions for me in accordance with this power of attorney for health care, any instructions I give in Part 2 of this form, and my other wishes to the extent known to my agent. To the extent my wishes are unknown, my agent shall make health care decisions for me in accordance with what my agent determines to be in my best interest. In determining my best interest, my agent shall consider my personal values to the extent known to my agent.

(5) NOMINATION OF GUARDIAN: If a guardian of my person needs to be appointed for me by a court, I nominate the agent designated in this form. If that agent is not willing, able, or reasonably available to act as guardian, I nominate the alternate agents whom I have named, in the order designated.

## PART 2
## INSTRUCTIONS FOR HEALTH CARE

If you are satisfied to allow your agent to determine what is best for you in making end-of-life decisions, you need not fill out this part of the form. If you do fill out this part of the form, you may strike any wording you do not want.

(6) END-OF-LIFE DECISIONS: I direct that my health care providers and others involved in my care provide, withhold or withdraw treatment in accordance with the choice I have marked below:

[ ] (a) Choice Not To Prolong Life

I do not want my life to be prolonged if (i) I have an incurable and irreversible condition that will result in my death within a relatively short time, (ii) I become unconscious and, to a reasonable degree of medical certainty, I will not regain consciousness, or (iii) the likely risks and burdens of treatment would outweigh the expected benefits, or

[ ] (b) Choice To Prolong Life

I want my life to be prolonged as long as possible within the limits of generally accepted health care standards.

(7) ARTIFICIAL NUTRITION AND HYDRATION: Artificial nutrition and hydration must be provided, withheld or withdrawn in accordance with the choice I have made in paragraph (6) unless I mark the following box. If I mark this box [ ], artificial nutrition and hydration must be provided regardless of my condition and regardless of the choice I have made in paragraph (6).

(8) RELIEF FROM PAIN: Except as I state in the following space, I direct that treatment for alleviation of pain or discomfort be provided at all times, even if it hastens my death:

_____

_____

(9) OTHER WISHES: (If you do not agree with any of the optional choices above and wish to write your own, or if you wish to add to the instructions you have given above, you may do so here.) I direct that:

_____

(Add additional sheets if needed.)

## PART 3
## PRIMARY PHYSICIAN
### (OPTIONAL)

(10) I designate the following physician as my primary physician:

_____
(name of physician)

_____
(address)                          (city)              (state)        (zip code)

_____
(phone)

OPTIONAL: If the physician I have designated above is not willing, able, or reasonably available to act as my primary physician, I designate the following physician as my primary physician:

_____
(name of physician)

_____
(address)                          (city)              (state)        (zip code)

_____
(phone)

(11) EFFECT OF COPY: A copy of this form has the same effect as the original.

(12) SIGNATURES: Sign and date the form here:

_____        _____
(date)                                        (sign your name)

_____        _____
(address)                                    (print your name)

_____
(city)                         (state)

## PART 4
## CERTIFICATION OF AUTHORIZATION FOR ORGAN DONATION
### (OPTIONAL)

I, the undersigned, this _____ day of _____, 20_____, desire that my
_____ organ(s) be made available after my demise for:

   (a) Any licensed hospital, surgeon or physician, for medical education, research, advancement of medical science, therapy or transplantation to individuals;

   (b) Any accredited medical school, college or university engaged in medical education or research, for therapy, educational research or medical science purposes or any accredited school of mortuary science;

   (c) Any person operating a bank or storage facility for blood, arteries, eyes, pituitaries, or other human parts, for use in medical education, research, therapy or transplantation to individuals;

(d) The donee specified below, for therapy or transplantation needed by him or her, do donate my _____ for that purpose to _____ (name) at _____ (address).

I authorize a licensed physician or surgeon to remove and preserve for use my _____ for that purpose.

I specifically provide that this declaration shall supersede and take precedence over any decision by my family to the contrary.

Witnessed this _____ day of _____, 20_____.

_____
(donor)

_____
(address)

_____
(telephone)

_____
(witness)

_____
(witness)

(13) WITNESSES: This power of attorney will not be valid for making health care decisions unless it is either (a) signed by two (2) qualified adult witnesses who are personally known to you and who are present when you sign or acknowledge your signature; or (b) acknowledged before a notary public in the state.

ALTERNATIVE NO. 1

Witness

I declare under penalty of perjury pursuant to Section 97-9-61, Mississippi Code of 1972, that the principal is personally known to me, that the principal signed or acknowledged this power of attorney in my presence, that the principal appears to be of sound mind and under no duress, fraud or undue influence, that I am not the person appointed as agent by this document, and that I am not a health care provider, nor an employee of a health care provider or facility. I am not related to the principal by blood, marriage or adoption, and to the best of my knowledge, I am not entitled to any part of the estate of the principal upon the death of the principal under a will now existing or by operation of law.

_____          _____
(date)                                    (signature of witness)

_____          _____
(address)                                 (print name of witness)

_____
(city)                    (state)

Witness

I declare under penalty of perjury pursuant to Section 97-9-61, Mississippi Code of 1972, that the principal is personally known to me, that the principal signed or acknowledged this power of attorney in my presence, that the principal appears to be of sound mind and under no duress, fraud or undue influence, that I am not the person appointed as agent by this document, and that I am not a health care provider, nor an employee of a health care provider or facility.

_____          _____
(date)                                    (signature of witness)


_____          _____
(address)                                 (print name of witness)


_____
(city)                 (state)


ALTERNATIVE NO. 2

State of _____

County of _____

On this _____ day of _____, in the year _____, before me, _____ (insert name of notary public) appeared _____, personally known to me (or proved to me on the basis of satisfactory evidence) to be the person whose name is subscribed to this instrument, and acknowledged that he or she executed it. I declare under the penalty of perjury that the person whose name is subscribed to this instrument appears to be of sound mind and under no duress, fraud or undue influence.

Notary Seal


_____
(Signature of Notary Public)

## Power of Attorney

**NOTICE: THE POWERS GRANTED BY THIS DOCUMENT ARE BROAD AND SWEEPING. THEY ARE EXPLAINED IN THIS PART. IF YOU HAVE ANY QUESTIONS ABOUT THESE POWERS, OBTAIN COMPETENT LEGAL ADVICE. THIS DOCUMENT DOES NOT AUTHORIZE ANYONE TO MAKE MEDICAL AND OTHER HEALTH CARE DECISIONS FOR YOU. YOU MAY REVOKE THIS POWER OF ATTORNEY IF YOU LATER WISH TO DO SO.**

I _____ (insert your name and address) appoint _____ _____ (insert the name and address of the person appointed) as my agent (attorney-in-fact) to act for me in any lawful way with respect to the following initialed subjects:

TO GRANT ALL OF THE FOLLOWING POWERS, INITIAL THE LINE IN FRONT OF (N) AND IGNORE THE LINES IN FRONT OF THE OTHER POWERS.

TO GRANT ONE OR MORE, BUT FEWER THAN ALL, OF THE FOLLOWING POWERS, INITIAL THE LINE IN FRONT OF EACH POWER YOU ARE GRANTING.

TO WITHHOLD A POWER, DO NOT INITIAL THE LINE IN FRONT OF IT. YOU MAY, BUT NEED NOT, CROSS OUT EACH POWER WITHHELD.

INITIAL

_____ (A)  real property transactions;
_____ (B)  tangible personal property transactions;
_____ (C)  stock and bond transactions;
_____ (D)  commodity and option transactions;
_____ (E)  banking and other financial institution transactions;
_____ (F)  business operating transactions;
_____ (G)  insurance and annuity transactions;
_____ (H)  estate, trust, and other beneficiary transactions;
_____ (I)  claims and litigation;
_____ (J)  personal and family maintenance;
_____ (K)  benefits from social security, medicare, medicaid, or other governmental programs or from military service;
_____ (L)  retirement plan transactions;
_____ (M)  tax matters;
_____ (N)  ALL OF THE POWERS LISTED ABOVE. YOU NEED NOT INITIAL ANY OTHER LINES IF YOU INITIAL LINE (N).

SPECIAL INSTRUCTIONS:
ON THE FOLLOWING LINES, YOU MAY GIVE SPECIAL INSTRUCTIONS LIMITING OR EXTENDING THE POWERS GRANTED TO YOUR AGENT.

_____
_____
_____
_____
_____
_____
_____
_____

UNLESS YOU DIRECT OTHERWISE ABOVE, THIS POWER OF ATTORNEY IS EFFECTIVE IMMEDIATELY AND WILL CONTINUE UNTIL IT IS REVOKED.

This power of attorney revokes all previous powers of attorney signed by me.

STRIKE THE PRECEDING SENTENCE IF YOU DO NOT WANT THIS POWER OF ATTORNEY TO REVOKE ALL PREVIOUS POWERS OF ATTORNEY SIGNED BY YOU.

IF YOU DO WANT THIS POWER OF ATTORNEY TO REVOKE ALL PREVIOUS POWERS OF ATTORNEY SIGNED BY YOU, YOU SHOULD READ THOSE POWERS OF ATTORNEY AND SATISFY THEIR PROVISIONS CONCERNING REVOCATION. THIRD PARTIES WHO RECEIVED COPIES OF THOSE POWERS OF ATTORNEY SHOULD BE NOTIFIED.

This power of attorney will continue to be effective if I become disabled, incapacitated, or incompetent.

STRIKE THE PRECEDING SENTENCE IF YOU DO NOT WANT THIS POWER OF ATTORNEY TO CONTINUE IF YOU BECOME DISABLED, INCAPACITATED, OR INCOMPETENT.

If it becomes necessary to appoint a conservator of my estate or guardian of my person, I nominate my agent.

STRIKE THE PRECEDING SENTENCE IF YOU DO NOT WANT TO NOMINATE YOUR AGENT AS CONSERVATOR OR GUARDIAN.

If any agent named by me dies, becomes incompetent, resigns or refuses to accept the office or agent, I name the following (each to act and successively, in the order named) as successor(s) to the agent:

1. _____
2. _____
3. _____

For purposes of this subsection, a person is considered to be incompetent if and while: (1) the person is a minor; (2) the person is an adjudicated incompetent or disabled person; (3) a conservator has been appointed to act for the person; (4) a guardian has been appointed to act for the person; or (5) the person is unable to give prompt and intelligent consideration to business matters as certified by a licensed physician.

I agree that any third party who receives a copy of this document may act under it. I may revoke this power of attorney by a written document that expressly indicates my intent to revoke. Revocation of the power of attorney is not effective as to a third party until the third party learns of the revocation. I agree to indemnify the third party for any claims that arise against the third party because of reliance on this power of attorney.

Signed this _____ day of _____, 20_____

_____
(Your Signature)

State of _____

(County) of _____

This document was acknowledged before me on _____ (date) by

_____
(Name of Principal)

_____
(Signature of Notarial Officer)

(Seal, if any)                _____
(Title (and Rank))

[My commission expires: _____]

BY SIGNING, ACCEPTING, OR ACTING UNDER THE APPOINTMENT, THE AGENT ASSUMES THE FIDUCIARY AND OTHER LEGAL RESPONSIBILITIES OF AN AGENT. THE AGENT WORKS EXCLUSIVELY FOR THE BENEFIT OF THE PRINCIPAL. THE FOREMOST DUTY AS THE AGENT IS THAT OF LOYALTY TO AND PROTECTION OF THE BEST INTERESTS OF THE PRINCIPAL. THE AGENT SHALL DIRECT ANY BENEFITS DERIVED FROM THE POWER OF ATTORNEY TO THE PRINCIPAL. THE AGENT HAS A DUTY TO AVOID CONFLICTS OF INTEREST AND TO USE ORDINARY SKILL AND PRUDENCE IN THE EXERCISE OF THESE DUTIES.

_____
(Signature of Agent)

Signed this _____ day of _____, 20_____

## DECLARATION

If I should have an incurable and irreversible condition that, without the administration of life-sustaining treatment, will, in the opinion of my attending physician or attending advanced practice registered nurse, cause my death within a relatively short time and I am no longer able to make decisions regarding my medical treatment, I appoint _____ or, if he or she is not reasonably available or is unwilling to serve, _____, to make decisions on my behalf regarding withholding or withdrawal of treatment that only prolongs the process of dying and is not necessary for my comfort or to alleviate pain, pursuant to the Montana Rights of the Terminally Ill Act.

If the individual I have appointed is not reasonably available or is unwilling to serve, I direct my attending physician or attending advanced practice registered nurse, pursuant to the Montana Rights of the Terminally Ill Act, to withhold or withdraw treatment that only prolongs the process of dying and is not necessary for my comfort or to alleviate pain.

Signed this _____ day of _____, _____.

Signature _____

City, County, and State of Residence _____

The declarant voluntarily signed this document in my presence.

Witness

_____

Address

_____

Witness

_____

Address

_____

Name and address of designee.

Name

_____

Address

_____

## Directive to Physicians

If I should have an incurable or irreversible condition that, without the administration of life-sustaining treatment, will, in the opinion of my attending physician, cause my death within a relatively short time and I am no longer able to make decisions regarding my medical treatment, I direct my attending physician, pursuant to the Montana Rights of the Terminally Ill Act, to withhold or withdraw treatment that only prolongs the process of dying and is not necessary to my comfort or to alleviate pain.

Signed this _____ day of _____, 200_____.

Signature _____

City, County, and State of Residence _____

_____

The declarant voluntarily signed this document in my presence.

Witness: _____

Address: _____

Witness: _____

Address: _____

## Power of Attorney

_____, a domiciliary of _____ County, Nebraska, Principal, desiring and intending to establish a Power of Attorney operative under the Nebraska Short Form Act, does hereby appoint, constitute, and designate _____, a _____ of or with an office in _____ County, Nebraska, and _____, a _____ of or with an office in _____ County, Nebraska, Agent, the lawful and true Agent and attorney in fact for Principal; and Principal does hereby further provide and stipulate in connection therewith as follows:

1.    This Power of Attorney is, as marked, a
   ( )    Durable Power of Attorney and a
         ( )    Contingent Durable Power of Attorney, upon the contingency of,
             ( )    Incompetence of Principal, or
             ( )    Other Contingency:_____, or
   ( )    Present Durable Power of Attorney
   ( )    Nondurable Power of Attorney.

2.    By this Power of Attorney, Principal confers upon and grants to Agent plenary power, plenary power subject to limitations, or all and each of the listed general powers as individually marked:
   ( )    Plenary Power; or
   ( )    Plenary Power Subject to Limitations, exclusive of General Powers for Domestic and Personal Concerns and for Fiduciary Relationships and
         ( )    No Other Restrictions, or
         ( )    Other Restrictions:_____; or
         ( )    General Power for Bank and Financial Transactions.
         ( )    General Power for Business Interests.
         ( )    General Power for Chattels and Goods.
         ( )    General Power for Disputes and Litigation.
         ( )    General Power for Domestic and Personal Concerns.
         ( )    General Power for Fiduciary Relationships.
         ( )    General Power for Governmental and Other Benefits.
         ( )    General Power for Insurance Coverage and Policies.
         ( )    General Power for Proprietary Interests and Materials.
         ( )    General Power for Real Estate.
         ( )    General Power for Securities.
         ( )    General Power for Records, Reports, and Statements.

3.    By this Power of Attorney, Principal makes the following additional provision or provisions:

   _____
   _____
   _____

4.    This Power of Attorney revokes and supersedes all prior executed instruments of like import and remains operative until revoked.

EXECUTED AT _____, _____ County, Nebraska, on _____, _____.

_____
Principal

STATE OF NEBRASKA      )
                         ) ss.
COUNTY OF _____  )

The foregoing instrument was acknowledged before me on _____, _____, by the Principal _____.

_____
Notary Public

## Power of Attorney for Health Care

I appoint _____, whose address is _____ _____, and whose telephone number is _____, as my attorney in fact for health care. I appoint _____, whose address is _____ _____, and whose telephone number is _____, as my successor attorney in fact for health care. I authorize my attorney in fact appointed by this document to make health care decisions for me when I am determined to be incapable of making my own health care decisions. I have read the warning which accompanies this document and understand the consequences of executing a power of attorney for health care.

I direct that my attorney in fact comply with the following instructions or limitations:

_____
_____
_____

I direct that my attorney in fact comply with the following instructions on life-sustaining treatment: (optional) _____
_____
_____

I direct that my attorney in fact comply with the following instructions on artificially administered nutrition and hydration: (optional) _____
_____
_____

I HAVE READ THIS POWER OF ATTORNEY FOR HEALTH CARE. I UNDERSTAND THAT IT ALLOWS ANOTHER PERSON TO MAKE LIFE AND DEATH DECISIONS FOR ME IF I AM INCAPABLE OF MAKING SUCH DECISIONS. I ALSO UNDERSTAND THAT I CAN REVOKE THIS POWER OF ATTORNEY FOR HEALTH CARE AT ANY TIME BY NOTIFYING MY ATTORNEY IN FACT, MY PHYSICIAN, OR THE FACILITY IN WHICH I AM A PATIENT OR RESIDENT. I ALSO UNDERSTAND THAT I CAN REQUIRE IN THIS POWER OF ATTORNEY FOR HEALTH CARE THAT THE FACT OF MY INCAPACITY IN THE FUTURE BE CONFIRMED BY A SECOND PHYSICIAN.

_____
(Signature of person making designation/date)

### DECLARATION OF WITNESSES

We declare that the principal is personally known to us, that the principal signed or acknowledged his or her signature on this power of attorney for health care in our presence, that the principal appears to be of sound mind and not under duress or undue influence, and that neither of us not the principal's attending physician is the person appointed as attorney in fact by this document.

Witnessed By:

_____     _____
(Signature of Witness/Date)          (Printed Name of Witness)


_____     _____
(Signature of Witness/Date)          (Printed Name of Witness)


OR


State of Nebraska,                              )
                                                ) ss.
County of _____       )

    On this _____ day of _____, _____, before me, _____
_____, a notary public in and for _____ County,
personally came _____, personally to me
known to be the identical person whose name is affixed to the above power of attorney
for health care as principal, and I declare that he or she appears in sound mind and not
under duress or undue influence, that he or she acknowledges the execution of the
same to be his or her voluntary act and deed, and that I am not the attorney in fact or
successor attorney in fact designated by this power of attorney for health care.

    Witness my hand and notarial seal at _____ in
such county the day and year last above written.



                                     _____
Seal                                       Signature of Notary Public

## Durable Power of Attorney for Health Care Decisions

WARNING TO PERSON EXECUTING THIS DOCUMENT

THIS IS AN IMPORTANT LEGAL DOCUMENT.  IT CREATES A DURABLE POWER OF ATTORNEY FOR HEALTH CARE.  BEFORE EXECUTING THIS DOCUMENT, YOU SHOULD KNOW THESE IMPORTANT FACTS:

1. THIS DOCUMENT GIVES THE PERSON YOU DESIGNATE AS YOUR ATTORNEY-IN-FACT THE POWER TO MAKE HEALTH CARE DECISIONS FOR YOU.  THIS POWER IS SUBJECT TO ANY LIMITATIONS OR STATEMENT OF YOUR DESIRES THAT YOU INCLUDE IN THIS DOCUMENT.  THE POWER TO MAKE HEALTH CARE DECISIONS FOR YOU MAY INCLUDE CONSENT, REFUSAL OF CONSENT, OR WITHDRAWAL OF CONSENT TO ANY CARE, TREATMENT, SERVICE, OR PROCEDURE TO MAINTAIN, DIAGNOSE, OR TREAT A PHYSICAL OR MENTAL CONDITION.  YOU MAY STATE IN THIS DOCUMENT ANY TYPES OF TREATMENT OR PLACEMENTS THAT YOU DO NOT DESIRE.

2. THE PERSON YOU DESIGNATE IN THIS DOCUMENT HAS A DUTY TO ACT CONSISTENT WITH YOUR DESIRES AS STATED IN THIS DOCUMENT OR OTHERWISE MADE KNOWN OR, IF YOUR DESIRES ARE UNKNOWN, TO ACT IN YOUR BEST INTERESTS.

3. EXCEPT AS YOU OTHERWISE SPECIFY IN THIS DOCUMENT, THE POWER OF THE PERSON YOU DESIGNATE TO MAKE HEALTH CARE DECISIONS FOR YOU MAY INCLUDE THE POWER TO CONSENT TO YOUR DOCTOR NOT GIVING TREATMENT OR STOPPING TREATMENT WHICH WOULD KEEP YOU ALIVE.

4. UNLESS YOU SPECIFY A SHORTER PERIOD IN THIS DOCUMENT, THIS POWER WILL EXIST INDEFINITELY FROM THE DATE YOU EXECUTE THIS DOCUMENT AND, IF YOU ARE UNABLE TO MAKE HEALTH CARE DECISIONS FOR YOURSELF, THIS POWER WILL CONTINUE TO EXIST UNTIL THE TIME WHEN YOU BECOME ABLE TO MAKE HEALTH CARE DECISIONS FOR YOURSELF.

5. NOTWITHSTANDING THIS DOCUMENT, YOU HAVE THE RIGHT TO MAKE MEDICAL AND OTHER HEALTH CARE DECISIONS FOR YOURSELF SO LONG AS YOU CAN GIVE INFORMED CONSENT WITH RESPECT TO THE PARTICULAR DECISION.  IN ADDITION, NO TREATMENT MAY BE GIVEN TO YOU OVER YOUR OBJECTION, AND HEALTH CARE NECESSARY TO KEEP YOU ALIVE MAY NOT BE STOPPED IF YOU OBJECT.

6. YOU HAVE THE RIGHT TO REVOKE THE APPOINTMENT OF THE PERSON DESIGNATED IN THIS DOCUMENT TO MAKE HEALTH CARE DECISIONS FOR YOU BY NOTIFYING THAT PERSON OF THE REVOCATION ORALLY OR IN WRITING.

7. YOU HAVE THE RIGHT TO REVOKE THE AUTHORITY GRANTED TO THE PERSON DESIGNATED IN THIS DOCUMENT TO MAKE HEALTH CARE DECISIONS FOR YOU BY NOTIFYING THE TREATING PHYSICIAN, HOSPITAL, OR OTHER PROVIDER OR HEALTH CARE ORALLY OR IN WRITING.

8. THE PERSON DESIGNATED IN THIS DOCUMENT TO MAKE HEALTH CARE DECISIONS FOR YOU HAS THE RIGHT TO EXAMINE YOUR MEDICAL RECORDS AND TO CONSENT TO THEIR DISCLOSURE UNLESS YOU LIMIT THIS RIGHT IN THIS DOCUMENT.

9. THIS DOCUMENT REVOKES ANY PRIOR DURABLE POWER OF ATTORNEY FOR HEALTH CARE.

10. IF THERE IS ANYTHING IN THIS DOCUMENT THAT YOU DO NOT UNDERSTAND, YOU SHOULD ASK A LAWYER TO EXPLAIN IT TO YOU.

1. DESIGNATION OF HEALTH CARE AGENT.

I, _____,
(insert your name) do hereby designate and appoint:

      Name: _____

      Address: _____

      Telephone Number: _____

as my attorney-in-fact to make health care decisions for me as authorized in this document.

      (Insert the name and address of the person you wish to designate as your attorney-in-fact to make health care decisions for you.  Unless the person is also your spouse, legal guardian or the person most closely related to you by blood, none of the following may be designated as your attorney-in-fact: (1) your treating provider of health care, (2) an employee of your treating provider of health care, (3) an operator of a health care facility, or (4) an employee of an operator of a health care facility.)

## 2. CREATION OF DURABLE POWER OF ATTORNEY FOR HEALTH CARE.

By this document I intend to create a durable power of attorney by appointing the person designated above to make health care decisions for me. This power of attorney shall not be affected by my subsequent incapacity.

## 3. GENERAL STATEMENT OF AUTHORITY GRANTED.

In the event that I am incapable of giving informed consent with respect to health care decisions, I hereby grant to the attorney-in-fact named above full power and authority to make health care decisions for me before, or after my death, including: consent, refusal or consent, or withdrawal of consent to any care, treatment, service, or procedure to maintain, diagnose, or treat a physical or mental condition, subject only to the limitations and special provisions, if any, set forth in paragraph 4 or 6.

## 4. SPECIAL PROVISIONS AND LIMITATIONS.

(Your attorney-in-fact is not permitted to any of the following: commitment to or placement in a mental health treatment facility, convulsive treatment, psychosurgery, sterilization, or abortion. If there are any other types of treatment or placement that you do not want your attorney-in-fact's authority to give consent for or other restrictions you wish to place on his or her attorney-in-fact's authority, you should list them in the space below. If you do not write any limitations, your attorney-in-fact will have the broad powers to make health care decisions on your behalf which are set forth in paragraph 3, except to the extent that there are limits provided by law.)

In exercising the authority under this durable power of attorney for health care, the authority of my attorney-in-fact is subject to the following special provisions and limitations: _____

_____

## 5. DURATION.

I understand that this power of attorney will exist indefinitely from the date I execute this document unless I establish a shorter time. If I am unable to make health care decisions for myself when this power of attorney expires, the authority I have granted my attorney-in-fact will continue to exist until the time when I become able to make health care decisions for myself.

(IF APPLICABLE)

I wish to have this power of attorney end on the following date: _____

## 6. STATEMENT OF DESIRES.

(With respect to decisions to withhold or withdraw life-sustaining treatment, your attorney-in-fact must make health care decisions that are consistent with your known desires. You can, but are not required to, indicate your desires below. If your desires are unknown, your attorney-in-fact has the duty to act in your best interests; and, under some circumstances, a judicial proceeding may be necessary so that a court can determine the health care decision that is in your best interests. If you wish to indicate your desires, you may INITIAL the statement or statements that reflect your desires and/or write your own statements in the space below.)

(If the statement reflects your desires, initial the box next to the statement.)

1. I desire that my life be prolonged to the greatest extent possible, without regard to my condition, the chances I have for recovery or long-term survival, or the cost of the procedures.   [_____]

2. If I am in a coma which my doctors have reasonably concluded is irreversible, I desire that life-sustaining or prolonging treatments not be used. (Also should utilize provisions of NRS 449.535 to 449.690, inclusive, if this subparagraph is initialed.)   [_____]

3. If I have an incurable or terminal condition or illness and no reasonable hope of long term recovery or survival, desire that life sustaining or prolonging treatments not be used. (Also should utilize provisions of NRS 449.535 to 449.690, inclusive, if this subparagraph is initialed.)   [_____]

4. Withholding or withdrawal of artificial nutrition and hydration may result in death by starvation or dehydration. I want to receive or continue receiving artificial nutrition and hydration by way of the gastro-intestinal tract after all other treatment is withheld.   [_____]

5. I do not desire treatment to be provided and/or continued if the burdens of the treatment outweigh the expected benefits. My attorney-in-fact is to consider the relief of suffering, the preservation or restoration or functioning, and the quality as well as the extent of the possible extension of my life.   [_____]

(If you wish to change your answer, you may do so by drawing an "X" through the answer you do not want, and circling the answer you prefer.)

Other or Additional Statements of Desires:

_____

_____

_____

**7. DESIGNATION OF ALTERNATIVE ATTORNEY-IN-FACT.**

(You are not required to designate any alternative attorney-in-fact but you may do so. Any alternative attorney-in-fact you designate will be able to make the same health care decisions as the attorney-in-fact designated in paragraph 1, page 2, in the event that he or she is unable or unwilling to act as your attorney-in-fact. Also, if the attorney-in-fact designated in paragraph 1 is your spouse, his or her designation as your attorney-in-fact is automatically revoked by law if your marriage is dissolved.)

If the person designated in paragraph 1 as my attorney-in-fact is unable to make health care decisions for me, then I designate the following persons to serve as my attorney-in-fact to make health care decisions for me as authorized in this document, such persons to serve in the order listed below:

A.  First Alternative Attorney-in-fact
Name: _____
Address: _____
_____
Telephone Number: _____

B.  Second Alternative Attorney-in-fact
Name: _____
Address: _____
_____
Telephone Number: _____

**8. PRIOR DESIGNATIONS REVOKED.** I revoke any prior durable power of attorney for health care.

(YOUR POWER OF ATTORNEY WILL NOT BE VALID FOR MAKING HEALTH CARE DECISIONS UNLESS IT IS EITHER (1) SIGNED BY AT LEAST TWO QUALIFIED WITNESSES WHO ARE PERSONALLY KNOWN TO YOU AND WHO ARE PRESENT WHEN YOU SIGN OR ACKNOWLEDGE YOUR SIGNATURE OR (2) ACKNOWLEDGED BEFORE A NOTARY PUBLIC.)

## CERTIFICATE OR ACKNOWLEDGMENT OF NOTARY PUBLIC

(You may use ACKNOWLEDGMENT before a notary public instead of the statement of witnesses.)

State of Nevada        )
                   ) ss.
County of _____)

On this _____ day of _____, in the year _____, before me, _____ (here insert name of notary public) personally appeared _____ (here insert name of principal) personally known to me (or proved to me on the basis of satisfactory evidence) to be the person whose name is subscribed to this instrument, and acknowledged that he or she executed it.  I declare under penalty or perjury that the person whose name is ascribed to this instrument appears to be of sound mind and under no duress, fraud, or undue influence.

NOTARY SEAL

_____
(Signature of Notary Public)

## STATEMENT OF WITNESSES

(You should carefully read and follow this witnessing procedure.  This document will not be valid unless you comply with the witnessing procedure.  If you elect to use witnesses instead of having this document notarized you must use two qualified adult witnesses.  None of the following may be used as a witness:  (1) a person you designate as the attorney-in-fact, (2) a provider of health care, (3) an employee of a provider of health care, (4) the operator of a health care facility, (5) an employee of an operator of a health care facility.  At least one of the witnesses must make the additional declaration set out following the place where the witnesses sign.)

I declare under penalty of perjury that the principal is personally known to me, that the principal signed or acknowledged this durable power of attorney in my presence, that the principal appears to be of sound mind and under no duress, fraud, or undue influence, that I am not the person appointed as attorney-in-fact by this document, and that I am not a provider of health care, an employee of a provider of health care, the operator of a community care facility, nor an employee of an operator of a health care facility.

Signature: _____    Signature: _____

Print Name: _____    Print Name: _____

Residence Address: _____    Residence Address: _____
_____    _____

Date: _____    Date: _____

(AT LEAST ONE OF THE ABOVE WITNESSES MUST ALSO SIGN THE FOLLOWING DECLARATION.)

I declare under penalty of perjury that I am not related to the principal by blood, marriage, or adoption, and to the best of my knowledge I am not entitled to any part of the estate of the principal upon the death or the principal under a will now existing or by operation of law.

Signature: _____

Print Name: _____

Residence Address: _____
_____

Date: _____

COPIES: You should retain an executed copy of this document and give one to your attorney-in-fact. The power of attorney should be available so a copy may be given to your providers of health care.

# INFORMATION CONCERNING THE DURABLE POWER OF ATTORNEY

THIS IS AN IMPORTANT LEGAL DOCUMENT. BEFORE SIGNING THIS DOCUMENT YOU SHOULD KNOW THESE IMPORTANT FACTS:

Notice to the Principal: As the "Principal," you are using this Durable Power of Attorney to grant power to another person (called the "Agent" or "Attorney in Fact") to make decisions, including, but not limited to, decisions concerning your money, property, or both, and to use your money, property, or both on your behalf. If this written Durable Power of Attorney does not limit the powers that you give to your Agent, your Agent will have broad and sweeping powers to sell or otherwise dispose of your property, and to spend your money without advance notice to you or approval by you. Under this document, your agent will continue to have these powers after you become incapacitated, and unless otherwise indicated your Agent will have these powers before you become incapacitated. You have the right to retain this Power and not to release this Power until you instruct your attorney or any other person who may hold this Power of Attorney to so release it to your Agent pursuant to written instructions. You have the right to revoke or take back this Durable Power of Attorney at any time, so long as you are of sound mind. If there is anything about this Durable Power of Attorney that you do not understand, you should seek professional advice.

_____

Principal

## Acknowledgment of Agent

I, _____, have read the attached power of attorney and am the person identified as the Agent for the Principal. I hereby acknowledge that when I act as Agent or "attorney in fact," I am given power under this Durable Power of Attorney to make decisions about money, property, or both belonging to the Principal, and to spend the Principal's money, property, or both on the Principal's behalf, in accordance with the terms of this Durable Power of Attorney. This Durable Power of Attorney is valid only if the Principal is of sound mind when the Principal signs it. When acting in the capacity of Agent, I am under a duty (called a "fiduciary duty") to observe the standards observed by a prudent person, which means the use of those powers that is reasonable in view of the interests of the Principal and in view of the way in which a person of ordinary judgment would act in carrying out that person's own affairs. If the exercise of my acts is called into question, the burden will be upon me to prove that I acted under the standards of a fiduciary. As the Agent, I am not entitled to use the money or property for my own benefit or to make gifts to myself or others unless the Durable Power of Attorney specifically gives me the authority to do so. As the Agent, my authority under this Durable Power of Attorney will end when the Principal dies and I will not have authority to manage or dispose of any property or administer the estate unless I am authorized to do so by a New Hampshire Probate Court. If I violate my fiduciary duty under this Durable Power of Attorney, I may be liable for damages and may be subject to criminal prosecution. If there is anything about this Durable Power of Attorney, or my duties under it, that I do not understand, I understand that I should seek professional advice.

_____
Agent

# Durable Power of Attorney for Health Care

INFORMATION CONCERNING THE DURABLE
POWER OF ATTORNEY FOR HEALTH CARE

THIS IS AN IMPORTANT LEGAL DOCUMENT.  BEFORE SIGNING THIS DOCUMENT YOU SHOULD KNOW THESE IMPORTANT FACTS:

Except to the extent you state otherwise, this document gives the person you name as your agent the authority to make any and all health care decisions for you when you are no longer capable of making them yourself.  "Health care" means any treatment, service or procedure to maintain, diagnose or treat your physical or mental condition.  Your agent, therefore, can have the poser to make a broad range of health care decisions for you.  Your agent may consent, refuse to consent, or withdraw consent to medical treatment and may make decisions about withdrawing or withholding life-sustaining treatment.  Your agent cannot consent or direct any of the following:  commitment to a state institution, sterilization, or termination of treatment if you are pregnant and if the withdrawal of that treatment is deemed likely to terminate the pregnancy unless the failure to withhold the treatment will be physically harmful to you or prolong severe pain which cannot be alleviated by medication.

You may state in this document any treatment you do not desire, except as stated above, or treatment you want to be sure you receive.  Your agent's authority will begin when your doctor certifies that you lack the capacity to make health care decisions.  If for moral or religious reasons you do not wish to be treated by a doctor or examined by a doctor for the certification that you lack capacity, you must say so in the document and name a person to be able to certify your lack of capacity.  That person may not be your agent or alternate agent or any person ineligible to be your agent.  You may attach additional pages if you need more space to complete your statement.

If you want to give your agent authority to withhold or withdraw the artificial providing of nutrition and fluids, your document must say so.  Otherwise, your agent will not be able to direct that.  Under no conditions will your agent be able to direct the withholding of food and drink for you to eat and drink normally.

Your agent will be obligated to follow your instructions when making decisions on your behalf.  Unless you state otherwise, your agent will have the same authority to make decisions about your health care as you would have had if made consistent with state law.

It is important that you discuss this document with your physician or other health care providers before you sign it to make sure that you understand the nature and range of decisions which may be made on your behalf.  If you do not have a physician, you should talk with someone else who is knowledgeable about these issues and can answer your questions.  You do not need a lawyer's assistance to complete this document, but if there is anything in this document that you do not understand, you should ask a lawyer to explain it to you.

The person you appoint as agent should be someone you know and trust and must be at least 18 years old.  If you appoint your health or residential care provider (e.g. your physician, or an employee of a home health agency, hospital, nursing home, or residential care home, other than a relative), that person will have to choose between acting as your agent or as your health or residential care provider; the law does not permit a person to do both at the same time.

You should inform the person you appoint that you want him or her to be your health care agent.  You should discuss this document with your agent and your physician and give each a signed copy.  You should indicate on the document itself the people and institutions who will have signed copies.  Your agent will not be liable for health care decisions made in good faith on your behalf.

Even after you have signed this document, you have the right to make health care decisions for yourself as long as you are able to do so, and treatment cannot be given to you or stopped over your objection.  You have the right to revoke the authority granted to your agent by informing him or her or your health care provider orally or in writing.

This document may not be changed or modified.  If you want to make changes in the document you must make an entirely new one.

You should consider designating an alternative agent in the event that your agent is unwilling, unable, unavailable, or ineligible to act as your agent. Any alternate agent you designate will have the same authority to make health care decisions for you.

THIS POWER OF ATTORNEY WILL NOT BE VALID UNLESS IT IS SIGNED IN THE PRESENCE OF TWO (2) OR MORE QUALIFIED WITNESSES WHO MUST BOTH BE PRESENT WHEN YOU SIGN AND ACKNOWLEDGE YOUR SIGNATURE. THE FOLLOWING PERSONS MAY NOT ACT AS WITNESSES:

—the person you have designated as your agent;

—your spouse;

—your lawful heirs or beneficiaries named in your will or a deed;

ONLY ONE OF THE TWO WITNESSES MAY BE YOUR HEALTH OR RESIDENTIAL CARE PROVIDER OR ONE OF THEIR EMPLOYEES.

I, _____, hereby appoint _____ of _____ as my agent to make any and all health care decisions for me, except to the extent I state otherwise in this document or as prohibited by law. This durable power of attorney for health care shall take effect in the event I become unable to make my own health care decisions.

STATEMENT OF DESIRES, SPECIAL PROVISIONS, AND LIMITATIONS REGARDING HEALTH CARE DECISIONS.

For your convenience in expressing your wishes, some general statements concerning the withholding or removal of life-sustaining treatment are set forth below. (Life-sustaining treatment is defined as procedures without which a person would die, such as but not limited to the following: cardiopulmonary resuscitation, mechanical respiration, kidney dialysis or the use of other external mechanical and technological devices, drugs to maintain blood pressure, blood transfusions, and antibiotics.) There is also a section which allows you to set forth specific directions for these or other matters. If you wish you may indicate your agreement or disagreement with any of the following statements and give your agent power to act in those specific circumstances.

1.    If I become permanently incompetent to make health care decisions, and if I am also suffering from a terminal illness, I authorize my agent to direct that life-sustaining treatment be discontinued. (YES) (NO) (Circle your choice and initial beneath it.)

2.    Whether terminally ill or not, if I become unconscious I authorize my agent to direct that life-sustaining treatment be discontinued. (YES) (NO) (Circle your choice and initial beneath it.)

3.    I realize that situations could arise in which the only way to allow me to die would be to discontinue artificial feeding (artificial nutrition and hydration). In carrying out any instructions I have given above in #1 or #2 or any instructions I may write in #4 below, I authorize my agent to direct that (circle your choice of (a) or (b) and initial beside it:

(a)    artificial nutrition and hydration not to be started or, if started, be discontinued,

-or-

(b)    although all other forms of life-sustaining treatment be withdrawn, artificial nutrition and hydration continue to be given to me. (If you fail to complete item 3, your agent will not have the power to direct the withdrawal of artificial nutrition and hydration.)

4.    Here you may include any specific desires or limitations you deem appropriate, such as when or what life-sustaining treatment you would want used or withheld, or instructions about refusing any specific types of treatment that are inconsistent with your religious beliefs or unacceptable to you for any other reason. You may leave this question blank if you desire.

_____

_____(attach additional pages as necessary)

In the event the person I appoint above is unable, unwilling or unavailable, or ineligible to act as my health care agent, I hereby appoint _____ of _____ as alternate agent.

I hereby acknowledge that I have been provided with a disclosure statement explaining the effect of this document. I have read and understand the information contained in the disclosure statement.

The original of this document will be kept at _____ _____and the following persons and institutions will have signed copies:

_____
_____

In witness whereof, I have hereunto signed my name this _____ day of _____, _____

_____
Signature

I declare that the principal appears to be of sound mind and free from duress at the time the durable power of attorney for health care is signed and that the principal has affirmed that he or she is aware of the nature of the document and is signing it freely and voluntarily.

Witness:_____ Address:_____

Witness:_____ Address:_____

STATE OF NEW HAMPSHIRE
COUNTY OF _____

The foregoing instrument was acknowledged before me this _____ day of _____, _____, by _____.

_____
Notary Public/Justice of the Peace
My Commission Expires:

## Statutory Power of Attorney

NOTICE: THIS IS AN IMPORTANT DOCUMENT. THE POWER GRANTED BY THIS DOCUMENT ARE BROAD AND SWEEPING. THEY ARE EXPLAINED IN THE UNIFORM STATUTORY FORM POWER OF ATTORNEY ACT, CHAPTER 45, ARTICLE 5, PART 6 NMSA 1978. IF YOU HAVE ANY QUESTIONS ABOUT THESE POWERS, YOU SHOULD ASK A LAWYER TO EXPLAIN THEM TO YOU. THIS FORM DOES NOT PROHIBIT THE USE OF ANY OTHER FORM. YOU MAY REVOKE THIS POWER OF ATTORNEY IF YOU LATER WISH TO DO SO.

I, _____ (Name) reside at

_____ (Address), New Mexico. I appoint _____

_____ (Name(s) and address(es))

to serve as my attorney(s)-in-fact.

If any attorney-in-fact appointed above is unable to serve, then I appoint _____

_____ to serve as successor attorney-in-fact in place of the person who is unable to serve.

This power of attorney shall not be affected by my incapacity but will terminate upon my death unless I have revoked it prior to my death. I intend by this power of attorney to avoid a court-supervised guardianship or conservatorship.

Should my attempt be defeated, I ask that my agent be appointed as guardian or conservator of my person or estate.

STRIKE THROUGH THE SENTENCE ABOVE IF YOU DO NOT WANT TO NOMINATE YOUR AGENT AS YOUR GUARDIAN OR CONSERVATOR.

CHECK AND INITIAL THE FOLLOWING PARAGRAPH ONLY IF YOU WANT YOUR ATTORNEY(S)-IN-FACT TO BE ABLE TO ACT ALONE AND INDEPENDENTLY OF EACH OTHER WITHOUT THE SIGNATURE OF THE OTHER(S). IF YOU DO NOT CHECK AND INITIAL THE FOLLOWING PARAGRAPH AND MORE THAN ONE PERSON IS NAMED TO ACT ON YOUR BEHALF THEN THEY MUST ACT JOINTLY.

( )        If more than one person is appointed to serve as my attorney-in-fact then they may act
_____    severally, alone and independently of each other.
initials

My attorney(s)-in-fact shall have the power to act in my name, place and stead in any way which I myself could do with respect to the following matters to the extent permitted by law:

INITIAL IN THE BOX IN FRONT OF EACH AUTHORIZATION WHICH YOU DESIRE TO GIVE TO YOUR ATTORNEY(S)-IN-FACT. YOUR ATTORNEY(S)-IN-FACT SHALL BE AUTHORIZED TO ENGAGE ONLY IN THOSE ACTIVITIES WHICH ARE INITIALED.

(_____)   1.    real estate transactions.
(_____)   2.    stock and bond transactions.
(_____)   3.    commodity and option transactions.
(_____)   4.    tangible personal property transactions.
(_____)   5.    banking and other financial institution transactions.
(_____)   6.    business operating transactions.
(_____)   7.    insurance and annuity transactions.
(_____)   8.    estate, trust and other beneficiary transactions.
(_____)   9.    claims and litigation.
(_____)  10.    personal and family maintenance.
(_____)  11.    benefits from social security, medicare, medicaid or other government programs or civil or military service.
(_____)  12.    retirement plan transactions.
(_____)  13.    tax matters, including any transactions with the Internal Revenue Service.
(_____)  14.    decisions regarding lifesaving and life prolonging medical treatment
(_____)  15.    decisions relating to medical treatment, surgical treatment, nursing care, medication, hospitalization, institutionalization in a nursing home or other facility and home health care.

(_____) 16.     transfer of property or income as a gift to the principal's spouse for the purpose of qualifying the principal for governmental medical assistance.

(_____) 17.     ALL OF THE ABOVE POWERS, INCLUDING FINANCIAL AND HEALTH CARE DECISIONS. IF YOU INITIAL THE BOX IN FRONT OF LINE 17, YOU NEED NOT INITIAL ANY OTHER LINES.

SPECIAL INSTRUCTIONS:
ON THE FOLLOWING LINES YOU MAY GIVE SPECIAL INSTRUCTIONS LIMITING OR EXTENDING THE POWERS YOU HAVE GRANTED TO YOUR AGENT.

_____

_____

CHECK AND INITIAL THE FOLLOWING PARAGRAPH IF YOU INTEND FOR THIS POWER OF ATTORNEY TO BECOME EFFECTIVE ONLY IF YOU BECOME INCAPACITATED. YOUR FAILURE TO DO SO WILL MEAN THAT YOUR ATTORNEY(S)-IN-FACT ARE EMPOWERED TO ACT ON YOUR BEHALF FROM THE TIME YOU SIGN THIS DOCUMENT UNTIL YOUR DEATH UNLESS YOU REVOKE THE POWER BEFORE YOUR DEATH.

( )            This power of attorney shall become effective only if I become incapacitated. My attorney(s)-in-fact shall be entitled to rely on notarized statements from two qualified health
_____   care professionals, one of whom shall be a physician, as to my incapacity. By incapacity
initials       I mean that among other things, I am unable to effectively manage my personal care, property or financial affairs.

      This power of attorney will not be affected by a lapse of time. I agree that any third party who receives a copy of this power of attorney my act under it.


_____
(Signature)


_____
(Optional, but preferred: Your Social Security number)

Dated: _____, _____

NOTICE: IF THIS POWER OF ATTORNEY AFFECTS REAL ESTATE, IT MUST BE RECORDED IN THE OFFICE OF THE COUNTY CLERK IN EACH COUNTY WHERE THE REAL ESTATE IS LOCATED.

## ACKNOWLEDGMENT

STATE OF NEW MEXICO_____       )
                                            ) SS.
County of _____   )

      The foregoing instrument was acknowledged before me on _____,
_____, by _____.
                                                     (seal)


_____
Notary Public

My Commission Expires:

_____

BY ACCEPTING OR ACTING UNDER THE POWER OF ATTORNEY, YOUR AGENT ASSUMES THE FIDUCIARY AND OTHER LEGAL RESPONSIBILITIES OF AN AGENT ACTING ON YOUR BEHALF.
and
THIS AFFIDAVIT IS FOR THE USE OF YOUR ATTORNEY(S)-IN-FACT
IF EVER YOUR ATTORNEY(S)-IN-FACT ACTS ON YOUR BEHALF
UNDER YOUR WRITTEN POWER OF ATTORNEY.

## AFFIDAVIT AS TO POWER OF ATTORNEY BEING IN FULL FORCE

STATE OF NEW MEXICO_____            )
                                                      ) SS.
COUNTY OF _____              )

I/we _____ being duly sworn, state:

1.      _____ ("Principal") of _____, County, New Mexico, signed a written Power of Attorney on _____, _____, appointing the undersigned as his/her attorney(s)-in-fact. (A true copy of the power of attorney is attached hereto and incorporated herein.)

2.      As attorney(s)-in-fact and under and by virtue of the Power of Attorney, I/we have this date executed the following described instrument: _____
_____

3.      At the time of executing the above described instrument I/we had no actual knowledge or actual notice of revocation or termination of the Power of Attorney by death or otherwise, or notice of any facts indicating the same.

4.      I/we represent that the principal is now alive; has not, at any time, revoked or repudiated the power of attorney; and the power of attorney still is in full force and effect.

5.      I/we make this affidavit for the purpose of inducing _____ _____ to accept delivery of the above described instrument, as executed by me/us in my/our capacity of attorney(s)-in-fact for the Principal.

_____, Attorney-in-fact

_____, Attorney-in-fact

Sworn to before me _____ this _____ day of _____, _____.

_____
Notary Public

My commission expires:
_____.

# Optional Advance Health-Care Directive

## Explanation

You have the right to give instructions about your own health care. You also have the right to name someone else to make health-care decisions for you. This form lets you do either or both of these things. It also lets you express your wishes regarding the designation of your primary physician.

THIS FORM IS OPTIONAL. Each paragraph and word of this form is also optional. If you use this form, you may cross out, complete or modify all or any part of it. You are free to use a different form. If you use this form, be sure to sign it and date it.

PART 1 of this form is a power of attorney for health care. PART 1 lets you name another individual as agent to make health-care decisions for you if you become incapable of making your own decisions or if you want someone else to make those decisions for you now even though you are still capable. You may also name an alternate agent to act for you if your first choice is not willing, able or reasonably available to make decisions for you. Unless related to you, your agent may not be an owner, operator or employee of a health-care institution at which you are receiving care.

Unless the form you sign limits the authority of your agent, your agent may make all health-care decisions for you. This form has a place for you to limit the authority of your agent. You need not limit the authority of your agent if you wish to rely on your agent for all health-care decisions that may have to be made. If you choose not to limit the authority of your agent, your agent will have the right to:

(a)  consent or refuse consent to any care, treatment, service or procedure to maintain, diagnose or otherwise affect a physical or mental condition;

(b)  select or discharge health-care providers and institutions;

(c)  approve or disapprove diagnostic tests, surgical procedures, programs of medication and orders not to resuscitate; and

(d)  direct the provision, withholding or withdrawal of artificial nutrition and hydration and all other forms of health care.

PART 2 of this form lets you give specific instructions about any aspect of your health care. Choices are provided for you to express your wishes regarding life-sustaining treatment, including the provision of artificial nutrition and hydration, as well as the provision of pain relief. In addition, you may express your wishes regarding whether you want to make an anatomical gift of some or all of your organs and tissue. Space is also provided for you to add to the choices you have made or for you to write out any additional wishes.

PART 3 of this form lets you designate a physician to have primary responsibility for your health care. After completing this form, sign and date the form at the end. It is recommended but not required that you request two other individuals to sign as witnesses. Give a copy of the signed and completed form to your physician, to any other health-care providers you may have, to any health-care institution at which you are receiving care and to any health-care agents you have named. You should talk to the person you have named as agent to make sure that he or she understands your wishes and is willing to take the responsibility.

You have the right to revoke this advance health-care directive or replace this form at any time.

# PART 1
# POWER OF ATTORNEY FOR HEALTH CARE

(1) DESIGNATION OF AGENT: I designate the following individual as my agent to make health-care decisions for me:

_____
(name of individual you choose as agent)

_____
(address)                          (city)                    (state)        (zip code)

_____
(home phone)                                   (work phone)

If I revoke my agent's authority or if my agent is not willing, able or reasonably available to make a health-care decision for me, I designate as my first alternate agent:

_____
(name of individual you choose as first alternate agent)

_____
(address)                          (city)                    (state)        (zip code)

_____
(home phone)                                   (work phone)

If I revoke the authority of my agent and first alternate agent or if neither is willing, able or reasonably available to make a health-care decision for me, I designate as my second alternate agent:

_____
(name of individual you choose as second alternate agent)

_____
(address)                          (city)                    (state)        (zip code)

_____
(home phone)                                   (work phone)

(2) AGENT'S AUTHORITY:  My agent is authorized to obtain and review medical records, reports and information about me and to make all health-care decisions for me, including decisions to provide, withhold or withdraw artificial nutrition, hydration and all other forms of health care to keep me alive, except as I state here:

_____
(Add additional sheets if needed.)

(3) WHEN AGENT'S AUTHORITY BECOMES EFFECTIVE: My agent's authority becomes effective when my primary physician and one other qualified health-care professional determine that I am unable to make my own health-care decisions. If I initial this box [  ], my agent's authority to make health-care decisions for me takes effect immediately.

(4) AGENT'S OBLIGATION:  My agent shall make health-care decisions for me in accordance with this power of attorney for health care, any instructions I give in Part 2 of this form and my other wishes to the extent known to my agent. To the extent my wishes are unknown, my agent shall make health-care decisions for me in accordance with what my agent determines to be in my best interest. In determining my best interest, my agent shall consider my personal values to the extent known to my agent.

(5) NOMINATION OF GUARDIAN:  If a guardian of my person needs to be appointed for me by a court, I nominate the agent designated in this form. If that agent is not willing, able or reasonably available to act as guardian, I nominate the alternate agents whom I have named, in the order designated.

## PART 2
## INSTRUCTIONS FOR HEALTH CARE

If you are satisfied to allow your agent to determine what is best for you in making end-of-life decisions, you need not fill out this part of the form. If you do fill out this part of the form, you may cross out any wording you do not want.

(6) END-OF-LIFE DECISIONS:  If I am unable to make or communicate decisions regarding my health care, and IF (i) I have an incurable or irreversible condition that will result in my death within a relatively short time, OR (ii) I become unconscious and, to a reasonable degree of medical certainty, I will not regain consciousness, OR (iii) the likely risks and burdens of treatment would outweigh the expected benefits, THEN I direct that my health-care providers and others involved in my care provide, withhold or withdraw treatment in accordance with the choice I have initialed below in one of the following three boxes:

[ ]  I CHOOSE NOT To Prolong Life
I do not want my life to be prolonged.

[ ]  I CHOOSE To Prolong Life
I want my life to be prolonged as long as possible within the limits of generally accepted health-care standards.

[ ]  I CHOOSE To Let My Agent Decide
My agent under my power of attorney for health care may make life-sustaining treatment decisions for me.

(7) ARTIFICIAL NUTRITION AND HYDRATION:  If I have chosen above NOT to prolong life, I also specify by marking my initials below:

[ ]  I DO NOT want artificial nutrition OR

[ ]  I DO want artificial nutrition.

[ ]  I DO NOT want artificial hydration unless required for my comfort OR

[ ]  I DO want artificial hydration.

(8) RELIEF FROM PAIN: Regardless of the choices I have made in this form and except as I state in the following space, I direct that the best medical care possible to keep me clean, comfortable and free of pain or discomfort be provided at all times so that my dignity is maintained, even if this care hastens my death: _____
_____

(9) ANATOMICAL GIFT DESIGNATION:  Upon my death I specify as marked below whether I choose to make an anatomical gift of all or some of my organs or tissue:

[ ]  I CHOOSE to make an anatomical gift of all of my organs or tissue to be determined by
medical suitability at the time of death, and artificial support may be maintained long enough for organs to be removed.

[ ]  I CHOOSE to make a partial anatomical gift of some of my organs and tissue as specified below, and artificial support may be maintained long enough for organs to be removed.
_____
_____

[ ]  I REFUSE to make an anatomical gift of any of my organs or tissue.

[ ]  I CHOOSE to let my agent decide.

(10) OTHER WISHES:  (If you wish to write your own instructions, or if you wish to add to the instructions you have given above, you may do so here.) I direct that:
_____
_____

(Add additional sheets if needed.)

# PART 3
# PRIMARY PHYSICIAN

(11) I designate the following physician as my primary physician:

_____
(name of physician)

_____
(address)                    (city)              (state)      (zip code)

_____
(phone)

If the physician I have designated above is not willing, able or reasonably available to act as my primary physician, I designate the following physician as my primary physician:

_____
(name of physician)

_____
(address)                    (city)              (state)      (zip code)

_____
(phone)

\* \* \* \* \* \* \* \* \* \* \* \* \* \* \* \* \* \* \*

(12) EFFECT OF COPY: A copy of this form has the same effect as the original.

(13) REVOCATION: I understand that I may revoke this OPTIONAL ADVANCE HEALTH-CARE DIRECTIVE at any time, and that if I revoke it, I should promptly notify my supervising health-care provider and any health-care institution where I am receiving care and any others to whom I have given copies of this power of attorney. I understand that I may revoke the designation of an agent either by a signed writing or by personally informing the supervising health-care provider.

(14) SIGNATURES: Sign and date the form here:

_____          _____
(date)                                     (sign your name)

_____          _____
(address)                                  (print your name)

_____          _____
(city)              (state)                (your Social Security number)

### (Optional) SIGNATURES OF WITNESSES:

First witness                              Second witness

_____          _____
(print name)                               (print name)

_____          _____
(address)                                  (address)

_____          _____
(city)              (state)                (city)              (state)

_____          _____
(signature of witness)                     (signature of witness)

_____          _____
(date)                                     (date)

# DURABLE GENERAL POWER OF ATTORNEY
## NEW YORK STATUTORY SHORT FORM

## THE POWERS YOU GRANT BELOW CONTINUE TO BE EFFECTIVE
## SHOULD YOU BECOME DISABLED OR INCOMPETENT

**(CAUTION: THIS IS AN IMPORTANT DOCUMENT. IT GIVES THE PERSON WHOM YOU DESIGNATE (YOUR "AGENT") BROAD POWERS TO HANDLE YOUR PROPERTY DURING YOUR LIFETIME, WHICH MAY INCLUDE POWERS TO MORTGAGE, SELL, OR OTHERWISE DISPOSE OF ANY REAL OR PERSONAL PROPERTY WITHOUT ADVANCE NOTICE TO YOU OR APPROVAL BY YOU. THESE POWERS WILL CONTINUE TO EXIST EVEN AFTER YOU BECOME DISABLED, OR INCOMPETENT. THESE POWERS ARE EXPLAINED MORE FULLY IN NEW YORK GENERAL OBLIGATIONS LAW, ARTICLE 5, TITLE 15, SECTIONS 5-1502A THROUGH 5-1503, WHICH EXPRESSLY PERMIT THE USE OF ANY OTHER OR DIFFERENT FORM OF POWER OF ATTORNEY.**

**THIS DOCUMENT DOES NOT AUTHORIZE ANYONE TO MAKE MEDICAL OR OTHER HEALTH CARE DECISIONS. YOU MAY EXECUTE A HEALTH CARE PROXY TO DO THIS.**

**IF THERE IS ANYTHING ABOUT THIS FORM THAT YOU DO NOT UNDERSTAND, YOU SHOULD ASK A LAWYER TO EXPLAIN IT TO YOU.)**

This is intended to constitute a DURABLE GENERAL POWER OF ATTORNEY pursuant to Article 5, Title 15 of the New York General Obligations Law:

I, _____,
*(insert your name and address)*

do hereby appoint: _____

_____
*(If 1 person is to be appointed agent, insert the name and address of your agent above)*

_____

_____

_____
*(If 2 or more persons are to be appointed agents by you, insert their names and addresses above)*

my attorney(s)-in-fact TO ACT
*(If more than one agent is designated, CHOOSE ONE of the following two choices by putting your initials in ONE of the blank spaces to the left of your choice:)*

(   ) Each agent may SEPARATELY act.

(   ) All agents must act TOGETHER.

*(If neither blank space is initialed, the agents will be required to act TOGETHER)*

IN MY NAME, PLACE AND STEAD in any way which I myself could do, if I were personally present, with respect to the following matters as each of them as defined in Title 15 of Article 5 of the New York General Obligations Law to the extent that I am permitted by law to act through an agent.

**(DIRECTIONS: Initial in the blank space to the left of your choice any one or more of the following lettered subdivisions as to which you WANT to give your agent authority. If the blank space to the left of any particular division is NOT initialed, NO AUTHORITY WILL BE GRANTED for matters that are included in that subdivision. Alternatively, the letter corresponding to each power you wish to grant may be written or typed on the blank line in subdivision "(Q)", and you may then put your initials in the blank space to the left of subdivision "(Q)" in order to grant each of the powers so indicated)**

(_____)    (A)     real estate transactions;

(_____)    (B)     chattel and goods transactions;

(_____)    (C)     bond, share and commodity transactions;

(_____)    (D)     banking transactions;

(_____)    (E)     business operating transactions;

(_____)    (F)     insurance transactions;

| | | |
|---|---|---|
| ( _____ ) | (G) | estate transactions; |
| ( _____ ) | (H) | claims and litigation |
| ( _____ ) | (I) | personal relationships and affairs; |
| ( _____ ) | (J) | benefits from military service; |
| ( _____ ) | (K) | records, reports and statements; |
| ( _____ ) | (L) | retirement benefit transactions; |
| ( _____ ) | (M) | making gifts to my spouse, children and more remote descendants, and parents, not to exceed in the aggregate $10,000 to each of such persons in any year; |
| ( _____ ) | (N) | tax matters; |
| ( _____ ) | (O) | all other matters; |
| ( _____ ) | (P) | full and unqualified authority to my attorney(s)-in-fact to delegate any or all of the foregoing powers to any person or persons whom my attorney(s)-in-fact shall select; |
| ( _____ ) | (Q) | each of the above matters identified by the following letters: |

_____
_____
_____

*(Special provisions and limitations may be included in the statutory short form durable power of attorney only if they conform to the requirements of section 5-1503 of the New York General Obligations Law.)*

This durable Power of Attorney shall not be affected by my subsequent disability or incompetence.

If every agent named above is unable or unwilling to serve, I appoint _____
_____
_____
*(insert name and address of successor)*
to be my agent for all purposes hereunder.

**TO INDUCE ANY THIRD PARTY TO ACT HEREUNDER, I HEREBY AGREE THAT ANY THIRD PARTY RECEIVING A DULY EXECUTED COPY OR FACSIMILE OF THIS INSTRUMENT MAY ACT HEREUNDER, AND THAT REVOCATION OR TERMINATION HEREOF SHALL BE INEFFECTIVE AS TO SUCH THIRD PARTY UNLESS AND UNTIL ACTUAL NOTICE OR KNOWLEDGE OF SUCH REVOCATION OR TERMINATION SHALL HAVE BEEN RECEIVED BY SUCH THIRD PARTY, AND I FOR MYSELF AND FOR MY HEIRS, EXECUTORS, LEGAL REPRESENTATIVES AND ASSIGNS, HEREBY AGREE TO INDEMNIFY AND HOLD HARMLESS ANY SUCH THIRD PARTY FROM AND AGAINST ANY AND ALL CLAIMS THAT MAY ARISE AGAINST SUCH THIRD PARTY BY REASON OF SUCH THIRD PARTY HAVING RELIED ON THE PROVISIONS OF THIS INSTRUMENT.**

THIS DURABLE GENERAL POWER OF ATTORNEY MAY BE REVOKED BY ME AT ANY TIME.

**IN WITNESS WHEREOF**, I have hereunto signed my name on _____, _____ (year)

(YOU SIGN HERE)==>   _____
*Signature of Principal*

## ACKNOWLEDGEMENT

STATE OF _____   COUNTY OF _____   ss.:

On _____ before me personally came _____
_____ to me known, and known to me to be the individual described in, and who executed the foregoing instrument, and he acknowledged to me that he executed the same.

_____
Notary Public

My commission expires:

# DURABLE GENERAL POWER OF ATTORNEY
EFFECTIVE AT A FUTURE TIME
NEW YORK STATUTORY SHORT FORM

## THE POWERS YOU GRANT BELOW CONTINUE TO BE EFFECTIVE SHOULD YOU BECOME DISABLED OR INCOMPETENT

**(CAUTION: THIS IS AN IMPORTANT DOCUMENT. IT GIVES THE PERSON WHOM YOU DESIGNATE (YOUR "AGENT") BROAD POWERS TO HANDLE YOUR PROPERTY DURING YOUR LIFETIME, WHICH MAY INCLUDE POWERS TO MORTGAGE, SELL, OR OTHERWISE DISPOSE OF ANY REAL OR PERSONAL PROPERTY WITHOUT ADVANCE NOTICE TO YOU OR APPROVAL BY YOU. THESE POWERS WILL CONTINUE TO EXIST EVEN AFTER YOU BECOME DISABLED, OR INCOMPETENT. THESE POWERS ARE EXPLAINED MORE FULLY IN NEW YORK GENERAL OBLIGATIONS LAW, ARTICLE 5, TITLE 15, SECTIONS 5-1502A THROUGH 5-1503, WHICH EXPRESSLY PERMIT THE USE OF ANY OTHER OR DIFFERENT FORM OF POWER OF ATTORNEY.**

**THIS DOCUMENT DOES NOT AUTHORIZE ANYONE TO MAKE MEDICAL OR OTHER HEALTH CARE DECISIONS. YOU MAY EXECUTE A HEALTH CARE PROXY TO DO THIS.**

**IF THERE IS ANYTHING ABOUT THIS FORM THAT YOU DO NOT UNDERSTAND, YOU SHOULD ASK A LAWYER TO EXPLAIN IT TO YOU.)**

This is intended to constitute a POWER OF ATTORNEY EFFECTIVE AT A FUTURE TIME pursuant to Article 5, Title 15 of the New York General Obligations Law:

I,_____

*(insert your name and address)*

do hereby appoint:_____

_____

*(If 1 person is to be appointed agent, insert the name and address of your agent above)*

_____

_____

_____

*(If 2 or more persons are to be appointed agents by you, insert their names and addresses above)*

my attorney(s)-in-fact TO ACT
(If more than one agent is designated, CHOOSE ONE of the following two choices by putting your initials in ONE of the blank spaces to the left of your choice:)

(    ) Each agent may SEPARATELY act.

(    ) All agents must act TOGETHER.

*(If neither blank space is initialed, the agents will be required to act TOGETHER)*

TO TAKE EFFECT upon the occasion of the signing of a written statement EITHER:

(INSTRUCTIONS: COMPLETE OR OMIT SECTION (I) -OR- SECTION (II) BELOW BUT NEVER COMPLETE BOTH SECTIONS (I) AND (II) BELOW. IF YOU DO NOT COMPLETE EITHER SECTION (I) OR SECTION (II) BELOW, IT SHALL BE PRESUMED THAT YOU WANT THE PROVISIONS OF SECTION (I) BELOW TO APPLY.)

(I) by a physician or physicians named herein by me at this point:

Dr. _____

_____

*(Insert full name(s) and address(es) of certifying Physician(s) chosen by you)*

or if no physician or physicians are named hereinabove, or if the physician or physicians named hereinabove are unable to act, by my regular physician, or by a physician who has treated me within one year preceding the date of such signing, or by a licensed psychologist or psychiatrist, certifying that I am suffering from diminished capacity that would preclude me from conducting my affairs in a competent manner;

-OR-

(II) by a person or persons named herein by me at this point: _____

_____

_____

*(Insert full name(s) and addresses of certifying Person(s) chosen by you)*

CERTIFYING that the following specified event has occurred:_____

_____

_____

*(Insert hereinabove the specified event the certification of which will cause THIS POWER OF ATTORNEY to take effect)*

IN MY NAME, PLACE AND STEAD in any way which I myself could do, if I were personally present, with respect to the following matters as each of them as defined in Title 15 of Article 5 of the New York General Obligations Law to the extent that I am permitted by law to act through an agent:

**(DIRECTIONS: Initial in the blank space to the left of your choice any one or more of the following lettered subdivisions as to which you WANT to give your agent authority. If the blank space to the left of any particular division is NOT initialed, NO AUTHORITY WILL BE GRANTED for matters that are included in that subdivision. Alternatively, the letter corresponding to each power you wish to grant may be written or typed on the blank line in subdivision "(Q)", and you may then put your initials in the blank space to the left of subdivision "(Q)" in order to grant each of the powers so indicated)**

( _____ )  (A)  real estate transactions;
( _____ )  (B)  chattel and goods transactions;
( _____ )  (C)  bond, share and commodity transactions;
( _____ )  (D)  banking transactions;
( _____ )  (E)  business operating transactions;
( _____ )  (F)  insurance transactions;
( _____ )  (G)  estate transactions;
( _____ )  (H)  claims and litigation
( _____ )  (I)  personal relationships and affairs;
( _____ )  (J)  benefits from military service;
( _____ )  (K)  records, reports and statements;
( _____ )  (L)  retirement benefit transactions;
( _____ )  (M)  making gifts to my spouse, children and more remote descendants, and

parents, not to exceed in the aggregate $10,000 to each of such persons in any year;

(_____) (N) tax matters;

(_____) (O) all other matters;

(_____) (P) full and unqualified authority to my attorney(s)-in-fact to delegate any or all of the foregoing powers to any person or persons whom my attorney(s)-in-fact shall select;

(_____) (Q) each of the above matters identified by the following letters:

This durable Power of Attorney shall not be affected by my subsequent disability or incompetence.

*(Special provisions and limitations may be included in the statutory short form durable power of attorney only if they conform to the requirements of section 5-1503 of the New York General Obligations Law.)*

If every agent named above is unable or unwilling to serve, I appoint _____

_____

_____

*(insert name and address of successor)*

to be my agent for all purposes hereunder.

**TO INDUCE ANY THIRD PARTY TO ACT HEREUNDER, I HEREBY AGREE THAT ANY THIRD PARTY RECEIVING A DULY EXECUTED COPY OR FACSIMILE OF THIS INSTRUMENT MAY ACT HEREUNDER, AND THAT REVOCATION OR TERMINATION HEREOF SHALL BE INEFFECTIVE AS TO SUCH THIRD PARTY UNLESS AND UNTIL ACTUAL NOTICE OR KNOWLEDGE OF SUCH REVOCATION OR TERMINATION SHALL HAVE BEEN RECEIVED BY SUCH THIRD PARTY, AND I FOR MYSELF AND FOR MY HEIRS, EXECUTORS, LEGAL REPRESENTATIVES AND ASSIGNS, HEREBY AGREE TO INDEMNIFY AND HOLD HARMLESS ANY SUCH THIRD PARTY FROM AND AGAINST ANY AND ALL CLAIMS THAT MAY ARISE AGAINST SUCH THIRD PARTY BY REASON OF SUCH THIRD PARTY HAVING RELIED ON THE PROVISIONS OF THIS INSTRUMENT.**

THIS DURABLE GENERAL POWER OF ATTORNEY MAY BE REVOKED BY ME AT ANY TIME.

IN WITNESS WHEREOF, I have hereunto signed my name on _____, _____(year)

(YOU SIGN HERE)==> _____
                              Signature of Principal

## ACKNOWLEDGEMENT

STATE OF _____        COUNTY OF _____ ss.:

On _____before me personally came _____ _____ to me known, and known to me to be the individual described in, and who executed the foregoing instrument, and he acknowledged to me that he executed the same.

_____
Notary Public

My commission expires:

# NONDURABLE GENERAL POWER OF ATTORNEY
## NEW YORK STATUTORY SHORT FORM

### THE POWERS YOU GRANT BELOW CEASE TO BE EFFECTIVE
### SHOULD YOU BECOME DISABLED OR INCOMPETENT

**(CAUTION: THIS IS AN IMPORTANT DOCUMENT. IT GIVES THE PERSON WHOM YOU DESIGNATE (YOUR "AGENT") BROAD POWERS TO HANDLE YOUR PROPERTY DURING YOUR LIFETIME, WHICH MAY INCLUDE POWERS TO MORTGAGE, SELL, OR OTHERWISE DISPOSE OF ANY REAL OR PERSONAL PROPERTY WITHOUT ADVANCE NOTICE TO YOU OR APPROVAL BY YOU. THESE POWERS WILL TERMINATE IF YOU BECOME DISABLED OR INCOMPETENT. THESE POWERS ARE EXPLAINED MORE FULLY IN NEW YORK GENERAL OBLIGATIONS LAW, ARTICLE 5, TITLE 15, SECTIONS 5-120A THROUGH 5-1503, WHICH EXPRESSLY PERMIT THE USE OF ANY OTHER OR DIFFERENT FORM OF POWER OF ATTORNEY.**

**THIS DOCUMENT DOES NOT AUTHORIZE ANYONE TO MAKE MEDICAL OR OTHER HEALTH CARE DECISIONS. YOU MAY EXECUTE A HEALTH CARE PROXY TO DO THIS.**

**IF THERE IS ANYTHING ABOUT THIS FORM THAT YOU DO NOT UNDERSTAND, YOU SHOULD ASK A LAWYER TO EXPLAIN IT TO YOU.)**

THIS is intended to constitute a NONDURABLE GENERAL POWER OF ATTORNEY pursuant to Article 5, Title 15 of the New York General Obligations Law:

I, _____
*(insert your name and address)*

do hereby appoint: _____
_____
*(If 1 person is to be appointed agent, insert the name and address of your agent above)*

_____
_____
_____
_____
*(If 2 or more persons are to be appointed agents by you, insert their names and addresses above)*

my attorney(s)-in-fact TO ACT

*(If more than one agent is designated, CHOOSE ONE of the following two choices by putting your initials in ONE of the blank spaces to the left of your choice:)*

(    ) Each agent may SEPARATELY act.

(    ) All agents must act TOGETHER.

*(If neither blank space is initialed, the agents will be required to act TOGETHER)*

IN MY NAME, PLACE AND STEAD in any way which I myself could do, if I were personally present, with respect to the following matters as each of them as defined in Title 15 of Article 5 of the New York General Obligations Law to the extent that I am permitted by law to act through an agent:

**(DIRECTIONS: Initial in the blank space to the left of your choice any one or more of the following lettered subdivisions as to which you WANT to give your agent authority.**

**If the blank space to the left of any particular division is NOT initialed, NO AUTHORITY WILL BE GRANTED for matters that are included in that subdivision. ALTERNATIVELY, the letter corresponding to each power you wish to grant may be written or typed on the blank line in subdivision "(Q)", and you may then put your initials in the blank space to the left of subdivision "(Q)" in order to grant each of the powers so indicated)**

| | | |
|---|---|---|
| (_____) | (A) | real estate transactions; |
| (_____) | (B) | chattel and goods transactions; |
| (_____) | (C) | bond, share and commodity transactions; |
| (_____) | (D) | banking transactions; |
| (_____) | (E) | business operating transactions; |
| (_____) | (F) | insurance transactions; |
| (_____) | (G) | estate transactions; |
| (_____) | (H) | claims and litigation |
| (_____) | (I) | personal relationships and affairs; |
| (_____) | (J) | benefits from military service; |
| (_____) | (K) | records, reports and statements; |
| (_____) | (L) | retirement benefit transactions; |
| (_____) | (M) | making gifts to my spouse, children and more remote descendants, and parents, not to exceed in the aggregate $10,000 to each of such persons in any year; |
| (_____) | (N) | tax matters; |
| (_____) | (O) | all other matters; |
| (_____) | (P) | full and unqualified authority to my attorney(s)-in-fact to delegate any or all of the foregoing powers to any person or persons whom my attorney(s)-in-fact shall select; |
| (_____) | (Q) | each of the above matters identified by the following letters: |

*(Special provisions and limitations may be included in the statutory short form durable power of attorney only if they conform to the requirements of section 5-1503 of the New York General Obligations Law.)*

If every agent named above is unable or unwilling to serve, I appoint _____
_____
(insert name and address of successor)

to be my agent for all purposes hereunder.

**TO INDUCE ANY THIRD PARTY TO ACT HEREUNDER, I HEREBY AGREE THAT ANY THIRD PARTY RECEIVING A DULY EXECUTED COPY OR FACSIMILE OF THIS INSTRUMENT MAY ACT HEREUNDER, AND THAT REVOCATION OR TERMINATION HEREOF SHALL BE INEFFECTIVE AS TO SUCH THIRD PARTY UNLESS AND UNTIL ACTUAL NOTICE OR KNOWLEDGE OF SUCH REVOCATION OR TERMINATION SHALL HAVE BEEN RECEIVED BY SUCH THIRD PARTY, AND I FOR MYSELF AND FOR MY HEIRS, EXECUTORS, LEGAL REPRESENTATIVES AND ASSIGNS, HEREBY AGREE TO INDEMNIFY AND HOLD HARMLESS ANY SUCH THIRD PARTY FROM AND AGAINST ANY AND ALL CLAIMS THAT MAY ARISE AGAINST SUCH THIRD PARTY BY REASON OF SUCH THIRD PARTY HAVING RELIED ON THE PROVISIONS OF THIS INSTRUMENT.**

THIS NONDURABLE GENERAL POWER OF ATTORNEY MAY BE REVOKED BY ME AT ANY TIME.

**IN WITNESS WHEREOF**, I have hereunto signed my name on _____, _____(year)

(YOU SIGN HERE)==> _____
*(Signature of Principal)*

## ACKNOWLEDGEMENT

STATE OF _____ COUNTY OF _____ ss.:

On _____ before me personally came _____
_____ to me known, and known to me to be the individual described in, and who executed the foregoing instrument, and he acknowledged to me that he executed the same.

_____
Notary Public

My commission expires:

# AFFIDAVIT THAT POWER OF ATTORNEY IS IN FULL FORCE
*(Sign before a notary public)*

STATE OF _____ COUNTY OF _____ ss.:

_____ , being duly sworn, deposes and says:

1.    The Principal within did, in writing, appoint me as the Principal's true and lawful ATTORNEY-IN-FACT in the within Power of Attorney.

2.    I have no actual knowledge or actual notice of revocation or termination of the Power of Attorney by death or otherwise, or knowledge of any facts indicating the same. I further represent that the Principal is alive, has not revoked or repudiated the Power of Attorney and the Power of Attorney still is in full force and effect.

3.    I make this affidavit for the purpose of inducing


to accept delivery of the following Instrument(s), as executed by me in my capacity as the ATTORNEY-IN-FACT, with full knowledge that this affidavit will be relied upon in accepting the execution and delivery of the Instrument(s) and in paying good and valuable consideration therefor:




_____

Sworn to before me on this
_____ day of _____ , _____


_____
Notary Public

My commission expires:

# Health Care Proxy

I _____ (name of principal) hereby
appoint _____
_____ (name, home address and telephone number of
agent) as my health care agent to make any and all health care decisions for me, except to the
extent I state otherwise.

This health care proxy shall take effect in the event I become unable to make my own
health care decisions.
NOTE: Although not necessary, and neither encouraged nor discouraged, you may wish to state
instructions or wishes, and limit your agent's authority.  Unless your agent knows your wishes
about artificial nutrition and hydration, your agent will not have authority to decide about artificial
nutrition and hydration.  If you choose to state instructions, wishes, or limits, please do so below:
_____
_____
_____
_____
_____
_____

I direct my agent to make health care decisions in accordance with my wishes and
instructions as stated above or as otherwise known to him or her.  I also direct my agent to abide
by any limitations on his or her authority as stated above or as otherwise known to him or her.

In the event the person I appoint is unable, unwilling or unavailable to act as my health
care agent, I hereby appoint _____
_____(name, home address and telephone number of alternate agent) as my
health care agent.

I understand that, unless I revoke it, this proxy will remain in effect indefinitely or until the
date or occurrence of the condition I have stated below:

(Please complete the following if you do NOT want this health care proxy to be in effect
indefinitely):

This proxy shall expire: _____
_____ (Specify date or condition)

Signature:_____

Address:_____

Date:_____

I declare that the person who signed or asked another to sign this document is personally
known to me and appears to be of sound mind and acting willingly and free from duress.  He or
she signed (or asked another to sign for him or her) this document in my presence and that
person signed in my presence.  I am not the person appointed as agent by this document.

Witness: _____

Witness: _____

Witness: _____

# North Carolina Statutory Short Form of General Power of Attorney

**NOTICE: THE POWERS GRANTED BY THIS DOCUMENT ARE BROAD AND SWEEPING. THEY ARE DEFINED IN CHAPTER 32A OF THE NORTH CAROLINA GENERAL STATUTES WHICH EXPRESSLY PERMITS THE USE OF ANY OTHER OR DIFFERENT FORM OF POWER OF ATTORNEY DESIRED BY THE PARTIES CONCERNED.**

State of _____

County of _____

I, _____ , appoint
_____ to be my attorney-in-fact to act in my name in any way which I myself could act for myself, with respect to the following matters as each of them is defined in Chapter 32A of the North Carolina General Statutes. (DIRECTIONS: Initial the line opposite any one or more of the subdivisions as to which the principal desires to give the attorney-in-fact authority.)

| | | |
|---|---|---|
| (1) | Real property transactions................................................................ | _____ |
| (2) | Personal property transactions ...................................................... | _____ |
| (3) | Bond, share, stock, securities and commodity transactions................ | _____ |
| (4) | Banking transactions....................................................................... | _____ |
| (5) | Safe deposits................................................................................. | _____ |
| (6) | Business operating transactions....................................................... | _____ |
| (7) | Insurance transactions.................................................................... | _____ |
| (8) | Estate transactions......................................................................... | _____ |
| (9) | Personal relationships and affairs.................................................... | _____ |
| (10) | Social security and unemployment.................................................. | _____ |
| (11) | Benefits from military service.......................................................... | _____ |
| (12) | Tax matters.................................................................................... | _____ |
| (13) | Employment of agents.................................................................... | _____ |
| (14) | Gifts to charities, and to individuals other than the attorney-in-fact.. | _____ |
| (15) | Gifts to the named attorney-in-fact................................................. | _____ |

(If power of substitution and revocation is to be given, add: 'I also give to such person full power to appoint another to act as my attorney-in-fact and full power to revoke such appointment.')

_____
_____
_____

(If period of power of attorney is to be limited, add: "This power terminates _____ , _____ .")

_____

(If power of attorney is to be a durable power of attorney under the provisions of Article 2 of Chapter 32A and is to continue in effect after the incapacity or mental incompetence of the principal, add: 'This power of a attorney shall not be affected by my subsequent incapacity or mental incompetence.')

_____
_____
_____

(If power of attorney is to take effect only after the incapacity or mental incompetence of the principal, add: 'This power of attorney shall become effective after I become incapacitated or mentally incompetent.')

_____
_____
_____

(If power of attorney is to be effective to terminate or direct the administration of a custodial trust created under the Uniform Custodial Trust Act, add: 'In the event of my subsequent incapacity or mental incompetence, the attorney-in-fact of this power of attorney shall have the power to terminate or to direct the administration of any custodial trust of which I am the beneficiary.')

_____

_____

_____

(If power of attorney is to be effective to determine whether a beneficiary under the Uniform Custodial Trust Act is incapacitated or ceases to be incapacitated, add: 'The attorney-in-fact of this power of attorney shall have the power to determine whether I am incapacitated or whether my incapacity has ceased for the purposes of any custodial trust of which I am the beneficiary.')

_____

_____

_____

I waive the requirement, set out in North Carolina Gen. Stat. § 32A-11, that the attorney-in-fact files this power of attorney with the clerk of the superior court and render inventories and accounts, after my incapacity or mental incompetence, to the clerk of the superior court.

Dated: _____, _____.

_____(SEAL)
Signature

STATE OF _____ COUNTY OF _____

On this _____ day of _____, _____, personally appeared before me, the said named _____ to me known and known to be the person described in and who executed the foregoing instrument and he (or she) acknowledged that he (or she) executed the same and being duly sworn by me, made oath that the statements in the foregoing instrument are true.

My Commission Expires: _____

_____
(Signature of Notary Public)

Notary Public (Official Seal)

# Health Care Power of Attorney

(Notice: This document gives the person you designate your health care agent broad powers to make health care decisions, including mental health treatment decisions, for you. Except to the extent that you express specific limitations or restrictions on the authority of your health care agent, this power includes the power to consent to your doctor not giving treatment or stopping treatment necessary to keep you alive, admit you to a facility, and administer certain treatments and medications. This power exists only as to those health care decisions for which you are unable to give informed consent.

This form does not impose a duty on your health care agent to exercise granted powers, but when a power is exercised, your health care agent will have to use due care to act in your best interests and in accordance with this document. For mental health treatment decisions, your health care agent will act according to how the health care agent believes you would act if you were making the decision. Because the powers granted by this document are broad and sweeping, you should discuss your wishes concerning life-sustaining procedures, mental health treatment, and other health care decisions with your health care agent.

Use of this form in the creation of a health care power of attorney is lawful and is authorized pursuant to North Carolina law. However, use of this form is an optional and nonexclusive method for creating a health care power of attorney and North Carolina law does not bar the use of any other or different form of power of attorney for health care that meets the statutory  requirements.)

1.  Designation of health care agent.
I, _____ , being of sound mind, hereby appoint
Name:_____ Home Address:_____
Home Telephone Number _____ Work Telephone Number_____
as my health care attorney-in-fact (herein referred to as my 'health care agent') to act for me and in my name (in any way I could act in person) to make health care decisions for me as authorized in this document.

If the person named as my health care agent is not reasonably available or is unable or unwilling to act as my agent, then I appoint the following persons (each to act alone and successively, in the order named), to serve in that capacity: (Optional)

A.      Name: _____
        Home Address: _____
        Home Telephone Number _____ Work Telephone Number _____

B.      Name: _____
        Home Address: _____
        Home Telephone Number _____ Work Telephone Number _____

Each successor health care agent designated shall be vested with the same power and duties as if originally named as my health care agent.

2.  Effectiveness of appointment.

(Notice: This health care power of attorney may be revoked by you at any time in any manner by which you are able to communicate your intent to revoke to your health care agent and your attending physician.)

Absent revocation, the authority granted in this document shall become effective when and if the physician or physicians designated below determine that I lack sufficient understanding or capacity to make or communicate decisions relating to my health care and will continue in effect during my incapacity, until my death. This determination shall be made by the following physician or physicians. For decisions related to mental health treatment, this determination shall be made by the following physician or eligible psychologist. (You may include here a designation of your choice, including your attending physician or eligible psychologist, or any other physician or eligible psychologist. You may also name two or more physicians or eligible psychologists, if desired, both of whom must make this determination before the authority granted to the health care agent becomes effective.):

_____

_____

3.  General statement of authority granted.

Except as indicated in section 4 below, I hereby grant to my health care agent named above full power and authority to make health care decisions, including mental health treatment decisions, on my behalf, including, but not limited to, the following:

A.    To request, review, and receive any information, verbal or written, regarding my physical or mental health, including, but not limited to, medical and hospital records, and to consent to the disclosure of this information.

B.    To employ or discharge my health care providers.

C.    To consent to and authorize my admission to and discharge from a hospital, nursing or convalescent home, or other institution.

D.    To consent to and authorize my admission to and retention in a facility for the care or treatment of mental illness.

E.    To consent to and authorize the administration of medications for mental health treatment and electroconvulsive treatment (ECT) commonly referred to as "shock treatment."

F.    To give consent for, to withdraw consent for, or to withhold consent for, X ray, anesthesia, medication, surgery, and all other diagnostic and treatment procedures ordered by or under the authorization of a licensed physician, dentist, or podiatrist. This authorization specifically includes the power to consent to measures for relief of pain.

G.    To authorize the withholding or withdrawal of life-sustaining procedures when and if my physician determines that I am terminally ill, permanently in a coma, suffer severe dementia, or am in a persistent vegetative state. Life-sustaining procedures are those forms of medical care that only serve to artificially prolong the dying process and may include mechanical ventilation, dialysis, antibiotics, artificial nutrition hydration, and other forms of medical treatment which sustain, restore or supplant vital bodily functions. Life-sustaining procedures do not include care necessary to provide comfort or alleviate pain.

I DESIRE THAT MY LIFE NOT BE PROLONGED BY LIFE-SUSTAINING PROCEDURES IF I AM TERMINALLY ILL, PERMANENTLY IN A COMA, SUFFER SEVERE DEMENTIA, OR AM IN A PERSISTENT VEGETATIVE STATE.

H.    To exercise any right I may have to make a disposition of any part or all of my body for medical purposes, to donate my organs, to authorize an autopsy, and to direct the disposition of my remains.

I.    To take any lawful actions that may be necessary to carry out these decisions, including the granting of releases of liability to medical providers.

4.  Special provisions and limitations. (Notice: The above grant of power is intended to be as broad as possible so that your health care agent will have authority to make any decisions you could make to obtain or terminate any type of health care. If you wish to limit the scope of your health care agent's powers, you may do so in this section.)

A.     In exercising the authority to make health care decisions on my behalf, the authority of my health care agent is subject to the following special provisions and limitations (Here you may include any specific limitations you deem appropriate such as: your own definition of when life-sustaining treatment should be withheld or discontinued, or instructions to refuse any specific types of treatment that are inconsistent with your religious beliefs, or unacceptable to you for any other reason.):

_____

_____

_____

_____

B.     In exercising the authority to make mental health decisions on my behalf, the authority of my health care agent is subject to the following special provisions and limitations. (Here you may include any specific limitations you deem appropriate such as: limiting the grant of authority to make only mental health treatment decisions, your own instructions regarding the administration or withholding of psychotropic medications and electroconvulsive treatment (ECT), instructions regarding your admission to and retention in a health care facility for mental health treatment, or instructions to refuse any specific types of treatment that are unacceptable to you):

_____

_____

_____

_____

C.     (Notice: This health care power of attorney may incorporate or be combined with an advance instruction for mental health treatment, executed in accordance with Part 2 of Article 3 of Chapter 122C of the General Statutes, which you may use to state your instructions regarding mental health treatment in the event you lack sufficient understanding or capacity to make or communicate mental health treatment decisions. Because your health care agent's decisions about decisions must be consistent with any statements you have expressed in an advance instruction, you should indicate here whether you have executed an advance instruction for mental health treatment.):

_____

_____

_____

_____

5.  Guardianship provision. If it becomes necessary for a court to appoint a guardian of my person, I nominate my health care agent acting under this document to be the guardian of my person, to serve without bond or security. The guardian shall act consistently with G.S. 35A-1201(a)(5).

6.  Reliance of third parties on health care agent.

A.     No person who relies in good faith upon the authority of or any representations by my health care agent shall be liable to me, my estate, my heirs, successors, assigns, or personal representatives, for actions or omissions by my health care agent.

B.     The powers conferred on my health care agent by this document may be exercised by my health care agent alone, and my health care agent's signature or act under the authority granted in this document may be accepted by persons as fully authorized by me and with the same force and effect as if I were personally present, competent, and acting on my own behalf. All acts performed in good faith by my health care agent pursuant to this power of attorney are done with my consent and shall have the same validity and effect as if I were present and exercised the powers myself, and shall inure to the benefit of and bind me, my estate, my heirs, successors, assigns, and personal representatives. The authority of my health care agent pursuant to this power of attorney shall be superior to and binding upon my family, relatives, friends, and others.

7. Miscellaneous provisions.

A.     I revoke any prior health care power of attorney.

B.     My health care agent shall be entitled to sign, execute, deliver, and acknowledge any contract or other document that may be necessary, desirable, convenient, or proper in order to exercise and carry out any of the powers described in this document and to incur reasonable costs on my behalf incident to the exercise of these powers; provided, however, that except as shall be necessary in order to exercise the powers described in this document relating to my health care, my health care agent shall not have any authority over my property or financial affairs.

C.     My health care agent and my health care agent's estate, heirs, successors, and assigns are hereby released and forever discharged by me, my estate, my heirs, successors, and assigns and personal representatives from all liability and from all claims or demands of all kinds arising out of the acts or omissions of my health care agent pursuant to this document, except for willful misconduct or gross negligence.

D.     No act or omission of my health care agent, or of any other person, institution, or facility acting in good faith in reliance on the authority of my health care agent pursuant to this health care power of attorney shall be considered suicide, nor the cause of my death for any civil or criminal purposes, nor shall it be considered unprofessional conduct or as lack of professional competence. Any person, institution, or facility against whom criminal or civil liability is asserted because of conduct authorized by this health care power of attorney may interpose this document as a defense.

8. Signature of principal. By signing here, I indicate that I am mentally alert and competent, fully informed as to the contents of this document, and understand the full import of this grant of powers to my health care agent.

(SEAL)

_____          _____
Signature of Principal                                   Date

9. Signatures of Witnesses. I hereby state that the Principal, _____, being of sound mind, signed the foregoing health care power of attorney in my presence, and that I am not related to the principal by blood or marriage, and I would not be entitled to any portion of the estate of the principal under any existing will or codicil of the principal or as an heir under the Intestate Succession Act, if the principal died on this date without a will. I also state that I am not the principal's attending physician, nor an employee of the principal's attending physician, nor an employee of the health facility in which the principal is a patient, nor an employee of a nursing home or any group care home where the principal resides. I further state that I do not have any claim against the principal.

Witness:_____          Date:_____

Witness:_____          Date:_____

STATE OF NORTH CAROLINA

COUNTY OF_____

CERTIFICATE

I,_____, a Notary Public for _____ County, North Carolina, hereby certify that _____ appeared before me and swore to me and to the witnesses in my presence that this instrument is a health care power of attorney, and that he/she willingly and voluntarily made and executed it as his/her free act and deed for the purposes expressed in it.

I further certify that_____ and _____, witnesses, appeared before me and swore that they witnessed _____ sign the attached health care power of attorney, believing him/her to be of sound mind; and also swore that at the time they witnessed the signing (i) they were not related within the third degree to him/her or his/her spouse, and (ii) they did not know nor have a reasonable expectation that they would be entitled to any portion of his/her estate upon his/her death under any will or codicil thereto then existing or under the Intestate Succession Act as it provided at that time, and (iii) they were not a physician attending him/her, nor an employee of an attending physician, nor an employee of a health facility in which he/she was a patient, nor an employee of a nursing home or any group-care home in which he/she resided, and (iv) they did not have a claim against him/her. I further certify that I am satisfied as to the genuineness and due execution of the instrument.

This the _____ day of _____, _____

_____
Notary Public
My Commission Expires:

(A copy of this form should be given to your health care agent and any alternate named in this power of attorney, and to your physician and family members.)

# HEALTH CARE DIRECTIVE

I_____, understand this document allows me to do ONE OR ALL of the following:

PART I: Name another person (called the health care agent) to make health care decisions for me if I am unable to make and communicate health care decisions for myself. My health care agent must make health care decisions for me based on the instructions I provide in this document (Part II), if any, the wishes I have made known to him or her, or my agent must act in my best interest if I have not made my health care wishes known.

### AND/OR

PART II: Give health care instructions to guide others making health care decisions for me. If I have named a health care agent, these instructions are to be used by the agent. These instructions may also be used by my health care providers, others assisting with my health care and my family, in the event I cannot make and communicate decisions for myself.

### AND/OR

PART III: Allows me to make an organ and tissue donation upon my death by signing a document of anatomical gift.

## PART I: APPOINTMENT OF HEALTH CARE AGENT

THIS IS WHO I WANT TO MAKE HEALTH CARE DECISIONS FOR ME IF I AM UNABLE TO MAKE AND COMMUNICATE HEALTH CARE DECISIONS FOR MYSELF (I know I can change my agent or alternate agent at any time and I know I do not have to appoint an agent or an alternate agent)
NOTE: If you appoint an agent, you should discuss this health care directive with your agent and give your agent a copy. If you do not wish to appoint an agent, you may leave Part I blank and go to Part II and/or Part III. None of the following may be designated as your agent: your treating health care provider, a nonrelative employee of your treating health care provider, an operator of a long-term care facility, or a nonrelative employee of a long-term care facility.

When I am unable to make and communicate health care decisions for myself, I trust and appoint _____ to make health care decisions for me. This person is called my health care agent.
Relationship of my health care agent to me: _____
Telephone number of my health care agent: _____
Address of my health care agent: _____

(OPTIONAL) APPOINTMENT OF ALTERNATE HEALTH CARE AGENT: If my health care agent is not reasonably available, I trust and appoint _____ to be my health care agent instead.
Relationship of my alternate health care agent to me: _____
Telephone number of my alternate health care agent: _____
Address of my alternate health care agent: _____

THIS IS WHAT I WANT MY HEALTH CARE AGENT TO BE ABLE TO DO IF I AM UNABLE TO MAKE AND COMMUNICATE HEALTH CARE DECISIONS FOR MYSELF (I know I can change these choices)

My health care agent is automatically given the powers listed below in (A) through (D).
My health care agent must follow my health care instructions in this document or any other instructions I have given to my agent. If I have not given health care instructions, then my agent must act in my best interest.
Whenever I am unable to make and communicate health care decisions for myself, my health care agent has the power to:

(A)    Make any health care decision for me. This includes the power to give, refuse, or withdraw consent to any care, treatment, service, or procedures. This includes deciding whether to stop or not start health care that is keeping me or might keep me alive and deciding about mental health treatment.

(B)     Choose my health care providers.

(C)     Choose where I live and receive care and support when those choices relate to my health care needs.

(D)     Review my medical records and have the same rights that I would have to give my medical records to other people.

If I DO NOT want my health care agent to have a power listed above in (A) through (D) OR if I want to LIMIT any power in (A) through (D), I MUST say that here:

_____
_____
_____

My health care agent is NOT automatically given the powers listed below in (1) and (2). If I WANT my agent to have any of the powers in (1) and (2), I must INITIAL the line in front of the power; then my agent WILL HAVE that power.

_____(1)     To decide whether to donate any parts of my body, including organs, tissues, and eyes, when I die.

_____(2)     To decide what will happen with my body when I die (burial, cremation).

If I want to say anything more about my health care agent's powers or limits on the powers, I can say it here:

_____
_____
_____

# PART II: HEALTH CARE INSTRUCTIONS

NOTE: Complete this Part II if you wish to give health care instructions. If you appointed an agent in Part I, completing this Part II is optional but would be very helpful to your agent. However, if you chose not to appoint an agent in Part I, you MUST complete, at a minimum, Part II (B) if you wish to make a valid health care directive.

These are instructions for my health care when I am unable to make and communicate health care decisions for myself. These instructions must be followed (so long as they address my needs).

(A)     THESE ARE MY BELIEFS AND VALUES ABOUT MY HEALTH CARE
        (I know I can change these choices or leave any of them blank)
        I want you to know these things about me to help you make decisions about my health care:

My goals for my health care:

_____
_____

My fears about my health care:

_____
_____

My spiritual or religious beliefs and traditions:

_____
_____

My beliefs about when life would be no longer worth living:

_____
_____

My thoughts about how my medical condition might affect my family:

_____
_____
_____

**(B)** THIS IS WHAT I WANT AND DO NOT WANT FOR MY HEALTH CARE
(I know I can change these choices or leave any of them blank)

Many medical treatments may be used to try to improve my medical condition or to prolong my life. Examples include artificial breathing by a machine connected to a tube in the lungs, artificial feeding or fluids through tubes, attempts to start a stopped heart, surgeries, dialysis, antibiotics, and blood transfusions. Most medical treatments can be tried for a while and then stopped if they do not help.

I have these views about my health care in these situations:

(Note: You can discuss general feelings, specific treatments, or leave any of them blank).

If I had a reasonable chance of recovery and were temporarily unable to make and communicate health care decisions for myself, I would want:

_____
_____
_____

If I were dying and unable to make and communicate health care decisions for myself, I would want:

_____
_____
_____

If I were permanently unconscious and unable to make and communicate health care decisions for myself, I would want:

_____
_____
_____

If I were completely dependent on others for my care and unable to make and communicate health care decisions for myself, I would want:

_____
_____
_____

In all circumstances, my doctors will try to keep me comfortable and reduce my pain. This is how I feel about pain relief if it would affect my alertness or if it could shorten my life:

_____
_____
_____

There are other things that I want or do not want for my health care, if possible:

Who I would like to be my doctor:

_____
_____

Where I would like to live to receive health care:

_____
_____
_____

Where I would like to die and other wishes I have about dying:

_____
_____
_____

My wishes about what happens to my body when I die (cremation, burial):

_____
_____
_____

Any other things:

_____
_____
_____

## PART III: MAKING AN ANATOMICAL GIFT

I would like to be an organ donor at the time of my death. I have told my family my decision and ask my family to honor my wishes. I wish to donate the following (initial one statement):

[        ] Any needed organs and tissue.

[        ] Only the following organs and tissue: _____

## PART IV: MAKING THE DOCUMENT LEGAL

PRIOR DESIGNATIONS REVOKED. I revoke any prior health care directive.

DATE AND SIGNATURE OF PRINCIPAL
(YOU MUST DATE AND SIGN THIS HEALTH CARE DIRECTIVE)

I sign my name to this Health Care Directive Form on _____ at
                                                                                        (date)

_____
(city)
_____
(state)
_____
(you sign here)

(THIS HEALTH CARE DIRECTIVE WILL NOT BE VALID UNLESS IT IS NOTARIZED OR SIGNED BY TWO QUALIFIED WITNESSES WHO ARE PRESENT WHEN YOU SIGN OR ACKNOWLEDGE YOUR SIGNATURE. IF YOU HAVE ATTACHED ANY ADDITIONAL PAGES TO THIS FORM, YOU MUST DATE AND SIGN EACH OF THE ADDITIONAL PAGES AT THE SAME TIME YOU DATE AND SIGN THIS HEALTH CARE DIRECTIVE.)

### NOTARY PUBLIC OR STATEMENT OF WITNESSES

This document must be (1) notarized or (2) witnessed by two qualified adult witnesses. The person notarizing this document may be an employee of a health care or long-term care provider providing your care. At least one witness to the execution of the document must not be a health care or long-term care provider providing you with direct care or an employee of the health care or long-term care provider providing you with direct care. None of the following may be used as a notary or witness:

1. A person you designate as your agent or alternate agent;
2. Your spouse;
3. A person related to you by blood, marriage, or adoption;
4. A person entitled to inherit any part of your estate upon your death; or
5. A person who has, at the time of executing this document, any claim against your estate.

### Option 1: Notary Public

In my presence on _____ (date), _____ (name of declarant) acknowledged the declarant's signature on this document or acknowledged that the declarant directed the person signing this document to sign on the declarant's behalf.

_____
(Signature of Notary Public)

My commission expires _____, 20____.

**Option 2: Two Witnesses**

**Witness One:**

(1)     In my presence on _____ (date), _____ (name of declarant) acknowledged the declarant's signature on this document or acknowledged that the declarant directed the person signing this document to sign on the declarant's behalf.

(2)     I am at least eighteen years of age.

(3)     If I am a health care provider or an employee of a health care provider giving direct care to the declarant, I must initial this box: [        ].
I certify that the information in (1) through (3) is true and correct.

_____
(Signature of Witness One)

_____
(Address)

**Witness Two:**

(1)     In my presence on_____(date), _____ (name of declarant) acknowledged the declarant's signature on this document or acknowledged that the declarant directed the person signing this document to sign on the declarant's behalf.

(2)     I am at least eighteen years of age.

(3)     If I am a health care provider or an employee of a health care provider giving direct care to the declarant, I must initial this box: [        ].

I certify that the information in (1) through (3) is true and correct.

_____
(Signature of Witness Two)

_____
(Address)

## ACCEPTANCE OF APPOINTMENT OF POWER OF ATTORNEY

I accept this appointment and agree to serve as agent for health care decisions. I understand I have a duty to act consistently with the desires of the principal as expressed in this appointment. I understand that this document gives me authority over health care decisions for the principal only if the principal becomes incapacitated. I understand that I must act in good faith in exercising my authority under this power of attorney. I understand that the principal may revoke this power of attorney at any time in any manner. If I choose to withdraw during the time the principal is competent, I must notify the principal of my decision. If I choose to withdraw when the principal is not able to make health care decisions, I must notify the principal's physician.

_____
(Signature of agent/date)

_____
(Signature of alternate agent/date)

## PRINCIPAL'S STATEMENT

I have read a written explanation of the nature and effect of an appointment of a health care agent that is attached to my health care directive.

Dated this _____ day of _____ , 20 _____ .

_____
(Signature of Principal)

STATEMENT AFFIRMING EXPLANATION OF DOCUMENT TO RESIDENT OF LONG-TERM CARE FACILITY. (Only necessary if person is a resident of long-term care facility and Part I is completed appointing an agent. This statement does not need to be completed if the resident has read a written explanation of the nature and effect of an appointment of a health care agent and completed the Principal's Statement above.)
I have explained the nature and effect of this health care directive to _____
(name of principal) who signed this document and who is a resident of _____
(name and city of facility). I am (check one of the following):

    [ ]    A recognized member of the clergy.

    [ ]    An attorney licensed to practice in North Dakota.

    [ ]    A person designated by the district court for the county in which the above-named facility is located.

    [ ]    A person designated by the North Dakota department of human services.

Dated on _____ , 20___ .

_____ (Signature)

STATEMENT AFFIRMING EXPLANATION OF DOCUMENT TO HOSPITAL PATIENT OR PERSON BEING ADMITTED TO HOSPITAL. (Only necessary if person is a patient in a hospital or is being admitted to a hospital and Part I is completed appointing an agent. This statement does not need to be completed if the patient or person being admitted has read a written explanation of the nature and effect of an appointment of a health care agent and completed the Principal's Statement above.)

I have explained the nature and effect of this health care directive to _____ (name of principal) who signed this document and who is a patient or is being admitted as a patient of _____ (name and city of hospital).
I am (check one of the following):

    [ ]    An attorney licensed to practice in North Dakota.

    [ ]    A person designated by the hospital to explain the health care directive.

Dated on _____ , 20___ .

_____ (Signature)

**Notice to Adult Executing This Document**

This is an important legal document. Before executing this document, you should know these facts:

This document gives the person you designate (the attorney in fact) the power to make **most** health care decisions for you if you lose the capacity to make informed health care decisions for yourself. This power is effective only when your attending physician determines that you have lost the capacity to make informed health care decisions for yourself and, notwithstanding this document, as long as you have the capacity to make informed health care decisions for yourself, you retain the right to make all medical and other health care decisions for yourself.

You may include specific limitations in this document on the authority of the attorney in fact to make health care decisions for you.

Subject to any specific limitations you include in this document, if your attending physician determines that you have lost the capacity to make an informed decision on a health care matter, the attorney in fact **generally** will be authorized by this document to make health care decisions for you to the same extent as you could make those decisions yourself, if you had the capacity to do so. The authority of the attorney in fact to make health care decisions for you **generally** will include the authority to give informed consent, to refuse to give informed consent, or to withdraw informed consent to any care, treatment, service, or procedure to maintain, diagnose, or treat a physical or mental condition.

However, even if the attorney in fact has general authority to make health care decisions for you under this document, the attorney in fact **never** will be authorized to do any of the following:

(1)     Refuse or withdraw informed consent to life-sustaining treatment (unless your attending physician and one other physician who examines you determine, to a reasonable degree of medical certainty and in accordance with reasonable medical standards, that either of the following applies:

(a)     You are suffering from an irreversible, incurable, and untreatable condition caused by disease, illness, or injury from which (i) there can be no recovery and (ii) your death is likely to occur within a relatively short time if life-sustaining treatment is not administered, and your attending physician additionally determines, to a reasonable degree of medical certainty and in accordance with reasonable medical standards, that there is no reasonable possibility that you will regain the capacity to make informed health care decisions for yourself.

(b)   You are in a state of permanent unconsciousness that is characterized by you being irreversibly unaware of yourself and your environment and by a total loss of cerebral cortical functioning, resulting in you having no capacity to experience pain or suffering, and your attending physician additionally determines, to a reasonable degree of medical certainty and in accordance with reasonable medical standards, that there is no reasonable possibility that you will regain the capacity to make informed health care decisions for yourself);

(2)   Refuse or withdraw informed consent to health care necessary to provide you with comfort care (except that, if the attorney in fact is not prohibited from doing so under (4) below, the attorney in fact could refuse or withdraw informed consent to the provision of nutrition or hydration to you as described under (4) below). **(You should understand that comfort care is defined in Ohio law to mean artificially or technologically administered sustenance (nutrition) or fluids (hydration) when administered to diminish your pain or discomfort, not to postpone your death, and any other medical or nursing procedure, treatment, intervention, or other measure that would be taken to diminish your pain or discomfort, not to postpone your death. Consequently, if your attending physician were to determine that a previously described medical or nursing procedure, treatment, intervention, or other measure will not or no longer will serve to provide comfort to you or alleviate your pain, then, subject to (4) below, your attorney in fact would be authorized to refuse or withdraw informed consent to the procedure, treatment, intervention, or other measure.);**

(3)   Refuse or withdraw informed consent to health care for you if you are pregnant and if the refusal or withdrawal would terminate the pregnancy (unless the pregnancy or health care would pose a substantial risk to your life, or unless your attending physician and at least one other physician who examines you determine, to a reasonable degree of medical certainty and in accordance with reasonable medical standards, that the fetus would not be born alive);

**(4)   Refuse or withdraw informed consent to the provision of artificially or technologically administered sustenance (nutrition) or fluids (hydration) to you, unless:**

**(a)   You are in a terminal condition or in a permanently unconscious state.**

**(b)   Your attending physician and at least one other physician who has examined you determine, to a reasonable degree of medical certainty and in accordance with reasonable medical**

**standards, that nutrition or hydration will not or no longer will serve to provide comfort to you or alleviate your pain.**

(c) **If, but only if, you are in a permanently unconscious state, you authorize the attorney in fact to refuse or withdraw informed consent to the provision of nutrition or hydration to you by doing both of the following in this document:**

(i) **Including a statement in capital letters or other conspicuous type, including, but not limited to, a different font, bigger type, or boldface type, that the attorney in fact may refuse or withdraw informed consent to the provision of nutrition or hydration to you if you are in a permanently unconscious state and if the determination that nutrition or hydration will not or no longer will serve to provide comfort to you or alleviate your pain is made, or checking or otherwise marking a box or line (if any) that is adjacent to a similar statement on this document;**

(ii) **Placing your initials or signature underneath or adjacent to the statement, check, or other mark previously described.**

(d) **Your attending physician determines, in good faith, that you authorized the attorney in fact to refuse or withdraw informed consent to the provision of nutrition or hydration to you if you are in a permanently unconscious state by complying with the requirements of (4)(c)(i) and (ii) above.**

(5) Withdraw informed consent to any health care to which you previously consented, unless a change in your physical condition has significantly decreased the benefit of that health care to you, or unless the health care is not, or is no longer, significantly effective in achieving the purposes for which you consented to its use.

Additionally, when exercising authority to make health care decisions for you, the attorney in fact will have to act consistently with your desires or, if your desires are unknown, to act in your best interest. You may express your desires to the attorney in fact by including them in this document or by making them known to the attorney in fact in another manner.

When acting pursuant to this document, the attorney in fact **generally** will have the same rights that you have to receive information about proposed health care, to review health care records, and to consent to the disclosure of health care records. You can limit that right in this document if you so choose.

Generally, you may designate any competent adult as the attorney in fact under this document. However, you **cannot** designate your attending physician or the administrator of any nursing home in which you are receiving care as the attorney in fact under this document. Additionally, you **cannot** designate an employee or agent of your attending physician, or an employee or agent of a health care facility at which you are being treated, as the attorney in fact under this document, unless either type of employee or agent is a competent adult and related to you by blood, marriage, or adoption, or unless either type of employee or agent is a competent adult and you and the employee or agent are members of the same religious order.

This document has no expiration date under Ohio law, but you may choose to specify a date upon which your durable power of attorney for health care generally will expire. However, if you specify an expiration date and then lack the capacity to make informed health care decisions for yourself on that date, the document and the power it grants to your attorney in fact will continue in effect until you regain the capacity to make informed health care decisions for yourself.

You have the right to revoke the designation of the attorney in fact and the right to revoke this entire document at any time and in any manner. Any such revocation generally will be effective when you express your intention to make the revocation. However, if you made your attending physician aware of this document, any such revocation will be effective only when you communicate it to your attending physician, or when a witness to the revocation or other health care personnel to whom the revocation is communicated by such a witness communicate it to your attending physician.

If you execute this document and create a valid durable power of attorney for health care with it, it will revoke any prior, valid durable power of attorney for health care that you created, unless you indicate otherwise in this document.

This document is not valid as a durable power of attorney for health care unless it is acknowledged before a notary public or is signed by at least two adult witnesses who are present when you sign or acknowledge your signature. No person who is related to you by blood, marriage, or adoption may be a witness. The attorney in fact, your attending physician, and the administrator of any nursing home in which you are receiving care also are ineligible to be witnesses.

If there is anything in this document that you do not understand, you should ask your lawyer to explain it to you.

## Signature Form for Financial Power of Attorney

Signed: _____(Principal's signature)

City, County, and State of Residence

_____

_____

The principal is personally known to me and I believe the principal to be of sound mind. I am eighteen (18) years of age or older. I am not related to the principal by blood or marriage, or related to the attorney-in-fact by blood or marriage. The principal has declared to me that this instrument is his power of attorney granting to the named attorney-in-fact the power and authority specified herein, and that he has willingly made and executed it as his free and voluntary act for the purposes herein expressed.

Witness:_____

Witness:_____

STATE OF OKLAHOMA                    )
                                     ) SS.
COUNTY OF _____)

Before me, the undersigned authority, on this _____ day of _____, 20_____, personally appeared _____ (principal), _____ (witness), and _____ (witness), whose names are subscribed to the foregoing instrument in their respective capacities, and all of said persons being by me duly sworn, the principal declared to me and to the said witnesses in my presence that the instrument is his or her power of attorney, and that the principal has willingly and voluntarily made and executed it as the free act and deed of the principal for the purposes therein expressed, and the witnesses declared to me that they were each eighteen (18) years of age or over, and that neither of them is related to the principal by blood or marriage, or related to the attorney-in-fact by blood or marriage.

_____

Notary Public

My Commission Expires:

_____

## Advance Directive for Health Care

I, _____, being of sound mind and eighteen (18) years of age or older, willfully and voluntarily make known my desire, by my instructions to others through my living will, or by my appointment of a health care proxy, or both, that my life shall not be artificially prolonged under the circumstances set forth below. I thus do hereby declare:

### I. Living Will

a.    If my attending physician and another physician determine that I am no longer able to make decisions regarding my medical treatment, I direct my attending physician and other health care providers, pursuant to the Oklahoma Rights of the Terminally III or Persistently Unconscious Act, to withhold or withdraw treatment from me under the circumstances I have indicated below by my signature. I understand that I will be given treatment that is necessary for my comfort or to alleviate my pain.

b.    If I have a terminal condition:

(1)    I direct that life-sustaining treatment shall be withheld or withdrawn if such treatment would only prolong my process of dying, and if my attending physician and another physician determine that I have an incurable and irreversible condition that even with the administration of life-sustaining treatment will cause my death within six (6) months.

_____ (initials)

(2)    I understand that the subject of the artificial administration of nutrition and hydration (food and water) that will only prolong the process of dying from an incurable and irreversible condition is of particular importance. I understand that if I do not sign this paragraph, artificially administered nutrition and hydration will be administered to me. I further understand that if I sign this paragraph, I am authorizing the withholding or withdrawal of artificially administered nutrition (food) and hydration (water).

_____ (initials)

(3)    I direct that (add other medical directives, if any) _____

_____

_____

_____

_____ (initials)

c.    If I am persistently unconscious:

(1)    I direct that life-sustaining treatment be withheld or withdrawn if such treatment will only serve to maintain me in an irreversible condition, as determined by my attending physician and another physician, in which thought and awareness of self and environment are absent.

_____ (initials)

(2) I understand that the subject of the artificial administration of nutrition and hydration (food and water) for individuals who have become persistently unconscious is of particular importance. I understand that if I do not sign this paragraph, artificially administered nutrition and hydration will be administered to me. I further understand that if I sign this paragraph, I am authorizing the withholding or withdrawal of artificially administered nutrition (food) and hydration (water).

_____ (initials)

(3) I direct that (add other medical directives, if any) _____
_____
_____
_____

_____ (initials)

## II. My Appointment of My Health Care Proxy

a. If my attending physician and another physician determine that I am no longer able to make decisions regarding my medical treatment, I direct my attending physician and other health care providers pursuant to the Oklahoma Rights of the Terminally Ill or Persistently Unconscious Act to follow the instructions of _____
_____, whom I appoint as my health care proxy. If my health care proxy is unable or unwilling to serve, I appoint _____ as my alternate health care proxy with the same authority. My health care proxy is authorized to make whatever medical treatment decisions I could make if I were able, except that decisions regarding life-sustaining treatment can be made by my health care proxy or alternate health care proxy only as I indicate in the following sections.

b. If I have a terminal condition:

(1) I authorize my health care proxy to direct that life-sustaining treatment be withheld or withdrawn if such treatment would only prolong my process of dying and if my attending physician and another physician determine that I have an incurable and irreversible condition that even with the administration of life-sustaining treatment will cause my death within six (6) months.

_____ (initials)

(2) I understand that the subject of the artificial administration of nutrition and hydration (food and water) is of particular importance. I understand that if I do not sign this paragraph, artificially administered nutrition (food) or hydration (water) will be administered to me. I further understand that if I sign this paragraph, I am authorizing the withholding or withdrawal of artificially administered nutrition and hydration.

_____ (initials)

(3)    I authorize my health care proxy to (add other medical directives, if any)

_____

_____

_____

_____ (initials)

c.    If I am persistently unconscious:

(1)    I authorize my health care proxy to direct that life-sustaining treatment be withheld or withdrawn if such treatment will only serve to maintain me in an irreversible condition, as determined by my attending physician and another physician, in which thought and awareness of self and environment are absent.

_____ (initials)

(2)    I understand that the subject of the artificial administration of nutrition and hydration (food and water) is of particular importance. I understand that if I do not sign this paragraph, artificially administered nutrition (food) and hydration (water) will be administered to me. I further understand that if I sign this paragraph, I am authorizing the withholding and withdrawal of artificially administered nutrition and hydration.

_____ (initials)

(3)    I authorize my health care proxy to (add other medical directives, if any)

_____

_____

_____

_____ (initials)

## III. Anatomical Gifts

I direct that at the time of my death my entire body or designated body organs or body parts be donated for purposes of transplantation, therapy, advancement or medical or dental science or research or education pursuant to the provisions of the Uniform Anatomical Gift Act. Death means either irreversible cessation of circulatory and respiratory functions or irreversible cessation of all functions of the entire brain, including the brain stem. I specifically donate:

[ ]    My entire body; or

[ ]    The following body organs or parts:
    ( ) lungs,   ( ) liver,   ( ) pancreas,   ( ) heart,   ( ) kidneys,
    ( ) brain,   ( ) skin,   ( ) bones/marrow,   ( ) bloods/fluids,
    ( ) tissue,   ( ) arteries,   ( ) eyes/cornea/lens,   ( ) glands,
    ( ) other: _____

_____ (initials)

## IV. Conflicting Provisions

I understand that if I have completed both a living will and have appointed a health care proxy, and if there is a conflict between my health care proxy's decision and my living will, my living will shall take precedence unless I indicate otherwise. _____
_____

_____ (initials)

## V. General Provisions

a.   I understand that if I have been diagnosed as pregnant and that diagnosis is known to my attending physician, this advance directive shall have no force or effect during the course of my pregnancy.

b.   In the absence of my ability to give directions regarding the use of life-sustaining procedures, it is my intention that this advance directive shall be honored by my family and physicians as the final expression of my legal right to refuse medical or surgical treatment including, but not limited to, the administration of any life-sustaining procedures, and I accept the consequences of such refusal.

c.   This advance directive shall be in effect until it is revoked.

d.   I understand that I may revoke this advance directive at any time.

e.   I understand and agree that if I have any prior directives, and, if I sign this advance directive, my prior directives are revoked.

f.   I understand the full importance of this advance directive and I am emotionally and mentally competent to make this advance directive.

# ADVANCE DIRECTIVE

## YOU DO NOT HAVE TO FILL OUT AND SIGN THIS FORM

## PART A: IMPORTANT INFORMATION ABOUT THIS ADVANCE DIRECTIVE

This is an important legal document. It can control critical decisions about your health care. Before signing, consider these important facts:

### Facts About Part B
### (Appointing a Health Care Representative)

You have the right to name a person to direct your health care when you cannot do so. This person is called your "health care representative." You can do this by using Part B of this form. Your representative must accept on Part E of this form.

You can write in this document any restrictions you want on how your representative will make decisions for you. Your representative must follow your desires as stated in this document or otherwise made known. If your desires are unknown, your representative must try to act in your best interest. Your representative can resign at any time.

### Facts About Part C
### (Giving Health Care Instructions)

You also have the right to give instructions for health care providers to follow if you become unable to direct your care. You can do this by using Part C of this form.

### Facts About Completing This Form

This form is valid only if you sign it voluntarily and when you are of sound mind. If you do not want an advance directive, you do not have to sign this form.

Unless you have limited the duration of this advance directive, it will not expire. If you have set an expiration date, and you become unable to direct your health care before that date, this advance directive will not expire until you are able to make those decisions again.

You may revoke this document at any time. To do so, notify your representative and your health care provider of the revocation.

Despite this document, you have the right to decide your own health care as long as you are able to do so.

If there is anything in this document that you do not understand, ask a lawyer to explain it to you.

You may sign PART B, PART C, or both parts. You may cross out words that don't express your wishes or add words that better express your wishes. Witnesses must sign PART D.

Print your NAME, BIRTHDATE AND ADDRESS here:

_____
(Name)

_____
(Birthdate)

_____
_____
(Address)

Unless revoked or suspended, this advance directive will continue for:

INITIAL ONE:

__ My entire life

__ Other period (__Years)

## PART B: APPOINTMENT OF HEALTH CARE REPRESENTATIVE

I appoint _____ as my health care representative. My representative's address is _____ and telephone number is _____.

I appoint _____ as my alternate health care representative. My alternate's address is _____ and telephone number is _____.

I authorize my representative (or alternate) to direct my health care when I can't do so.

NOTE: You may not appoint your doctor, an employee of your doctor, or an owner, operator or employee of your health care facility, unless that person is related to you by blood, marriage or adoption or that person was appointed before your admission into the health care facility.

1. Limits.

Special Conditions or Instructions:
_____
_____
_____

INITIAL IF THIS APPLIES:

    ____ I have executed a Health Care Instruction or Directive to Physicians. My
        representative is to honor it.

2. Life Support.

"Life support" refers to any medical means for maintaining life, including procedures, devices and medications. If you refuse life support, you will still get routine measures to keep you clean and comfortable.

INITIAL IF THIS APPLIES:

    ____ My representative MAY decide about life support for me. (If you don't initial this
        space, then your representative MAY NOT decide about life support.)

3. Tube Feeding.

One sort of life support is food and water supplied artificially by medical device, known as tube feeding.

INITIAL IF THIS APPLIES:

    ____ My representative MAY decide about tube feeding for me. (If you don't initial this
        space, then your representative MAY NOT decide about tube feeding.)

_____
(Date)

SIGN HERE TO APPOINT A HEALTH CARE REPRESENTATIVE

_____
(Signature of person making appointment)

## PART C: HEALTH CARE INSTRUCTIONS

NOTE: In filling out these instructions, keep the following in mind:

• The term "as my physician recommends" means that you want your physician to try life support if your physician believes it could be helpful and then discontinue it if it is not helping your health condition or symptoms.

• "Life support" and "tube feeding" are defined in Part B above.

• If you refuse tube feeding, you should understand that malnutrition, dehydration and death will probably result.

• You will get care for your comfort and cleanliness, no matter what choices you make.

•You may either give specific instructions by filling out Items 1 to 4 below, or you may use the general instruction provided by Item 5.

Here are my desires about my health care if my doctor and another knowledgeable doctor confirm that I am in a medical condition described below:

1. Close to Death. If I am close to death and life support would only postpone the moment of my death:

A. INITIAL ONE:

____ I want to receive tube feeding.

____ I want tube feeding only as my physician recommends.

____ I DO NOT WANT tube feeding.

B. INITIAL ONE:

____ I want any other life support that may apply.

____ I want life support only as my physician recommends.

____ I want NO life support.

2. Permanently Unconscious. If I am unconscious and it is very unlikely that I will ever become conscious again:

A. INITIAL ONE:

____ I want to receive tube feeding.

____ I want tube feeding only as my physician recommends.

____ I DO NOT WANT tube feeding.

B. INITIAL ONE:

____ I want any other life support that may apply.

____ I want life support only as my physician recommends.

____ I want NO life support.

3. Advanced Progressive Illness. If I have a progressive illness that will be fatal and is in an advanced stage, and I am consistently and permanently unable to communicate by any means, swallow food and water safely, care for myself and recognize my family and other people, and it is very unlikely that my condition will substantially improve:

A. INITIAL ONE:

____ I want to receive tube feeding.

____ I want tube feeding only as my physician recommends.

____ I DO NOT WANT tube feeding.

B. INITIAL ONE:

____ I want any other life support that may apply.

____ I want life support only as my physician recommends.

____ I want NO life support.

4. Extraordinary Suffering. If life support would not help my medical condition and would make me suffer permanent and severe pain:

A. INITIAL ONE:

____ I want to receive tube feeding.

____ I want tube feeding only as my physician recommends.

____ I DO NOT WANT tube feeding.

B. INITIAL ONE:

____ I want any other life support that may apply.

____ I want life support only as my physician recommends.

____ I want NO life support.

5. General Instruction.
   INITIAL IF THIS APPLIES:

   I do not want my life to be prolonged by life support. I also do not want tube feeding as life support. I want my doctors to allow me to die naturally if my doctor and another knowledgeable doctor confirm I am in any of the medical conditions listed in Items 1 to 4 above.

6. Additional Conditions or Instructions.

_____
_____
_____

[Insert description of what you want done.]

7. Other Documents. A "health care power of attorney" is any document you may have signed to appoint a representative to make health care decisions for you.

INITIAL ONE:

___ I have previously signed a health care power of attorney. I want it to remain in effect unless appointed a health care representative after signing the health care power of     attorney.

___ I have a health care power of attorney, and I REVOKE IT.

___ I DO NOT have a health care power of attorney.

_____
(Date)

SIGN HERE TO GIVE INSTRUCTIONS

_____
(Signature)

_____

## PART D: DECLARATION OF WITNESSES

We declare that the person signing this advance directive:

(a) Is personally known to us or has provided proof of identity;

(b) Signed or acknowledged that person's signature on this advance directive in our presence;

(c) Appears to be of sound mind and not under duress, fraud or undue influence;

(d) Has not appointed either of us as health care representative or alternative representative; and

(e) Is not a patient for whom either of us is attending physician.

Witnessed By:

_____     _____
(Signature of Witness/Date                    (Printed Name of Witness)

_____     _____
(Signature of Witness/Date                    (Printed Name of Witness)

NOTE: One witness must not be a relative (by blood, marriage or adoption) of the person signing this advance directive.

That witness must also not be entitled to any portion of the person's estate upon death. That witness must also not own, operate or be employed at a health care facility where the person is a patient or resident.

## PART E: ACCEPTANCE BY HEALTH CARE REPRESENTATIVE

I accept this appointment and agree to serve as health care representative. I understand I must act consistently with the desires of the person I represent, as expressed in this advance directive or otherwise made known to me. If I do not know the desires of the person I represent, I have a duty to act in what I believe in good faith to be that person's best interest. I understand that this document allows me to decide about that person's health care only while that person cannot do so. I understand that the person who appointed me may revoke this appointment. If I learn that this document has been suspended or revoked, I will inform the person's current health care provider if known to me.

_____
(Signature of Health Care Representative/Date)

_____
(Printed name)

_____
(Signature of Alternate Health Care Representative/Date)

_____
(Printed name)

# POWER OF ATTORNEY

## NOTICE

THE PURPOSE OF THIS POWER OF ATTORNEY IS TO GIVE THE PERSON YOU DESIGNATE (YOUR "AGENT") BROAD POWERS TO HANDLE YOUR PROPERTY, WHICH MAY INCLUDE POWERS TO SELL OR OTHERWISE DISPOSE OF ANY REAL OR PERSONAL PROPERTY WITHOUT ADVANCE NOTICE TO YOU OR APPROVAL BY YOU.

THIS POWER OF ATTORNEY DOES NOT IMPOSE A DUTY ON YOUR AGENT TO EXERCISE GRANTED POWERS, BUT WHEN POWERS ARE EXERCISED, YOUR AGENT MUST USE DUE CARE TO ACT FOR YOUR BENEFIT AND IN ACCORDANCE WITH THIS POWER OF ATTORNEY.

YOUR AGENT MAY EXERCISE THE POWERS GIVEN HERE THROUGHOUT YOUR LIFETIME, EVEN AFTER YOU BECOME INCAPACITATED, UNLESS YOU EXPRESSLY LIMIT THE DURATION OF THESE POWERS OR YOU REVOKE THESE POWERS OR A COURT ACTING ON YOUR BEHALF TERMINATES YOUR AGENT'S AUTHORITY.

YOUR AGENT MUST KEEP YOUR FUNDS SEPARATE FROM YOUR AGENT'S FUNDS.

A COURT CAN TAKE AWAY THE POWERS OF YOUR AGENT IF IT FINDS YOUR AGENT IS NOT ACTING PROPERLY.

THE POWERS AND DUTIES OF AN AGENT UNDER A POWER OF ATTORNEY ARE EXPLAINED MORE FULLY IN 20 PA.C.S. CH. 56.

IF THERE IS ANYTHING ABOUT THIS FORM THAT YOU DO NOT UNDERSTAND, YOU SHOULD ASK A LAWYER OF YOUR OWN CHOOSING TO EXPLAIN IT TO YOU.

I HAVE READ OR HAD EXPLAINED TO ME THIS NOTICE AND I UNDERSTAND ITS CONTENTS.

_____ (Principal)     _____(Date)

## Acknowledgment of Agent

I, _____, have read the attached power of attorney and am the person identified as the agent for the principal. I hereby acknowledge that in the absence of a specific provision to the contrary in the power of attorney or in 20 Pa.C.S. when I act as agent:

I shall exercise the powers for the benefit of the principal.

I shall keep the assets of the principal separate from my assets.

I shall exercise reasonable caution and prudence.

I shall keep a full and accurate record of all actions, receipts and disbursements on behalf of the principal.

_____ (Agent)        _____(Date)

# DECLARATION

I, _____, being of sound mind, willfully and voluntarily make this declaration to be followed if I become incompetent. This declaration reflects my firm and settled commitment to refuse life-sustaining treatment under the circumstances indicated below.

I direct my attending physician to withhold or withdraw life-sustaining treatment that serves only to prolong the process of my dying, if I should be in a terminal condition or in a state of permanent unconsciousness.

I direct that treatment be limited to measures to keep me comfortable and to relieve pain, including any pain that might occur by withholding or withdrawing life-sustaining treatment.

In addition, if I am in the condition described above, I feel especially strong about the following forms of treatment:

I ( ) do ( ) do not want cardiac resuscitation.
I ( ) do ( ) do not want mechanical respiration.
I ( ) do ( ) do not want tube feeding or any other artificial or invasive form of nutrition
         (food) or hydration (water).
I ( ) do ( ) do not want blood or blood products.
I ( ) do ( ) do not want any form of surgery or invasive diagnostic tests.
I ( ) do ( ) do not want kidney dialysis.
I ( ) do ( ) do not want antibiotics.

I realize that if I do not specifically indicate my preference regarding any of the forms of treatment listed above, I may receive that form of treatment.

Other instructions:
I ( ) do ( ) do not want to designate another person as my surrogate to make medical treatment decisions for me if I should be incompetent and in a terminal condition or in a state of permanent unconsciousness. Name and address of surrogate (if applicable):


Name and address of substitute surrogate (if surrogate above is unable to serve):


I ( ) do ( ) do not want to make an anatomical gift of all or part of my body, subject to the following limitations, if any:

I made this declaration on the _____ day of _____ (month) (year).


_____
Declarant's signature

_____
_____
Declarant's address

The declarant or the person on behalf of and at the direction of declarant knowingly and voluntarily signed this writing by signature or mark in my presence.

_____
Witness' signature

_____
Witness' signature

_____
Witness' address

_____
Witness' address

# Statutory Form Durable Power of Attorney for Health Care

### WARNING TO PERSON EXECUTING THIS DOCUMENT

This is an important legal document which is authorized by the general laws of this state. Before executing this document, you should know these important facts:

You must be at least eighteen (18) years of age and a resident of the state for this document to be legally valid and binding.

This document gives the person you designate as your agent (the attorney in fact) the power to make health care decisions for you. Your agent must act consistently with your desires as stated in this document or otherwise made known.

Except as you otherwise specify in this document, this document gives your agent the power to consent to your doctor not giving treatment or stopping treatment necessary to keep you alive.

Notwithstanding this document, you have the right to make medical and other health care decisions for yourself so long as you can give informed consent with respect to the particular decision. In addition, no treatment may be given to you over your objection at the time, and health care necessary to keep you alive may not be stopped or withheld if you object at the time.

This document gives your agent authority to consent, to refuse to consent, or to withdraw consent to any care, treatment, service, or procedure to maintain, diagnose, or treat a physical or mental condition. This power is subject to any statement of your desires and any limitation that you include in this document. You may state in this document any types of treatment that you do not desire. In addition, a court can take away the power of your agent to make health care decisions for you if your agent:

(1) Authorizes anything that is illegal,

(2) Acts contrary to your known desires, or

(3) Where your desires are not known, does anything that is clearly contrary to your best interests.

Unless you specify a specific period, this power will exist until you revoke it. Your agent's power and authority ceases upon your death except to inform your family or next of kin of your desire, if any, to be an organ and tissue owner.

You have the right to revoke the authority of your agent by notifying your agent or your treating doctor, hospital, or other health care provider orally or in writing of the revocation.

Your agent has the right to examine your medical records and to consent to their disclosure unless you limit this right in this document.

This document revokes any prior durable power of attorney for health care.

You should carefully read and follow the witnessing procedure described at the end of this form. This document will not be valid unless you comply with the witnessing procedure.

If there is anything in this document that you do not understand, you should ask a lawyer to explain it to you.

Your agent may need this document immediately in case of an emergency that requires a decision concerning your health care. Either keep this document where it is immediately available to your agent and alternate agents or give each of them an executed copy of this document. You may also want to give your doctor an executed copy of this document.

(1) DESIGNATION OF HEALTH CARE AGENT.   I,

_____,

(insert your name and address)

do hereby designate and appoint:

_____

(insert name, address, and telephone number of one individual only as your agent to make health care decisions for you)

(None of the following may be designated as your agent: (1) your treating health care provider, (2) a nonrelative employee of your treating health care provider, (3) an operator of a community care facility, or (4) a nonrelative employee of an operator of a community care facility.) as my attorney in fact (agent) to make health care decisions for me as authorized in this document. For the purposes of this document, "health care decision" means consent, refusal of consent, or withdrawal of consent to any care, treatment, service, or procedure to maintain, diagnose, or treat an individual's physical or mental condition.

(2) CREATION OF DURABLE POWER OF ATTORNEY FOR HEALTH CARE. By this document I intend to create a durable power of attorney for health care.

(3) GENERAL STATEMENT OF AUTHORITY GRANTED. Subject to any limitations in this document, I hereby grant to my agent full power and authority to make health care decisions for me to the same extent that I could make such decisions for myself if I had the capacity to do so. In exercising this authority, my agent shall make health care decisions that are consistent with my desires as stated in this document or otherwise made known to my agent, including, but not limited to, my desires concerning obtaining or refusing or withdrawing life-prolonging care, treatment, services, and procedures and informing my family or next of kin of my desire, if any, to be an organ or tissue donor.

(If you want to limit the authority of your agent to make health care decisions for you, you can state the limitations in paragraph (4) ("Statement of Desires, Special Provisions, and Limitations") below. You can indicate your desires by including a statement of your desires in the same paragraph.)

(4) STATEMENT OF DESIRES, SPECIAL PROVISIONS, AND LIMITATIONS. (Your agent must make health care decisions that are consistent with your known desires. You can, but are not required to, state your desires in the space provided below. You should consider whether you want to include a statement of your desires concerning life-prolonging care, treatment, services, and procedures. You can also include a statement of your desires concerning other matters relating to your health care. You can also make your desires known to your agent by discussing your desires with your agent or by some other means. If there are any types of treatment that you do not want to be used, you should state them in the space below. If you want to limit in any other way the authority given your agent by this document, you should state the limits in the space below. If you do not state any limits, your agent will have broad powers to make health care decisions for you, except to the extent that there are limits provided by law.)

In exercising the authority under this durable power of attorney for health care, my agent shall act consistently with my desires as stated below and is subject to the special provisions and limitations stated below:

(a) Statement of desires concerning life-prolonging care, treatment, services, and procedures:

_____

_____

_____

(b) Additional statement of desires, special provisions, and limitations regarding health care decisions:

_____

_____

_____

(c) Statement of desire regarding organ and tissue donation:

_____

_____

_____

Initial if applicable:

[      ] In the event of my death, I request that my agent inform my family/next of kin of my desire to be an organ and tissue donor, if possible.

(You may attach additional pages if you need more space to complete your statement. If you attach additional pages, you must date and sign EACH of the additional pages at the same time you date and sign this document.)

(5) INSPECTION AND DISCLOSURE OF INFORMATION RELATING TO MY PHYSICAL OR MENTAL HEALTH. Subject to any limitations in this document, my agent has the power and authority to do all of the following:

> (a) Request, review, and receive any information, verbal or written, regarding my physical or mental health, including, but not limited to, medical and hospital records.

> (b) Execute on my behalf any releases or other documents that may be required in order to obtain this information.

> (c) Consent to the disclosure of this information.

(If you want to limit the authority of your agent to receive and disclose information relating to your health, you must state the limitations in paragraph (4) ("Statement of desires, special provisions, and limitations") above.)

(6) SIGNING DOCUMENTS, WAIVERS, AND RELEASES. Where necessary to implement the health care decisions that my agent is authorized by this document to make, my agent has the power and authority to execute on my behalf all of the following:

> (a) Documents titled or purporting to be a "Refusal to Permit Treatment" and "Leaving Hospital Against Medical Advice."

> (b) Any necessary waiver or release from liability required by a hospital or physician.

(7) DURATION. (Unless you specify a shorter period in the space below, this power of attorney will exist until it is revoked.)

This durable power of attorney for health care expires on _____

_____ (Fill in this space ONLY if you want the authority of your agent to end on a specific date.)

(8) DESIGNATION OF ALTERNATE AGENTS. (You are not required to designate any alternate agents but you may do so. Any alternate agent you designate will be able to make the same health care decisions as the agent you designated in paragraph (1), above, in the event that agent is unable or ineligible to act as your agent. If the agent you designated is your spouse, he or she becomes ineligible to act as your agent if your marriage is dissolved.)

If the person designated as my agent in paragraph (1) is not available or becomes ineligible to act as my agent to make a health care decision for me or loses the mental capacity to make health care decisions for me, or if I revoke that person's appointment or authority to act as my agent to make health care decisions for me, then I designate and appoint the following persons to serve as my agent to make health care decisions for me as authorized in this document, such persons to serve in the order listed below:

(A) First Alternate Agent:

_____
(Insert name, address, and telephone number of first alternate agent.)

(B) Second Alternate Agent:

_____
(Insert name, address, and telephone number of second alternate agent.)

(9) PRIOR DESIGNATIONS REVOKED. I revoke any prior durable power of attorney for health care.

DATE AND SIGNATURE OF PRINCIPAL
(YOU MUST DATE AND SIGN THIS POWER OF ATTORNEY)

I sign my name to this Statutory Form Durable Power of Attorney for Health Care on _____
_____ at _____
(Date)

_____, _____.
(City)                              (State)

_____
(You sign here)

(THIS POWER OF ATTORNEY WILL NOT BE VALID UNLESS IT IS SIGNED BY TWO (2) QUALIFIED WITNESSES WHO ARE PRESENT WHEN YOU SIGN OR ACKNOWLEDGE YOUR SIGNATURE. IF YOU HAVE ATTACHED ANY ADDITIONAL PAGES TO THIS FORM, YOU MUST DATE AND SIGN EACH OF THE ADDITIONAL PAGES AT THE SAME TIME YOU DATE AND SIGN THIS POWER OF ATTORNEY.)

## STATEMENT OF WITNESSES

(This document must be witnessed by two (2) qualified adult witnesses. None of the following may be used as a witness:

(1) A person you designate as your agent or alternate agent,

(2) A health care provider,

(3) An employee of a health care provider,

(4) The operator of a community care facility,

(5) An employee of an operator of a community care facility.

You are not required to have this document witnessed by a notary public.

At least one of the witnesses must make the additional declaration set out following the place where the witnesses sign.)

I declare under penalty of perjury that the person who signed or acknowledged this document is personally known to me to be the principal, that the principal signed or acknowledged this durable power of attorney in my presence, that the principal appears to be of sound mind and under no duress, fraud, or undue influence, that I am not the person appointed as attorney in fact by this document, and that I am not a health care provider, an employee of a health care provider, the operator of a community care facility, nor an employee of an operator of a community care facility.

Signature: _____

Residence Address: _____

Print Name: _____

Date: _____

Signature: _____

Residence Address: _____

Print Name: _____

Date: _____

(AT LEAST ONE OF THE ABOVE WITNESSES MUST ALSO SIGN THE FOLLOWING DECLARATION.)

I further declare under penalty of perjury that I am not related to the principal by blood, marriage, or adoption, and, to the best of my knowledge, I am not entitled to any part of the estate of the principal upon the death of the principal under a will now existing or by operation of law.

Signature: _____

Print Name: _____

Signature: _____

Print Name: _____

# Health Care Power of Attorney
## (SOUTH CAROLINA STATUTORY FORM)

## INFORMATION ABOUT THIS DOCUMENT

THIS IS AN IMPORTANT LEGAL DOCUMENT. BEFORE SIGNING THIS DOCUMENT, YOU SHOULD KNOW THESE IMPORTANT FACTS:

1.	THIS DOCUMENT GIVES THE PERSON YOU NAME AS YOUR AGENT THE POWER TO MAKE HEALTH CARE DECISIONS FOR YOU IF YOU CANNOT MAKE THE DECISION FOR YOURSELF. THIS POWER INCLUDES THE POWER TO MAKE DECISIONS ABOUT LIFE-SUSTAINING TREATMENT. UNLESS YOU STATE OTHERWISE, YOUR AGENT WILL HAVE THE SAME AUTHORITY TO MAKE DECISIONS ABOUT YOUR HEALTH CARE AS YOU WOULD HAVE.

2.	THIS POWER IS SUBJECT TO ANY LIMITATIONS OR STATEMENTS OF YOUR DESIRES THAT YOU INCLUDE IN THIS DOCUMENT. YOU MAY STATE IN THIS DOCUMENT ANY TREATMENT YOU DO NOT DESIRE OR TREATMENT YOU WANT TO BE SURE YOU RECEIVE. YOUR AGENT WILL BE OBLIGATED TO FOLLOW YOUR INSTRUCTIONS WHEN MAKING DECISIONS ON YOUR BEHALF. YOU MAY ATTACH ADDITIONAL PAGES IF YOU NEED MORE SPACE TO COMPLETE THE STATEMENT.

3.	AFTER YOU HAVE SIGNED THIS DOCUMENT, YOU HAVE THE RIGHT TO MAKE HEALTH CARE DECISIONS FOR YOURSELF IF YOU ARE MENTALLY COMPETENT TO DO SO. AFTER YOU HAVE SIGNED THIS DOCUMENT, NO TREATMENT MAY BE GIVEN TO YOU OR STOPPED OVER YOUR OBJECTION IF YOU ARE MENTALLY COMPETENT TO MAKE THAT DECISION.

4.	YOU HAVE THE RIGHT TO REVOKE THIS DOCUMENT, AND TERMINATE YOUR AGENT'S AUTHORITY, BY INFORMING EITHER YOUR AGENT OR YOUR HEALTH CARE PROVIDER ORALLY OR IN WRITING.

5.	IF THERE IS ANYTHING IN THIS DOCUMENT THAT YOU DO NOT UNDERSTAND, YOU SHOULD ASK A SOCIAL WORKER, LAWYER, OR OTHER PERSON TO EXPLAIN IT TO YOU.

6.	THIS POWER OF ATTORNEY WILL NOT BE VALID UNLESS TWO PERSONS SIGN AS WITNESSES. EACH OF THESE PERSONS MUST EITHER WITNESS YOUR SIGNING OF THE POWER OF ATTORNEY OR WITNESS YOUR ACKNOWLEDGMENT THAT THE SIGNATURE ON THE POWER OF ATTORNEY IS YOURS.

THE FOLLOWING PERSONS MAY NOT ACT AS WITNESSES:

A.	YOUR SPOUSE; YOUR CHILDREN, GRANDCHILDREN, AND OTHER LINEAL DESCENDANTS; YOUR PARENTS, GRANDPARENTS, AND OTHER LINEAL ANCESTORS; YOUR SIBLINGS AND THEIR LINEAL DESCENDANTS; OR A SPOUSE OF ANY OF THESE PERSONS.

B.	A PERSON WHO IS DIRECTLY FINANCIALLY RESPONSIBLE FOR YOUR MEDICAL CARE.

C.	A PERSON WHO IS NAMED IN YOUR WILL, OR, IF YOU HAVE NO WILL, WHO WOULD INHERIT YOUR PROPERTY BY INTESTATE SUCCESSION.

D.	A BENEFICIARY OF A LIFE INSURANCE POLICY ON YOUR LIFE.

E.	THE PERSONS NAMED IN THE HEALTH CARE POWER OF ATTORNEY AS YOUR AGENT OR SUCCESSOR AGENT.

F.	YOUR PHYSICIAN OR AN EMPLOYEE OF YOUR PHYSICIAN.

G.	ANY PERSON WHO WOULD HAVE A CLAIM AGAINST ANY PORTION OF YOUR ESTATE (PERSONS TO WHOM YOU OWE MONEY).

IF YOU ARE A PATIENT IN A HEALTH FACILITY, NO MORE THAN ONE WITNESS MAY BE AN EMPLOYEE OF THAT FACILITY.

7.	YOUR AGENT MUST BE A PERSON WHO IS 18 YEARS OLD OR OLDER AND OF SOUND MIND. IT MAY NOT BE YOUR DOCTOR OR ANY OTHER HEALTH CARE PROVIDER THAT IS NOW PROVIDING YOU WITH TREATMENT; OR AN EMPLOYEE OF

YOUR DOCTOR OR PROVIDER; OR A SPOUSE OF THE DOCTOR, PROVIDER, OR EMPLOYEE; UNLESS THE PERSON IS A RELATIVE OF YOURS.

      8. YOU SHOULD INFORM THE PERSON THAT YOU WANT HIM OR HER TO BE YOUR HEALTH CARE AGENT. YOU SHOULD DISCUSS THIS DOCUMENT WITH YOUR AGENT AND YOUR PHYSICIAN AND GIVE EACH A SIGNED COPY. IF YOU ARE IN A HEALTH CARE FACILITY OR A NURSING CARE FACILITY, A COPY OF THIS DOCUMENT SHOULD BE INCLUDED IN YOUR MEDICAL RECORD.

## 1. DESIGNATION OF HEALTH CARE AGENT

I,_____, hereby appoint:
    (Principal)

_____(Agent)
_____ (Address)
Home Telephone:_____ Work Telephone:_____
as my agent to make health care decisions for me as authorized in this document.

## 2. EFFECTIVE DATE AND DURABILITY  By this document I intend to create a durable power of attorney effective upon, and only during, any period of mental incompetence.

## 3. AGENT'S POWERS  I grant to my agent full authority to make decisions for me regarding my health care. In exercising this authority, my agent shall follow my desires as stated in this document or otherwise expressed by me or known to my agent. In making any decision, my agent shall attempt to discuss the proposed decision with me to determine my desires if I am able to communicate in any way. If my agent cannot determine the choice I would want made, then my agent shall make a choice for me based upon what my agent believes to be in my best interests. My agent's authority to interpret my desires is intended to be as broad as possible, except for any limitations I may state below.

    Accordingly, unless specifically limited by Section E, below, my agent is authorized as follows:

A. To consent, refuse, or withdraw consent to any and all types of medical care, treatment, surgical procedures, diagnostic procedures, medication, and the use of mechanical or other procedures that affect any bodily function, including, but not limited to, artificial respiration, nutritional support and hydration, and cardiopulmonary resuscitation;

B. To authorize, or refuse to authorize, any medication or procedure intended to relieve pain, even though such use may lead to physical damage, addiction, or hasten the moment of, but not intentionally cause, my death;

C. To authorize my admission to or discharge, even against medical advice, from any hospital, nursing care facility, or similar facility or service;

D. To take any other action necessary to making, documenting, and assuring implementation of decisions concerning my health care, including, but not limited to, granting any waiver or release from liability required by any hospital, physician, nursing care provider, or other health care provider; signing any documents relating to refusals of treatment or the leaving of a facility against medical advice, and pursuing any legal action in my name, and at the expense of my estate to force compliance with my wishes as determined by my agent, or to seek actual or punitive damages for the failure to comply;

E. The powers granted above do not include the following powers or are subject to the following rules or limitations: _____

_____
_____

## 4. ORGAN DONATION (INITIAL ONLY ONE)

My agent may _____; may not _____ consent to the donation of all or any of my tissue or organs for purposes of transplantation.

## 5. EFFECT ON DECLARATION OF A DESIRE FOR A NATURAL DEATH (LIVING WILL)

I understand that if I have a valid Declaration of a Desire for a Natural Death, the instructions contained in the Declaration will be given effect in any situation to which they are applicable. My agent will have authority to make decisions concerning my health care only in situations to which the Declaration does not apply.

## 6. STATEMENT OF DESIRES AND SPECIAL PROVISIONS With respect to any Life-Sustaining Treatment, I direct the following: (INITIAL ONLY ONE OF THE FOLLOWING 4 PARAGRAPHS)

(1) _____ GRANT OF DISCRETION TO AGENT. I do not want my life to be prolonged nor do I want life-sustaining treatment to be provided or continued if my agent believes the burdens of the treatment outweigh the expected benefits. I want my agent to consider the relief of suffering, my personal beliefs, the expense involved and the quality as well as the possible extension of my life in making decisions concerning life-sustaining treatment.

OR

(2) _____ DIRECTIVE TO WITHHOLD OR WITHDRAW TREATMENT. I do not want my life to be prolonged and I do not want life-sustaining treatment:

a. if I have a condition that is incurable or irreversible and, without the administration of life-sustaining procedures, expected to result in death within a relatively short period of time; or

b. if I am in a state of permanent unconsciousness.

OR

(3) _____ DIRECTIVE FOR MAXIMUM TREATMENT. I want my life to be prolonged to the greatest extent possible, within the standards of accepted medical practice, without regard to my condition, the chances I have for recovery, or the cost of the procedures.

OR

(4) _____ DIRECTIVE IN MY OWN WORDS: _____

_____

_____

## 7. STATEMENT OF DESIRES REGARDING TUBE FEEDING

With respect to Nutrition and Hydration provided by means of a nasogastric tube or tube into the stomach, intestines, or veins, I wish to make clear that (INITIAL ONLY ONE)

_____ I do not want to receive these forms of artificial nutrition and hydration, and they may be withheld or withdrawn under the conditions given above;

OR

_____ I do want to receive these forms of artificial nutrition and hydration.

IF YOU DO NOT INITIAL EITHER OF THE ABOVE STATEMENTS, YOUR AGENT WILL NOT HAVE AUTHORITY TO DIRECT THAT NUTRITION AND HYDRATION NECESSARY FOR COMFORT CARE OR ALLEVIATION OF PAIN BE WITHDRAWN.

## 8. SUCCESSORS

If an agent named by me dies, becomes legally disabled, resigns, refuses to act, becomes unavailable, or if an agent who is my spouse is divorced or separated from me, I name the following as successors to my agent, each to act alone and successively, in the order named.

A.     First Alternate Agent: _____
       Name: _____
       Address: _____
       Telephone: _____

B.     Second Alternate Agent: _____
       Name: _____
       Address: _____
       Telephone: _____

## 9.  ADMINISTRATIVE PROVISIONS

A.       I revoke any prior Health Care Power of Attorney and any provisions relating to health care of any other prior power of attorney.

B.       This power of attorney is intended to be valid in any jurisdiction in which it is presented.

## 10. UNAVAILABILITY OF AGENT

If at any relevant time the Agent or Successor Agents named herein are unable or unwilling to make decisions concerning my health care, and those decision are to be made by a guardian, by the Probate Court, or by a surrogate pursuant to the Adult Health Care Consent Act, it is my intention that the guardian, Probate Court, or surrogate make those decisions in accordance with my directions as stated in this document.

BY SIGNING HERE I INDICATE THAT I UNDERSTAND THE CONTENT OF THIS DOCUMENT AND THE EFFECT OF THIS GRANT OF POWERS TO MY AGENT.

I sign my name to this Health Care Power of Attorney on this _____ day of _____, _____. My current home address is: _____
_____

Signature: _____

Name: _____

WITNESS STATEMENT

I declare, on the basis of information and belief, that the person who signed or acknowledged this document (the principal) is personally known to me, that he/she signed or acknowledged this Health Care Power of Attorney in my presence, and that he/she appears to be of sound mind and under no duress, fraud, or undue influence. I am not related to the principal by blood, marriage, or adoption, either as a spouse, a lineal ancestor, descendant of the parents of the principal, or spouse of any of them. I am not directly financially responsible for the principal's medical care. I am not entitled to any portion of the principal's estate upon his decease, whether under any will or as an heir by intestate succession, nor am I the beneficiary of an insurance policy on the principal's life, nor do I have a claim against the principal's estate as of this time. I am not the principal's attending physician, nor an employee of the attending physician. No more than one witness is an employee of a health facility in which the principal is a patient. I am not appointed as Health Care Agent or Successor Health Care Agent by this document.

| Witness No. 1 | Witness No. 2 |
|---|---|
| Date: _____ | Date: _____ |
| Signature: _____ | Signature: _____ |
| Print Name: _____ | Print Name: _____ |
| Residence Address: _____ | Residence Address: _____ |
| _____ | _____ |
| _____ | _____ |
| Telephone: _____ | Telephone: _____ |

# LIVING WILL DECLARATION

This is an important legal document. This document directs the medical treatment you are to receive in the event you are unable to participate in your own medical decisions and you are in a terminal condition. This document may state what kind of treatment you want or do not want to receive.

This document can control whether you live or die. Prepare this document carefully. If you use this form, read it completely. You may want to seek professional help to make sure the form does what you intend and is completed without mistakes.

This document will remain valid and in effect until and unless you revoke it. Review this document periodically to make sure it continues to reflect your wishes. You may amend or revoke this document at any time by notifying your physician and other health-care providers. You should give copies of this Document to your physician and your family. This form is entirely optional. If you choose to use this form, please note that the form provides signature lines for you, the two witnesses whom you have selected and a notary public.

TO MY FAMILY, PHYSICIANS, AND ALL THOSE CONCERNED WITH MY CARE:

I, _____, willfully and voluntarily make this declaration as a directive to be followed if I am in a terminal condition and become unable to participate in decisions regarding my medical care.

With respect to any life-sustaining treatment, I direct the following:

(Initial only one of the following optional directives if you agree. If you do not agree with any of the following directives, space is provided below for you to write your own directives).

_____ NO LIFE-SUSTAINING TREATMENT. I direct that no life-sustaining treatment be provided. If life-sustaining treatment is begun, terminate it.

_____ TREATMENT FOR RESTORATION. Provide life-sustaining treatment only if and for so long as you believe treatment offers a reasonable possibility of restoring to me the ability to think and act for myself.

_____ TREAT UNLESS PERMANENTLY UNCONSCIOUS. If you believe that I am permanently unconscious and are satisfied that this condition is irreversible, then do not provide me with life-sustaining treatment, and if life-sustaining treatment is being provided to me, terminate it. If and so long as you believe that treatment has a reasonable possibility of restoring consciousness to me, then provide life-sustaining treatment.

_____ MAXIMUM TREATMENT. Preserve my life as long as possible, but do not provide treatment that is not in accordance with accepted medical standards as then in effect. (Artificial nutrition and hydration is food and water provided by means of a nasogastric tube or tubes inserted into the stomach, intestines, or veins. If you do not wish to receive this form of treatment, you must initial the statement below which reads: "I intend to include this treatment, among the 'life-sustaining treatment' that may be withheld or withdrawn.")

With respect to artificial nutrition and hydration, I wish to make clear that (Initial only one)

_____ I intend to include this treatment among the "life-sustaining treatment" that may be withheld or withdrawn.

_____ I do not intend to include this treatment among the "life-sustaining treatment" that may be withheld or withdrawn.

(If you do not agree with any of the printed directives and want to write your own, or if you want to write directives in addition to the printed provisions, or if you want to express some of your other thoughts, you can do so here.)

_____
_____
_____

Date: _____     _____
                                (your signature)


_____   _____
(your address)                        (type or print your signature)

The declarant voluntarily signed this document in my presence.

Witness_____   Witness_____

Address _____   Address _____


On this _____ day of _____, 200_____, the declarant, _____, and witnesses _____, and _____, personally appeared before the undersigned officer and signed the foregoing instrument in my presence. Dated this _____ day of _____, 200____.


_____
Notary Public
My commission expires: _____

# Power of Attorney

I, _____

_____(insert your name and address),

appoint _____

_____ (insert the name and address of the person appointed) as my attorney-in-fact (agent) to act for me in any lawful way with respect to the powers set forth, defined, and described in the Tennessee Code Annotated, Section 34-6-109, which is incorporated by reference herein; subject to any special instructions or limitations contained in paragraph 2 below. If my agent designated above shall be unable or unwilling to serve, I appoint _____

_____

_____ (insert name and address of alternate agent) as my alternate agent.

1.   **Effective Date** (CHECK ONE OF THE FOLLOWING BOXES):

&#9633;     This power of attorney shall become effective immediately, and (check one):

&#9633;     shall not be affected by subsequent disability or incapacity of the principal.

&#9633;     shall terminate upon the subsequent disability or incapacity of the principal.

&#9633;     This power of attorney shall become effective upon the disability or incapacity of the principal.

2.   **Special Instructions and Limitations** (if none, type in the word "none"): _____

_____

_____

3.   **Conservator:** In the event a court appoints a conservator, guardian of the estate, or guardian of the person for me, I nominate _____

_____ (insert name and address of person nominated) to serve as such conservator or guardian.

Signed this _____ day of _____, _____.

_____        _____
(Your signature)                                              (Your social security number)

ACKNOWLEDGMENT

State of _____          )
(County) of _____          )

On this _____ day of _____, _____, before me, personally appeared _____ (name of principal), who is personally known to me or provided _____ as identification, and acknowledged that he or she executed it.

_____
Notary Public

## Durable Power of Attorney for Health Care

### WARNING TO PERSON EXECUTING THIS DOCUMENT

This is an important legal document. Before executing this document you should know these important facts.

This document gives the person you designate as your agent (the attorney in fact) the power to make health care decisions for you. Your agent must act consistently with your desires as stated in this document.

Except as you otherwise specify in this document, this document gives your agent the power to consent to your doctor not giving treatment or stopping treatment necessary to keep you alive.

Notwithstanding this document, you have the right to make medical and other health care decisions for yourself so long as you can give informed consent with respect to the particular decision. In addition, no treatment may be given to you over your objection, and health care necessary to keep you alive may not be stopped or withheld if you object at the time.

This document gives your agent authority to consent, to refuse to consent, or to withdraw consent to any care, treatment, service, or procedure to maintain, diagnose or treat a physical or mental condition. This power is subject to any limitations that you include in this document. You may state in this document any types of treatment that you do not desire. In addition, a court can take away the power of your agent to make health care decisions for you if your agent: (1) authorizes anything that is illegal; or (2) acts contrary to your desires as stated in this document.

You have the right to revoke the authority of your agent by notifying your agent or your treating physician, hospital or other health care provider orally or in writing of the revocation.

Your agent has the right to examine your medical records and to consent to their disclosure unless you limit this right in this document.

Unless you otherwise specify in this document, this document gives your agent the power after you die to: (1) authorize an autopsy; (2) donate your body or parts thereof for transplant or therapeutic or educational or scientific purposes; and (3) direct the disposition of your remains.

If there is anything in this document that you do not understand, you should ask an attorney to explain it to you.

I, _____

_____ (insert your name and address),

appoint _____

_____ (insert name, address, and telephone number of agent), as my attorney in fact (agent) for health care decisions. I appoint _____

_____(insert name, address, and telephone number of alternate agent), as my alternative agent for health care decisions. I authorize my agent  to make health care decisions for me when I am incapable of making my own health care decisions, with all of the authority permitted under the laws of Tennessee, except as may be limited in the following paragraph. I understand the consequences of appointing an agent for health care.

**Special Instructions and Limitations:** I direct that my agent comply with the following instructions or limitations (if none, write in the word "none"): _____

_____

_____

In addition, I direct that my agent have authority to make decisions regarding the enforcement of my intentions regarding life-prolonging procedures as stated in any living will I have executed or may execute in the future.

Dated:_____          _____

                                                                  Signature of Principal

## WITNESS STATEMENT

I declare under penalty of perjury under the laws of Tennessee that the person who signed this document is personally known to me to be the principal; that the principal signed this durable power of attorney in my presence; that the principal appears to be of sound mind and under no duress, fraud or undue influence; that I am not the person appointed as attorney in fact by this document; that I am not a health care provider, an employee of a health care provider, the operator of a health care institution nor an employee of an operator of a health care institution; that I am not related to the principal by blood, marriage, or adoption; that, to the best of my knowledge, I do not, at the present time, have a claim against any portion of the estate of the principal upon the principal's death; and that, to the best of my knowledge, I am not entitled to any part of the estate of the principal upon the death of the principal under a will or codicil thereto now existing, or by operation of law.

Witness_____          Witness_____

STATE OF TENNESSEE
COUNTY OF _____

Subscribed, sworn to and acknowledged before me by _____ _____, the declarant, and subscribed and sworn to before me by _____ and _____, witnesses, this _____ day of _____, _____.

                                                       _____

                                                                  Notary Public

My Commission Expires:_____

# LIVING WILL

I, _____, willfully and voluntarily make known my desire that my dying shall not be artificially prolonged under the circumstances set forth below, and do hereby declare:

If at any time I should have a terminal condition and my attending physician has determined there is no reasonable medical expectation of recovery and which, as a medical probability, will result in my death, regardless of the use or discontinuance of medical treatment implemented for the purpose of sustaining life, or the life process, I direct that medical care be withheld or withdrawn, and that I be permitted to die naturally with only the administration of medications or the performance of any medical procedure deemed necessary to provide me with comfortable care or to alleviate pain.

## ARTIFICIALLY PROVIDED NOURISHMENT AND FLUIDS:

By checking the appropriate line below, I specifically:

_____Authorize the withholding or withdrawal of artificially provided food, water or other nourishment or fluids.

_____DO NOT authorize the withholding or withdrawal of artificially provided food, water or other nourishment or fluids.

## ORGAN DONOR CERTIFICATION:

Notwithstanding my previous declaration relative to the withholding or withdrawal of life-prolonging procedures, if as indicated below I have expressed my desire to donate my organs and/or tissues for transplantation, or any of them as specifically designated herein, I do direct my attending physician, if I have been determined dead according to Tennessee Code Annotated, § 68-3-501(b), to maintain me on artificial support systems only for the period of time required to maintain the viability of and to remove such organs and/or tissues.

By checking the appropriate line below, I specifically:

_____Desire to donate my organs and/or tissues for transplantation.

_____Desire to donate my _____
                                   (insert specific organs and/or tissues for transplantation)

_____DO NOT desire to donate my organs or tissues for transplantation.

In the absence of my ability to give directions regarding my medical care, it is my intention that this declaration shall be honored by my family and physician as the final expression of my legal right to refuse medical care and accept the consequences of such refusal.

The definitions of terms used herein shall be as set forth in the Tennessee Right to Natural Death Act, Tennessee Code Annotated, § 32-11-103.

I understand the full import of this declaration, and I am emotionally and mentally competent to make this declaration.

In acknowledgment whereof, I do hereinafter affix my signature on this the _____ day of _____, 200____.


_____
Declarant


We, the subscribing witnesses hereto, are personally acquainted with and subscribe our names hereto at the request of the declarant, an adult, whom we believe to be of sound mind, fully aware of the action taken herein and its possible consequence.

We, the undersigned witnesses, further declare that we are not related to the declarant by blood or marriage; that we are not entitled to any portion of the estate of the declarant upon the declarant's decease under any will or codicil thereto presently existing or by operation of law then existing; that we are not the attending physician, an employee of the attending physician or, health facility in which the declarant is a patient; and that we are not persons who, at the present time, have a claim against any portion of the estate of the declarant upon the declarant's death.

_____      _____
Witness                                         Witness

STATE OF TENNESSEE
COUNTY OF _____

Subscribed, sworn to and acknowledged before me by _____, the declarant, and subscribed and sworn to before me by _____ and _____, witnesses, this _____ day of _____, 200_____.

_____
Notary Public

My Commission Expires: _____

## Statutory Durable Power of Attorney

NOTICE: THE POWERS GRANTED BY THIS DOCUMENT ARE BROAD AND SWEEPING. THEY ARE EXPLAINED IN THE DURABLE POWER OF ATTORNEY ACT, CHAPTER XII, TEXAS PROBATE CODE. IF YOU HAVE ANY QUESTIONS ABOUT THESE POWERS, OBTAIN COMPETENT LEGAL ADVICE. THIS DOCUMENT DOES NOT AUTHORIZE ANYONE TO MAKE MEDICAL AND OTHER HEALTH-CARE DECISIONS FOR YOU. YOU MAY REVOKE THIS POWER OF ATTORNEY IF YOU LATER WISH TO DO SO.

I, _____
_____ (insert your name and address),
appoint _____
_____(insert the name and address of the person appointed) as my agent (attorney-in-fact) to act for me in any lawful way with respect to all of the following powers except for a power that I have crossed out below:

TO WITHHOLD A POWER, YOU MUST CROSS OUT EACH POWER WITHHELD.
Real property transactions;
Tangible personal property transactions;
Stock and bond transactions;
Commodity and option transactions;
Banking and other financial institution transactions;
Business operating transactions;
Insurance and annuity transactions;
Estate, trust, and other beneficiary transactions;
Claims and litigation;
Personal and family maintenance;
Benefits from social security, Medicare, Medicaid, or other governmental programs or
    civil or military service;
Retirement plan transactions;
Tax matters;

IF NO POWER LISTED ABOVE IS CROSSED OUT, THIS DOCUMENT SHALL BE CONSTRUED AND INTERPRETED AS A GENERAL POWER OF ATTORNEY AND MY AGENT (ATTORNEY IN FACT) SHALL HAVE THE POWER AND AUTHORITY TO PERFORM OR UNDERTAKE ANY ACTION I COULD PERFORM OR UNDERTAKE IF I WERE PERSONALLY PRESENT.

SPECIAL INSTRUCTIONS:

Special instructions applicable to gifts (initial in front of the following sentence to have it apply):
I grant my agent (attorney in fact) the power to apply my property to make gifts, except that the amount of a gift to an individual may not exceed the amount of annual exclusions allowed from the federal gift tax for the calendar year of the gift.

ON THE FOLLOWING LINES YOU MAY GIVE SPECIAL INSTRUCTIONS LIMITING OR EXTENDING THE POWERS GRANTED TO YOUR AGENT.

_____
_____
_____
_____
_____
_____

UNLESS YOU DIRECT OTHERWISE ABOVE, THIS POWER OF ATTORNEY IS EFFECTIVE IMMEDIATELY AND WILL CONTINUE UNTIL IT IS REVOKED.

CHOOSE ONE OF THE FOLLOWING ALTERNATIVES BY CROSSING OUT THE ALTERNATIVE NOT CHOSEN:

(A)  This power of attorney is not affected by my subsequent disability or incapacity.

(B)  This power of attorney becomes effective upon my disability or incapacity.

YOU SHOULD CHOOSE ALTERNATIVE (A) IF THIS POWER OF ATTORNEY IS TO BECOME EFFECTIVE ON THE DATE IT IS EXECUTED.

IF NEITHER (A) NOR (B) IS CROSSED OUT, IT WILL BE ASSUMED THAT YOU CHOSE ALTERNATIVE (A).

If alternative (B) is chosen and a definition o my disability or incapacity is not contained in this power of attorney, I shall be considered disabled or incapacitated for purposes of this power of attorney if a physician certifies in writing at a date later than the date this power of attorney is executed that, based on the physician's medical examination of me, I am mentally incapable of managing my financial affairs. I authorize the physician who examines me for this purpose to disclose my physical or mental condition to another person for purposes of this power of attorney. A third party who accepts this power of attorney is fully protected from any action taken under this power of attorney that is based on the determination made by a physician or my disability or incapacity.

I agree that any third party who receives a copy of this document may act under it. Revocation of the durable power of attorney is not effective as to a third party until the third party receives actual notice of the revocation. I agree to indemnify the third party for any claims that arise against the third party because of reliance on this power of attorney.

If any agent named by me dies, becomes legally disabled, resigns, or refuses to act, I name the following (each to act alone and successively, in the order named) as successor(s) to that agent: _____

_____.

Signed this _____ day of _____, _____.


_____
(your signature)


State of _____

County of _____

This document was acknowledged before me on _____
(date), by _____ (name of principal).


_____
(signature of notarial officer)

(Seal, if any, of notary)    _____
(printed name)

My commission expires: _____


THE ATTORNEY IN FACT OR AGENT, BY ACCEPTING OR ACTING UNDER THE APPOINTMENT, ASSUMES THE FIDUCIARY AND OTHER LEGAL RESPONSIBILITIES OF AN AGENT.

# Medical Power of Attorney Designation of Health Care Agent

INFORMATION CONCERNING THE DURABLE POWER
OF ATTORNEY FOR HEALTH CARE

THIS IS AN IMPORTANT LEGAL DOCUMENT.   BEFORE SIGNING THIS DOCUMENT, YOU SHOULD KNOW THESE IMPORTANT FACTS:

Except to the extent you state otherwise, this document gives the person you name as your agent the authority to make any and all health care decisions for you in accordance with your wishes, including your religious and moral beliefs, when you are no longer capable of making them yourself.  Because "health care" means any treatment, service, or procedure to maintain, diagnose, or treat your physical or mental condition, your agent has the power to make a broad range of health care decisions for you.  Your agent may consent, refuse to consent, or withdraw consent to medical treatment and may make decisions about withdrawing or withholding life-sustaining treatment.   Your agent may not consent to voluntary inpatient mental health services, convulsive treatment, psychosurgery, or abortion.  A physician must comply with your agent's instructions or allow you to be transferred to another physician.

Your agent's authority begins when your doctor certifies that you lack the capacity to make health care decisions.

Your agent is obligated to follow your instructions when making decisions on your behalf.  Unless you state otherwise, your agent has the same authority to make decisions about your health care as you would have had.

It is important that you discuss this document with your physician or other health care provider before you sign it to make sure that you understand the nature and range of decisions that may be made on your behalf.  If you do not have a physician, you should talk with someone else who is knowledgeable about these issues and can answer your questions.  You do not need a lawyer's assistance to complete this document, but if there is anything in this document that you do not understand, you should ask a lawyer to explain it to you.

The person you appoint as agent should be someone you know and trust.  The person must be 18 years of age or older or a person under 18 years of age who has had the disabilities of minority removed.  If you appoint your health or residential care provider (e.g., your physician or an employee of a home health agency, hospital, nursing home, or residential care home, other than a relative), that person has to choose between acting as your agent or as your health or residential care provider; the law does not permit a person to do both at the same time.

You should inform the person you appoint that you want the person to be your health care agent.  You should discuss this document with your agent and your physician and give each a signed copy.  You should indicate on the document itself the people and institutions who have signed copies.  Your agent is not liable for health care decisions made in good faith on your behalf.

Even after you have signed this document, you have the right to make health care decisions for yourself as long as you are able to do so and treatment cannot be given to you or stopped over your objection. You have the right to revoke the authority granted to your agent by informing your agent or your health or residential care provider orally or in writing or by your execution of a subsequent durable power of attorney for health care. Unless you state otherwise, your appointment of a spouse dissolves on divorce.

This document may not be changed or modified.  If you want to make changes in the document, you must make an entirely new one.

You may wish to designate an alternate agent in the event that your agent is unwilling, unable, or ineligible to act as your agent.  Any alternate agent you designate has the same authority to make health care decisions for you.

THIS POWER OF ATTORNEY IS NOT VALID UNLESS IT IS SIGNED IN THE PRESENCE OF TWO OR MORE QUALIFIED WITNESSES.  THE FOLLOWING PERSONS MAY NOT ACT AS WITNESSES:

(1) the person you have designated as your agent;

(2) a person related to you by blood or marriage;

(3) a person entitled to any part of your estate after your death under a will or codicil executed by you or by operation of law;

(4) your attending physician;

(5) an employee of your attending physician;

(6) an employee of a health care facility in which you are a patient if the employee is providing direct patient care to you or is an officer, director, partner, or business office employee of the health care facility or of any parent organization of the health care facility; or

(7) a person who, at the time this power of attorney is executed, has a claim against any part of your estate after your death.

DESIGNATION OF HEALTH CARE AGENT.

I, _____ (insert your name) appoint:

Name: _____

Address: _____

Phone: _____

as my agent to make any and all health care decisions for me, except to the extent I state otherwise in this document.  This durable power of attorney for health care takes effect if I become unable to make my own health care decisions and this fact is certified in writing by my physician.

LIMITATIONS ON THE DECISION-MAKING AUTHORITY OF MY AGENT ARE AS FOLLOWS:

_____

_____

DESIGNATION OF ALTERNATE AGENT.

(You are not required to designate an alternate agent but you may do so.  An alternate agent may make the same health care decisions as the designated agent if the designated agent is unable or unwilling to act as your agent.  If the agent designated is your spouse, the designation is automatically revoked by law if your marriage is dissolved.)

If the person designated as my agent is unable or unwilling to make health care decisions for me, I designate the following persons to serve as my agent to make health care decisions for me as authorized by this document, who serve in the following order:

A.      First Alternate Agent

Name: _____

Address: _____

_____ Phone: _____

B.      Second Alternate Agent

Name: _____

Address: _____

_____ Phone: _____

The original of this document is kept at _____

_____

_____

The following individuals or institutions have signed copies:

Name: _____

Address: _____

_____

Name: _____

Address: _____

_____

DURATION.

I understand that this power of attorney exists indefinitely from the date I execute this document unless I establish a shorter time or revoke the power of attorney. If I am unable to make health care decisions for myself when this power of attorney expires, the authority I have granted my agent continues to exist until the time I become able to make health care decisions for myself.

(IF APPLICABLE) This power of attorney ends on the following date: _____

PRIOR DESIGNATIONS REVOKED.

I revoke any prior durable power of attorney for health care.

ACKNOWLEDGMENT OF DISCLOSURE STATEMENT.

I have been provided with a disclosure statement explaining the effect of this document. I have read and understand that information contained in the disclosure statement.

(YOU MUST DATE AND SIGN THIS POWER OF ATTORNEY.)

I sign my name to this durable power of attorney for health care on _____ day of_____, _____, at

_____
(City and State)

_____
(Signature)

_____
(Print Name)

STATEMENT OF FIRST WITNESS.

I am not the person appointed as agent by this document. I am not related to the principal by blood or marriage. I would not be entitled to any portion of the principal's estate on the principal's death. I am not the attending physician of the principal or an employee of the attending physician. I have no claim against any portion of the principal's estate on the principal's death. Furthermore, if I am an employee of a health care facility in which the principal is a patient, I am not involved in providing direct patient care to the principal and am not an officer, director, partner, or business office employee of the health care facility or of any parent organization of the health care facility.

Signature: _____

Print Name: _____ Date: _____

Address: _____

SIGNATURE OF SECOND WITNESS.

Signature: _____

Print Name:_____ Date: _____

Address: _____

# DIRECTIVE TO PHYSICIANS AND FAMILY OR SURROGATES

Instructions for completing this document:

This is an important legal document known as an Advance Directive. It is designed to help you communicate your wishes about medical treatment at some time in the future when you are unable to make your wishes known because of illness or injury. These wishes are usually based on personal values. In particular, you may want to consider what burdens or hardships of treatment you would be willing to accept for a particular amount of benefit obtained if you were seriously ill.

You are encouraged to discuss your values and wishes with your family or chosen spokesperson, as well as your physician. Your physician, other health care provider, or medical institution may provide you with various resources to assist you in completing your advance directive. Brief definitions are listed below and may aid you in your discussions and advance planning. Initial the treatment choices that best reflect your personal preferences. Provide a copy of your directive to your physician, usual hospital, and family or spokesperson. Consider a periodic review of this document. By periodic review, you can best assure that the directive reflects your preferences.

In addition to this advance directive, Texas law provides for two other types of directives that can be important during a serious illness. These are the Medical Power of Attorney and the Out-of-Hospital Do-Not-Resuscitate Order. You may wish to discuss these with your physician, family, hospital representative, or other advisers. You may also wish to complete a directive related to the donation of organs and tissues.

DIRECTIVE

I, _____, recognize that the best health care is based upon a partnership of trust and communication with my physician. My physician and I will make health care decisions together as long as I am of sound mind and able to make my wishes known. If there comes a time that I am unable to make medical decisions about myself because of illness or injury, I direct that the following treatment preferences be honored:

If, in the judgment of my physician, I am suffering with a terminal condition from which I am expected to die within six months, even with available life-sustaining treatment provided in accordance with prevailing standards of medical care:

_____ I request that all treatments other than those needed to keep me comfortable be discontinued or withheld and my physician allow me to die as gently as possible; OR

_____ I request that I be kept alive in this terminal condition using available life-sustaining treatment. (THIS SELECTION DOES NOT APPLY TO HOSPICE CARE.)

If, in the judgment of my physician, I am suffering with an irreversible condition so that I cannot care for myself or make decisions for myself and am expected to die without life-sustaining treatment provided in accordance with prevailing standards of care:

_____ I request that all treatments other than those needed to keep me comfortable by discontinued or withheld and my physician allow me to die as gently as possible; OR

_____ I request that I be kept alive in this irreversible condition using available life-sustaining treatment. (THIS SELECTION DOES NOT APPLY TO HOSPICE CARE.)

Additional requests: (After discussion with your physician, you may wish to consider listing particular treatments in this space that you do or do not want in specific circumstances, such as artificial nutrition and fluids, intravenous antibiotics, etc. Be sure to state whether you do or do not want the particular treatment.) _____

_____

_____

After signing this directive, if my representative or I elect hospice care, I understand and agree that only those treatments needed to keep me comfortable would be provided and I would not be given available life-sustaining treatments.

If I do not have a Medical Power of Attorney, and I am unable to make my wishes known, I designate the following person(s) to make treatment decisions with my physician compatible with my personal values:

1. _____

2. _____

(If a Medical Power of Attorney has been executed, then an agent already has been named and you should not list additional names in this document.)

If the above persons are not available, or if I have not designated a spokesperson, I understand that a spokesperson will be chosen for me following standards specified in the laws of Texas. If, in the judgment of my physician, my death is imminent within minutes to hours, even with the use of all available medical treatment provided within the prevailing standard of care, I acknowledge that all treatments may be withheld or removed except those needed to maintain my comfort. I understand that under Texas law this directive has no effect if I have been diagnosed as pregnant. This directive will remain in effect until I revoke it. No other person may do so.

Signed _____ Date _____

City, County, State of Residence _____

Two competent adult witnesses must sign below, acknowledging the signature of the declarant. The witness designated as Witness 1 may not be a person designated to make a treatment decision for the patient and may not be related to the patient by blood or marriage. This witness may not be entitled to any part of the estate and may not have a claim against the estate of the patient. This witness may not be the attending physician or an employee of the attending physician. If this witness is an employee of a health care facility in which the patient is being cared for, this witness may not be involved in providing direct patient care to the patient. This witness may not be an officer, director, partner, or business office employee of a health care facility in which the patient is being cared for or of any parent organization of the health care facility.

Witness 1 _____ Witness 2 _____

Definitions:

"Artificial nutrition and hydration" means the provision of nutrients or fluids by a tube inserted in a vein, under the skin in the subcutaneous tissues, or in the stomach (gastrointestinal tract).

"Irreversible condition" means a condition, injury, or illness:

(1) that may be treated, but is never cured or eliminated;

(2) that leaves a person unable to care for or make decisions for the person's own self; and

(3) that, without life-sustaining treatment provided in accordance with the prevailing standard of medical care, is fatal.

Explanation: Many serious illnesses such as cancer, failure of major organs (kidney, heart, liver, or lung), and serious brain disease such as Alzheimer's dementia may be considered irreversible early on. There is no cure, but the patient may be kept alive for prolonged periods of time if the patient receives life-sustaining treatments. Late in the course of the same illness, the disease may be considered terminal when, even with treatment, the patient is expected to die. You may wish to consider which burdens of treatment you would be willing to accept in an effort to achieve a particular outcome. This is a very personal decision that you may wish to discuss with your physician, family, or other important persons in your life.

"Life-sustaining treatment" means treatment that, based on reasonable medical judgment, sustains the life of a patient and without which the patient will die. The term includes both life-sustaining medications and artificial life support such as mechanical breathing machines, kidney dialysis treatment, and artificial hydration and nutrition. The term does not include the administration of pain management medication, the performance of a medical procedure necessary to provide comfort care, or any other medical care provided to alleviate a patient's pain.

"Terminal condition" means an incurable condition caused by injury, disease, or illness that according to reasonable medical judgment will produce death within six months, even with available life-sustaining treatment provided in accordance with the prevailing standard of medical care.

Explanation: Many serious illnesses may be considered irreversible early in the course of the illness, but they may not be considered terminal until the disease is fairly advanced. In thinking about terminal illness and its treatment, you again may wish to consider the relative benefits and burdens of treatment and discuss your wishes with your physician, family, or other important persons in your life.

# MEDICAL POWER OF ATTORNEY

## INFORMATION CONCERNING THE MEDICAL POWER OF ATTORNEY

THIS IS AN IMPORTANT LEGAL DOCUMENT. BEFORE SIGNING THIS DOCUMENT, YOU SHOULD KNOW THESE IMPORTANT FACTS:

Except to the extent you state otherwise, this document gives the person you name as your agent the authority to make any and all health care decisions for you in accordance with your wishes, including your religious and moral beliefs, when you are no longer capable of making them yourself. Because "health care" means any treatment, service, or procedure to maintain, diagnose, or treat your physical or mental condition, your agent has the power to make a broad range of health care decisions for you. Your agent may consent, refuse to consent, or withdraw consent to medical treatment and may make decisions about withdrawing or withholding life-sustaining treatment. Your agent may not consent to voluntary inpatient mental health services, convulsive treatment, psychosurgery, or abortion. A physician must comply with your agent's instructions or allow you to be transferred to another physician.

Your agent's authority begins when your doctor certifies that you lack the competence to make health care decisions.

Your agent is obligated to follow your instructions when making decisions on your behalf. Unless you state otherwise, your agent has the same authority to make decisions about your health care as you would have had.

It is important that you discuss this document with your physician or other health care provider before you sign it to make sure that you understand the nature and range of decisions that may be made on your behalf. If you do not have a physician, you should talk with someone else who is knowledgeable about these issues and can answer your questions. You do not need a lawyer's assistance to complete this document, but if there is anything in this document that you do not understand, you should ask a lawyer to explain it to you.

The person you appoint as agent should be someone you know and trust. The person must be 18 years of age or older or a person under 18 years of age who has had the disabilities of minority removed. If you appoint your health or residential care provider (e.g., your physician or an employee of a home health agency, hospital, nursing home, or residential care home, other than a relative), that person has to choose between acting as your agent or as your health or residential care provider; the law does not permit a person to do both at the same time.

You should inform the person you appoint that you want the person to be your health care agent. You should discuss this document with your agent and your physician and give each a signed copy. You should indicate on the document itself the people and institutions who have signed copies. Your agent is not liable for health care decisions made in good faith on your behalf.

Even after you have signed this document, you have the right to make health care decisions for yourself as long as you are able to do so and treatment cannot be given to you or stopped over your objection. You have the right to revoke the authority granted to your agent by informing your agent or your health or residential care provider orally or in writing or by your execution of a subsequent medical power of attorney. Unless you state otherwise, your appointment of a spouse dissolves on divorce.

This document may not be changed or modified. If you want to make changes in the document, you must make an entirely new one.

You may wish to designate an alternate agent in the event that your agent is unwilling, unable, or ineligible to act as your agent. Any alternate agent you designate has the same authority to make health care decisions for you.

THIS POWER OF ATTORNEY IS NOT VALID UNLESS IT IS SIGNED IN THE PRESENCE OF TWO COMPETENT ADULT WITNESSES. THE FOLLOWING PERSONS MAY NOT ACT AS ONE OF THE WITNESSES:

(1) the person you have designated as your agent;

(2) a person related to you by blood or marriage;

(3) a person entitled to any part of your estate after your death under a will or codicil executed by you or by operation of law;

(4) your attending physician;

(5) an employee of your attending physician;

(6) an employee of a health care facility in which you are a patient if the employee is providing direct patient care to you or is an officer, director, partner, or business office employee of the health care facility or of any parent organization of the health care facility; or

(7) a person who, at the time this power of attorney is executed, has a claim against any part of your estate after your death.

MEDICAL POWER OF ATTORNEY DESIGNATION OF HEALTH CARE AGENT

I, _____(insert your name), appoint:
Name: _____
Address: _____
Phone: _____

as my agent to make any and all health care decisions for me, except to the extent I state otherwise in this document. This medical power of attorney takes effect if I become unable to make my own health care decisions and this fact is certified in writing by my physician.

LIMITATIONS ON THE DECISION-MAKING AUTHORITY OF MY AGENT ARE AS FOLLOWS:
_____
_____
_____

### DESIGNATION OF ALTERNATE AGENT.

(You are not required to designate an alternate agent but you may do so. An alternate agent may make the same health care decisions as the designated agent if the designated agent is unable or unwilling to act as your agent. If the agent designated is your spouse, the designation is automatically revoked by law if your marriage is dissolved.)
If the person designated as my agent is unable or unwilling to make health care decisions for me, I designate the following persons to serve as my agent to make health care decisions for me as authorized by this document, who serve in the following order:
A.      First Alternate Agent
              Name: _____
              Address: _____
              Phone: _____

B.      Second Alternate Agent
              Name: _____
              Address: _____
              Phone: _____

The original of this document is kept at: _____
                                          _____
                                          _____

The following individuals or institutions have signed copies:
              Name: _____
              Address: _____
              Phone: _____

              Name: _____
              Address: _____
              Phone: _____

### DURATION.

I understand that this power of attorney exists indefinitely from the date I execute this document unless I establish a shorter time or revoke the power of attorney. If I am unable to make health care decisions for myself when this power of attorney expires, the authority I have granted my agent continues to exist until the time I become able to make health care decisions for myself.

(IF APPLICABLE) This power of attorney ends on the following date:
_____

PRIOR DESIGNATIONS REVOKED.

I revoke any prior medical power of attorney.

ACKNOWLEDGMENT OF DISCLOSURE STATEMENT.

I have been provided with a disclosure statement explaining the effect of this document. I have read and understand that information contained in the disclosure statement.

(YOU MUST DATE AND SIGN THIS POWER OF ATTORNEY.)

I sign my name to this medical power of attorney on _____ day of _____(month, year) at _____
(City and State)

_____
(Signature)

_____
(Printed Name)

STATEMENT OF FIRST WITNESS.

I am not the person appointed as agent by this document. I am not related to the principal by blood or marriage. I would not be entitled to any portion of the principal's estate on the principal's death. I am not the attending physician of the principal or an employee of the attending physician. I have no claim against any portion of the principal's estate on the principal's death. Furthermore, if I am an employee of a health care facility in which the principal is a patient, I am not involved in providing direct patient care to the principal and am not an officer, director, partner, or business office employee of the health care facility or of any parent organization of the health care facility.

Signature: _____

Printed Name: _____ Date: _____

Address: _____

SIGNATURE OF SECOND WITNESS.

Signature: _____

Printed Name: _____ Date: _____

Address: _____

## Special Power of Attorney

I, _____, of _____,
this _____ day of _____, _____, being of sound mind,
willfully and voluntarily appoint _____,
of _____, as my agent and
attorney-in-fact, without substitution, with lawful authority to execute a directive on my
behalf under Section 75-2-1105, governing the care and treatment to be administered to
or withheld from me at any time after I incur an injury, disease, or illness which renders
me unable to give current directions to attending physicians and other providers of
medical services.

I have carefully selected my above-named agent with confidence in the belief
that this person's familiarity with my desires, beliefs, and attitudes will result in directions
to attending physicians and providers of medical services which would probably be the
same as I would give if able to do so.

This power of attorney shall be and remain in effect from the time my attending
physician certifies that I have incurred a physical or mental condition rendering me
unable to give current directions to attending physicians and other providers of medical
services as to my care and treatment.


_____
Signature of Principal


State of _____ )
County of _____ )

On the _____ day of _____, _____, personally
appeared before me _____, who duly
acknowledged to me that he has read and fully understands the foregoing power of
attorney, executed the same of his own volition and for the purposes set forth, and that
he was acting under no constraint or undue influence whatsoever.


_____
Notary Public

My commission expires:      Residing at: _____

_____

# DIRECTIVE TO PHYSICIANS AND PROVIDERS OF MEDICAL SERVICES

(Pursuant to Section 75-2-1104, UCA)

This directive is made this _____ day of _____, 200____.

1.     I, _____, being of sound mind, willfully and voluntarily make known my desire that my life not be artificially prolonged by life-sustaining procedures except as I may otherwise provide in this directive.

2.     I declare that if at any time I should have an injury, disease, or illness, which is certified in writing to be a terminal condition or persistent vegetative state by two physicians who have personally examined me, and in the opinion of those physicians the application of life-sustaining procedures would serve only to unnaturally prolong the moment of my death and to unnaturally postpone or prolong the dying process, I direct that these procedures be withheld or withdrawn and my death be permitted to occur naturally.

3.     I expressly intend this directive to be a final expression of my legal right to refuse medical or surgical treatment and to accept the consequences from this refusal which shall remain in effect notwithstanding my future inability to give current medical directions to treating physicians and other providers of medical services.

4.     I understand that the term "life-sustaining procedure" includes artificial nutrition and hydration and any other procedures that I specify below to be considered life-sustaining but does not include the administration of medication or the performance of any medical procedure which is intended to provide comfort care or to alleviate pain: _____

_____.

5.     I reserve the right to give current medical directions to physicians and other providers of medical services so long as I am able, even though these directions may conflict with the above written directive that life-sustaining procedures be withheld or withdrawn.

6.     I understand the full import of this directive and declare that I am emotionally and mentally competent to make this directive.


_____          _____
Declarant's signature                                          City, County, and State of Residence

        We witnesses certify that each of us is 18 years of age or older and each personally witnessed the declarant sign or direct the signing of this directive; that we are acquainted with the declarant and believe him to be of sound mind; that the declarant's desires are as expressed above; that neither of us is a person who signed the above directive on behalf of the declarant; that we are not related to the declarant by blood or marriage nor are we entitled to any portion of declarant's estate according to the laws of intestate succession of this state or under any will or codicil of declarant; that we are not directly financially responsible for declarant's medical care; and that we are not agents of any health care facility in which the declarant may be a patient at the time of signing this directive.


_____          _____
Signature of Witness                                         Signature of Witness


_____          _____


_____          _____
Address                                                        Address

# Durable Power of Attorney for Health Care

## INFORMATION CONCERNING THE DURABLE POWER OF ATTORNEY FOR HEALTH CARE

THIS IS AN IMPORTANT LEGAL DOCUMENT.  BEFORE SIGNING THIS DOCUMENT, YOU SHOULD KNOW THESE IMPORTANT FACTS:

Except to the extent you state otherwise, this document gives the person you name as your agent the authority to make any and all health care decisions for you when you are no longer capable of making them yourself.  "Health care" means any treatment, service or procedure to maintain, diagnose or treat your physical or mental condition.  Your agent therefore can have the power to make a broad range of health care decisions for you.  Your agent may consent, refuse to consent, or withdraw consent to medical treatment and may make decisions about withdrawing or withholding life-sustaining treatment.

You may state in this document any treatment you do not desire or treatment you want to be sure you receive.  Your agent's authority will begin when your doctor certifies that you lack the capacity to make health care decisions.  You may attach additional pages if you need more space to complete your statement.

Your agent will be obligated to follow your instructions when making decisions on your behalf.  Unless you state otherwise, your agent will have the same authority to make decisions about your health care as you would have had.

It is important that you discuss this document with your physician or other health care providers before you sign it to make sure that you understand the nature and range of decisions which may be made on your behalf.  If you do not have a physician, you should talk with someone else who is knowledgeable about these issues and can answer your questions.  You do not need a lawyer's assistance to complete this document, but if there is anything in this document that you do not understand, you should ask a lawyer to explain it to you.

The person you appoint as agent should be someone you know and trust and must be at least 18 years old.  If you appoint your health or residential care provider (e.g. your physician, or an employee of a home health agency, hospital, nursing home, or residential care home, other than a relative), that person will have to choose between acting as your agent or as you health or residential care provider; the law does not permit a person to do both at the same time.

You should inform the person you appoint that you want him or her to be your health care agent.  You should discuss this document with your agent and your physician and give each a signed copy.  You should indicate on the document itself the people and institutions who will have signed copies.  Your agent will not be liable for health care decisions for yourself as long as you are able to do so, and treatment cannot be given to you or stopped over your objection.  You have the right to revoke the authority granted to your agent by informing him or her or your health care provider orally or in writing.

This document may not be changed or modified.  If you want to make changes in the document you must make an entirely new one.

You may wish to designate an alternate agent in the event that your agent is unwilling, unable or ineligible to act as your agent.  Any alternate agent you designate will have the same authority to make health care decisions for you.

THIS POWER OF ATTORNEY WILL NOT BE VALID UNLESS IT IS SIGNED IN THE PRESENCE OF TWO (2) OR MORE QUALIFIED WITNESSES WHO MUST BOTH BE PRESENT WHEN YOU SIGN OR ACKNOWLEDGE YOUR SIGNATURE.  THE FOLLOWING PERSONS MAY NOT ACT AS WITNESSES:
— the person you have designated as your agent;
— your health or residential care provider or one of their employees;
— your spouse;
— your lawful heirs or beneficiaries named in your will or a deed;
— creditors or persons who have a claim against you.

I, _____ , hereby appoint _____

_____ as my agent to make any and all health care decisions for me, except to the extent I state otherwise in this document. This durable power of attorney for health care shall take effect in the event I become unable to make my own health care decisions.

(a) **STATEMENT OF DESIRES, SPECIAL PROVISIONS, AND LIMITATIONS REGARDING HEALTH CARE DECISIONS.**

Here you may include any specific desires or limitations you deem appropriate, such as when or what life-sustaining measures should be withheld; directions whether to continue or discontinue artificial nutrition and hydration; or instructions to refuse any specific types of treatment that are inconsistent with your religious beliefs or unacceptable to you for any reason.

_____

_____

_____

_____

(attach additional pages as necessary)

(b) **THE SUBJECT OF LIFE-SUSTAINING TREATMENT IS OF PARTICULAR IMPORTANCE.** For your convenience in dealing with that subject, some general statements concerning the withholding or removal of life-sustaining treatment are set forth below.

IF YOU AGREE WITH ONE OF THESE STATEMENTS, YOU MAY INCLUDE THE STATEMENT IN THE BLANK SPACE ABOVE:

- If I suffer a conditions from which there is no reasonable prospect of regaining my ability to think and act for myself, I want only care directed to my comfort and dignity, and authorize my agent to decline all treatment (including artificial nutrition and hydration) the primary purpose of which is to prolong my life.
- If I suffer a condition from which there is no reasonable prospect of regaining my ability to think and act for myself, I want care directed to my comfort and dignity and also want artificial nutrition and hydration if needed, but authorize my agent to decline all other treatment the primary purpose of which is to prolong my life.
- I want my life sustained by any reasonable medical measures, regardless of my condition.

In the event the person I appoint above is unable, unwilling or unavailable to act as my health care agent, I hereby appoint _____ of _____ as alternate agent.

I hereby acknowledge that I have been provided with a disclosure statement explaining the effect of this document. I have read and understand the information contained in the disclosure statement.

The original of this document will be kept at _____

_____ and the following persons and institutions will have signed copies:

_____

_____

In witness whereof, I have hereunto signed my name this _____ day of _____,

_____ .

_____

Signature

I declare that the principal appears to be of sound mind and free from duress at the time the durable power of attorney for health care is signed and that the principal has affirmed that he or she is aware of the nature of the document and is signing it freely and voluntarily.

Witness: _____ Address: _____

Witness: _____ Address: _____

State of ombudsman, hospital representative or other authorized person (to be signed only if the principal is in or is being admitted to a hospital, nursing home or residential care home):

I declare that I have personally explained the nature and effect of this durable power of attorney to the principal and that the principal understands the same.

Date: _____

Name:_____ Address: _____

## Terminal Care Document

To my family, my physician, my lawyer, my clergyman.  To any medical facility in whose care I happen to be.  To any individual who may become responsible for my health, welfare or affairs.

Death is as much a reality as birth, growth, maturity and old age—it is the one certainty of life.  If the time comes when I, _____, can no longer take part in decisions of my own future, let this statement stand as an expression of my wishes, while I am still of sound mind.

If the situation should arise in which I am in a terminal state and there is no reasonable expectation of my recovery, I direct that I be allowed to die a natural death and that my life not be prolonged by extraordinary measures.  I do, however, ask that medication be mercifully administered to me to alleviate suffering even though this may shorten my remaining life.

This statement is made after careful consideration and is in accordance with my strong convictions and beliefs.  I want the wishes and directions here expressed carried out to the extent permitted by law.  Insofar as they are not legally enforceable, I hope that those to whom this will is addressed will regard themselves as morally bound by these provisions.

Signed: _____

Date: _____

Witness: _____    Witness: _____

Copies of this request have been given to:

_____

_____

_____

# ADVANCE MEDICAL DIRECTIVE

I, _____, willfully and voluntarily make known my desire and do hereby declare: If at any time my attending physician should determine that I have a terminal condition where the application of life-prolonging procedures would serve only to artificially prolong the dying process, I direct that such procedures be withheld or withdrawn, and that I be permitted to die naturally with only the administration of medication or the performance of any medical procedure deemed necessary to provide me with comfort care or to alleviate pain. (OPTION: I specifically direct that the following procedures or treatments be provided to me: _____ )

In the absence of my ability to give directions regarding the use of such life-prolonging procedures, it is my intention that this advance directive shall be honored by my family and physician as the final expression of my legal right to refuse medical or surgical treatment and accept the consequences of such refusal.

OPTION: APPOINTMENT OF AGENT (CROSS THROUGH IF YOU DO NOT WANT TO APPOINT AN AGENT TO MAKE HEALTH CARE DECISIONS FOR YOU.)

I hereby appoint _____ (primary agent), of _____
_____
(address and telephone number), as my agent to make health care decisions on my behalf as authorized in this document. If _____ (primary agent) is not reasonably available or is unable or unwilling to act as my agent, then I appoint _____
_____ (successor agent), of _____
_____ (address and telephone number), to serve in that capacity.

I hereby grant to my agent, named above, full power and authority to make health care decisions on my behalf as described below whenever I have been determined to be incapable of making an informed decision about providing, withholding or withdrawing medical treatment. The phrase "incapable of making an informed decision" means unable to understand the nature, extent and probable consequences of a proposed medical decision or unable to make a rational evaluation of the risks and benefits of a proposed medical decision as compared with the risks and benefits of alternatives to that decision, or unable to communicate such understanding in any way. My agent's authority hereunder is effective as long as I am incapable of making an informed decision.

The determination that I am incapable of making an informed decision shall be made by my attending physician and a second physician or licensed clinical psychologist after a personal examination of me and shall be certified in writing. Such certification shall be required before treatment is withheld or withdrawn, and before, or as soon as reasonably practicable after, treatment is provided, and every 180 days thereafter while the treatment continues.

In exercising the power to make health care decisions on my behalf, my agent shall follow my desires and preferences as stated in this document or as otherwise known to my agent. My agent shall be guided by my medical diagnosis and prognosis and any information provided by my physicians as to the intrusiveness, pain, risks, and side effects associated with treatment or nontreatment. My agent shall not authorize a course of treatment which he knows, or upon reasonable inquiry ought to know, is contrary to my religious beliefs or my basic values, whether expressed orally or in writing. If my agent cannot determine what treatment choice I would have made on my own behalf, then my agent shall make a choice for me based upon what he believes to be in my best interests.

OPTION: POWERS OF MY AGENT (CROSS THROUGH ANY LANGUAGE YOU DO NOT WANT AND ADD ANY LANGUAGE YOU DO WANT.)

The powers of my agent shall include the following:

A. To consent to or refuse or withdraw consent to any type of medical care, treatment, surgical procedure, diagnostic procedure, medication and the use of mechanical or other procedures that affect any bodily function, including, but not limited to, artificial respiration, artificially administered nutrition and hydration, and cardiopulmonary resuscitation. This authorization specifically includes the power to consent to the administration of dosages of pain-relieving medication in excess of recommended dosages in an amount sufficient to relieve pain, even if such medication carries the risk of addiction or inadvertently hastens my death;

B. To request, receive, and review any information, verbal or written, regarding my physical or mental health, including but not limited to, medical and hospital records, and to consent to the disclosure of this information;

C. To employ and discharge my health care providers;

D. To authorize my admission to or discharge (including transfer to another facility) from any hospital, hospice, nursing home, adult home or other medical care facility for services other than those for treatment of mental illness requiring admission procedures provided in Article 1 (§ 37.2-800 et seq.) of Chapter 8 of Title 37.2; and

E. To take any lawful actions that may be necessary to carry out these decisions, including the granting of releases of liability to medical providers.

Further, my agent shall not be liable for the costs of treatment pursuant to his authorization, based solely on that authorization.

OPTION: APPOINTMENT OF AN AGENT TO MAKE AN ANATOMICAL GIFT OR ORGAN, TISSUE OR EYE DONATION (CROSS THROUGH IF YOU DO NOT WANT TO APPOINT AN AGENT TO MAKE AN ANATOMICAL GIFT OR ANY ORGAN, TISSUE OR EYE DONATION FOR YOU).

Upon my death, I direct that an anatomical gift of all of my body or certain organ, tissue or eye donations may be made pursuant to Article 2 (§ 32.1-289 et seq.) of Chapter 8 of Title 32.1 and in accordance with my directions, if any. I hereby appoint _____ as my agent, of _____ (address and telephone number), to make any such anatomical gift or organ, tissue or eye donation following my death. I further direct that: _____
(declarant's directions concerning anatomical gift or organ, tissue or eye donation).

This advance directive shall not terminate in the event of my disability.

By signing below, I indicate that I am emotionally and mentally competent to make this advance directive and that I understand the purpose and effect of this document.

_____
(Date)

_____
(Signature of Declarant)

The declarant signed the foregoing advance directive in my presence. I am not the spouse or a blood relative of the declarant.

(Witness) _____

(Witness) _____

# Mental Health Advance Directive

NOTICE TO PERSONS CREATING A MENTAL HEALTH ADVANCE DIRECTIVE

This is an important legal document. It creates an advance directive for mental health treatment. Before signing this document you should know these important facts:

(1) This document is called an advance directive and allows you to make decisions in advance about your mental health treatment, including medications, short-term admission to inpatient treatment and electroconvulsive therapy.

YOU DO NOT HAVE TO FILL OUT OR SIGN THIS FORM.
IF YOU DO NOT SIGN THIS FORM, IT WILL NOT TAKE EFFECT.

If you choose to complete and sign this document, you may still decide to leave some items blank.

(2) You have the right to appoint a person as your agent to make treatment decisions for you. You must notify your agent that you have appointed him or her as an agent. The person you appoint has a duty to act consistently with your wishes made known by you. If your agent does not know what your wishes are, he or she has a duty to act in your best interest. Your agent has the right to withdraw from the appointment at any time.

(3) The instructions you include with this advance directive and the authority you give your agent to act will only become effective under the conditions you select in this document. You may choose to limit this directive and your agent's authority to times when you are incapacitated or to times when you are exhibiting symptoms or behavior that you specify. You may also make this directive effective immediately. No matter when you choose to make this directive effective, your treatment providers must still seek your informed consent at all times that you have capacity to give informed consent.

(4) You have the right to revoke this document in writing at any time you have capacity.

YOU MAY NOT REVOKE THIS DIRECTIVE WHEN YOU HAVE BEEN FOUND TO BE INCAPACITATED UNLESS YOU HAVE SPECIFICALLY STATED IN THIS DIRECTIVE THAT YOU WANT IT TO BE REVOCABLE WHEN YOU ARE INCAPACITATED.

(5) This directive will stay in effect until you revoke it unless you specify an expiration date. If you specify an expiration date and you are incapacitated at the time it expires, it will remain in effect until you have capacity to make treatment decisions again unless you chose to be able to revoke it while you are incapacitated and you revoke the directive.

(6) You cannot use your advance directive to consent to civil commitment. The procedures that apply to your advance directive are different than those provided for in the Involuntary Treatment Act. Involuntary treatment is a different process.

(7) If there is anything in this directive that you do not understand, you should ask a lawyer to explain it to you.

(8) You should be aware that there are some circumstances where your provider may not have to follow your directive.

(9) You should discuss any treatment decisions in your directive with your provider.

(10) You may ask the court to rule on the validity of your directive.

PART I.
STATEMENT OF INTENT TO CREATE A MENTAL HEALTH ADVANCE DIRECTIVE

I, _____, being a person with capacity, willfully and voluntarily execute this mental health advance directive so that my choices regarding my mental health care will be carried out in circumstances when I am unable to express my instructions and preferences regarding my mental health care. If a guardian is appointed by a court to make mental health decisions for me, I intend this document to take precedence over all other means of ascertaining my intent.

The fact that I may have left blanks in this directive does not affect its validity in any way. I intend that all completed sections be followed. If I have not expressed a choice, my agent should make the decision that he or she determines is in my best interest. I intend this directive to take precedence over any other directives I have previously executed, to the extent that they are inconsistent with this document, or unless I expressly state otherwise in either document.

I understand that I may revoke this directive in whole or in part if I am a person with capacity. I understand that I cannot revoke this directive if a court, two health care providers, or one mental health professional and one health care provider find that I am an incapacitated person, unless, when I executed this directive, I chose to be able to revoke this directive while incapacitated.

I understand that, except as otherwise provided in law, revocation must be in writing. I understand that nothing in this directive, or in my refusal of treatment to which I consent in this directive, authorizes any health care provider, professional person, health care facility, or agent appointed in this directive to use or threaten to use abuse, neglect, financial exploitation, or abandonment to carry out my directive.

I understand that there are some circumstances where my provider may not have to follow my directive.

## PART II.
## WHEN THIS DIRECTIVE IS EFFECTIVE
### YOU MUST COMPLETE THIS PART FOR YOUR DIRECTIVE TO BE VALID.

I intend that this directive become effective (YOU MUST CHOOSE ONLY ONE):

_____ Immediately upon my signing of this directive.

_____ If I become incapacitated.

_____ When the following circumstances, symptoms, or behaviors occur:

_____

_____

## PART III.
## DURATION OF THIS DIRECTIVE
### YOU MUST COMPLETE THIS PART FOR YOUR DIRECTIVE TO BE VALID.

I want this directive to (YOU MUST CHOOSE ONLY ONE):

_____ Remain valid and in effect for an indefinite period of time.

_____ Automatically expire _____ years from the date it was created.

## PART IV.
## WHEN I MAY REVOKE THIS DIRECTIVE
### YOU MUST COMPLETE THIS PART FOR THIS DIRECTIVE TO BE VALID.

I intend that I be able to revoke this directive (YOU MUST CHOOSE ONLY ONE):

_____ Only when I have capacity. I understand that choosing this option means I may only revoke this directive if I have capacity. I further understand that if I choose this option and become incapacitated while this directive is in effect, I may receive treatment that I specify in this directive, even if I object at the time.

_____ Even if I am incapacitated. I understand that choosing this option means that I may revoke this directive even if I am incapacitated. I further understand that if I choose this option and revoke this directive while I am incapacitated I may not receive treatment that I specify in this directive, even if I want the treatment.

PART V.
PREFERENCES AND INSTRUCTIONS ABOUT TREATMENT, FACILITIES, AND PHYSICIANS

A. Preferences and Instructions About Physician(s) to be Involved in My Treatment.

I would like the physician(s) named below to be involved in my treatment decisions:

Dr _____ Contact information: _____

Dr _____ Contact information: _____

I do not wish to be treated by Dr _____

B. Preferences and Instructions About Other Providers:

I am receiving other treatment or care from providers who I feel have an impact on my mental health care. I would like the following treatment provider(s) to be contacted when this directive is effective:

Name: _____ Profession: _____
Contact information: _____

Name: _____ Profession: _____
Contact information: _____

C. Preferences and Instructions About Medications for Psychiatric Treatment (initial and complete all that apply):

_____ I consent, and authorize my agent (if appointed) to consent, to the following medications: _____
_____

_____ I do not consent, and I do not authorize my agent (if appointed) to consent, to the administration of the following medications: _____
_____
_____

_____ I am willing to take the medications excluded above if my only reason for excluding them is the side effects which include: _____
_____
and these side effects can be eliminated by dosage adjustment or other means.

_____ I am willing to try any other medication the hospital doctor recommends

_____ I am willing to try any other medications my outpatient doctor recommends

_____ I do not want to try any other medications.

Medication Allergies:

I have allergies to, or severe side effects from, the following: _____
_____

Other Medication Preferences or Instructions:

_____ I have the following other preferences or instructions about medications:
_____

D. Preferences and Instructions About Hospitalization and Alternatives (initial all that apply and, if desired, rank "1" for first choice, "2" for second choice, and so on):

_____ In the event my psychiatric condition is serious enough to require 24-hour care and I have no physical conditions that require immediate access to emergency medical care, I prefer to receive this care in programs/facilities designed as alternatives to psychiatric hospitalizations

_____ I would also like the interventions below to be tried before hospitalization is considered:

_____ Calling someone or having someone call me when needed

Name: _____
Telephone: _____

_____ Staying overnight with someone

Name: _____
Telephone: _____

_____ Having a mental health service provider come to see me

_____ Going to a crisis triage center or emergency room

_____ Staying overnight at a crisis respite (temporary) bed

_____ Seeing a service provider for help with psychiatric medications

_____ Other, specify: _____
_____

Authority to Consent to Inpatient Treatment. I consent, and authorize my agent (if appointed) to consent, to voluntary admission to inpatient mental health treatment for _____ days (not to exceed 14 days)

(Sign one):

_____ If deemed appropriate by my agent (if appointed) and treating physician
_____ (Signature)
  or
_____ Under the following circumstances (specify symptoms, behaviors, or circumstances that indicate the need for hospitalization)
_____ (Signature)

_____ I do not consent, or authorize my agent (if appointed) to consent, to inpatient treatment
_____ (Signature)

Hospital Preferences and Instructions:

If hospitalization is required, I prefer the following hospitals: _____
_____

I do not consent to be admitted to the following hospitals: _____
_____

E. Preferences and Instructions About Preemergency. I would like the interventions below to be tried before use of seclusion or restraint is considered (initial all that apply):

_____ "Talk me down" one-on-one

_____ More medication

_____ Time out/privacy

_____ Show of authority/force

_____ Shift my attention to something else

_____ Set firm limits on my behavior

_____ Help me to discuss/vent feelings

_____ Decrease stimulation

_____ Offer to have neutral person settle dispute

_____ Other, specify_____

F. Preferences and Instructions About Seclusion, Restraint, and Emergency Medications. If it is determined that I am engaging in behavior that requires seclusion, physical restraint, and/or emergency use of medication, I prefer these interventions in the order I have chosen (choose "1" for first choice, "2" for second choice, and so on):

_____ Seclusion

_____ Seclusion and physical restraint (combined)

_____ Medication by injection

_____ Medication in pill or liquid form

In the event that my attending physician decides to use medication in response to an emergency situation after due consideration of my preferences and instructions for emergency treatments stated above, I expect the choice of medication to reflect any preferences and instructions I have expressed in Part III C of this form.

The preferences and instructions I express in this section regarding medication in emergency situations do not constitute consent to use of the medication for nonemergency treatment.

G. Preferences and Instructions About Electroconvulsive Therapy (ECT or Shock Therapy). My wishes regarding electroconvulsive therapy are (sign one):

\_\_\_\_\_ I do not consent, nor authorize my agent (if appointed) to consent, to the administration of electroconvulsive therapy _____ (Signature)

\_\_\_\_\_ I consent, and authorize my agent (if appointed) to consent, to the administration of electroconvulsive therapy _____ (Signature)

\_\_\_\_\_ I consent, and authorize my agent (if appointed) to consent, to the administration of electroconvulsive therapy, but only under the following conditions: _____

_____(Signature)

H. Preferences and Instructions About Who is Permitted to Visit. If I have been admitted to a mental health treatment facility, the following people are not permitted to visit me there:

Name: _____
Name: _____
Name: _____

I understand that persons not listed above may be permitted to visit me.

I. Additional Instructions About My Mental Health Care:

Other instructions about my mental health care: _____
_____

In case of emergency, please contact:
Name: _____
Address: _____
Work telephone: _____
Home telephone: _____

Physician: _____
Address: _____
Telephone: _____

The following may help me to avoid a hospitalization: _____
_____

I generally react to being hospitalized as follows: _____
_____

Staff of the hospital or crisis unit can help me by doing the following: _____
_____
_____

J. Refusal of Treatment

I do not consent to any mental health treatment.

_____ (Signature)

PART VI.
DURABLE POWER OF ATTORNEY (APPOINTMENT OF MY AGENT)

(Fill out this part only if you wish to appoint an agent or nominate a guardian.)

I authorize an agent to make mental health treatment decisions on my behalf. The authority granted to my agent includes the right to consent, refuse consent, or withdraw consent to any mental health care, treatment, service, or procedure, consistent with any instructions and/or limitations I have set forth in this directive. I intend that those decisions should be made in accordance with my expressed wishes as set forth in this document. If I have not expressed a choice in this document and my agent does not otherwise know my wishes, I authorize my agent to make the decision that my agent determines is in my best interest. This agency shall not be affected by my incapacity. Unless I state otherwise in this durable power of attorney, I may revoke it unless prohibited by other state law.

A. Designation of an Agent

I appoint the following person as my agent to make mental health treatment decisions for me as authorized in this document and request that this person be notified immediately when this directive becomes effective:

Name: _____
Address: _____
Work telephone: _____
Home telephone: _____
Relationship: _____

B. Designation of Alternate Agent

If the person named above is unavailable, unable, or refuses to serve as my agent, or I revoke that person's authority to serve as my agent, I hereby appoint the following person as my alternate agent and request that this person be notified immediately when this directive becomes effective or when my original agent is no longer my agent:

Name: _____
Address: _____
Work telephone: _____
Home telephone: _____
Relationship: _____

C. When My Spouse is My Agent (initial if desired)

_____ If my spouse is my agent, that person shall remain my agent even if we become legally separated or our marriage is dissolved, unless there is a court order to the contrary or I have remarried.

D. Limitations on My Agent's Authority

I do not grant my agent the authority to consent on my behalf to the following:

_____

_____

E. Limitations on My Ability to Revoke this Durable Power of Attorney

I choose to limit my ability to revoke this durable power of attorney as follows:

_____

_____

F. Preference as to Court-Appointed Guardian

In the event a court appoints a guardian who will make decisions regarding my mental health treatment, I nominate the following person as my guardian:

Name: _____

Address: _____

Work telephone: _____

Home telephone: _____

Relationship: _____

The appointment of a guardian of my estate or my person or any other decision maker shall not give the guardian or decision maker the power to revoke, suspend, or terminate this directive or the powers of my agent, except as authorized by law.

_____

(Signature required if nomination is made)

PART VII.
OTHER DOCUMENTS

(Initial all that apply)

I have executed the following documents that include the power to make decisions regarding health care services for myself:

_____ Health care power of attorney (chapter 11.94 RCW)

_____ "Living will" (Health care directive; chapter 70.122 RCW)

_____ I have appointed more than one agent. I understand that the most recently appointed agent controls except as stated below:

_____

_____

PART VIII.
NOTIFICATION OF OTHERS AND CARE OF PERSONAL AFFAIRS

(Fill out this part only if you wish to provide nontreatment instructions.)

I understand the preferences and instructions in this part are NOT the responsibility of my treatment provider and that no treatment provider is required to act on them.

A. Who Should Be Notified

I desire my agent to notify the following individuals as soon as possible when this directive becomes effective:

Name: _____
Address: _____
Day telephone: _____
Evening telephone: _____

Name: _____
Address: _____
Day telephone: _____
Evening telephone: _____

B. Preferences or Instructions About Personal Affairs

I have the following preferences or instructions about my personal affairs (e.g., care of dependents, pets, household) if I am admitted to a mental health treatment facility: _____
_____
_____

C. Additional Preferences and Instructions:

_____
_____
_____
_____
_____

PART IX.
SIGNATURE

By signing here, I indicate that I understand the purpose and effect of this document and that I am giving my informed consent to the treatments and/or admission to which I have consented or authorized my agent to consent in this directive. I intend that my consent in this directive be construed as being consistent with the elements of informed consent under chapter 7.70 RCW.

Signature: _____
Date: _____
Printed Name: _____

This directive was signed and declared by the "Principal," to be his or her directive, in our presence who, at his or her request, have signed our names below as witnesses. We declare that, at the time of the creation of this instrument, the Principal is personally known to us, and, according to our best knowledge and belief, has capacity at this time and does not appear to be acting under duress, undue influence, or fraud. We further declare that none of us is:

(A) A person designated to make medical decisions on the principal's behalf;

(B) A health care provider or professional person directly involved with the provision of care to the principal at the time the directive is executed;

(C) An owner, operator, employee, or relative of an owner or operator of a health care facility or long-term care facility in which the principal is a patient or resident;

(D) A person who is related by blood, marriage, or adoption to the person, or with whom the principal has a dating relationship as defined in RCW 26.50.010;

(E) An incapacitated person;

(F) A person who would benefit financially if the principal undergoes mental health treatment; or

(G) A minor.

Witness 1: Signature: _____
Date: _____
Printed Name: _____
Telephone: _____
Address: _____

Witness 2: Signature: _____
Date: _____
Printed Name: _____
Telephone: _____
Address: _____

## PART X.
## RECORD OF DIRECTIVE

I have given a copy of this directive to the following persons: _____
_____

DO NOT FILL OUT PART XI UNLESS YOU INTEND TO REVOKE THIS DIRECTIVE IN PART OR IN WHOLE

## PART XI.
## REVOCATION OF THIS DIRECTIVE

(Initial any that apply): _____
_____

_____ I am revoking the following part(s) of this directive (specify):

_____ I am revoking all of this directive.

By signing here, I indicate that I understand the purpose and effect of my revocation and that no person is bound by any revoked provision(s). I intend this revocation to be interpreted as if I had never completed the revoked provision(s).

Signature: _____
Date: _____
Printed Name: _____

DO NOT SIGN THIS PART UNLESS YOU INTEND TO REVOKE THIS DIRECTIVE IN PART OR IN WHOLE

# HEALTH CARE DIRECTIVE

Directive made this _____ day of _____ (month, year).

I, _____, having the capacity to make health care decisions, willfully, and voluntarily make known my desire that my dying shall not be artificially prolonged under the circumstances set forth below, and do hereby declare that:

(a) If at any time I should be diagnosed in writing to be in a terminal condition by the attending physician, or in a permanent unconscious condition by two physicians, and where the application of life-sustaining treatment would serve only to artificially prolong the process of my dying, I direct that such treatment be withheld or withdrawn, and that I be permitted to die naturally. I understand by using this form that a terminal condition means an incurable and irreversible condition caused by injury, disease, or illness, that would within reasonable medical judgment cause death within a reasonable period of time in accordance with accepted medical standards, and where the application of life-sustaining treatment would serve only to prolong the process of dying. I further understand in using this form that a permanent unconscious condition means an incurable and irreversible condition in which I am medically assess within reasonable medical judgment as having no reasonable probability of recovery from an irreversible coma or a persistent vegetative state.

(b) In the absence of my ability to give directions regarding the use of such life-sustaining treatment, it is my intention that this directive shall be honored by my family and physician(s) as the final expression of my legal right to refuse medical or surgical treatment and I accept the consequences of such refusal. If another person is appointed to make these decisions for me, whether through a durable power of attorney or otherwise, I request that the person be guided by this directive and any other clear expressions of my desires.

(c) If I am diagnosed to be in a terminal condition or a permanent unconscious condition (check one):
　　　　　_____ I DO want to have artificially provided nutrition and hydration.
　　　　　_____ I DO NOT want to have artificially provided nutrition and hydration.

(d) If I have been diagnosed as pregnant and that diagnosis is known to my physician, this directive shall have no force or effect during the course of my pregnancy.

(e) I understand the full import of this directive and I am emotionally and mentally capable to make the health care decisions contained in this directive.

(f) I understand that before I sign this directive, I can add to or delete from or otherwise change the wording of this directive and that I may add to or delete from this directive at any time and that any changes shall be consistent with Washington state law or federal constitutional law to be legally valid.

(g) It is my wish that every part of this directive be fully implemented. If for any reason any part is held invalid it is my wish that the remainder of my directive be implemented.

Signed_____

_____
City, County, and State of Residence

The declarer has been personally known to me and I believe him or her to be capable of making health care decisions.

Witness_____
Witness_____

## State of West Virginia
## Medical Power of Attorney

The Person I Want to Make Health Care Decisions For Me When I Can't Make Them for Myself

Dated: _____, 20_____

I, _____,
(Insert your name and address)

hereby appoint as my representative to act on my behalf to give, withhold or withdraw informed consent to health care decisions in the event that I am not able to do so myself.

**The person I choose as my representative is:**

_____
(Insert the name, address, area code and telephone number of the person you wish to designate as your representative)

**The person I choose as my successor representative is:** If my representative is unable, unwilling or disqualified to serve, then I appoint:

_____
(Insert the name, address, area code and telephone number of the person you wish to designate as your successor representative)

This appointment shall extend to, but not be limited to, health care decisions relating to medical treatment, surgical treatment, nursing care, medication, hospitalization, care and treatment in a nursing home or other facility, and home health care. The representative appointed by this document is specifically authorized to be granted access to my medical records and other health information and to act on my behalf to consent to, refuse or withdraw any and all medical treatment or diagnostic procedures, or autopsy if my representative determines that I, if able to do so, would consent to, refuse or withdraw such treatment or procedures. Such authority shall include, but not be limited to, decisions regarding the withholding or withdrawal of life-prolonging interventions.

I appoint this representative because I believe this person understands my wishes and values and will act to carry into effect the health care decisions that I would make if I were able to do so, and because I also believe that this person will act in my best interest when my wishes are unknown. It is my intent that my family, my physician and all legal authorities be bound by the decisions that are made by the representative appointed by this document, and it is my intent that these decisions should not be the subject of review by any health care provider or administrative or judicial agency.

It is my intent that this document be legally binding and effective and that this document be taken as a formal statement of my desire concerning the method by which any health care decisions should be made on my behalf during any period when I am unable to make such decisions.

In exercising the authority under this medical power of attorney, my representative shall act consistently with my special directives or limitations as stated below.

I am giving the following SPECIAL DIRECTIVES OR LIMITATIONS ON THIS POWER: (Comments about tube feedings, breathing machines, cardiopulmonary resuscitation and dialysis may be placed here. My failure to provide special directives or limitations does not mean that I want or refuse certain treatments.)

THIS MEDICAL POWER OF ATTORNEY SHALL BECOME EFFECTIVE ONLY UPON MY INCAPACITY TO GIVE, WITHHOLD OR WITHDRAW INFORMED CONSENT TO MY OWN MEDICAL CARE.

_____

(Signature of the Principal)

I did not sign the principal's signature above. I am at least eighteen years of age and am not related to the principal by blood or marriage. I am not entitled to any portion of the estate of the principal or to the best of my knowledge under any will of the principal or codicil thereto, or legally responsible for the costs of the principal's medical or other care. I am not the principal's attending physician, nor am I the representative or successor representative of the principal.

Witness: _____  DATE: _____

Witness: _____  DATE: _____

STATE OF _____
COUNTY OF _____

I, _____, a Notary Public of said _____ County, do certify that _____, as principal, and _____ and _____, as witnesses, whose names are signed to the writing above bearing date on the _____ day of _____, 20_____, have this day acknowledged the same before me.

Given under my hand this _____ day of _____, 20_____.

My commission expires: _____.

_____

(Notary Public)

# Wisconsin Basic Power of Attorney for Finances and Property

NOTICE: THIS IS AN IMPORTANT DOCUMENT. BEFORE SIGNING THIS DOCUMENT, YOU SHOULD KNOW THESE IMPORTANT FACTS. BY SIGNING THIS DOCUMENT, YOU ARE NOT GIVING UP ANY POWERS OR RIGHTS TO CONTROL YOU FINANCES AND PROPERTY YOURSELF. IN ADDITION TO YOUR OWN POWERS AND RIGHTS, YOU ARE GIVING ANOTHER PERSON, YOUR AGENT, BROAD POWERS TO HANDLE YOUR FINANCES AND PROPERTY. THIS BASIC POWER OF ATTORNEY FOR FINANCES AND PROPERTY MAY GIVE THE PERSON WHOM YOU DESIGNATE (YOUR "AGENT") BROAD POWERS TO HANDLE YOUR FINANCES AND PROPERTY, WHICH MAY INCLUDE POWERS TO ENCUMBER, SELL OR OTHERWISE DISPOSE OF ANY REAL OR PERSONAL PROPERTY WITHOUT ADVANCE NOTICE TO YOU OR APPROVAL BY YOU. THE POWER WILL EXIST AFTER YOU BECOME DISABLED, OR INCAPACITATED, IF YOU CHOOSE THAT PROVISION. THIS DOCUMENT DOES NOT AUTHORIZE ANYONE TO MAKE MEDICAL OR OTHER HEALTH CARE DECISIONS FOR YOU. IF YOU OWN COMPLEX OR SPECIAL ASSETS SUCH AS A BUSINESS, OR IF THERE IS ANYTHING ABOUT THIS FORM THAT YOU DO NOT UNDERSTAND, YOU SHOULD ASK A LAWYER TO EXPLAIN THIS FORM TO YOU BEFORE YOU SIGN IT.

IF YOU WISH TO CHANGE YOUR BASIC POWER OF ATTORNEY FOR FINANCES AND PROPERTY, YOU MUST COMPLETE A NEW DOCUMENT AND REVOKE THIS ONE. YOU MAY REVOKE THIS DOCUMENT AT ANY TIME BY DESTROYING IT, BY DIRECTING ANOTHER PERSON TO DESTROY IT IN YOUR PRESENCE OR BY SIGNING A WRITTEN AND DATED STATEMENT EXPRESSING YOUR INTENT TO REVOKE THIS DOCUMENT. IF YOU REVOKE THIS DOCUMENT, YOU SHOULD NOTIFY YOUR AGENT AND ANY OTHER PERSON TO WHOM YOU HAVE GIVEN A COPY OF THE FORM. YOU ALSO SHOULD NOTIFY ALL PARTIES HAVING CUSTODY OF YOUR ASSETS. THESE PARTIES HAVE NO RESPONSIBILITY TO YOU UNLESS YOU ACTUALLY NOTIFY THEM OF THE REVOCATION. IF YOUR AGENT IS YOUR SPOUSE AND YOUR MARRIAGE IS ANNULLED, OR YOU ARE DIVORCED AFTER SIGNING THIS DOCUMENT, THIS DOCUMENT IS INVALID.

SINCE SOME 3RD PARTIES OR SOME TRANSACTIONS MAY NOT PERMIT USE OF THIS DOCUMENT, IT IS ADVISABLE TO CHECK IN ADVANCE, IF POSSIBLE, FOR ANY SPECIAL REQUIREMENTS THAT MAY BE IMPOSED.

YOU SHOULD SIGN THIS FORM ONLY IF THE AGENT YOU NAME IS RELIABLE, TRUSTWORTHY AND COMPETENT TO MANAGE YOUR AFFAIRS.

I, _____, (insert your name and address) appoint _____ (insert the name and address of the person appointed) as my agent to act for me in any lawful way with respect to the powers initialed below. If the person appointed is unable or unwilling to act as my agent, I appoint _____ (insert name and address of alternate person appointed) to act for me in any lawful way with respect to the powers initialed below.

TO GRANT ONE OR MORE OF THE FOLLOWING POWERS, INITIAL THE LINE IN FRONT OF EACH POWER YOU ARE GRANTING.

TO WITHHOLD A POWER, DO NOT INITIAL THE LINE IN FRONT OF IT. YOU MAY, BUT NEED NOT, CROSS OUT EACH POWER WITHHELD.

## HANDLING MY MONEY AND PROPERTY

Initials

_____ 1.  PAYMENTS OF BILLS: My agent may make payments that are necessary or appropriate in connection with the administration of my affairs.

_____ 2.  BANKING: My agent may conduct business with financial institutions, including endorsing all checks and drafts made payable to my order and collecting the proceeds; signing in my name checks or orders on all accounts in my name or for my benefit; withdrawing funds from accounts in my name; opening accounts in my name; and entering into and removing articles from my safe deposit box.

_____ 3.  INSURANCE: My agent may obtain insurance of all types, as considered necessary or appropriate, settle and adjust insurance claims and borrow from insurers and 3rd parties using insurance policies as collateral.

_____ 4.     ACCOUNTS: My agent may ask for, collect and receive money, dividends, interest, legacies and property due or that may become due and owning to me and give receipt for those payments.

_____ 5.     REAL ESTATE: My agent may manage real property; sell, convey and mortgage realty for prices and on terms as considered advisable; foreclose mortgages and take title to property in my name; and execute deeds, mortgages, releases, satisfactions and other instruments relating to realty.

_____ 6.     BORROWING: My agent may borrow money and encumber my assets for loans as considered necessary.

_____ 7.     SECURITIES: My agent may buy, sell, pledge and exchange securities of all kinds in my name; sign and deliver in my name transfers and assignments of securities; and consent in my name to reorganizations, mergers or exchange of securities for new securities.

_____ 8.     INCOME TAXES: My agent may make and sign tax returns; represent me in all income tax matters before any federal, state, or local tax collecting agency; and receive confidential information and perform any acts that I may perform, including receiving refund checks and the signing of returns.

_____ 9.     TRUSTS: My agent may transfer at any time any of my property to a living trust that has been established by me before the execution of this document.

## PROFESSIONAL AND TECHNICAL ASSISTANCE

Initials

_____ 10.     LEGAL ACTIONS: My agent may retain attorneys on my behalf; appear for me in all actions and proceedings to which I may be a party; commence actions and proceedings in my name; and sign in my name all documents or pleadings of every description.

_____ 11.     PROFESSIONAL ASSISTANCE: My agent may hire accountants, attorneys, clerks, workers and others for the management, preservation and protection of my property and estate.

## GENERAL AUTHORITY

Initials

_____ 12.     GENERAL: My agent may do any act or thing that I could do in my own proper person if personally present, including managing or selling tangible assets, disclaiming a probate or non-probate inheritance and providing support for a minor child or dependent adult. The specifically enumerated powers of the basic power of attorney for finances and property are not a limitation of this intended broad general power except that my agent may not take any action prohibited by law and my agent under this document may not:

    a.     Make medical or health care decisions for me.

    b.     Make, modify or revoke a will for me.

    c.     Other than a burial trust agreement under section 445.125, Wisconsin Statutes, enter
into a trust agreement on my behalf or amend or revoke a trust agreement, entered into by me.

    d.     Change any beneficiary designation of any life insurance policy, qualified
retirement plan, individual retirement account or payable on death account or the like whether directly or by canceling and replacing the policy or rollover to another plan or account.

    e.     Forgive debts owed to me or disclaim or waive benefits payable to me, except a
probate or non-probate inheritance.

    f.     Appoint a substitute or successor agent for me.

    g.     Make gifts.

## COMPENSATION TO AGENT FROM PRINCIPAL'S FUNDS

Initials

_____ 13.     COMPENSATION: My agent may receive compensation only in an amount not greater than that usual for the services to be performed if expressly authorized in the special instructions portion of this document.

# ACCOUNTING

Initials

_____ 14. ACCOUNTING: My agent shall render an accounting (monthly) (quarterly) (annually) (CIRCLE ONE) to me or to _____ _____ (insert name and address) during my lifetime and a final accounting to the personal representative of my estate, if any is appointed, after my death.

# NOMINATION OF GUARDIAN

Initials

_____ 15. GUARDIAN: If necessary, I nominate _____ (name) of _____ (address) as guardian of my person and I nominate _____ (name) of _____ _____ (address) as guardian of my estate.

# SPECIAL INSTRUCTIONS

Initials

_____ 16. SPECIAL INSTRUCTIONS:
ON THE FOLLOWING LINES YOU MAY GIVE SPECIAL INSTRUCTIONS REGARDING THE POWERS GRANTED TO YOUR AGENT.

_____
_____
_____

TO ESTABLISH WHEN, AND FOR HOW LONG, THE BASIC POWER OF ATTORNEY FOR FINANCES AND PROPERTY IS IN EFFECT, YOU MUST INITIAL ONLY ONE OF THE FOLLOWING 3 OPTIONS. IF YOU DO NOT INITIAL ONE, OR IF YOU INITIAL MORE THAN ONE, THIS BASIC POWER OF ATTORNEY FOR FINANCES AND PROPERTY WILL NOT TAKE EFFECT.

Initials

_____ This basic power of attorney for finances and property becomes effective when I sign it and will continue in effect as a durable power of attorney under section 243.07, Wisconsin Statutes, if I become disabled or incapacitated.

_____ This basic power of attorney for finances and property becomes effective only when both of the following apply:

      a.      I have signed it; and

      b.      I become disabled or incapacitated.

_____ This basic power of attorney for finances and property becomes effective when I sign it BUT WILL CEASE TO BE EFFECTIVE IF I BECOME DISABLED OR INCAPACITATED.

I agree that any 3rd party who receives a copy of this document may act under it. Revocation of this basic power of attorney is not effective as to a 3rd party until the 3rd party learns of the revocation. I agree to reimburse the 3rd party for any loss resulting from claims that arise against the 3rd party because of reliance on this basic power of attorney.

Signed this _____ day of _____, 20___.

_____
(Your Signature)

By signing as a witness, I am acknowledging the signature of the principal who signed in my presence and the presence of the other witness, and the fact that he or she has stated that this power of attorney reflects his or her wishes and is being executed voluntarily. I believe him or her to be of sound mind and capable of creating this power of attorney. I am not related to him or her by blood, marriage or adoption, and, to the best of my knowledge, I am not entitled to any portion of his or her estate under his or her will.

Witness _____     Witness _____

Dated: _____     Dated: _____

Signature: _____     Signature: _____

Print Name: _____     Print Name: _____

Address: _____     Address: _____


State of _____

County of _____

This document was acknowledged before me on _____ (date) by _____ (name of principal).

(Seal, if any)

_____
(Signature of Notarial Officer)

_____
(Title)

My commission is permanent or expires: _____

BY ACCEPTING OR ACTING UNDER THE APPOINTMENT, THE AGENT ASSUMES THE FIDUCIARY AND OTHER LEGAL RESPONSIBILITIES AND LIABILITIES OF AN AGENT.

_____
(Name of Agent)

_____
(Signature of Agent)

This document was drafted by _____ (signature of person preparing the document).

# Power of Attorney for Health Care

### NOTICE TO PERSON MAKING THIS DOCUMENT

YOU HAVE THE RIGHT TO MAKE DECISIONS ABOUT YOUR HEALTH CARE. NO HEALTH CARE MAY BE GIVEN TO YOU OVER YOUR OBJECTION, AND NECESSARY HEALTH CARE MAY NOT BE STOPPED OR WITHHELD IF YOU OBJECT.

BECAUSE YOUR HEALTH CARE PROVIDERS IN SOME CASES MAY NOT HAVE HAD THE OPPORTUNITY TO ESTABLISH A LONG-TERM RELATIONSHIP WITH YOU, THEY ARE OFTEN UNFAMILIAR WITH YOUR BELIEFS AND VALUES AND THE DETAILS OF YOUR FAMILY RELATIONSHIPS. THIS POSES A PROBLEM IF YOU BECOME PHYSICALLY OR MENTALLY UNABLE TO MAKE DECISIONS ABOUT YOUR HEALTH CARE.

IN ORDER TO AVOID THIS PROBLEM, YOU MAY SIGN THIS LEGAL DOCUMENT TO SPECIFY THE PERSON WHOM YOU WANT TO MAKE HEALTH CARE DECISIONS FOR YOU IF YOU ARE UNABLE TO MAKE THOSE DECISIONS PERSONALLY. THAT PERSON IS KNOWN AS YOUR HEALTH CARE AGENT. YOU SHOULD TAKE SOME TIME TO DISCUSS YOUR THOUGHTS AND BELIEFS ABOUT MEDICAL TREATMENT WITH THE PERSON OR PERSONS WHOM YOU HAVE SPECIFIED. YOU MAY STATE IN THIS ANY TYPES OF HEALTH CARE THAT YOU DO OR DO NOT DESIRE, AND YOU MAY LIMIT THE AUTHORITY OF YOUR HEALTH CARE AGENT. IF YOUR HEALTH CARE AGENT IS UNAWARE OF YOUR DESIRES WITH RESPECT TO A PARTICULAR HEALTH CARE DECISION, HE OR SHE IS REQUIRED TO DETERMINE WHAT WOULD BE IN YOUR BEST INTERESTS IN MAKING THE DECISION.

THIS IS AN IMPORTANT LEGAL DOCUMENT. IT GIVES YOUR AGENT BROAD POWERS TO MAKE HEALTH CARE DECISIONS FOR YOU. IT REVOKES ANY PRIOR POWER OF ATTORNEY FOR HEALTH CARE THAT YOU MAY HAVE MADE. IF YOU WISH TO CHANGE YOUR POWER OF ATTORNEY FOR HEALTH CARE, YOU MAY REVOKE THIS DOCUMENT AT ANY TIME BY DESTROYING IT, BY DIRECTING ANOTHER PERSON TO DESTROY IT IN YOUR PRESENCE, BY SIGNING A WRITTEN AND DATED STATEMENT OR BY STATING THAT IT IS REVOKED IN THE PRESENCE OF TWO WITNESSES. IF YOU REVOKE, YOU SHOULD NOTIFY YOUR AGENT, YOUR HEALTH CARE PROVIDERS AND ANY OTHER PERSON TO WHOM YOU HAVE GIVEN A COPY. IF YOUR AGENT IS YOUR SPOUSE AND YOUR MARRIAGE IS ANNULLED OR YOU ARE DIVORCED AFTER SIGNING THIS DOCUMENT, THE DOCUMENT IS INVALID.

YOU MAY ALSO USE THIS DOCUMENT TO MAKE OR REFUSE TO MAKE AN ANATOMICAL GIFT UPON YOUR DEATH. IF YOU USE THIS DOCUMENT TO MAKE OR REFUSE TO MAKE AN ANATOMICAL GIFT, THIS DOCUMENT REVOKES ANY PRIOR DOCUMENT OF GIFT THAT YOU MAY HAVE MADE. YOU MAY REVOKE OR CHANGE ANY ANATOMICAL GIFT THAT YOU MAKE BY THIS DOCUMENT BY CROSSING OUT THE ANATOMICAL GIFT PROVISION IN THIS DOCUMENT.

DO NOT SIGN THIS DOCUMENT UNLESS YOU CLEARLY UNDERSTAND IT.

IT IS SUGGESTED THAT YOU KEEP THE ORIGINAL OF THIS DOCUMENT ON FILE WITH YOUR PHYSICIAN.

## POWER OF ATTORNEY FOR HEALTH CARE

Document made this _____ day of _____ (month), _____ (year).

### CREATION OF POWER OF ATTORNEY FOR HEALTH CARE

I, _____ (print name, address and date of birth), being of sound mind, intend by this document to create a power of attorney for health care. My executing this power of attorney for health care is voluntary. Despite the creation of this power of attorney for health care, I expect to be fully informed about and allowed to participate in any health care decision for me, to the extent that I am able. For the purposes of this document, "health care decision" means an informed decision to accept, maintain, discontinue or refuse any care, treatment, service or procedure to maintain, diagnose or treat my physical or mental condition.

In addition, I may, by this document, specify my wishes with respect to making an anatomical gift upon my death.

# DESIGNATION OF HEALTH CARE AGENT

If I am no longer able to make health care decisions for myself, due to my incapacity, I hereby designate

_____

_____ (print name, address and telephone number) to be my health care agent for the purpose of making health care decisions on my behalf. If he or she is ever unable or unwilling to do so, I hereby designate _____

_____ (print name, address and telephone number) to be my alternate health care agent for the purpose of making health care decisions on my behalf. Neither my health care agent nor my alternate health care agent whom I have designated is my health care provider, an employee of my health care provider, an employee of a health care facility in which I am a patient or a spouse of any of those persons, unless he or she is also my relative. For purposes of this document, "incapacity" exists if 2 physicians or a physician and a psychologist who have personally examined me sign a statement that specifically expresses their opinion that I have a condition that means that I am unable to receive and evaluate information effectively or to communicate decisions to such an extent that I lack the capacity to manage my health care decisions. A copy of that statement must be attached to this document.

## GENERAL STATEMENT OF AUTHORITY GRANTED

Unless I have specified otherwise in this document, if I ever have incapacity I instruct my health care provider to obtain the health care decision of my health care agent, if I need treatment, for all of my health care and treatment. I have discussed my desires thoroughly with my health care agent and believe that he or she understands my philosophy regarding the health care decisions I would make if I were able. I desire that my wishes be carried out through the authority given to my health care agent under this document.

If I am unable, due to my incapacity, to make a health care decision, my health care agent is instructed to make the health care decision for me, but my health care agent should try to discuss with me any specific proposed health care if I am able to communicate in any manner, including by blinking my eyes. If this communication cannot be made, my health care agent shall base his or her decision on any health care choices that I have expressed prior to the time of the decision. If I have not expressed a health care choice about the health care in question and communication cannot be made, my health care agent shall base his or her health care decision on what he or she believes to be in my best interest.

## LIMITATIONS ON MENTAL HEALTH TREATMENT

My health care agent may not admit or commit me on an inpatient basis to an institution for mental diseases, an intermediate care facility for the mentally retarded, a state treatment facility or a treatment facility. My health care agent may not consent to experimental mental health research or psychosurgery, electro-convulsive treatment or drastic mental health treatment procedures for me.

## ADMISSION TO NURSING HOMES OR COMMUNITY-BASED RESIDENTIAL FACILITIES

My health care agent may admit me to a nursing home or community-based residential facility for short-term stays for recuperative care or respite care.

If I have checked "Yes" to the following, my health care agent may admit me for a purpose other than recuperative care or respite care, but if I have checked "No" to the following, my health care agent may not so admit me:

    1. A nursing home - Yes ___    No ___

    2. A community-based residential facility - Yes ___    No ___

If I have not checked either "Yes" or "No" immediately above, my health care agent may admit me only for short-term stays for recuperative care or respite care.

## PROVISION OF A FEEDING TUBE

If I have checked "Yes" to the following, my health care agent may have a feeding tube withheld or withdrawn from me, unless my physician has advised that, in his or her professional judgment, this will cause me pain or will reduce my comfort. If I have checked "No" to the following, my health care agent may not have a feeding tube withheld or withdrawn from me.

My health care agent may not have orally ingested nutrition or hydration withheld or withdrawn from me unless the provision of the nutrition or hydration is medically contraindicated.

Withhold or withdraw a feeding tube - Yes \_\_\_ No \_\_\_

If I have not checked either "Yes" or "No immediately above, my health care agent may not have a feeding tube withdrawn from me.

## HEALTH CARE DECISIONS FOR PREGNANT WOMEN

If I have checked "Yes" to the following, my health care agent may make health care decisions for me even if my health care agent knows I am pregnant. If I have checked "No" to the following, my health care agent may not make health care decisions for me if my health care agent knows I am pregnant.

Health care decision if I am pregnant- Yes \_\_\_ No \_\_\_

If I have not checked either "Yes" or "No" immediately above, my health care agent may not make health care decisions for me if my health care agent knows I am pregnant.

## STATEMENT OF DESIRES, SPECIAL PROVISIONS OR LIMITATIONS

In exercising authority under this document, my health care agent shall act consistently with my following stated desires, if any, and is subject to any special provisions or limitations that I specify. The following are specific desires, provisions or limitations that I wish to state:

_____

_____

_____

## INSPECTION AND DISCLOSURE OF INFORMATION
## RELATING TO MY PHYSICAL OR MENTAL HEALTH

Subject to any limitations in this document, my health care agent has the authority to do all of the following:

(a) Request, review and receive any information, oral or written, regarding my physical or mental health, including medical and hospital records.

(b) Execute on my behalf any documents that may be required in order to obtain this information.

(c) Consent to the disclosure of this information.

(The principal and the witnesses all must sign the document at the same time.)
## SIGNATURE OF PRINCIPAL

(person creating the power of attorney for health care)

Signature _____ Date _____

(The signing of this document by the principal revokes all previous powers of attorney for health care documents.)

## STATEMENT OF WITNESSES

I know the principal personally and I believe him or her to be of sound mind and at least 18 years of age. I believe that his or her execution of this power of attorney for health care is voluntary. I am at least 18 years of age, am not related to the principal by blood, marriage or adoption and am not directly financially responsible for the principal's health care. I am not a health care provider who is serving the principal at this time, an employee of the health care provider, other than a chaplain or a social worker, of an inpatient health care facility in which the declarant is a patient. I am not the principal's health care agent. To the best of my knowledge, I am not entitled to and do not have a claim on the principal's estate.

Witness No. 1:

Print Name _____    Date _____

Address _____

_____

Signature _____

Witness No. 2:

Print Name _____    Date _____

Address _____

_____

Signature _____

## STATEMENT OF HEALTH CARE AGENT AND ALTERNATE HEALTH CARE AGENT

I understand that _____ (name of principal) has designated me to be his or her health care agent or alternate health care agent if he or she is ever found to have incapacity and unable to make health care decisions himself or herself. _____ (name of principal) has discussed his or her desires regarding health care decisions with me.

Agent's signature _____

Address _____

_____

Alternate's signature _____

Address _____

_____

Failure to execute a power of attorney for health care document under chapter 155 of the Wisconsin Statutes creates no presumption about the intent of any individual with regard to his or her health care decisions. This power of attorney for health care is executed as provided in chapter 155 of the Wisconsin Statutes.

## ANATOMICAL GIFTS (optional)

Upon my death:

____ I wish to donate only the following organs or parts (specify the organs or parts):

_____

____ I wish to donate any needed organ or part.

____ I with to donate my body for anatomical study if needed.

____ I refuse to make an anatomical gift. (If this revokes a prior commitment that I have made to make an anatomical gift to a designated donee, I will attempt to notify the donee to which or to whom I agreed to donate.)

Failing to check any of the lines immediately above creates no presumption about my desire to make or refuse to make an anatomical gift.

Signature _____    Date _____

# Advance Health Care Directive
## Explanation

You have the right to give instructions about your own health care. You also have the right to name someone else to make health care decisions for you. This form lets you do either or both of these things. It also lets you express your wishes regarding donation of organs and the designation of your supervising health care provider. If you use this form, you may complete or modify all or any part of it. You are free to use a different form.

Part 1 of this form is a power of attorney for health care. Part 1 lets you name another individual as agent to make health care decisions for you if you become incapable of making your own decisions or if you want someone else to make those decisions for you now even though you are still capable.

You may also name an alternate agent to act for you if your first choice is not willing, able or reasonably available to make decisions for you. Unless related to you, your agent may not be an owner, operator or employee of a residential or community care facility at which you are receiving care.

Unless the form you sign limits the authority of your agent, your agent may make all health care decisions for you. This form has a place for you to limit the authority of your agent. You need not limit the authority of your agent if you wish to rely on your agent for all health care decisions that may have to be made. If you choose not to limit the authority of your agent, your agent will have the right to:

(a) Consent or refuse consent to any care, treatment, service or procedure to maintain, diagnose or otherwise affect a physical or mental condition;

(b) Select or discharge health care providers and institutions;

(c) Approve or disapprove diagnostic tests, surgical procedures, programs of medication and orders not to resuscitate; and

(d) Direct the provision, withholding or withdrawal of artificial nutrition and hydration and all other forms of health care.

Part 2 of this form lets you give specific instructions about any aspect of your health care. Choices are provided for you to express your wishes regarding the provision, withholding or withdrawal of treatment to keep you alive, including the provision of artificial nutrition and hydration, as well as the provision of pain relief. Space is also provided for you to add to the choices you have made or for you to write out any additional wishes.
Part 3 of this form lets you express an intention to donate your bodily organs and tissues following your death.

Part 4 of this form lets you designate a supervising health care provider to have primary responsibility for your health care.

After completing this form, sign and date the form at the end. This form must either be signed before a notary public or, in the alternative, be witnessed by two (2) witnesses. Give a copy of the signed and completed form to your physician, to any other health care providers you may have, to any health care institution at which you are receiving care, and to any health care agents you have named. You should talk to the person you have named as agent to make sure that he or she understands your wishes and is willing to take the responsibility.

You have the right to revoke this advance health care directive or replace this form at any time.

* * * * * * * * * * * * * * * * * * * * *

## PART 1
## POWER OF ATTORNEY FOR HEALTH CARE

(1) DESIGNATION OF AGENT: I designate the following individual as my agent to make health care decisions for me:

_____
(name of individual you choose as agent)

_____
(address)                    (city)              (state)      (zip code)

_____
(home phone)                        (work phone)

OPTIONAL: If I revoke my agent's authority or if my agent is not willing, able or reasonably available to make a health care decision for me, I designate as my first alternate agent:

_____
(name of individual you choose as first alternate agent)

_____
(address)                    (city)              (state)      (zip code)

_____
(home phone)                        (work phone)

OPTIONAL: If I revoke the authority of my agent and first alternate agent or if neither is willing, able or reasonably available to make a health care decision for me, I designate as my second alternate agent:

_____
(name of individual you choose as second alternate agent)

_____
(address)                    (city)              (state)      (zip code)

_____
(home phone)                        (work phone)

(2) AGENT'S AUTHORITY: My agent is authorized to make all health care decisions for me, including decisions to provide, withhold or withdraw artificial nutrition and hydration and all other forms of health care to keep me alive, except as I state here:

_____
_____
_____
(Add additional sheets if needed.)

(3) WHEN AGENT'S AUTHORITY BECOMES EFFECTIVE: My agent's authority becomes effective when my supervising health care provider determines that I lack the capacity to make my own health care decisions unless I initial the following box. If I initial this box [          ], my agent's authority to make health care decisions for me takes effect immediately.

(4) AGENT'S OBLIGATION: My agent shall make health care decisions for me in accordance with this power of attorney for health care, any instructions I give in Part 2 of this form, and my other wishes to the extent known to my agent. To the extent my wishes are unknown, my agent shall make health care decisions for me in accordance with what my agent determines to be in my best interest. In determining my best interest, my agent shall consider my personal values to the extent known to my agent.

(5) NOMINATION OF GUARDIAN: If a guardian of my person needs to be appointed for me by a court, (please initial one):

[      ]          I nominate the agent(s) whom I named in this form in the order designated to act as guardian.

[      ]          I nominate the following to be guardian in the order designated:

_____

_____

_____

[      ]          I do not nominate anyone to be guardian.

PART 2
INSTRUCTIONS FOR HEALTH CARE

Please strike any wording that you do not want.

(6) END-OF-LIFE DECISIONS: I direct that my health care providers and others involved in my care provide, withhold or withdraw treatment in accordance with the choice I have initialed below:

[      ]          (a) Choice Not To Prolong Life
I do not want my life to be prolonged if (i) I have an incurable and irreversible condition that will result in my death within a relatively short time, (ii) I become unconscious and, to a reasonable degree of medical certainty, I will not regain consciousness, or (iii) the likely risks and burdens of treatment would outweigh the expected benefits, OR

[      ]          (b) Choice To Prolong Life
I want my life to be prolonged as long as possible within the limits of generally accepted health care standards.

(7) ARTIFICIAL NUTRITION AND HYDRATION: Artificial nutrition and hydration must be provided, withheld or withdrawn in accordance with the choice I have made in paragraph (6) unless I initial the following box. If I initial this box [      ], artificial nutrition must be provided regardless of my condition and regardless of the choice I have made in paragraph (6). If I initial this box [      ], artificial hydration must be provided regardless of my condition and regardless of the choice I have made in paragraph (6).

(8) RELIEF FROM PAIN: Except as I state in the following space, I direct that treatment for alleviation of pain or discomfort be provided at all times:

_____

_____

(9) OTHER WISHES: (If you do not agree with any of the optional choices above and wish to write your own, or if you wish to add to the instructions you have given above, you may do so here.) I direct that:

_____

(Add additional sheets if needed.)

PART 3
DONATION OF ORGANS AT DEATH
(OPTIONAL)

(10) Upon my death (initial applicable box):
[      ]          (a) I give my body, or
[      ]          (b) I give any needed organs, tissues or parts, or
[      ]          (c) I give the following organs, tissues or parts only

_____

[      ]          (d) My gift is for the following purposes (strike any of the following you do not want):
                    (i) Any purpose authorized by law;
                    (ii) Transplantation;
                    (iii) Therapy;
                    (iv) Research;
                    (v) Medical education.

(11) I designate the following physician as my primary physician:

_____
(name of physician)

_____
(address)                    (city)              (state)      (zip code)

_____
(phone)

If the physician I have designated above is not willing, able or reasonably available to act as my primary physician, I designate the following as my primary physician:

_____
(name of physician)

_____
(address)                    (city)              (state)      (zip code)

_____
(phone)

* * * * * * * * * * * * * * * * * * *

(12) EFFECT OF COPY: A copy of this form has the same effect as the original.

(13) SIGNATURES: Sign and date the form here:

_____          _____
(sign your name)                              (date)

_____
(print your name)

_____
(address)

_____
(city)                    (state)

(Optional) SIGNATURES OF WITNESSES:

First witness

_____          _____
(print name)                                  (address)

_____          _____
(signature of witness)                        (city)              (state)

_____
(date)

Second witness

_____          _____
(print name)                                  (address)

_____          _____
(signature of witness)                        (city)              (state)

_____
(date)

_____
(Signature of notary public in lieu of witnesses)

_____
(date)

# Index

## A

advance directive. *See living wills*
affidavit, 21, 29, 32, 38
Affidavit of Attorney in Fact, 21, 32
agent, 1, 2, 3, 4, 5, 6, 7, 8, 9, 10, 11, 12, 13,
    15, 17, 19, 20, 21, 22, 23, 24, 25, 26, 27,
    28, 29, 30, 31, 32, 34, 35, 37, 38, 39, 40,
    41, 43, 44, 45, 48, 49, 50
Alabama, 31, 36
Alaska, 20, 26
all-inclusive power of attorney, 9, 40
Alzheimer's disease, 4, 45
anatomical gifts, 33, 46
Arizona, 20, 26, 31, 36
Arkansas, 20, 25, 26
artificial, 8, 39, 40

assets, 3, 21
attorneys. *See lawyers*
authority of agent, 1, 3, 4, 6, 7, 8, 11, 12,
    13, 19, 21, 22, 24, 27, 30, 31, 36, 37, 38,
    45, 46, 47, 49
autopsy, 37

## B

banks, 1, 2, 9, 14, 15, 19
boats, 22
bonds, 27
brokers, 1, 2, 14, 21
businesses, 1, 2, 3, 6, 13, 14, 19, 21, 24, 25,
    27, 48, 49

## C

California, 16, 20, 25, 26, 36
car accident, 34, 44
case reporters, 17
child care, 3, 10, 47, 48
children, 3, 4, 9, 10, 11, 41, 47, 48
code. *See statutes*
Colorado, 20, 25, 26
Connecticut, 9, 20, 26, 36, 37
contracts, 19
court, 3, 5, 16, 17, 21, 23, 37, 41, 45

## D

declaration regarding life-prolonging procedures. *See living wills*
deed, 6, 15, 23, 24, 32
Delaware, 36
digests, 16
disclosure statements, 25
District of Columbia, 20, 26, 36
do not resuscitate orders (DNR), 33, 44, 45
doctors, 1, 7, 8, 10, 34, 35, 39, 40, 44, 45, 46
Durable Financial Power of Attorney, 3, 20, 24
durable power of attorney, 2, 3, 20, 24, 25, 28, 29, 31, 32, 33, 34, 39, 40, 44
Durable Power of Attorney for Health Care, 33, 34, 39, 44

## E

elderly person, 3, 4, 5
emergency, 3, 10, 20, 48
end-stage condition, 34, 42

## F

feeding tube, 44
fiduciary, 21
financial matters, 1, 4, 5, 6, 10, 14, 19, 21, 30
financial power of attorney, 2, 3, 6, 10, 11, 12, 19, 20, 21, 23, 24, 25, 30, 36
Florida, 16, 17, 31, 35, 36, 37

## G

Georgia, 20, 27, 28, 36, 37
government agencies, 1, 46
guardianship, 3, 4, 5, 37, 41, 45

## H

Hawaii, 31, 36
health care, 1, 3, 5, 6, 7, 8, 9, 11, 12, 14, 15, 17, 21, 26, 28, 29, 30, 32, 33, 34, 35, 36, 37, 38, 39, 40, 41, 42, 43, 44, 45, 46, 47, 50
health care power of attorney, 3, 7, 8, 9, 11, 12, 17, 21, 26, 28, 29, 30, 33, 34, 35, 37, 38, 40, 41, 42, 43, 44, 45
homestead, 7
hospitals, 1, 7, 8, 10, 35, 44, 45, 46

# I

Illinois, 20, 26, 28, 36, 38
incapacitated, 2, 3, 6, 7, 24, 28, 31, 45
Indiana, 9, 20, 25, 28, 36, 38
insurance, 1, 11, 23
investing, 1, 11, 19, 21
Iowa, 36

# J

judge, 3, 4, 8

# K

Kansas, 36
Kentucky, 9, 16

# L

laws, 7, 14, 15, 16, 17, 36, 40, 41, 42, 43
lawsuits, 12, 14, 19, 44
lawyers, 3, 31
    fees, 14
legal encyclopedia, 17
legal research, 14, 15, 16, 17
lender, 1, 23, 27
liability, 13
life support, 11
life-prolonging procedures, 5, 8, 17, 34, 39,
    40, 42, 43
Limited Power of Attorney, 21, 22, 48
Limited Power of Attorney for Child Care,
    48

living trusts, 6, 7
living wills, 7, 8, 14, 33, 34, 35, 36, 37, 38,
    40, 41, 42, 43, 44
Louisiana, 9, 31

# M

Maine, 20, 28, 36
Maryland, 36
medical procedures, 40, 43
medical treatment, 5, 7, 8, 10, 12, 40, 41,
    42, 43
mental incapability, 41
Michigan, 17
Minnesota, 20, 25, 28, 36
Mississippi, 16, 36
Missouri, 9, 31
Montana, 20, 25, 28
mortgage, 1

# N

Nebraska, 20, 25, 29, 36
Nevada, 31, 36
New Hampshire, 31, 36
New Jersey, 9
New Mexico, 9, 20, 25, 29, 36, 38
New York, 20, 25, 29, 36
no code order. *See do not resuscitate
    orders (DNR)*
North Carolina, 20, 25, 29, 36
North Dakota, 36
notary public, 15, 20, 22, 23, 24, 26, 32, 38,
    39, 48, 50

# O

Ohio, 9, 31
Oklahoma, 36, 38
Oregon, 31, 36, 38
organ donation, 37, 46

# P

parents, 3, 4, 5, 10, 34, 41, 44, 48
Parkinson's disease, 4
patients, 41, 44, 45, 46
Pennsylvania, 9, 16, 31
permanent coma, 8, 34, 40, 44
persistent vegetative state, 34, 42
power of attorney for child care, 10, 47, 48
Power of Attorney for Real Estate, 23
practice manuals, 16
principal, 3, 6, 7, 17, 21, 24, 29, 32, 49
property, 2, 6, 7, 19, 23, 24, 32

# R

real estate, 6, 15, 19, 23, 24, 32
religious beliefs, 41, 43
return-receipt mail, 49
Revocation of Power of Attorney, 49
revoking a power of attorney, 9, 47, 49, 50
Rhode Island, 36

# S

securities, 1, 27
siblings, 5, 41
Social Security number, 32
South Carolina, 36
South Dakota, 9
spouse, 2, 4, 9, 25, 41
springing power of attorney, 6, 7, 20, 31
statutes, 16, 17, 25, 30, 38, 40
statutory forms, 9, 20, 23, 25, 26, 27, 28, 36
stocks, 14, 27
successor agent, 12
supplement, 16
surgery, 34
surrogate, 37, 40, 45

# T

taxes, 2, 3, 7
Tennessee, 20, 36
terminal illness, 8, 34, 40, 42, 43, 44, 45
termination, 28, 49
Terri Schiavo, 35
Texas, 20, 26, 30, 36
third party, 1, 9, 13, 14, 21, 32
title to property, 6, 16, 22, 23, 32, 50

# U

Utah, 9, 31, 36

# V

Vermont, 36
Virginia, 31, 36

# W

Washington, 9
West Virginia, 36
Wisconsin, 20, 25, 30, 36
witnesses, 15, 20, 23, 24, 26, 31, 32, 37, 39,
    50
Wyoming, 9

# Y

your medical wishes, 8, 12, 31, 34, 35, 41,
    42, 43, 44

# Sphinx® Publishing's National Titles
*Valid in All 50 States*

## LEGAL SURVIVAL IN BUSINESS

| | |
|---|---|
| The Complete Book of Corporate Forms (2E) | $29.95 |
| The Complete Hiring and Firing Handbook | $19.95 |
| The Complete Limited Liability Kit | $24.95 |
| The Complete Partnership Book | $24.95 |
| The Complete Patent Book | $26.95 |
| The Complete Patent Kit | $39.95 |
| The Entrepreneur's Internet Handbook | $21.95 |
| The Entrepreneur's Legal Guide | $26.95 |
| Financing Your Small Business | $16.95 |
| Fired, Laid-Off or Forced Out | $14.95 |
| Form Your Own Corporation (5E) | $29.95 |
| The Home-Based Business Kit | $14.95 |
| How to Buy a Franchise | $19.95 |
| How to Form a Nonprofit Corporation (3E) | $24.95 |
| How to Register Your Own Copyright (5E) | $24.95 |
| HR for Small Business | $14..95 |
| Incorporate in Delaware from Any State | $26.95 |
| Incorporate in Nevada from Any State | $24.95 |
| The Law (In Plain English)® for Restaurants | $16.95 |
| The Law (In Plain English)® for Small Business | $19.95 |
| The Law (In Plain English)® for Writers | $14.95 |
| Making Music Your Business | $18.95 |
| Minding Her Own Business (4E) | $14.95 |
| Most Valuable Business Legal Forms You'll Ever Need (3E) | $21.95 |
| Profit from Intellectual Property | $28.95 |
| Protect Your Patent | $24.95 |
| The Small Business Owner's Guide to Bankruptcy | $21.95 |
| Start Your Own Law Practice | $16.95 |
| Tax Power for the Self-Eemployed | $17.95 |
| Tax Smarts for Small Business | $21.95 |
| Your Rights at Work | $14.95 |

## LEGAL SURVIVAL IN COURT

| | |
|---|---|
| Attorney Responsibilities & Client Rights | $19.95 |
| Crime Victim's Guide to Justice (2E) | $21.95 |
| Legal Research Made Easy (4E) | $24.95 |
| Winning Your Personal Injury Claim (3E) | $24.95 |

## LEGAL SURVIVAL IN REAL ESTATE

| | |
|---|---|
| The Complete Kit to Selling Your Own Home | $18.95 |
| The Complete Book of Real Estate Contracts | $18.95 |
| Essential Guide to Real Estate Leases | $18.95 |
| Homeowner's Rights | $19.95 |
| How to Buy a Condominium or Townhome (2E) | $19.95 |
| How to Buy Your First Home (2E) | $14.95 |
| How to Make Money on Foreclosures | $16.95 |
| The Mortgage Answer Book | $14.95 |
| Sell Your Own Home Without a Broker | $14.95 |
| The Weekend Landlord | $16.95 |
| The Weekend Real Estate Investor | $14.95 |
| Working with Your Homeowners Association | $19.95 |

## LEGAL SURVIVAL IN SPANISH

| | |
|---|---|
| Cómo Comprar su Primera Casa | $8.95 |
| Cómo Conseguir Trabajo en los Estados Unidos | $8.95 |
| Cómo Hacer su Propio Testamento | $16.95 |
| Cómo Iniciar su Propio Negocio | $8.95 |
| Cómo Negociar su Crédito | $8.95 |
| Cómo Organizar un Presupuesto | $8.95 |
| Cómo Solicitar su Propio Divorcio | $24.95 |
| Guía de Inmigración a Estados Unidos (4E) | $24.95 |
| Guía de Justicia para Víctimas del Crimen | $21.95 |
| Guía Esencial para los Contratos de Arrendamiento de Bienes Raices | $22.95 |
| Inmigración y Ciudadanía en los EE.UU. Preguntas y Respuestas | $16.95 |
| Inmigración a los EE.UU. Paso a Paso (2E) | $24.95 |
| Manual de Beneficios del Seguro Social | $18.95 |
| El Seguro Social Preguntas y Respuestas | $16.95 |
| ¡Visas! ¡Visas! ¡Visas! | $9.95 |

## LEGAL SURVIVAL IN PERSONAL AFFAIRS

| | |
|---|---|
| 101 Complaint Letters That Get Results | $18.95 |
| The 529 College Savings Plan (2E) | $18.95 |
| The 529 College Savings Plan Made Simple | $7.95 |
| The Alternative Minimum Tax | $14.95 |
| The Antique and Art Collector's Legal Guide | $24.95 |
| The Childcare Answer Book | $12.95 |
| Child Support | $18.95 |
| The Complete Book of Insurance | $18.95 |
| The Complete Book of Personal Legal Forms | $24.95 |
| The Complete Credit Repair Kit | $19.95 |
| The Complete Legal Guide to Senior Care | $21.95 |
| The Complete Personal Bankruptcy Guide | $21.95 |
| Credit Smart | $18.95 |
| The Easy Will and Living Will Kit | $16.95 |
| Fathers' Rights | $19.95 |
| File Your Own Divorce (6E) | $24.95 |
| The Frequent Traveler's Guide | $14.95 |
| Gay & Lesbian Rights | $26.95 |
| Grandparents' Rights (4E) | $24.95 |
| How to Parent with Your Ex | $12.95 |
| How to Write Your Own Living Will (4E) | $18.95 |
| How to Write Your Own Premarital Agreement (3E) | $24.95 |
| The Infertility Answer Book | $16.95 |
| Law 101 | $16.95 |
| Law School 101 | $16.95 |
| The Living Trust Kit | $21.95 |
| Living Trusts and Other Ways to Avoid Probate (3E) | $24.95 |
| Make Your Own Simple Will (4E) | $26.95 |
| Mastering the MBE | $16.95 |
| Nursing Homes and Assisted Living Facilities | $19.95 |
| Power of Attorney Handbook (6E) | $24.95 |
| Quick Cash | $14.95 |
| Seniors' Rights | $19.95 |
| Sexual Harassment in the Workplace | $18.95 |
| Sexual Harassment:Your Guide to Legal Action | $18.95 |
| Sisters-in-Law | $16.95 |
| The Social Security Benefits Handbook (4E) | $18.95 |
| Social Security Q&A | $12.95 |
| Starting Out or Starting Over | $14.95 |
| Teen Rights (and Responsibilities) (2E) | $14.95 |
| Unmarried Parents' Rights (and Responsibilities)(3E) | $16.95 |
| U.S. Immigration and Citizenship Q&A | $18.95 |
| U.S. Immigration Step by Step (2E) | $24.95 |
| U.S.A. Immigration Guide (5E) | $26.95 |
| What They Don't Teach You in College | $12.95 |
| What to Do—Before "I DO" | $14.95 |
| The Wills and Trusts Kit (2E) | $29.95 |
| Win Your Unemployment Compensation Claim (2E) | $21.95 |
| Your Right to Child Custody, Visitation and Support (3E) | $24.95 |

# SPHINX® PUBLISHING ORDER FORM

| BILL TO: | | SHIP TO: | |
|---|---|---|---|
| | | | |
| | | | |
| Phone # | Terms | F.O.B. Chicago, IL | Ship Date |

**Charge my:** ☐ VISA  ☐ MasterCard  ☐ American Express

☐ **Money Order or Personal Check**

Credit Card Number

Expiration Date

| Qty | ISBN | Title | Retail | Ext. | Qty | ISBN | Title | Retail | Ext. |
|---|---|---|---|---|---|---|---|---|---|
| | | **SPHINX PUBLISHING NATIONAL TITLES** | | | | 1-57248-520-5 | How to Make Money on Foreclosures | $16.95 | |
| | 1-57248-363-6 | 101 Complaint Letters That Get Results | $18.95 | | | 1-57248-479-9 | How to Parent with Your Ex | $12.95 | |
| | 1-57248-361-X | The 529 College Savings Plan (2E) | $18.95 | | | 1-57248-379-2 | How to Register Your Own Copyright (5E) | $24.95 | |
| | 1-57248-483-7 | The 529 College Savings Plan Made Simple | $7.95 | | | 1-57248-394-6 | How to Write Your Own Living Will (4E) | $18.95 | |
| | 1-57248-460-8 | The Alternative Minimum Tax | $14.95 | | | 1-57248-156-0 | How to Write Your Own Premarital Agreement (3E) | $24.95 | |
| | 1-57248-349-0 | The Antique and Art Collector's Legal Guide | $24.95 | | | 1-57248-504-3 | HR for Small Business | $14.95 | |
| | 1-57248-347-4 | Attorney Responsibilities & Client Rights | $19.95 | | | 1-57248-230-3 | Incorporate in Delaware from Any State | $26.95 | |
| | 1-57248-482-9 | The Childcare Answer Book | $12.95 | | | 1-57248-158-7 | Incorporate in Nevada from Any State | $24.95 | |
| | 1-57248-382-2 | Child Support | $18.95 | | | 1-57248-531-0 | The Infertility Answer Book | $16.95 | |
| | 1-57248-487-X | Cómo Comprar su Primera Casa | $8.95 | | | 1-57248-474-8 | Inmigración a los EE.UU. Paso a Paso (2E) | $24.95 | |
| | 1-57248-488-8 | Cómo Conseguir Trabajo en los Estados Unidos | $8.95 | | | 1-57248-400-4 | Inmigración y Ciudadanía en los EE.UU. | $16.95 | |
| | 1-57248-148-X | Cómo Hacer su Propio Testamento | $16.95 | | | | Preguntas y Respuestas | | |
| | 1-57248-532-9 | Cómo Iniciar su Propio Negocio | $8.95 | | | 1-57248-453-5 | Law 101 | $16.95 | |
| | 1-57248-462-4 | Cómo Negociar su Crédito | $8.95 | | | 1-57248-374-1 | Law School 101 | $16.95 | |
| | 1-57248-463-2 | Cómo Organizar un Presupuesto | $8.95 | | | 1-57248-523-X | The Law (In Plain English)® for Restaurants | $16.95 | |
| | 1-57248-147-1 | Cómo Solicitar su Propio Divorcio | $24.95 | | | 1-57248-377-6 | The Law (In Plain English)® for Small Business | $19.95 | |
| | 1-57248-507-8 | The Complete Book of Corporate Forms (2E) | $29.95 | | | 1-57248-476-4 | The Law (In Plain English)® for Writers | $14.95 | |
| | 1-57248-383-0 | The Complete Book of Insurance | $18.95 | | | 1-57248-509-4 | Legal Research Made Easy (4E) | $24.95 | |
| | 1-57248499-3 | The Complete Book of Personal Legal Forms | $24.95 | | | 1-57248-449-7 | The Living Trust Kit | $21.95 | |
| | 1-57248-528-0 | The Complete Book of Real Estate Contracts | $18.95 | | | 1-57248-165-X | Living Trusts and Other Ways to | $24.95 | |
| | 1-57248-500-0 | The Complete Credit Repair Kit | $19.95 | | | | Avoid Probate (3E) | | |
| | 1-57248-458-6 | The Complete Hiring and Firing Handbook | $18.95 | | | 1-57248-511-6 | Make Your Own Simple Will (4E) | $26.95 | |
| | 1-57248-484-5 | The Complete Home-Based Business Kit | $16.95 | | | 1-57248-486-1 | Making Music Your Business | $18.95 | |
| | 1-57248-353-9 | The Complete Kit to Selling Your Own Home | $18.95 | | | 1-57248-186-2 | Manual de Beneficios para el Seguro Social | $18.95 | |
| | 1-57248-229-X | The Complete Legal Guide to Senior Care | $21.95 | | | 1-57248-220-6 | Mastering the MBE | $16.95 | |
| | 1-57248-498-5 | The Complete Limited Liability Company Kit | $24.95 | | | 1-57248-455-1 | Minding Her Own Business, 4E | $14.95 | |
| | 1-57248-391-1 | The Complete Partnership Book | $24.95 | | | 1-57248-480-2 | The Mortgage Answer Book | $14.95 | |
| | 1-57248-201-X | The Complete Patent Book | $26.95 | | | 1-57248-167-6 | Most Val. Business Legal Forms | $21.95 | |
| | 1-57248-514-0 | The Complete Patent Kit | $39.95 | | | | You'll Ever Need (3E) | | |
| | 1-57248-545-0 | The Complete Personal Bankruptcy Guide | $21.95 | | | 1-57248-535-3 | Power of Attorney Handbook (6E) | $24.95 | |
| | 1-57248-480-2 | The Mortgage Answer Book | $14.95 | | | 1-57248-332-6 | Profit from Intellectual Property | $28.95 | |
| | 1-57248-369-5 | Credit Smart | $18.95 | | | 1-57248-329-6 | Protect Your Patent | $24.95 | |
| | 1-57248-163-3 | Crime Victim's Guide to Justice (2E) | $21.95 | | | 1-57248-376-8 | Nursing Homes and Assisted Living Facilities | $19.95 | |
| | 1-57248-481-0 | The Easy Will and Living Will Kit | $16.95 | | | 1-57248-385-7 | Quick Cash | $14.95 | |
| | 1-57248-251-6 | The Entrepreneur's Internet Handbook | $21.95 | | | 1-57248-350-4 | El Seguro Social Preguntas y Respuestas | $16.95 | |
| | 1-57248-235-4 | The Entrepreneur's Legal Guide | $26.95 | | | 1-57248-529-9 | Sell Your Home Without a Broker | $14.95 | |
| | 1-57248-160-9 | Essential Guide to Real Estate Leases | $18.95 | | | 1-57248386-5 | Seniors' Rights | $19.95 | |
| | 1-57248-375-X | Fathers' Rights | $19.95 | | | 1-57248-527-2 | Sexual Harassment in the Workplace | $18.95 | |
| | 1-57248-517-5 | File Your Own Divorce (6E) | $24.95 | | | 1-57248-217-6 | Sexual Harassment: Your Guide to Legal Action | $18.95 | |
| | 1-57248-553-1 | Financing Your Small Business | $16.95 | | | 1-57248-378-4 | Sisters-in-Law | $16.95 | |
| | 1-57248-459-4 | Fired, Laid Off or Forced Out | $14.95 | | | 1-57248-219-2 | The Small Business Owner's Guide to Bankruptcy | $21.95 | |
| | 1-57248-516-7 | Form Your Own Corporation (4E) | $29.95 | | | 1-57248-395-4 | The Social Security Benefits Handbook (4E) | $18.95 | |
| | 1-57248-502-7 | The Frequent Traveler's Guide | $14.95 | | | 1-57248-216-8 | Social Security Q&A | $12.95 | |
| | 1-57248-331-8 | Gay & Lesbian Rights | $26.95 | | | 1-57248-521-3 | Start Your Own Law Practice | $16.95 | |
| | 1-57248-526-4 | Grandparents' Rights (4E) | $24.95 | | | 1-57248-328-8 | Starting Out or Starting Over | $14.95 | |
| | 1-57248-475-6 | Guía de Inmigración a Estados Unidos (4E) | $24.95 | | | 1-57248-525-6 | Teen Rights (and Responsibilities) (2E) | $14.95 | |
| | 1-57248-187-0 | Guía de Justicia para Víctimas del Crimen | $21.95 | | | 1-57248-457-8 | Tax Power for the Self-Employed | $17.95 | |
| | 1-57248-253-2 | Guía Esencial para los Contratos de | $22.95 | | | 1-57248-366-0 | Tax Smarts for Small Business | $21.95 | |
| | | Arrendamiento de Bienes Raices | | | | 1-57248-530-0 | Unmarried Parents' Rights (3E) | $16.95 | |
| | 1-57248-334-2 | Homeowner's Rights | $19.95 | | | 1-57248-362-8 | U.S. Immigration and Citizenship Q&A | $18.95 | |
| | 1-57248-164-1 | How to Buy a Condominium or Townhome (2E) | $19.95 | | | 1-57248-387-3 | U.S. Immigration Step by Step (2E) | $24.95 | |
| | 1-57248-197-7 | How to Buy Your First Home (2E) | $14.95 | | | 1-57248-392-X | U.S.A. Immigration Guide (5E) | $26.95 | |
| | 1-57248-384-9 | How to Buy a Franchise | $19.95 | | | 1-57248-178-0 | ¡Visas! ¡Visas! ¡Visas! | $9.95 | |
| | 1-57248-390-3 | How to Form a Nonprofit Corporation (3E) | $24.95 | | | 1-57248-554-X | What They Don't Teach You in College | $12.95 | |
| | | | | | | | **(Form Continued on Following Page)** | **Subtotal** | |

To order, call Sourcebooks at 1-800-432-7444 or FAX (630) 961-2168 (Bookstores, libraries, wholesalers—please call for discount)
*Prices are subject to change without notice.*
Find more legal information at: **www.SphinxLegal.com**

# SPHINX® PUBLISHING ORDER FORM

| Qty | ISBN | Title | Retail | Ext. |
|---|---|---|---|---|
| ___ | 1-57248-177-2 | The Weekend Landlord | $16.95 | ___ |
| ___ | 1-57248-557-4 | The Weekend Real Estate Investor | $14.95 | ___ |
| ___ | 1-57248-451-9 | What to Do — Before "I DO" | $14.95 | ___ |
| ___ | 1-57248-225-7 | Win Your Unemployment Compensation Claim (2E) | $21.95 | ___ |
| ___ | 1-57248-518-3 | The Wills and Trusts Kit | $29.95 | ___ |
| ___ | 1-57248-473-X | Winning Your Personal Injury Claim (3E) | $24.95 | ___ |
| ___ | 1-57248-333-4 | Working with Your Homeowners Association | $19.95 | ___ |
| ___ | 1-57248-380-6 | Your Right to Child Custody, Visitation and Support (3E) | $24.95 | ___ |
| ___ | 1-57248-505-1 | Your Rights at Work | $14.95 | ___ |

### CALIFORNIA TITLES

| Qty | ISBN | Title | Retail | Ext. |
|---|---|---|---|---|
| ___ | 1-57248-489-6 | How to File for Divorce in CA (5E) | $26.95 | ___ |
| ___ | 1-57248-464-0 | How to Settle and Probate an Estate in CA (2E) | $28.95 | ___ |
| ___ | 1-57248-336-9 | How to Start a Business in CA (2E) | $21.95 | ___ |
| ___ | 1-57248-194-3 | How to Win in Small Claims Court in CA (2E) | $18.95 | ___ |
| ___ | 1-57248-246-X | Make Your Own CA Will | $18.95 | ___ |
| ___ | 1-57248-397-0 | Landlords' Legal Guide in CA (2E) | $24.95 | ___ |
| ___ | 1-57248-515-9 | Tenants' Rights in CA (2E) | $24.95 | ___ |

### FLORIDA TITLES

| Qty | ISBN | Title | Retail | Ext. |
|---|---|---|---|---|
| ___ | 1-57248-396-2 | How to File for Divorce in FL (8E) | $28.95 | ___ |
| ___ | 1-57248-490-X | How to Form a Limited Liability Co. in FL (4E) | $24.95 | ___ |
| ___ | 1-57071-401-0 | How to Form a Partnership in FL | $22.95 | ___ |
| ___ | 1-57248-456-X | How to Make a FL Will (7E) | $16.95 | ___ |
| ___ | 1-57248-339-3 | How to Start a Business in FL (7E) | $21.95 | ___ |
| ___ | 1-57248-204-4 | How to Win in Small Claims Court in FL (7E) | $18.95 | ___ |
| ___ | 1-57248-540-X | Incorporate in FL (7E) | $29.95 | ___ |
| ___ | 1-57248-381-4 | Land Trusts in Florida (7E) | $29.95 | ___ |
| ___ | 1-57248-491-8 | Landlords' Rights and Duties in FL (10E) | $24.95 | ___ |
| ___ | 1-57248-558-2 | Probate and Settle an Estate in FL (6E) | $29.95 | ___ |

### GEORGIA TITLES

| Qty | ISBN | Title | Retail | Ext. |
|---|---|---|---|---|
| ___ | 1-57248-340-7 | How to File for Divorce in GA (5E) | $21.95 | ___ |
| ___ | 1-57248-493-4 | How to Start a Business in GA (4E) | $21.95 | ___ |

### ILLINOIS TITLES

| Qty | ISBN | Title | Retail | Ext. |
|---|---|---|---|---|
| ___ | 1-57248-244-3 | Child Custody, Visitation, and Support in IL | $24.95 | ___ |
| ___ | 1-57248-510-8 | File for Divorce in IL (4E) | $26.95 | ___ |
| ___ | 1-57248-170-6 | How to Make an IL Will (3E) | $16.95 | ___ |
| ___ | 1-57248-265-9 | How to Start a Business in IL (4E) | $21.95 | ___ |
| ___ | 1-57248-252-4 | Landlords' Legal Guide in IL | $24.95 | ___ |

### MARYLAND, VIRGINIA AND THE DISTRICT OF COLUMBIA

| Qty | ISBN | Title | Retail | Ext. |
|---|---|---|---|---|
| ___ | 1-57248-240-0 | How to File for Divorce in MD, VA, and DC | $28.95 | ___ |
| ___ | 1-57248-359-8 | How to Start a Business in MD, VA, or DC | $21.95 | ___ |

### MASSACHUSETTS TITLES

| Qty | ISBN | Title | Retail | Ext. |
|---|---|---|---|---|
| ___ | 1-57248-115-3 | How to Form a Corporation in MA | $24.95 | ___ |
| ___ | 1-57248-466-7 | How to Start a Business in MA (4E) | $21.95 | ___ |
| ___ | 1-57248-398-9 | Landlords' Legal Guide in MA (2E) | $24.95 | ___ |

### MICHIGAN TITLES

| Qty | ISBN | Title | Retail | Ext. |
|---|---|---|---|---|
| ___ | 1-57248-467-5 | How to File for Divorce in MI (4E) | $24.95 | ___ |
| ___ | 1-57248-182-X | How to Make a MI Will (3E) | $16.95 | ___ |
| ___ | 1-57248-468-3 | How to Start a Business in MI (4E) | $18.95 | ___ |

### MINNESOTA TITLES

| Qty | ISBN | Title | Retail | Ext. |
|---|---|---|---|---|
| ___ | 1-57248-142-0 | How to File for Divorce in MN | $21.95 | ___ |
| ___ | 1-57248-179-X | How to Form a Corporation in MN | $24.95 | ___ |
| ___ | 1-57248-178-1 | How to Make a MN Will (2E) | $16.95 | ___ |

### NEW JERSEY TITLES

| Qty | ISBN | Title | Retail | Ext. |
|---|---|---|---|---|
| ___ | 1-57248-512-4 | File for Divorce in NJ (2E) | $24.95 | ___ |

| Qty | ISBN | Title | Retail | Ext. |
|---|---|---|---|---|
| ___ | 1-57248-448-9 | How to Start a Business in NJ | $21.95 | ___ |

### NEW YORK TITLES

| Qty | ISBN | Title | Retail | Ext. |
|---|---|---|---|---|
| ___ | 1-57248-193-5 | Child Custody, Visitation and Support in NY | $26.95 | ___ |
| ___ | 1-57248-351-2 | File for Divorce in NY | $26.95 | ___ |
| ___ | 1-57248-249-4 | How to Form a Corporation in NY (2E) | $24.95 | ___ |
| ___ | 1-57248-401-2 | How to Make a NY Will (3E) | $16.95 | ___ |
| ___ | 1-57248-469-1 | How to Start a Business in NY (3E) | $21.95 | ___ |
| ___ | 1-57248-198-6 | How to Win in Small Claims Court in NY (2E) | $18.95 | ___ |
| ___ | 1-57248-122-6 | Tenants' Rights in NY | $21.95 | ___ |

### NORTH CAROLINA AND SOUTH CAROLINA TITLES

| Qty | ISBN | Title | Retail | Ext. |
|---|---|---|---|---|
| ___ | 1-57248-508-6 | How to File for Divorce in NC (4E) | $26.95 | ___ |
| ___ | 1-57248-371-7 | How to Start a Business in NC or SC | $24.95 | ___ |
| ___ | 1-57248-091-2 | Landlords' Rights & Duties in NC | $21.95 | ___ |

### OHIO TITLES

| Qty | ISBN | Title | Retail | Ext. |
|---|---|---|---|---|
| ___ | 1-57248-503-5 | How to File for Divorce in OH (3E) | $24.95 | ___ |
| ___ | 1-57248-174-9 | How to Form a Corporation in OH | $24.95 | ___ |
| ___ | 1-57248-173-0 | How to Make an OH Will | $16.95 | ___ |

### PENNSYLVANIA TITLES

| Qty | ISBN | Title | Retail | Ext. |
|---|---|---|---|---|
| ___ | 1-57248-242-7 | Child Custody, Visitation and Support in PA | $26.95 | ___ |
| ___ | 1-57248-495-0 | How to File for Divorce in PA (4E) | $24.95 | ___ |
| ___ | 1-57248-358-X | How to Form a Corporation in PA | $24.95 | ___ |
| ___ | 1-57248-094-7 | How to Make a PA Will (2E) | $16.95 | ___ |
| ___ | 1-57248-357-1 | How to Start a Business in PA (3E) | $21.95 | ___ |
| ___ | 1-57248-245-1 | Landlords' Legal Guide in PA | $24.95 | ___ |

### TEXAS TITLES

| Qty | ISBN | Title | Retail | Ext. |
|---|---|---|---|---|
| ___ | 1-57248-171-4 | Child Custody, Visitation, and Support in TX | $22.95 | ___ |
| ___ | 1-57248-399-7 | How to File for Divorce in TX (4E) | $24.95 | ___ |
| ___ | 1-57248-470-5 | How to Form a Corporation in TX (3E) | $24.95 | ___ |
| ___ | 1-57248-496-9 | How to Probate and Settle an Estate in TX (4E) | $26.95 | ___ |
| ___ | 1-57248-471-3 | How to Start a Business in TX (4E) | $21.95 | ___ |
| ___ | 1-57248-111-0 | How to Win in Small Claims Court in TX (2E) | $16.95 | ___ |
| ___ | 1-57248-355-5 | Landlords' Legal Guide in TX | $24.95 | ___ |
| ___ | 1-57248-513-2 | Write Your Own TX Will (4E) | $16.95 | ___ |

### WASHINGTON TITLES

| Qty | ISBN | Title | Retail | Ext. |
|---|---|---|---|---|
| ___ | 1-57248-522-1 | File for Divorce in WA | $24.95 | ___ |

SubTotal This page ___

SubTotal previous page ___

Shipping — $5.00 for 1st book, $1.00 each additional ___

Illinois residents add 6.75% sales tax ___

Connecticut residents add 6.00% sales tax ___

**Total** ___

To order, call Sourcebooks at 1-800-432-7444 or FAX (630) 961-2168 (Bookstores, libraries, wholesalers—please call for discount)

*Prices are subject to change without notice.*

Find more legal information at: **www.SphinxLegal.com**

# How to Use the CD-ROM

Thank you for purchasing *Power of Attorney Handbook*. In this book, we have worked hard to compile exactly what you need to determine which powers of attorney you need, how to fill out the necessary forms, and how to file them. To make this material even more useful, we have included every document in the book on the CD-ROM that is attached to the inside back cover of the book.

You can use these forms just as you would the forms in the book. Print them out, fill them in, and use them however you need. You can also fill in the forms directly on your computer. Just identify the form you need, open it, click on the space where the information should go, and input your information. Customize each form for your particular needs. Use them over and over again.

The CD-ROM is compatible with both PC and Mac operating systems. (While it should work with either operating system, we cannot guarantee that it will work with your particular system and we cannot provide technical assistance.) To use the forms on your computer, you will need to use Microsoft Word or another word processing program that can read Word files. The CD-ROM does not contain any such program.

Insert the CD-ROM into your computer. Double-click on the icon representing the disc on your desktop or go through your hard drive to identify the drive that contains the disc and click on it.

Once opened, you will see the files contained on the CD-ROM listed as "Form #: [Form Title]." Open the file you need. You may print the form to fill it out manually at this point, or you can click on the appropriate line to fill it in using your computer. Once all your information is filled in, you can print your filled-in form.

•    •    •    •    •

Purchasers of this book are granted a license to use the forms contained in it for their own personal use. By purchasing this book, you have also purchased a limited license to use all forms on the accompanying CD-ROM. The license limits you to personal use only and all other copyright laws must be adhered to. No claim of copyright is made in any government form reproduced in the book or on the CD-ROM. You are free to modify the forms and tailor them to your specific situation.

The author and publisher have attempted to provide the most current and up-to-date information available. However, the courts, Congress, and your state's legislatures review, modify, and change laws on an ongoing basis, as well as create new laws from time to time. Due to the very nature of the information and the continual changes in our legal system, to be sure that you have the current and best information for your situation, you should consult a local attorney or research the current laws yourself.

This publication is designed to provide accurate and authoritative information in regard to the subject matter covered. It is sold with the understanding that the publisher is not engaged in rendering legal, accounting, or other professional service. If legal advice or other expert assistance is required, the services of a competent professional person should be sought.

*—From a Declaration of Principles Jointly Adopted by a Committee of the American Bar Association and a Committee of Publishers and Associations*

This product is not a substitute for legal advice.

*—Disclaimer required by Texas statutes*